Decoding Global Marketing Decisions

Decoding Global Marketing Decisions: Leveraging AI and Emotional Intelligence for Entrepreneurial Success offers an in-depth exploration of how Artificial Intelligence and Emotional Intelligence are reshaping the future of global marketing and entrepreneurship.

As organizations compete in highly volatile and culturally diverse markets, success increasingly depends on the ability to integrate data-driven intelligence with human-centered emotional insight. This book presents cutting-edge research and practical frameworks that reveal how entrepreneurs and marketers can harness AI-powered tools, emotionally intelligent strategies, and innovative digital models to drive sustainable business growth across borders.

Key topics include:

- Empowered and data-driven decision-making in global markets
- Emotional intelligence as a driver of entrepreneurial success
- AI-powered marketing strategies and analytics
- Cross-cultural consumer behavior and engagement
- AI transformation in finance, influencer marketing, and sports branding
- Emotionally intelligent chatbots and human–AI collaboration
- Ethical, governance, and trust considerations in AI adoption

Edited by a distinguished international panel of experts, this volume is an essential resource for scholars, practitioners, and advanced students seeking to understand the intersection of technology, emotion, and entrepreneurship in the modern global economy.

This book is particularly valuable for:

- Marketing and entrepreneurship researchers
- MBA and postgraduate students
- Business leaders and startup founders
- Digital strategists and innovation managers
- Policy-makers and AI governance professionals

Together, these contributions decode the complex interplay between intelligence, emotion, and innovation, offering a roadmap for entrepreneurial success in the era of intelligent global marketing.

Advances in Computational Collective Intelligence

Series Editor: Dr. Subhendu Kumar Pani

Intelligent Business Analytics
Edited by Nitendra Kumar, Lakhwinder Kaur Dhillon, Mridul Dharwal, Elena Korchagina, and Vishal Jain

Augmented Reality and Sustainability: Goals and Challenges
Edited by Sonal Trivedi, Vishal Jain, Balamurugan Balusamy, Subhendu Pani, and Danish Ather

Patient-Centric 6G: A New Era in Smart Healthcare
Edited by Rajeev Kumar, Ankush Joshi, Preeti Bajaj, and Danila Parygin

Generative AI Tools: From Algorithms to Applications
Edited by Priyanka Sharma, Senthil Kumar AV, Monika Jyotiyana, and Adnan Alrabea

IoT Cybersecurity: Trends, Challenges, and Solutions
Edited by Laxmi Shaw, D. Ajitha, Chinmay Chakraborty, and S.M. Prabin

Smarter Healthcare through Generative Intelligence
Edited by Vibha Jain, Aditya Gupta, Amritpal Singh, Prabal Verma, and Tawseef Ayoub Shaik

Metaverse and Blockchain: Real-World Applications
By Dileep Kumar Murala and Sandeep Kumar Panda

Artificial Intelligence for Renewable Energy Systems
Edited by Srikanta Kumar Mohapatra, Abhineet Anand, Monit Kapoor, Anita Sardana, Abhishek Kumar, and Jayashree Mohanty

Smarter Healthcare through Generative Intelligence
Edited by Vibha Jain, Aditya Gupta, Amritpal Singh, Prabal Verma, and Tawseef Ayoub Shaikh

AI for Environmental Innovation and Stewardship
Edited by Rajeev Kumar, Saurabh Srivastava, and Sheng-Lung Peng

Decoding Global Marketing Decisions: Leveraging AI and Emotional Intelligence for Entrepreneurial Success
Edited by Thomas Heinrich Musiolik, Jose Esteves, Hemachandran Kannan, and Raul Villamarin Rodriguez

https://www.routledge.com/Advances-in-Computational-Collective-Intelligence/book-series/ACCICRC

Decoding Global Marketing Decisions

Leveraging AI and Emotional Intelligence for Entrepreneurial Success

Edited by
Thomas Heinrich Musiolik
Jose Esteves
Hemachandran Kannan
Raul Villamarin Rodriguez

CRC Press
Taylor & Francis Group
Boca Raton London New York

CRC Press is an imprint of the
Taylor & Francis Group, an **informa** business
AN AUERBACH BOOK

Designed cover image: Shutterstock

First edition published 2027
by CRC Press
2385 NW Executive Center Drive, Suite 320, Boca Raton FL 33431

and by CRC Press
4 Park Square, Milton Park, Abingdon, Oxon, OX14 4RN

CRC Press is an imprint of Taylor & Francis Group, LLC

Library of Congress Cataloging-in-Publication Data
Names: Musiolik, Thomas Heinrich, 1980- editor
Title: Decoding global marketing decisions : leveraging AI and emotional intelligence for entrepreneurial success / edited by Thomas Heinrich Musiolik, Jose Esteves, Hemachandran Kannan, and Raul Villamarin Rodriguez.
Description: First edition. | Boca Raton, FL : CRC Press, 2027. | Series: Computational collective intelligence | Includes bibliographical references and index. |
Identifiers: LCCN 2026016023 (print) | LCCN 2026016024 (ebook) | ISBN 9781041093169 hardback | ISBN 9781041095682 paperback | ISBN 9781003650775 ebook
Subjects: LCSH: Marketing–Management–Technological innovations | Artificial intelligence–Business applications | Decision making | Emotional intelligence | Entrepreneurship–Technological innovations
Classification: LCC HF5415.13 .D384 2027 (print) | LCC HF5415.13 (ebook) | DDC 658.8–dc23/eng/20260610
LC record available at https://lccn.loc.gov/2026016023
LC ebook record available at https://lccn.loc.gov/2026016024

ISBN: 978-1-041-09316-9 (hbk)
ISBN: 978-1-041-09568-2 (pbk)
ISBN: 978-1-003-65077-5 (ebk)

DOI: 10.1201/9781003650775

Typeset in Times
by SPi Technologies India Pvt Ltd (Straive)

Contents

About the Editors

Thomas Heinrich Musiolik is Chair Professor of Marketing and Technology at Woxsen University in Hyderabad, India, as well as Visiting Professor at the European University of Applied Sciences, Germany, HTW Berlin, and i-University in Tokyo, Japan. He holds a Master of Arts in Management with a focus on Marketing and Communication from FOM University of Applied Sciences for Economics and Management in Germany, a Bachelor of Business Administration from Avans University of Applied Sciences in the Netherlands, and a diploma in Business Administration, along with a qualification as a Marketing and Sales Economist from the Academy for Management and Economics in Berlin.

Musiolik is an expert for the European Commission and editor of the *Journal of Future Robot Life*. He is also a scientific ambassador for Brain City Berlin. Since 2011, he has been conducting research in the fields of marketing and technology, with a particular focus on how the brain functions and the influence of digital media. His core research question is which variables influence our experiences, regardless of the medium or technology used, and how unique and sustainable worlds of experience are created from this. His goal is to better understand the development of brand-related experiences and to develop innovative research methods to gain deeper insights into consumer behavior.

Furthermore, Musiolik explores societal changes resulting from digitalization. He analyzes user behavior in dealing with digital media such as websites, e-learning platforms, knowledge management systems, and e-commerce tools. A key focus is on investigating how interfaces can influence user behavior. His aim is to understand the impacts of digitalization on the human brain and to generate societal benefits from these insights.

His research interests include consumer and experiential behavior, experience design, digital media, digital marketing, digital communication, and artificial intelligence. As a scientist and personality, he advocates for clear decision-making, innovative ideas, and continuous questioning of the status quo.

Jose Esteves is Dean and President of the Executive Board at Porto Business School, where he leads the institution's strategy, governance, and international positioning. Under his leadership, all three MBA programs entered the *Financial Times* global rankings, and the school renewed major accreditations, including Association of MBAs (AMBA), European Foundation for Management Development (EFMD), and Business School Impact System (BSIS). With more than 30 years of experience across academia and industry, he works at the intersection of artificial intelligence, digital leadership, cybersecurity, and business strategy. He is also Professor of Information Systems and Innovation at IE Business School, where he teaches MBA, EMBA, and executive programs. His research and advisory work focus on helping organizations align strategy, culture, and operating models with emerging technologies to drive measurable outcomes. Recognized by Thinkers50 as one of the top digital thinkers, he frequently speaks globally on digital transformation, AI, analytics, and innovation in management education.

Hemachandran Kannan is the Director of the AI Research Centre and Vice Dean of the School of Business at Woxsen University in Hyderabad, India. He holds advanced qualifications in artificial intelligence, machine learning, and data science, and is recognized for his research and practice in applying AI to complex organizational, sectoral, and regional challenges, with particular focus on emerging market contexts and equitable development.

At Woxsen University, Dr. Hemachandran leads a team of researchers working on AI applications in regional development, smart cities, tourism analytics, and crisis prediction. His work combines advanced technical expertise with deep engagement with policy contexts, development challenges, and ensuring that AI serves equity and inclusive growth rather than concentration of opportunity. He has collaborated with development agencies, regional governments, and international organizations on AI-enabled development initiatives.

Dr. Hemachandran's particular interest in this project stems from his belief that regions—especially in emerging markets, island economies, and tourism-dependent contexts—have enormous potential to leverage AI for competitive advantage and resilience but often lack the frameworks, institutional capacity, and policy guidance to do so responsibly. He brings cutting-edge technical expertise, experience in emerging market contexts, and commitment to ensuring that technological innovation serves equitable regional development.

Raul Villamarin Rodriguez is Vice President of Woxsen University and a leader in strategic planning, policy development, and institutional governance. With extensive experience in higher education leadership, regional development partnerships, and international policy advisory work, Dr. Villamarin brings a strategic, systems-thinking lens to regional development and technology governance.

His work focuses on aligning institutional and policy strategies with contemporary regional challenges and opportunities, including the thoughtful adoption and governance of AI and emerging technologies at regional and national scales. He is deeply committed to ensuring that technological innovations serve equitable development, support peripheral and disadvantaged regions, and strengthen regional autonomy and agency rather than creating new forms of dependence or inequality. Dr. Villamarin's involvement ensures that the frameworks and recommendations are grounded in implementation reality and policy context, making them actionable for regional governments, policy-makers, and development professionals.

Contributors

Shyam Sunder Agrawal
School of Business
Lovely Professional University
Phagwara, India

Iftikhar Ahmed
UE Innovation Hub
University of Europe for Applied Sciences
Berlin, Germany

Raja Hashim Ali
UE Innovation Hub
University of Europe for Applied Sciences
Berlin, Germany

Souradipta Bandyopadhayay
Department of Law
Brainware University
Barasat, India

Yogita Bansal
School of Business
Inderprastha Engineering College
Delhi, India

Vijay Prakash Gupta
Institute of Business Management
GLA University
Mathura, India

Zareen Hossain
Research Scholar, Department of Law
Brainware University
Barasat, India

Danish Javed
Faculty of Computer Science & Engineering
GIK Institute of Engineering Sciences & Technology
Swabi, Pakistan

Solomon Jeresa
School of Business
University of Huddersfield
Huddersfield, UK

Talha Ali Khan
UE Innovations Hub
University of Europe for Applied Sciences
Berlin, Germany

Aman Kumar
School of Business
Woxsen University
Hyderabad, India

Rajesh Kumar K.V.
School of Business
Woxsen University
Hyderabad, India

Sai Adarsh Maddu
School of Business
Woxsen University
Hyderabad, India

Ismail A. Mageed
Faculty of Engineering and Digital Technologies
School of Computer Science, AI, and Electronics
University of Bradford
Bradford, UK

Anitha Mani
School of Business
SR University
Warangal, India

Geetha Manoharan
School of Business
SR University
Warangal, India

Michael Oyedele Oyenuga
School of Business
Woxsen University
Hyderabad, India

Sarita Peddi
School of Business
SR University
Warangal, India

Anil Pise
X-idian, Cumulus Solutions, and Deloitte
Johannesburg, South Africa

Sneha Polaki
School of Business
Woxsen University
Hyderabad, India

Richa Rajshree
School of Business
Inderprastha Engineering College
Delhi, India

Anshu Rani
REVA Business School
REVA University
Bengaluru, India

Manjeet Rege
Department of Software Engineering and Data Science
Center for Applied Artificial Intelligence
University of St. Thomas
St Paul, Minnesota

Pavithra Salanke
School of Commerce and Management Studies
Dayananda Sagar University
Bengaluru, India

Anushree Saxena
School of Business
Shri Vaishnav Institute of Management and Science
Indore, India

Kokila Saxena
School of Management Studies and Commerce
SDGI Global University
Ghaziabad, India

Mushtaq Ahmad Shah
Department of Management Studies
Lovely Professional University
Phagwara, India

Ruchika Sharma
School of Management Studies
REVA University
Bengaluru, India

Anchal Singh
School of Business
Woxsen University
Hyderabad, India

Abhinav Sinha
School of Business
Woxsen University
Hyderabad, India

Ritu Soryan
Dronacharya Group of Institutions, Greater Noida
Noida, India

Nagaraj Arakalgud Subbarao
School of Commerce and Management Studies
Dayananda Sagar University
Bengaluru, India

Amanjot Singh Syan
School of Business
Canadore Stanford International College
North Bay, Ontario, Canada

Shalu Tyagi
School of Business
ITS Engineering College
Greater Noida, India

Aparna Vajpayee
School of Liberal Arts and Management
P Savani University
Dhamdod, India

Preface

The global marketing landscape is undergoing a profound transformation driven by the convergence of Artificial Intelligence (AI) and Emotional Intelligence (EI). As digital technologies accelerate market dynamics and consumer expectations evolve across cultural and geographical boundaries, marketers and entrepreneurs must now integrate analytical intelligence with emotional awareness to make effective strategic decisions. Traditional marketing frameworks are no longer sufficient in a world where consumer engagement is shaped by algorithms, data-driven insights, and human emotions.

This edited volume, *Decoding Global Marketing Decisions: Leveraging AI and Emotional Intelligence for Entrepreneurial Success*, brings together a diverse group of international scholars and practitioners to explore how AI technologies and emotionally intelligent practices are redefining entrepreneurial marketing worldwide. The chapters in this book present theoretical foundations, empirical insights, and applied perspectives that collectively illustrate how global enterprises can decode consumer behavior, enhance customer engagement, and build sustainable competitive advantage in the digital age.

The book is structured to guide readers from fundamental concepts of empowered decision-making and emotional intelligence to advanced applications such as AI-powered marketing strategies, data-driven decision frameworks, virtual influencers, emotionally intelligent chatbots, and fan engagement in global sports marketing. Special emphasis is placed on cross-border consumer behavior, ethical considerations, influencer ecosystems, finance transformation, and the integration of mindfulness and emotional development into AI-enabled entrepreneurial practice.

By combining multidisciplinary viewpoints from marketing, psychology, information systems, and entrepreneurship, this volume serves as a comprehensive reference for researchers, educators, graduate students, industry professionals, and policy-makers. It is our hope that this book will inspire responsible innovation and encourage the creation of globally adaptive, emotionally aware, and technologically empowered entrepreneurial ecosystems.

1 Introduction to Empowered Decision-Making

Raja Hashim Ali, Danish Javed, Talha Ali Khan, Iftikhar Ahmed, and Thomas Heinrich Musiolik

1.1 THE EVOLVING NATURE OF DECISION-MAKING IN GLOBAL MARKETS

In a globalized and hyper-connected world, the nature of entrepreneurial decision-making has undergone a significant transformation. Traditional business decisions were largely intuitive, based on experience, gut feelings, and slow-moving data. However, with the proliferation of digital technologies, the rise of big data, and rapidly shifting market dynamics, decision-making has become more data-driven, fast-paced, and responsive than ever before [1]. Modern global markets are characterized by complexity and volatility. Entrepreneurs are not just contending with local competitors but navigating a vast international playing field influenced by geopolitical shifts, cultural expectations, and fluctuating economic indicators [2]. In this dynamic landscape, empowered decision-making is emerging as a critical capability, one that integrates data analytics, artificial intelligence (AI), emotional intelligence (EI), and real-time insights to guide strategic actions (Figure 1.1). Table 1.1 displays a comparative analysis of traditional and modern decision-making paradigms.

The key drivers behind this shift include the explosion of accessible data, increased customer expectations for personalization, and the speed at which markets now move [3]. Companies that leverage data to identify patterns, simulate scenarios, and anticipate change gain a clear edge over those relying on outdated methods. As illustrated in recent trends, decision support systems (DSS) powered by AI allow entrepreneurs to shift from reactive to proactive stances, making informed choices swiftly without compromising on accuracy. This evolution also signals a paradigm shift in the organizational decision structure from hierarchical, top-down models to more decentralized, collaborative systems, where insights are shared across functions. Real-time dashboards, machine learning (ML) predictions, and cognitive automation are increasingly enabling cross-functional teams to contribute to strategy formulation in ways that were previously unimaginable.

Yet, this transformation is not without its challenges [4]. Decision-makers now face the paradox of choice: having too much information can lead to analysis paralysis. Moreover, ethical concerns around algorithmic bias, data privacy, and explainability

DOI: 10.1201/9781003650775-1

FIGURE 1.1 Evolution of decision-making tools in entrepreneurship – milestones in the technological evolution of decision-making tools, emphasizing the rise of AI-driven agility.

TABLE 1.1
Traditional vs. Modern Decision-Making Approaches – Comparative Analysis of Decision-Making Paradigms, Highlighting Shifts in Speed, Inclusivity, and Technological Integration

Key Aspect	Traditional Decision-Making	Modern-Empowered Decision-Making
Foundation	Experience-based, intuition	Data-driven, AI/ML insights
Speed	Slow & manual (weeks/months for consensus)	Real time or near real time & automated
Risk Management Style	Reactive (post-crisis adjustments)	Proactive (predictive risk modeling)
Data Usage	Limited data	Big data insights
Stakeholder Inclusion	Hierarchical (top-down decisions)	Decentralized, collaborative (cross-functional input)
Example	A retailer expanding based on gut feel	Airbnb's dynamic pricing algorithm

are raising new questions about trust and transparency in AI-augmented decisions. The synergy between AI and EI addresses the limitations of purely data-driven or intuition-based models. AI excels at processing vast datasets, identifying market trends, predicting risks, and automating routine choices, while EI ensures decisions align with stakeholder values, cultural contexts, and ethical imperatives. For instance, an AI system might flag a cost-cutting opportunity by reducing a supplier workforce, but EI compels leaders to assess the human impact and brand reputation (Figure 1.2). Tools like sentiment analysis algorithms now incorporate emotional cues from customer feedback, enabling brands like Starbucks to tailor campaigns that resonate emotionally while optimizing return on investment (ROI). This balance fosters trust, innovation, and long-term resilience in global markets, as shown in Table 1.2.

Understanding the evolving nature of decision-making lays the foundation for exploring deeper frameworks that drive empowered decisions. The upcoming sections will delve into four foundational components that enable such empowered strategies in modern entrepreneurial environments. These include AI-powered DSS for real-time insights, ML algorithms for risk assessment, deep learning (DL) models for scenario simulation, and pattern recognition techniques in historical data for trend-based decisions. Together, these tools help entrepreneurs unlock value, mitigate uncertainty, and stay agile in the face of relentless change (Table 1.3).

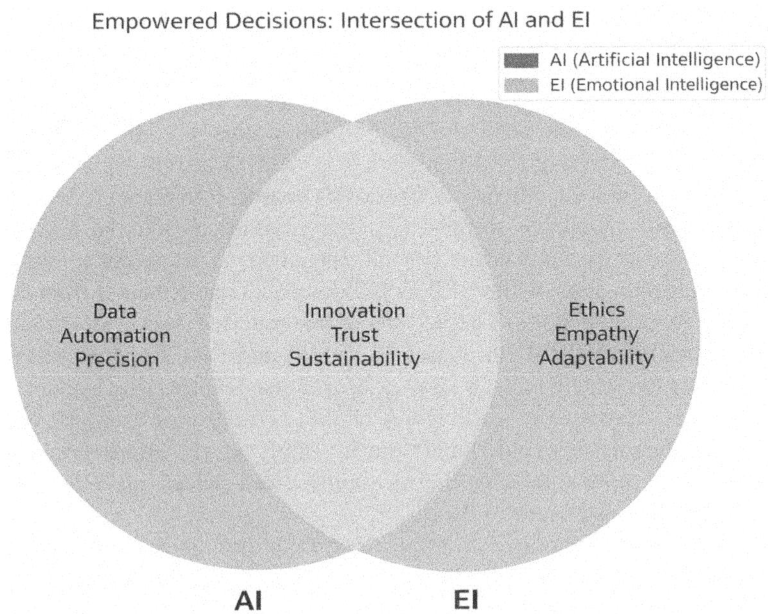

FIGURE 1.2 Integration of AI and emotional intelligence – synergy between AI and emotional intelligence, demonstrating how their integration fosters balanced, innovative outcomes.

TABLE 1.2
Roles of AI and Emotional Intelligence in Decision-Making – Complementary Roles of AI and Emotional Intelligence in Bridging Data-Driven and Human-Centric Decision-Making

AI Contributions	Emotional Intelligence Contributions
Predictive analytics for trends	Ethical judgment and cultural sensitivity
Automated risk quantification	Stakeholder empathy and conflict resolution
Real-time data processing	Balancing logic with human-centric values
Pattern recognition in big data	Interpreting unstructured feedback (e.g., surveys)

TABLE 1.3
A Short Summary of Drivers of Change and Demands of Digital Transformation

Aspect	Details
Drivers of Change	Digital transformation, globalization, customer-centric demands
Benefits	Faster response, increased accuracy, competitive edge
Challenges	Information overload, AI bias, decision fatigue

1.2 THE FRAMEWORK OF AI-POWERED DECISION SUPPORT SYSTEMS

AI-powered DSS are revolutionizing how businesses process and act on data in real time [5]. Modern tools like predictive analytics platforms (e.g., SAS, RapidMiner), natural language processing (NLP) engines (e.g., IBM Watson) [6], and interactive dashboards (e.g., Tableau, Microsoft Power BI) enable entrepreneurs to synthesize vast datasets into actionable insights [7]. For instance, predictive analytics can forecast sales trends by analyzing historical sales data, social media sentiment, and macroeconomic indicators, while NLP tools extract actionable themes from customer reviews or competitor reports. These systems integrate IoT sensors, customer relationship management (CRM) databases, and third-party for Application Programming Interfaces to create a holistic view of operations, empowering leaders to make informed choices under tight deadlines. A clothing retailer, for example, might use AI-driven dashboards to monitor real-time inventory levels, adjust pricing during flash sales, and reroute shipments during supply chain delays, all within a unified interface (Table 1.4 and Figure 1.3).

Netflix exemplifies the power of AI-powered DSS through its hyper-personalized recommendation engine and dynamic pricing strategies. The platform employs collaborative filtering algorithms and DL models to analyze user behavior (watch history, ratings, pause/rewind patterns) and recommend content with 80% accuracy in user engagement. For pricing, Netflix uses A/B testing powered by reinforcement learning to experiment with tiered subscription models across regions, balancing affordability with revenue goals. During the 2020 pandemic surge, real-time analytics helped Netflix adjust content budgets based on shifting viewer preferences, prioritizing local-language productions in high-growth markets like India and South Korea. This AI-driven agility contributed to a 21% year-over-year revenue increase, showcasing how DSS tools turn data into a competitive advantage (Figure 1.4).

TABLE 1.4
Popular AI Tools for Decision Support Systems – Key AI Tools Enabling Real-Time Decision Support across Industries, Categorized by Functionality and Application

Tool Category	Key Features	Use Cases	Examples
Predictive Analytics	Trend forecasting, risk modeling	Demand planning, fraud detection	SAS, RapidMiner, Google AI
NLP and Sentiment Analytics	Text mining, emotion detection	Customer feedback analysis	IBM Watson, MonkeyLearn
Dashboard Analytics	Real-time visualization, Key Performance Indicator (KPI) tracking	Inventory management, sales monitoring	Tableau, Power BI, Looker
Automated A/B Testing	Experimentation, multivariate testing	Pricing optimization, User Experience (UX) improvements	Optimizely, Visual Website Optimizer (VWO), Adobe Target

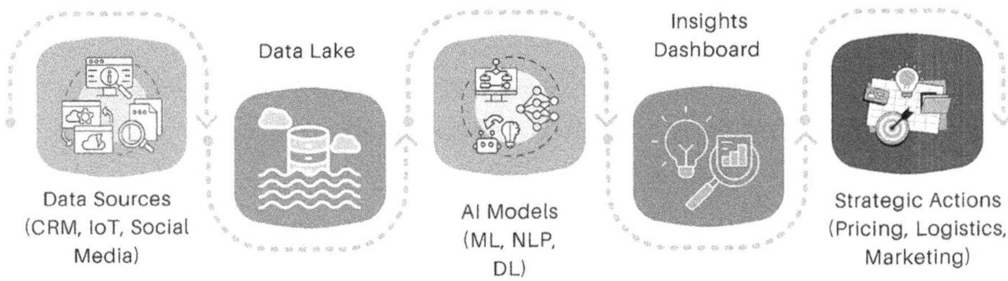

FIGURE 1.3 Architecture of an AI-powered decision support system – end-to-end architecture of a modern DSS, illustrating how raw data is transformed into actionable strategies through AI integration.

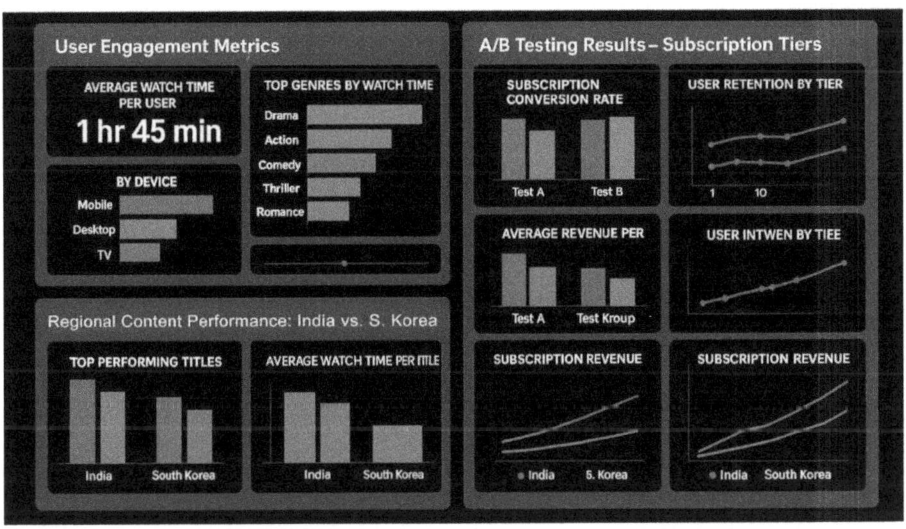

FIGURE 1.4 Netflix recommendation engine dashboard – simplified visualization of Netflix's AI-driven dashboard, highlighting real-time user behavior analytics and regional content optimization.

To assess the ROI of AI-powered DSS, businesses track three core metrics:

1. Speed: Time from data input to actionable insight (e.g., reducing supply chain risk assessments from days to minutes).
2. Accuracy: Precision of predictions (e.g., 95% accuracy in demand forecasting for a retail chain).
3. Scalability: Ability to handle growing data volumes without performance loss (e.g., supporting 10x user growth on a cloud-based platform).

Additional metrics include user adoption rates (e.g., 80% of teams using the DSS daily) and cost savings (e.g., 30% reduction in operational waste via predictive maintenance). Startups like Ocado, a UK-based grocery tech firm, use these metrics

TABLE 1.5
Metrics for Evaluating DSS Effectiveness – Quantitative and Qualitative Metrics to Assess the Impact of AI-Powered Decision Support Systems

Metric	Definition	Measurement Example
Speed	Time to generate insights from raw data	Reduced supply chain analysis from 48h to 2h
Accuracy	Precision of predictions or classifications	92% accuracy in customer churn prediction
Scalability	System performance under data load growth	Handled 10M to 100M transactions without lag
User Adoption	Percentage of teams actively using the DSS	75% of marketing teams daily usage
Cost Savings	Operational efficiencies gained	25% reduction in logistics costs

to validate their AI warehouse management systems, which process 3.5 million data points per second to optimize delivery routes (Table 1.5).

1.3 MACHINE LEARNING FOR RISK ASSESSMENT: QUANTIFYING UNCERTAINTY – BALANCING DATA-DRIVEN PRECISION AND ETHICAL RESPONSIBILITY

ML [8] has become indispensable for quantifying risks in entrepreneurship, offering tools to model uncertainty with unprecedented precision. Bayesian networks, for instance, enable probabilistic reasoning by mapping dependencies between variables (e.g., market demand, regulatory changes, competitor actions) to calculate the likelihood of adverse outcomes. Monte Carlo simulations help in this situation by considering thousands of situations/scenarios to estimate/predict the outcome under different conditions. These different conditions may include currency fluctuations or a disruption in the supply chain process. Supervised ML techniques are used to classify risks (e.g., low vs. high credit risk) based on historical data. For example, fintech companies like Klarna employ ML to evaluate borrower reliability in real time, reducing default rates by 25% while expanding into volatile markets (Table 1.6).

Expanding into emerging economies demands rigorous risk assessment, where ML models analyze multifaceted datasets to guide decisions [9]. Consider Coca-Cola's entry into Myanmar: ML algorithms processed satellite imagery, social media sentiment, and local economic indicators to predict demand and regulatory hurdles. Similarly, ride-hailing startup Grab uses ensemble models to evaluate political stability and consumer purchasing power in Southeast Asian markets. These tools quantify risks such as:

- Regulatory compliance costs: Predicting legal barriers using NLP on government documents.
- Cultural misalignment: Using social media sentiment analysis to take the pulse of public opinion toward a brand.
- Logistical bottlenecks: Applying computer vision [10] to satellite imagery to gauge the health of roads, ports, and other infrastructure.

TABLE 1.6
ML Techniques for Risk Assessment – Comparison of ML Techniques for Risk Modeling, Highlighting Trade-Offs between Interpretability, Accuracy, and Resource Demands

Technique	Application	Strengths	Limitations
Bayesian Networks	Probabilistic dependency mapping	Handles incomplete data	Computationally intensive
Monte Carlo Simulations	Scenario testing under uncertainty	Captures complex interactions	Requires high computational power
Decision Trees	Binary risk classification	Interpretable, fast	Prone to overfitting
Gradient Boosting	Credit scoring, fraud detection	High accuracy, handles imbalanced data	Black-box nature

By running "what-if" drills, such as a sudden tariff hike or an outbreak of civil unrest, ML helps firms steer resources to the right places and sidestep expensive mistakes. Yet the same tools can magnify injustice if their training data carry hidden biases. A telling example is the 2019 Apple Card controversy, in which historical lending patterns appear to have short-changed women applicants. To keep models fair:

1. Diverse data sourcing: Make sure every demographic is represented, for instance, fold rural economic data into emerging-market analyses.
2. Algorithmic audits: Deploy toolkits such as IBM's AI Fairness 360 to spot and fix skewed risk scores.
3. Explainable AI (XAI): Techniques like SHapley Additive exPlanations (SHAP) values lay bare how the model weighs each variable, building confidence and accountability.

Fintech firms such as ZestFinance now merge fairness constraints straight into their pipelines, cutting discriminatory outcomes by 40% without sacrificing accuracy (Table 1.7 and Figures 1.5 and 1.6).

TABLE 1.7
Bias Mitigation Strategies in ML Risk Models – Proactive Approaches to Address Ethical Challenges in ML-Driven Risk Assessment

Strategy	Description	Example
Diverse Data Sourcing	Incorporate underrepresented data	Adding rural economic data for emerging markets
Algorithmic Audits	Regular bias detection audits	IBM AI Fairness 360 toolkit
Explainable AI (XAI)	Transparent model decision-making	SHAP values for loan approval explanations
Fairness Constraints	Embed equity metrics into ML pipelines	ZestFinance's fairness-aware underwriting

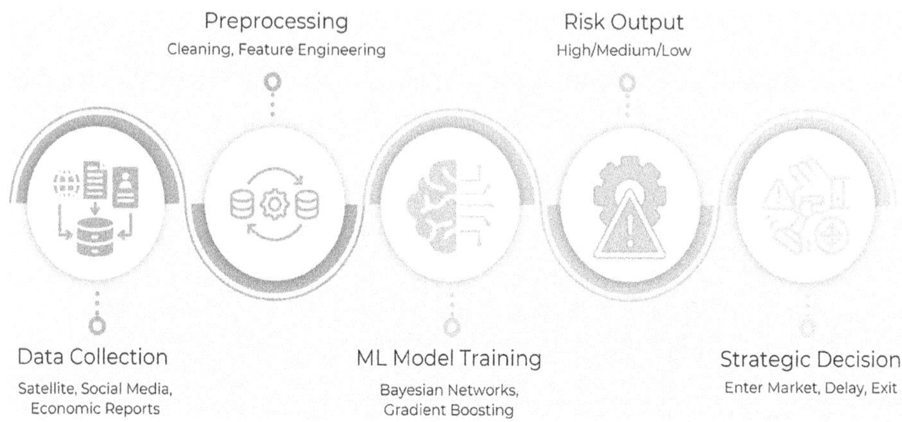

FIGURE 1.5 ML-driven market-entry risk assessment workflow – end-to-end workflow for assessing market-entry risks using ML, emphasizing data diversity and model interpretability.

FIGURE 1.6 Bias detection and correction in risk models – framework for identifying and resolving biases in risk assessment algorithms, ensuring ethical and equitable results.

1.4 DEEP LEARNING FOR SCENARIO SIMULATION – FROM PREDICTIVE ANALYTICS TO PRESCRIPTIVE STRATEGY

DL techniques are extremely useful when the traditional methods are used to capture the messy and non-linear relationships. These techniques are more powerful than the classical methods and are thus more data hungry as well as computationally intensive. One such DL-based technique is Convolutional Neural Networks (CNNs) [11], which can be used in a variety of situations. One particular use case is for the identification of a retail site using inputs from satellite imagery. Recurrent Neural Networks (RNN) are used where the requirement is to capture the relationship over a period of time, such as stock market intricacies or rolling supply chain issues. Generative Adversarial Networks (GANs) can be used to generate synthetic datasets to replicate extreme conditions such as market crashes or sudden competitor exits (Table 1.8).

A useful case study is the partnership between DeepMind and Google, where deep-reinforcement models were trained on sensory data from Google's data center with the objective to reduce the cooling costs. Using the deep-reinforcement models, an energy saving of 40% was achieved.

TABLE 1.8
Traditional vs. DL-Based Scenario Simulation – Contrasting Capabilities of Traditional and Deep Learning Approaches in Scenario Simulation

Aspect	Traditional Simulation	DL-Based Simulation
Data Input	Structured, limited variables	Structured + unstructured (text, images)
Complexity Handling	Linear approximations	Nonlinear, dynamic interactions
Adaptability	Static models, manual updates	Self-learning, real-time adjustments
Use Case Example	Excel-based financial forecasting	Simulating COVID-19 supply chain shocks
Tool Example	Monte Carlo in @RISK	TensorFlow with GANs

Key tools democratizing DL-driven scenario simulation include:

- TensorFlow/PyTorch: Open-source libraries for custom model development (e.g., simulating pricing wars using reinforcement learning).
- Keras: User-friendly interface for rapid prototyping of neural networks.
- AnyLogic: Multi-method simulation software integrating DL for hybrid scenarios.
- Proprietary Platforms: Salesforce's Einstein Analytics for CRM scenario testing.

For example, a startup in renewable energy might use PyTorch to simulate grid stability under varying weather conditions, while a fintech firm employs AnyLogic to stress-test loan portfolios against economic downturns (Table 1.9 and Figures 1.7 and 1.8).

TABLE 1.9
Deep Learning Tools for Scenario Simulation – Tools Enabling Entrepreneurs to Deploy DL for Scenario Simulation across Industries

Tool	Key Features	Entrepreneurial Application
TensorFlow	Scalable, custom neural networks	Demand forecasting for e-commerce
PyTorch	Dynamic computation graphs, research-friendly	Product launch risk simulation
AnyLogic	Hybrid modeling (agent-based + deep learning)	Supply chain disruption planning
Google's DeepMind	Reinforcement learning for optimization	Energy cost reduction in manufacturing

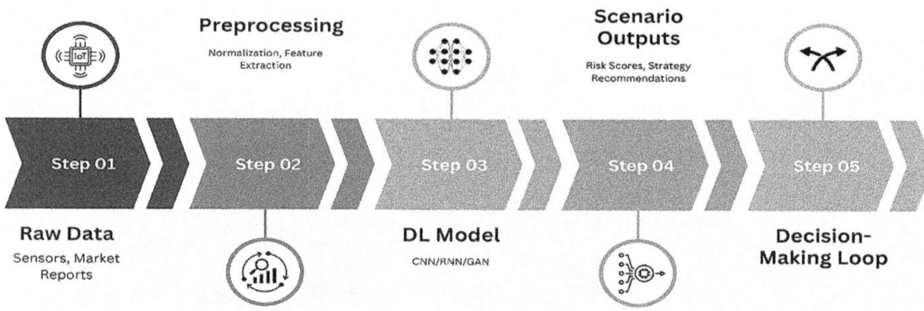

FIGURE 1.7 Architecture of a DL-based scenario simulation model – end-to-end workflow of a DL-driven simulation system, highlighting iterative learning and strategic adaptation.

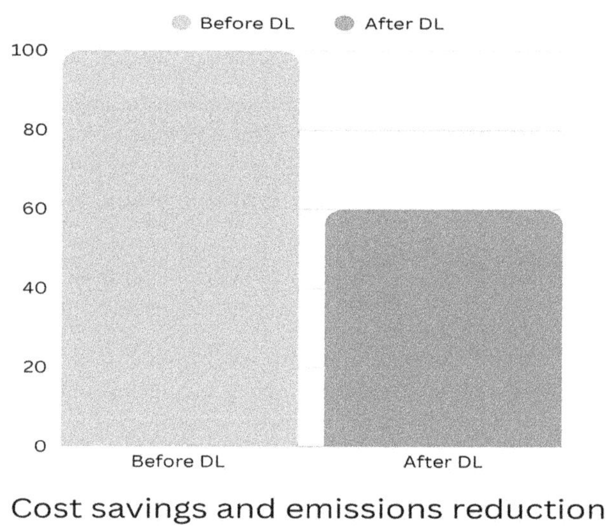

FIGURE 1.8 DeepMind's energy savings in Google data centers – impact of DeepMind's DL model on Google's energy efficiency, demonstrating scalable sustainability gains.

1.5 PATTERN RECOGNITION IN HISTORICAL DATA: IDENTIFYING TRENDS FOR PROACTIVE DECISION-MAKING – FROM RETROSPECTION TO FORESIGHT

Pattern recognition in historical data leverages advanced analytical techniques to transform raw information into strategic foresight. Time-series analysis (e.g., ARIMA, LSTM networks) identifies cyclical trends, such as seasonal sales spikes or quarterly revenue fluctuations, enabling businesses to align inventory and staffing. For instance, Starbucks uses time-series models to predict daily coffee demand across 30,000 locations. Clustering algorithms (e.g., K-means, DBSCAN) segment customers or markets based on historical behavior, such as grouping high-value clients for targeted

TABLE 1.10
Pattern Recognition Techniques and Applications – Key Pattern Recognition Methods, Their Entrepreneurial Applications, and Trade-Offs

Technique	Application	Strengths	Limitations
Time-Series Analysis	Demand forecasting, revenue prediction	Captures seasonality, trends	Struggles with abrupt market shifts
Clustering	Customer segmentation, market analysis	Unsupervised, scalable	Sensitive to initial parameters
Anomaly Detection	Fraud prevention, system monitoring	Real-time alerts, high precision	High false positives in noisy data
Association Rule Mining	Market basket analysis (e.g., Walmart)	Identifies product correlations	Computationally intensive

retention campaigns. Anomaly detection (e.g., Isolation Forest, Autoencoders) flags deviations like fraud or supply chain disruptions. PayPal employs anomaly detection to block 80% of fraudulent transactions preemptively. Together, these techniques convert passive data into actionable intelligence (Table 1.10).

Analyzing historical data shifts decision-making from reactive firefighting to proactive strategy. By identifying patterns in past consumer behavior, such as purchase cycles, brand loyalty shifts, or response to promotions, businesses anticipate future actions. For example, Netflix's recommendation engine analyzes viewing histories to predict what users will watch next, driving 80% of content engagement. Similarly, retailers like Zara use historical sales data to forecast fashion trends, reducing overstock by 20%. Proactive frameworks also mitigate risks [12]: financial institutions like JPMorgan Chase apply pattern recognition to predict loan defaults, adjusting credit policies before crises emerge. This approach reduces costs, enhances customer satisfaction, and fosters agility in volatile markets (Table 1.11).

Amazon's anticipatory shipping system epitomizes proactive decision-making through pattern recognition. By analyzing historical purchase data, browsing

TABLE 1.11
Proactive vs. Reactive Decision-Making – Strategic and Operational Contrasts between Proactive and Reactive Models

Aspect	Proactive Approach	Reactive Approach
Data Usage	Predictive analytics, historical trends	Crisis-driven, real-time data
Response Time	Pre-emptive actions (e.g., pre-stocking)	Post-crisis adjustments
Cost Efficiency	Reduces waste (e.g., 20% lower inventory)	High emergency costs (e.g., rush shipping)
Example	Amazon's anticipatory shipping	Recall management in automotive

behavior, and regional demographics, ML models predict demand for specific products before customers click "buy." Items are pre-shipped to nearby warehouses, slashing delivery times from days to hours. During peak seasons, this system reduces logistics costs by 15% and improves customer retention by 25%. However, challenges like data privacy concerns (e.g., profiling user behavior) and overstock risks persist, requiring continuous model refinement. Amazon's success underscores the balance between predictive accuracy and ethical data usage (Figures 1.9 and 1.10).

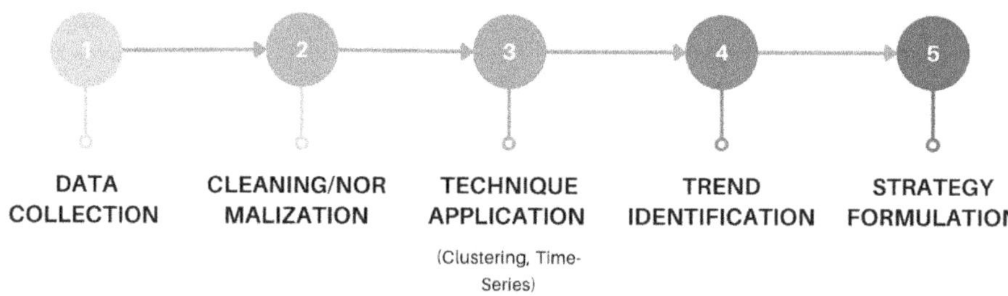

FIGURE 1.9 Pattern recognition workflow in historical data – end-to-end process of extracting actionable trends from historical data for proactive decision-making.

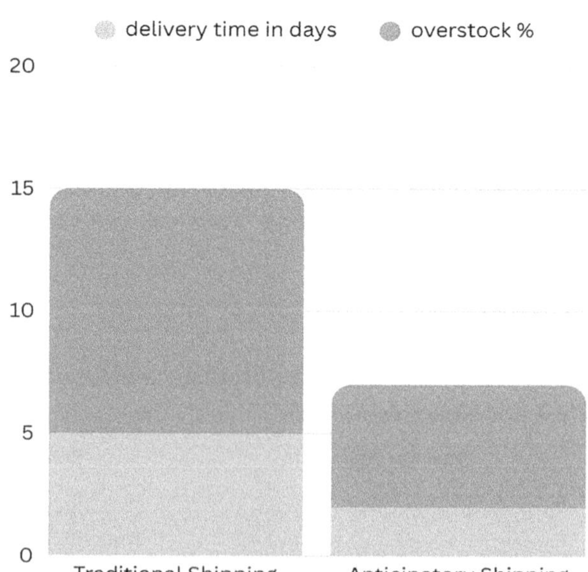

FIGURE 1.10 Impact of Amazon's anticipatory shipping – comparative performance of Amazon's proactive logistics model, emphasizing speed and cost reduction.

1.6 INTEGRATING AI WITH HUMAN JUDGMENT – HARMONIZING LOGIC AND EMPATHY IN ENTREPRENEURIAL DECISIONS

Machines excel at crunching data; humans excel at reading context. Suppose an algorithm asks to discontinue a low-margin product. Leaders still have to weigh how that move affects jobs, customer loyalty, and brand equity. EI ensures the final call matches the organization's values. Sentiment-aware tools help: Salesforce Einstein marries real-time sentiment cues with CRM records so sales teams know when a softer touch is needed. Unilever likewise automates résumé screening with AI [13] but keeps humans in the loop to judge cultural fit and soft skills, protecting trust in a global marketplace [14] (Table 1.12).

A human-in-the-loop (HITL) setup lets AI handle the heavy lifting while people remain the ultimate arbiters, especially when the stakes are high or the data ambiguous. Core features include feedback loops models learning from human corrections and confidence thresholds that pass low-certainty cases to experts [15]. Startups like Scale AI build such guardrails into training workflows to keep autonomous systems accountable (Figure 1.11 and Table 1.13).

- Healthcare: IBM Watson for Oncology proposes treatment options, but oncologists tailor plans to each patient's wishes.
- Finance: JPMorgan's COiN combs through contracts, flagging thorny clauses for legal review.
- Autonomous vehicles: Tesla Autopilot covers routine driving, yet hands control back to the driver when conditions turn unpredictable.

Putting too much faith in algorithms can create "tunnel vision," where decisions are efficient on paper but blind to real-world fallout.

- Bias amplification: Amazon shelved a résumé-screening tool when it started favoring male applicants.
- Ethical blind spots: Facebook's engagement engine prioritized divisive content because it drove clicks, not because it served society.
- Contextual ignorance: Uber's surge pricing during crises looked exploitative to riders who needed help most.

TABLE 1.12
Scenarios Requiring Human Judgment vs. AI Efficiency – Contextual Balance between AI Efficiency and Human Judgment in Critical Scenarios

Scenario	AI Strengths	Human Judgment Necessity
Customer Service	Chatbots resolving routine queries	Handling escalations requiring empathy
Financial Forecasting	Real-time market trend analysis	Ethical investment decisions
Healthcare Diagnosis	Identifying patterns in medical imaging	Patient's emotional state and preferences
Hiring	Résumé screening for keywords	Assessing cultural fit and creativity

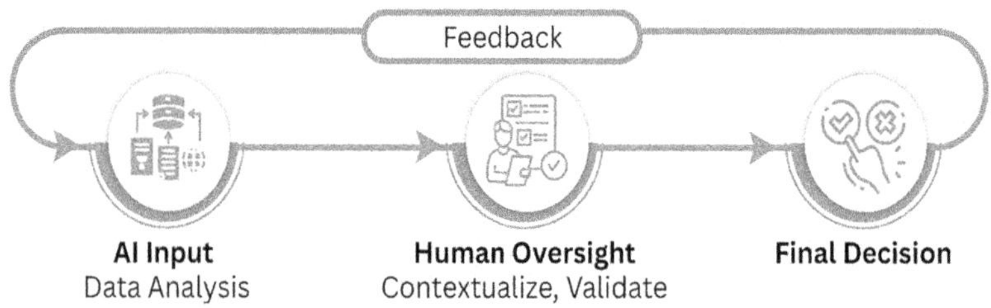

FIGURE 1.11 Human-in-the-loop decision workflow – iterative process of human–AI collaboration, emphasizing continuous learning and ethical alignment.

TABLE 1.13
Components of a Human-in-the-Loop Framework – Pillars of Effective Human–AI Collaboration, Ensuring Accountability and Adaptability

Component	Function	Example
Feedback Loops	Refine AI models using human corrections	Tesla's Autopilot driver interventions
Confidence Thresholds	Defer low-confidence AI outputs to humans	Medical AI flagging uncertain diagnoses
Ethical Audits	Ensure AI aligns with organizational values	Microsoft's Aether Committee reviews
Hybrid Validation	Cross-verify AI insights with teams	Unilever's AI–human hiring panels

The antidote is hybrid validation–run AI recommendations past diverse teams and leadership training in EI so that decision-makers feel comfortable challenging the math. Microsoft's Aether Committee is a strong model, vetting every AI project against ethical standards before launch (Figure 1.12).

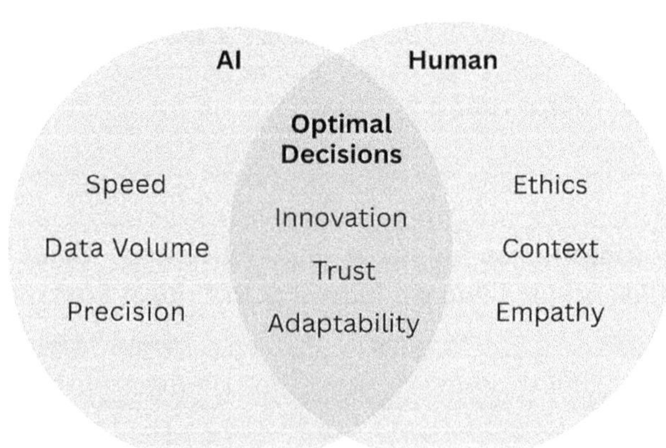

FIGURE 1.12 Balancing AI and human decision factors – symbiosis of AI capabilities and human values for holistic, ethical decision-making.

1.7 CASE STUDIES OF SUCCESSFUL ENTREPRENEURS – AI-DRIVEN INNOVATION, CRISIS PIVOTS, AND SCALING PATTERNS

Hypergrowth startups like Grammarly and UiPath demonstrate how AI adoption accelerates scaling. Grammarly's NLP algorithms analyze user writing patterns across 30M+ daily users, offering real-time suggestions that improve user retention by 50% (Table 1.14). UiPath leveraged robotic process automation (RPA) powered by ML to automate workflows for enterprises, achieving a $35B valuation within five years. Key lessons include:

- **Focus on user-centric AI:** Tools must solve clear pain points (e.g., Grammarly's grammar checks).
- **Scalability via cloud infrastructure:** UiPath's Amazon Web Services (AWS) integration allowed seamless global expansion.
- **Iterative model refinement:** Continuous feedback loops ensure AI stays relevant to evolving needs.

The COVID-19 pandemic forced startups to pivot rapidly using ML insights. Airbnb employed ML to shift focus from urban rentals to rural stays, analyzing booking cancellations and regional demand spikes. This pivot recovered 95% of pre-pandemic revenue by 2022. Similarly, Peloton used sentiment analysis on social media to identify home fitness trends, optimizing ad spend and inventory (Table 1.15 and Figure 1.13). These examples highlight ML's role in crisis agility [16]:

- Dynamic demand prediction: Adjusting offerings to real-time market shifts.
- Sentiment-driven marketing: Aligning campaigns with consumer emotions.

DL enables startups to dominate niche markets through precision [17]. DeepMind (now part of Google) used DL to revolutionize protein folding with AlphaFold, capturing the biotech research market. OpenAI's GPT-3 carved a niche in

TABLE 1.14
AI Adoption Strategies in Hypergrowth Startups – AI Strategies Driving Hypergrowth, Emphasizing Scalability and User-Centric Design

StartUp	AI Application	Outcome	Key Lesson
Grammarly	NLP for real-time writing feedback	50% increase in user retention	Solve specific pain points
UiPath	ML-driven RPA automation	$35B valuation in 5 years	Scalability via cloud infrastructure
DeepMind	DL for protein folding (AlphaFold)	Dominated biotech research tools	Invest in proprietary models

TABLE 1.15
Crisis Pivot Patterns Enabled by ML – ML's Role in Transforming Crises into Growth Opportunities through Agile Adaptation

Company	Crisis	ML-Driven Pivot	Result
Airbnb	COVID-19 travel ban	Shifted to rural/long-term rentals	95% revenue recovery by 2022
Peloton	Pandemic lockdowns	Targeted home fitness demand	172% YoY revenue growth (2020)
Slack	Remote work surge	Enhanced collaboration AI features	50% increase in enterprise contracts

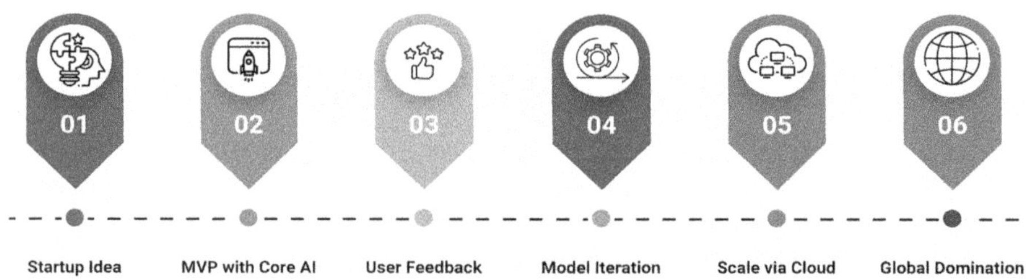

FIGURE 1.13 AI-driven scaling framework – iterative scaling process for AI startups, emphasizing continuous learning and infrastructure agility.

AI-generated content, empowering tools like Jasper.ai for marketers. DL's edge lies in:

- Processing unstructured data: Images, text, and genomics sequences.
- Creating defensible moats: Proprietary models that competitors cannot easily replicate.

Scaling success often hinges on recognizing patterns from historical data. Netflix identified binge-watching trends using clustering algorithms, driving original content investments (Figure 1.14). Stripe analyzed global payment failures to optimize checkout flows, reducing transaction drop-offs by 20% [18]. Common scaling patterns include:

- Network effects: Platforms like Slack grew by incentivizing team-wide adoption.
- Localized customization: Spotify's region-specific playlists boosted global subscriptions.

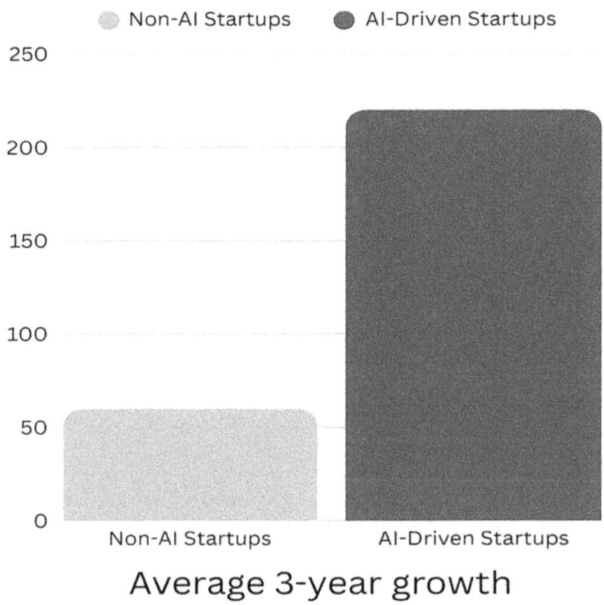

FIGURE 1.14 Revenue impact of AI adoption in startups – comparative revenue growth highlighting AI's transformative impact on scaling speed.

1.8 ETHICAL AND CULTURAL CHALLENGES – NAVIGATING AI'S MORAL MAZE IN GLOBAL MARKETS

Entrepreneurs leveraging AI must navigate a fragmented landscape of data privacy laws, such as the EU's GDPR, California's CCPA, and India's PDP Bill. These regulations dictate how data is collected, stored, and processed, with non-compliance risking fines (up to 4% of global revenue under GDPR) and reputational damage [19]. For example, Meta's $1.3B GDPR fine in 2023 underscores the cost of mishandling cross-border data transfers. Startups like DuckDuckGo differentiate themselves by prioritizing privacy-first AI, anonymizing user data to comply with regional norms. However, balancing compliance with innovation remains challenging, particularly in regions like China, where data localization laws conflict with global cloud infrastructures [20] (Table 1.16).

TABLE 1.16
Global Data Privacy Regulations and AI Implications – Regional Data Privacy Laws Shaping AI Development and Operational Constraints

Region	Regulation	Key Requirements	AI Impact
EU	GDPR	Data anonymization, user consent	Limits training data diversity
USA (CA)	CCPA	Opt-out of data sale, transparency	Increases compliance costs for startups
China	Data Security Law	Data localization, government access	Restricts cloud-based AI deployment
India	PDP Bill	Data minimization, breach reporting	Delays AI product launches

AI models trained on Western-centric datasets often fail in culturally diverse markets. Facial recognition systems [21], like those from Amazon Rekognition, exhibit higher error rates for non-Caucasian faces due to skewed training data. Similarly, NLP tools misinterpret dialects or idioms. Google Translate's gender bias in languages like Turkish sparked backlash (Table 1.17 and Figure 1.15). Mitigating these biases requires:

1. **Diverse Training Data:** Partnering with local experts to curate region-specific datasets.
2. **Cultural Audits:** Tools like IBM's AI Fairness 360 to evaluate model outputs across demographics.
3. **Inclusive Design:** Involving diverse teams in AI development, as seen in Microsoft's Inclusive Design Toolkit (Figure 1.16).

TABLE 1.17
Mitigating Cultural Bias in AI Models – Common Cultural Biases in AI and Strategies to Address Them, Emphasizing Inclusivity

Bias Type	Example	Mitigation Strategy	Tool/Initiative
Racial Bias	Facial recognition errors	Diverse training datasets	IBM AI Fairness 360
Gender Bias	Gendered translations in NLP	Gender-neutral algorithm design	Google's Gender Decoder
Linguistic Bias	Dialect misinterpretation	Local linguist partnerships	Microsoft's Z-Code Mixture of Experts
Socioeconomic Bias	Credit scoring disparities	Inclusive feature engineering	ZestFinance's fairness-aware underwriting

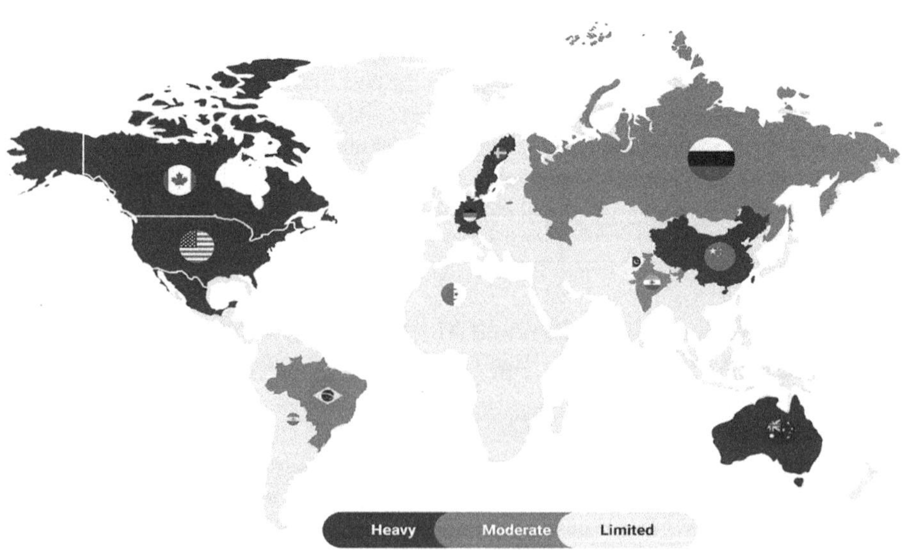

FIGURE 1.15 Global data privacy compliance map – visualization of data privacy regulations worldwide, illustrating compliance complexity for AI-driven businesses.

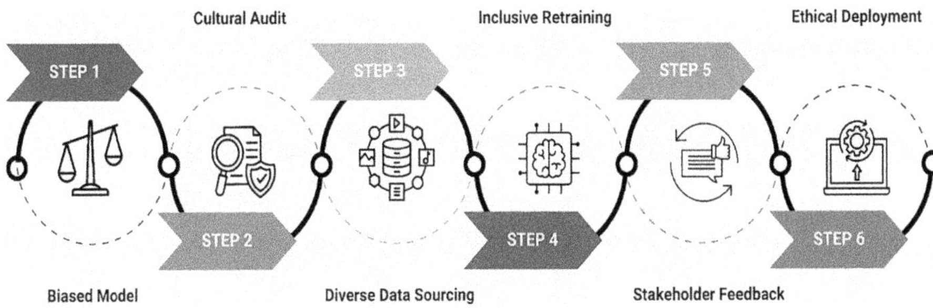

FIGURE 1.16 Cultural bias mitigation workflow – Iterative process for reducing cultural biases in AI systems, ensuring ethical global applicability.

1.9 THE FUTURE OF EMPOWERED DECISION-MAKING – COLLABORATIVE INTELLIGENCE, ETHICAL INNOVATION, AND SELF-OPTIMIZING SYSTEMS

The future of decision-making lies in decentralized, real-time AI systems [22]. Edge AI processes data locally on devices (e.g., sensors, smartphones), reducing latency and bandwidth costs. For example, Tesla's autonomous vehicles use edge computing to make split-second driving decisions without relying on cloud servers. Federated Learning trains AI models across distributed devices while keeping data localized, addressing privacy concerns. Google's Gboard uses this to improve predictive text without accessing personal messages. These technologies empower entrepreneurs with faster insights and compliance in data-sensitive markets like healthcare and finance (Table 1.18 and Figure 1.17).

Emotional AI (or affective computing) is poised to revolutionize decision-making by integrating human emotions into AI systems [23]. Startups like Affectiva analyze facial expressions and voice tones [24] to gauge customer sentiment during sales calls, enabling empathetic marketing. In mental health, Woebot uses NLP to detect emotional distress and offer tailored support. However, ethical challenges such as cultural differences in emotional expression and privacy risks require frameworks like the EU's proposed AI Act to regulate affective data usage. The synergy of EI and AI will foster trust in human-machine partnerships, particularly in high-stakes fields like healthcare and education (Table 1.19 and Figure 1.18).

TABLE 1.18
Edge AI vs. Federated Learning – Comparative Strengths of Edge AI and Federated Learning in Enabling Secure, Real-Time Decision-Making

Aspect	Edge AI	Federated Learning
Data Processing	Local device processing	Distributed model training
Latency	Near-zero (real-time decisions)	Depends on model aggregation speed
Privacy	Enhanced (data stays on-device)	Enhanced (raw data never centralized)
Use Case	Autonomous vehicles, IoT diagnostics	Healthcare (e.g., patient data analysis)
Example	Tesla Autopilot	Google's Gboard

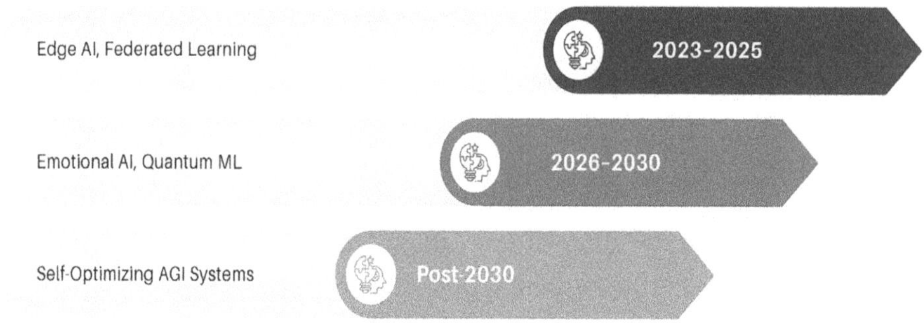

FIGURE 1.17 Roadmap for AI adoption in entrepreneurship – evolution of AI technologies shaping entrepreneurial decision-making, emphasizing scalability and ethical integration.

TABLE 1.19
Future Skills for AI-Augmented Entrepreneurs – Critical Competencies for Entrepreneurs to Harness AI Responsibly and Innovatively

Skill	Description	Tools/Resources
AI Literacy	Understanding AI/ML fundamentals	Coursera's *AI for Everyone*
Ethical Governance	Auditing algorithms for fairness	IBM's AI Fairness 360 Toolkit
Adaptive Leadership	Navigating AI-driven market shifts	MIT Sloan's *AI in Business* course
Collaborative Design	Building human–AI workflows	Notion AI, Zapier

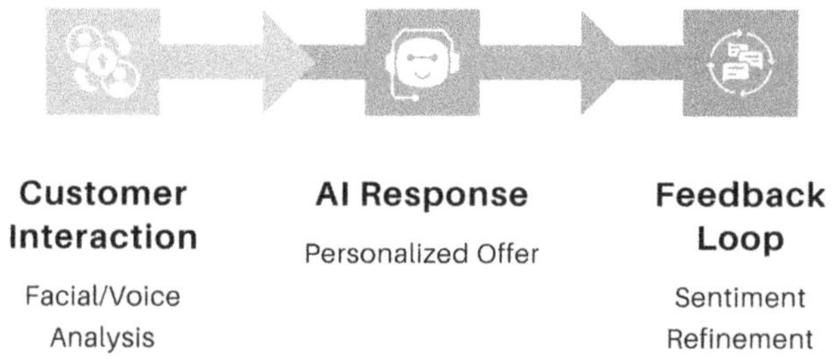

FIGURE 1.18 Emotional AI in customer decision-making – role of emotional AI in enhancing customer engagement through real-time empathy and personalization.

Entrepreneurs must adopt adaptive mindsets and ethical fluency to thrive. Key strategies include:

1. **Upskilling:** Leveraging platforms like Coursera or LinkedIn Learning for AI literacy.
2. **Ethical Governance:** Implementing AI ethics boards to audit algorithms for bias and transparency.
3. **Human–AI Symbiosis:** Using tools like Notion AI to enhance creativity while retaining critical oversight.

For instance, startups like Runway ML democratize generative AI for content creation, enabling small teams to compete with corporate giants. The future demands leaders who can balance innovation with accountability, ensuring AI amplifies human potential rather than replacing it [25].

REFERENCES

[1] Juan Camilo Serna-Zuluaga, David Juárez-Varón, Ana Mengual-Recuerda, and Ana Medina-López. Analysis of the influence of emotions on the decision-making of entrepreneurs using neurotechnologies. *International Entrepreneurship and Management Journal*, 20(3):2169–2186, 2024.

[2] Favour Oluwadamilare Usman, Nsisong Louis Eyo-Udo, Emmanuel Augustine Etukudoh, Beryl Odonkor, Chidera Victoria Ibeh, and Ayodeji Adegbola. A critical review of AI-driven strategies for entrepreneurial success. *International Journal of Management & Entrepreneurship Research*, 6(1):200–215, 2024.

[3] Liridon Kryeziu, Besnik A Krasniqi, Mehmet Bağış, Vjose Hajrullahu, Genc Zhushi, Donika Bytyçi, and Mirsim Ismajli. The effects of institutions, firm-level factors and rational decision-making on entrepreneurial behaviors of MSMES: lessons and opportunities for transition communities. *Journal of Enterprising Communities: People and Places in the Global Economy*, 18(4):771–797, 2024.

[4] Sara Baroncelli, Andrea Caputo, Erica Santini, and Christina Theodoraki. Resilience and entrepreneurial decision-making: the heterogeneity among Italian innovative start-ups. *Entrepreneurship & Regional Development*, 36(5–6):798–815, 2024.

[5] Maqsood Ahmed, Raja Hashim Ali, and Nisar Ali. Traffic sign recognition system. In *2024 International Conference on IT and Industrial Technologies (ICIT)*, Dubai, United Arab Emirates, pp. 1–6. IEEE, 2024.

[6] Pascal Adomako, Talha Ali Khan, Raja Hashim Ali, and Rand Koutaly. Comparison of leading AI models an analytical study of ChatGPT, Google Bard, and Microsoftbing. *ADCAIJ: Advances in Distributed Computing and Artificial Intelligence Journal*, 14: e31857, 2025.

[7] Shaheer Abbas, Ahmad Maaz, Raja Hashim Ali, Talha Ali Khan, and Iftikhar Ahmed. Automatic timetable generation using neural networks trained by genetic algorithms. In *2024 18th International Conference on Open Source Systems and Technologies (ICOSST)*, Lahore, Pakistan, pp. 1–6. IEEE, 2024.

[8] Alishba Ramzan, Raja Hashim Ali, Nisar Ali, and Ayesha Khan. Enhancing fake news detection using BERT: a comparative analysis of logistic regression, RFC, LSTM and BERT. In *2024 International Conference on IT and Industrial Technologies (ICIT)*, Dubai, United Arab Emirates, pp. 1–6. IEEE, 2024.

[9] Reiaan Mazhar Mian, Sohaib Khan, and Raja Hashim Ali. Bank note authentication using deep learning. In *2024 International Conference on IT and Industrial Technologies (ICIT)*, Dubai, United Arab Emirates, pp. 1–6. IEEE, 2024.

[10] Ahmad Maaz, Shaheer Abbas, Raja Hashim Ali, Iftikhar Ahmed, and Talha Ali Khan. VGG models in image captioning: which architecture delivers better descriptions? In *2024 18th International Conference on Open Source Systems and Technologies (ICOSST)*, Lahore, Pakistan, pp. 1–6. IEEE, 2024.

[11] Waqar Babar, Raja Hashim Ali, Alishba Faheem, and Syed Ahmed Mansoor. Using convolutional neural networks for enhanced pneumonia detection via chest x-rays. In *2024 International Conference on IT and Industrial Technologies (ICIT)*, Dubai, United Arab Emirates, pp. 1–6. IEEE, 2024.

[12] Robert J. Pidduck, David M. Townsend, and Lowell W. Busenitz. Non- probabilistic reasoning in navigating entrepreneurial uncertainty: a psychology of religious faith lens. *Journal of Business Venturing*, 39(4):106392, 2024.

[13] Arpita Agnihotri and Saurabh Bhattacharya. *Artificial Intelligence for Hiring and Induction: The Unilever Experience*. SAGE Publications: SAGE Business Cases Originals, 2024.

[14] Oluwaseun Peter Oyeyemi, Azeez Jason Kess-Momoh, Ganiyu Bolawale Omotoye, Binaebi Gloria Bello, Sunday Tubokirifuruar Tula, and Andrew Ifesinachi Daraojimba. Entrepreneurship in the digital age: a comprehensive review of start-up success factors and technological impact. *International Journal of Science and Research Archive*, 11(1):182–191, 2024.

[15] Brady Lund, Zeynep Orhan, Nishith Reddy Mannuru, Ravi Varma Kumar Bevara, Brett Porter, Meka Kasi Vinaih, and Padmapadanand Bhaskara. Standards, frameworks, and legislation for artificial intelligence (AI) transparency. *AI and Ethics*, 5(4):3639–3655, 2025.

[16] Shweta Sinha, Aarti Chugh, Ajantha Devi Vairamani, and Akshat Agarwal. Intelligent electric vehicles: leveraging ai-iot for sustainable mobility. In M. Balasubramanian, S. R. N. Reddy, & A. K. Bansal (Eds.), *Sustainable IoT and Data Analytics Enabled Machine Learning Techniques and Applications*, pp. 21–40. Springer, 2024.

[17] Stephen Lile, Shahzad Ansari, and Florian Urmetzer. Rethinking disruptive innovation: unravelling theoretical controversies and charting new research frontiers. *Innovation*, 27(3):394–416, 2024.

[18] Suddhasvatta Das and Kevin Gary. Challenges and success factors in large scale agile transformation—a systematic literature review. In *International Conference on Information Technology-New Generations*, pp. 405–416. Springer, Las Vegas, NV, 2024.

[19] Eugénie Coche, Ans Kolk, and Václav Ocelík. Unravelling cross-country regulatory intricacies of data governance: the relevance of legal insights for digitalization and international business. *Journal of International Business Policy*, 7(1):112–127, 2024.

[20] Dinesh Kumar and Nidhi Suthar. Ethical and legal challenges of AI in marketing: an exploration of solutions. *Journal of Information, Communication and Ethics in Society*, 22(1):124–144, 2024.

[21] Haris Anjum, Usama Arshad, Raja Hashim Ali, Zain Ul Abideen, Muhammad Huzaifa Shah, Talha Ali Khan, Ali Zeeshan Ijaz, Abu Bakar Siddique, and Muhammad Imad. Robust and reliable liveness detection models for facial recognition systems. In *2023 International Conference on Frontiers of Information Technology (FIT)*, Islamabad, Pakistan, pp. 292–297. IEEE, 2023.

[22] Gülay Demir, Prasenjit Chatterjee, and Dragan Pamucar. Sensitivity analysis in multi-criteria decision making: a state-of-the-art research perspective using bibliometric analysis. *Expert Systems with Applications*, 237:121660, 2024.

[23] Elias G Carayannis and Fernando AF Ferreira. Guest editorial: entrepreneurship and resource-based view: emerging issues, new trends and innovative decision support tools. *Management Decision*, 63(4):1121– 1123, 2025.

[24] Noor Ali, Khadija Ali, Fatimah Ali, Aaminah Ali, Nisar Ali, and Raja Hashim Ali. Streamlining attendance with voice recognition via Gaussian mixture model. In *2024 International Conference on IT and Industrial Technologies (ICIT)*, Dubai, United Arab Emirates, pp. 1–6. IEEE, 2024.

[25] Zeliha Merve Semerci and Selmi Yardımcı. Empowering modern dentistry: the impact of artificial intelligence on patient care and clinical decision making. *Diagnostics*, 14(12):1260, 2024.

2 Understanding Emotional Intelligence

Anil Pise and Hemachandran Kannan

2.1 INTRODUCTION TO EMOTIONAL INTELLIGENCE

In the rapidly changing environment of global marketing, in which artificial intelligence (AI) processes millions of data points in seconds and algorithms forecast consumer behavior with greater precision than ever, the reader may even think that human emotional ability is outdated. However, it is ironic that, in the ever-more digitized and data-centric business world, emotional intelligence (EI) has never been so important. Emotional awareness, empathy, and control of our emotions and those of others have become one of the central skills that define the difference between the successful and the less successful entrepreneurs and marketers.

The EI concept, though it is rather intuitive, is a complex model of thinking about the role of emotions in cognition, decision-making, and interactions between individuals. EI contrasts the traditionally defined intelligence quotient (IQ), which measures cognitive and analytical skills, with the oftentimes-ignored aspect of human capacity, namely the aspect that deals with emotions, interpersonal interactions, and social interaction. EI is a guide and a communication tool for any global entrepreneurs working in various cultural settings and with any multi-layered stakeholder setup. It helps to make the strategic choices, but most importantly to make a connection with a customer, a business partner, and a team employee on a global level. The EI process of translation of academic concepts to business necessity is indicative of larger trends in the way we conceive of success and effectiveness in the business environment. Traditionally, business training and corporate culture focused on technical skills, analytical quality, and rational decision-making. Emotions were considered most of the time as distractive elements that blurred vision and obstructed rational analysis. Yet, the last several decades of scientific studies in the fields of psychology, neuroscience, and organizational behavior have seriously questioned this viewpoint, showing that emotions do not hinder clear thinking but represent rather essential elements of proper reasoning and decision-making. EI is a concept that became popular in the 1990s due to the efforts of psychologists Peter Salovey and John Mayer, who defined it as the capacity to monitor personal and others' feelings and emotions, to discriminate between these feelings and emotions, and to utilize this information to direct thinking and behavior. Their definition gave them a strict theoretical basis in the objective of the emotional competencies as quantifiable and trainable skills, and not an intrinsic trait of personality. Soon after, the mainstream business communities were introduced to these concepts by Daniel Goleman

DOI: 10.1201/9781003650775-2

in his bestselling book, *Emotional Competency*, showing that emotional competencies can be more important than cognitive skills in the determination of leadership performance and professional achievement.

EI has infinite applications in the modern business world, where entrepreneurs have to operate at the global level. Take the case of the entrepreneur who has to present the investors with her innovative product that has a different cultural background to achieve success. One does not need only the technical merits of her offering but also the skills to read the room, identify the hidden issues, adjust to different communication styles, and establish genuine connections that will prompt trust and confidence. Or look at the marketing director who is required to manage a diverse, dispersed organization under the uncertainty of entering new international marketplaces – his success depends greatly on the emotional skills of empathy, self-awareness, and an ability to inspire others when they are in tough times. The importance of EI cannot be limited to personal leadership skills only but has far-reaching implications for the marketing strategy and implementation. At a time when the average consumer is being bombarded with thousands of marketing messages a day, emotional connection has become the key point of differentiation that makes its way through the noise. Marketers who are sensitive to emotional motivators – aspiration, a sense of belonging, security, or happiness – build stronger, longer-lasting relationships with their consumers than those merely competing on the functional features of their product or price. To gain knowledge regarding these emotional aspects, marketers must have advanced EI themselves as well as create mechanisms and processes for capturing and reacting to consumer emotional conditions. The situation with global entrepreneurs is a special case of the EI dilemma that is caused by the complexity of working beyond the limits of cultural boundaries. What is understood as trust in a particular culture can be interpreted as arrogance in another; display of emotion that is viewed as genuine and interesting in another culture will be viewed as unprofessional or over the top in another culture. General emotional competencies are only part of the emotionally intelligent global marketer: they should also have culturally adaptive emotional competencies – the competencies to understand how emotional standards, expressions, and interpretations differ among markets and to adapt their respective approaches. This cultural EI is an important competitive strength towards the construction of truly global brands and businesses.

Another strong argument in favor of enhancing EI that has been fronted by the contemporary business environment is the necessity to combine human judgment with AI systems. With the AIs replacing the routine analytical work and data processing, the uniquely human skills and abilities related to emotional and social intelligence gain even more importance, rather than losing them. The ability of machines to quickly process sentiment information on millions of social media posts is noteworthy, but perceiving the underlying emotional undertones, being able to distinguish between contextual factors that can influence emotional reactions, and making ethically justifiable decisions regarding the response are all the most inherently human abilities that can be based on EI. The best businesspeople and marketing companies will be those that can use the analytical power of AI and human emotional wisdom.

2.2 THEORETICAL FOUNDATIONS OF EMOTIONAL INTELLIGENCE

EI theoretical landscape consists of several models and frameworks that have different perspectives on the nature and structure of emotional competencies as well as measurement. The knowledge of these theoretical underpinnings helps entrepreneurs and marketers to have a more advanced understanding of the way EI functions and how it can be developed and implemented in a business format in an organized way [1].

Another model that theorizes EI conceptualized EI as an intelligence equivalent to cognitive capabilities, known as the ability-based model of EI, which was developed by Mayer and Salovey. This model explains EI in terms of four capabilities–linked branches. The first branch, which is the perception of emotions, consists of the correct identification of emotions in a person and others based on facial expressions, voice tone, body language, and other signals. The second branch, which employs emotion to support thinking, is associated with the ability to utilize emotional conditions to support cognitive functions such as problem-solving and creativity [2]. The third branch, knowledge of emotions, is the knowledge of emotional vocabularies, understanding emotional transitions and development, and intricate connections between various emotional conditions. The fourth and the most advanced branch is the ability to control one's emotions and the emotions of other people in order to get the desired results in other people, which is known as managing emotions. This ability-based model of EI views EI as a system of mental capacities and can be measured in an objective manner as separate cognitive capacity facets are in a traditional intelligence test. The advocates of this model claim that EI must be placed under strict psychometric criteria and show convergent and discriminant validity with other intelligences. This scientificity has seen the ability-based model especially effective in research terms, but critics observe that the objectivity of the assessment of emotional abilities is highly problematic, especially in the context of various cultures where emotional norms and manifestations differ greatly [3].

On the contrary, trait-based models view EI as a set of personality traits and the perception of emotional capabilities. Instead of tests of actual emotional functioning that measure the performance of individuals, trait models test the self-reported emotional functioning of individuals by use of questionnaires and self-assessment. Trait EI is composed of a number of dispositions such as emotional self-efficacy, emotional expression, empathy, relationship skills, and stress management [4]. This paradigm considers EI as comparatively stable traits with influence on the way people normally think and react to emotional experiences. Trait perspective has practical benefits to a business setting because self-report measures are simpler and less costly to conduct as compared to ability-based performance measures. Nonetheless, this dependence on self-assessment generates the risks of bias – people may not have a realistic understanding of their own emotional capabilities, or they may act in social desirability as opposed to acting in a truthful manner. As an entrepreneur and marketer, it is important to understand this difference; a person may view himself as extremely empathetic according to measures of traits but exhibit little actual skill in discerning the emotions of others in practice [5]. Mixed theories of EI, the most popular of which is the framework developed by Daniel Goleman, combine both skills and traits and different personality traits, motivational variables, and skills. The model by Goleman has established five key areas of EI that are specifically applicable to business and leadership situations. The basis of self-awareness is the skill of perceiving one's own feelings and understanding how these influence thoughts and actions. Self-regulation is the control of disruptive emotions and impulses and the adaptation to changing situations. Motivation does not only include the desire to achieve and get some external rewards but also involves achievement in its own right. Empathy refers to being able to know the emotional composition of others and the way people respond emotionally to individuals. Lastly, there are the social skills that relate to competence in dealing with relationships, networking, and motivating others. This blended model method has been especially effective in the organizational context as it links EI to competencies that influence performance in the workplace. This framework is actionable and common sense to the business leaders and human resource professionals to develop. Opponents of mixed models, however, claim that in including such broad constructs, they lose theoretical clarity and possess the possibility of containing things that are not necessarily EI but are related personality characteristics or general competencies [6].

The fundamental dimensions of EI should be investigated further, and each of them is unique in terms of marketing performance and business achievements. Self-awareness is the general dimension since it helps people identify their emotional conditions when they arise and comprehend the impact that the said emotions have on their perception and decision-making [7]. Self-awareness can be very useful to an entrepreneur in situations that require a lot of stakes, like when one feels that fear or overconfidence is clouding judgment about the opportunities in the market, or when personal emotional pitfalls are becoming a problem in the way that negotiation is going, or when the interaction between personal emotional process and the behavior of the team is involved. Self-regulation is a result of self-awareness since it helps an individual to control the way his/her emotions work instead of being subdued by them. This dimension is especially vital to those entrepreneurs who, by necessity, endure highs and lows of business development, the capacity to remain sensible and level-headed even at the moments when business seems to be going well, or to get excited and at the same time apply reasonable due diligence to circumstances even when there is extreme uncertainty on the outside. Self-regulation in the marketing context allows marketing professionals to react to negative feedback or failures of campaigns in a constructive way other than defensively, uphold ethical standards even when under short-term outcome pressure, and continue on with the long-term timelines that so many marketing strategies need before realizing results [8].

The EI dimension of motivation is intrinsic motivation, as motivation is a desire to accomplish something because it is right and not because of extrinsic benefits. More than the external motivations themselves would spur them to commit, emotionally intelligent people find significance and fulfillment in the job and keep their head on a swivel when faced with failure. In the case of entrepreneurs, this internal drive is critical in keeping them going during the long durations of uncertainty and difficulty that define venture creation. Intrinsically motivated professionals in marketing are more creative, persistent in the refinement of campaigns, sincere, and enthusiastic, which can easily be converted to more genuine and effective communication with customers. Empathy is probably the most directly applicable EI dimension in marketing. The capacity to read the emotions of others and their views and react properly to their moods directly makes marketers come up with messages and experiences that the target audience will associate with. Empathy helps in the profound customer insight that exists between customer-centric organizations and those that only do customer research. In the case of entrepreneurs who conduct business internationally, empathy is even more important; the skills of defining how the cultural context influences emotional experiences and expectations allow for communicating more effectively and adjusting to the market conditions (Table 2.1).

There are theoretical and practical challenges in measuring EI that ought to be known by the entrepreneur and marketer when measuring the EI of himself or herself or others. The ability-based measures usually introduce people to conditions and

TABLE 2.1
Core Dimensions of Emotional Intelligence and Marketing Applications

EI Dimension	Definition	Key Marketing Applications	Entrepreneurial Relevance
Self-Awareness	Recognition and understanding of one's own emotions and their effects	Recognizing personal biases in campaign evaluation; understanding how emotional state affects creative judgment; awareness of stress impact on decision quality	Identifying emotional triggers in negotiations; understanding personal risk tolerance; recognizing when emotions cloud strategic judgment
Self-Regulation	Managing disruptive emotions and adapting to change	Maintaining composure when campaigns underperform; responding constructively to criticism; adapting strategies without defensive reactions	Staying composed during setbacks; managing stress without affecting team morale; maintaining ethical standards under pressure
Motivation	Intrinsic drive to achieve beyond external rewards	Persistence in refining campaigns; creative problem-solving; genuine enthusiasm in customer communications	Sustained effort through uncertainty; resilience through failures; commitment to long-term vision
Empathy	Understanding others' emotions and perspectives	Deep customer insight; culturally sensitive messaging; anticipating audience reactions; relationship-based selling	Reading investor concerns; understanding team member needs; cross-cultural business development
Social Skills	Managing relationships and building networks	Cross-functional collaboration; agency relationship management; influencing stakeholders; team leadership	Recruiting talent; building partnerships; investor relations; creating organizational culture

make them recognize emotions in facial expression, anticipate emotional outcomes of behavior, or choose the right approach to emotional control. These performance-based tests provide objectivity but have problems with having the right answers to such emotional situations, which have several responses that may be relevant. The difference in the emotional expression and rules in cultures also makes the establishment of really universal measures of ability even more difficult. Self-report measures are easier to administer but present many issues of validity. Social desirability bias makes some respondents overrate their emotional competencies. Low self-awareness refers to the possibility that people can be really convinced they have skills in their emotions, which they might not have. The styles of response are different within different cultures; some cultures promote humble self-evaluation, while others promote confidence and self-promotion. When the entrepreneur is interested in assessing EI in the hiring or development process, the measurement problems discussed above are critical to perceiving the results in a proper way. Multi-source or 360-degree feedback provides a useful supplement to self-assessment as they provide the views of workmates, supervisors, subordinates, and other stakeholders. These techniques can show discrepancies between individual beliefs and the viewpoints of others regarding emotional abilities. Yet, they bring their own issues; raters might not be able to see all the factors involved, might be subject to some influences other than EI per se, or might be influenced by the quality of relationships they have with the individual being assessed.

New developments in EI testing involve behavioral observation and real-time emotional analysis. These methods see people in real work situations or in realistic simulations and evaluate them in dealing with emotionally charged situations. Behavioral assessment is more valid, and although costly and time-consuming as opposed to questionnaires, it provides more enriched information about actual emotional competencies. In the case of entrepreneurs who seek to create teams or work on their own abilities, integrating the various methods of assessing EI is the only way to obtain the most comprehensive and accurate description of it.

The theoretical bases of EI are not simply theoretical knowledge but a guideline for development. In contrast to cognitive intelligence, which actually does not change much during adulthood, EI can be trained significantly with the help of conscious practice, contemplation, and experience. This is a potential for growth that makes EI especially important to the business entrepreneur and marketer who aim at improving their performance. One can develop self-awareness by practicing mindfulness, journaling, and seeking feedback. Self-regulation is enhanced by means of stress management skills, cognitive reassessment, and rehearsal of other responses to emotional stimuli. Empathy can be developed through various social exposures, exercise of active listening, and perspective taking. Social skills are enhanced in terms of relationship-building experiences, communication training, and leadership opportunities. The knowledge of these theoretical bases is to help the entrepreneur to treat EI in a systematic way instead of assuming it is an inherent and immutable trait. By acknowledging that EI is made up of particular competitive skills that are developed, and not an overall people person aspect, business leaders can focus the development efforts on areas that have the most significant impact in their specific contexts and situations.

2.3 EMOTIONAL INTELLIGENCE IN GLOBAL MARKETING CONTEXTS

The crossroad of EI and global marketing is one of the most significant implementations of EI principles in business. In its purest meaning, marketing is the art and science of understanding and manipulating human behavior, which is an emotional task in its own right. Some marketers tend to emphasize more on the cognitive approach to persuasion by use of reason and features comparison, but in research, it has always been proven that emotions have a major influence on consumer decision-making in virtually all product categories and purchase situations.

The studies on consumer neuroscience have transformed the way in which we comprehend the process of decision-making within the human brain. In opposition to the models of rational economic actors, which previously prevailed in marketing theory, neurological data show that emotional processing is the preceding and determining factor of cognitive assessment when making decisions in the extremely large majority. The emotional center of the limbic system reacts to stimuli and starts to create preferences before the prefrontal region, which does logical analysis, has even been consulted. Emotion-first processing implies that consumers are actually limited in terms of the consideration set by the time they actually deliberate on rational factors such as price or features; the emotional responses have greatly limited the set of consideration and have biased the evaluation process. This decision-making emotional primacy has far-reaching consequences for global entrepreneurs. Marketing plans should not be merely informative on the functional benefits but should employ emotional appeals where brands seem correct, preferable, and personally pertinent to the consumer. This involves sophisticated EI on the part of marketers: the capacity to diagnose the emotional motives that apply to the target markets, to create messages and experiences that resonate with those motives in an authentic manner, and to know when their strategies are producing the intended emotional reaction. Consumer emotions that motivate consumer behavior depend on the type of product and the buying situation. Insurance purchases and security products are encouraged by fear and anxiety. Luxury goods and high-brand choices are affected by aspiration and status-seeking. The sense of belonging and social connection lead to the adoption of social media platforms and products related to communities. Entertainment decisions and spontaneous buying are driven by happiness and pleasure. Food and heritage brand preference are influenced by nostalgia and comfort. Marketers with EI are able to identify these emotional triggers and will develop strategies that are sensitive to them and will address them instead of focusing on rational product characteristics.

Take the case of an international business person who is striving to establish a high-quality coffee brand in more than one foreign country. Purely rational could be focused on coffee bean quality, practices in sourcing, and taste profiles – all are valid differentiators. Nonetheless, the emotionally understanding strategy acknowledges that coffee drinking in most societies has a strong emotional aspect: the physical warmth of the mornings, the social bond of coffee shop discussions, the aspirational linking to classiness and discerningness, or the nostalgic linking to the traditions of family. Marketing that appeals to such emotional associations, when conveying rational differentiators, will be much more successful as compared to marketing strategies that assume that the emotional dimensions do not matter at all. The key factors that drive the experience, expression, perception, and regulation of emotions in global markets are those of cultural influence. What is considered to be appropriate emotional expression in one culture is radically different in another. Open shows of enthusiasm and excitement can be taken as a sign of authenticity and interest in a certain culture, whereas in others the same actions can be viewed as immature and unprofessional. Some cultures place importance on emotional control and restraint, whereas others have more dramatic and emotional communication. The differences in these cultures present both opportunities and traps for the global marketers.

The concept of cultural display rules the informal norms governing which emotions can be expressed, in what intensity, and in which contexts they prove particularly relevant for global marketing. Display rules influence not only interpersonal interactions but also advertising effectiveness and brand communication. Marketing messages that violate cultural display rules risk alienating audiences or being dismissed as inappropriate, regardless of their other merits. Conversely, marketing that demonstrates cultural EI by aligning with local display rules and emotional norms can build deep connections and trust.

EI enables marketers to navigate these cultural complexities through several mechanisms. First, culturally intelligent marketers recognize that their own emotional norms and assumptions may not translate to other markets. This awareness prevents the assumption that emotional appeals effective in home markets will work universally. Second, EI facilitates the empathy necessary to understand how emotions function differently across cultures, not just what emotions people feel but how those emotions connect to behaviors and decisions in culturally specific ways. Third, EI supports relationship-building that enables marketers to develop trusted local partnerships and insights that guide culturally appropriate emotional marketing (Table 2.2).

Trust represents perhaps the most consequential emotional outcome that marketers seek to create, and EI plays a central role in building and maintaining consumer trust. Trust forms when customers believe that a company understands their needs, cares about their welfare, and will deliver on its promises. Each of these trust components has emotional dimensions that require EI to cultivate effectively.

Understanding customer needs demands empathy, the ability to see situations from customer perspectives and grasp not just what people want but why they want it and how it makes them feel. Many companies conduct extensive customer research yet fail to develop genuine empathy because they treat customers as data sources rather than humans with emotional experiences. Emotionally intelligent marketers bring qualitative understanding to complement quantitative data, spending time with customers in natural contexts, listening deeply to their stories, and developing genuine appreciation for customer experiences. Demonstrating care requires authentic emotional connection that customers can perceive in company communications and behaviors. Consumers have become increasingly sophisticated at detecting inauthentic corporate empathy, the "we care about you" messages that ring hollow because they're not backed by genuine organizational values or employee experiences. Emotionally intelligent marketing organizations create cultures where customer care is

TABLE 2.2
Cultural Variations in Emotional Expression and Marketing Implications

Cultural Dimension	High-Context Cultures (e.g., Japan, China)	Low-Context Cultures (e.g., USA, Germany)	Marketing Implications
Emotional Display	Subtle, restrained emotional expression; emphasis on harmony and group cohesion	More explicit, direct emotional expression; individual emotional authenticity valued	High-context: use suggestion and implicit emotional cues; low-context: more direct emotional appeals acceptable
Emotional Language	Indirect communication of emotions; reading between the lines expected	Direct verbal expression of emotions; explicit communication preferred	High-context: visual and symbolic emotional communication; low-context: verbal emotional messaging effective
Emotional Regulation	Strong emphasis on emotional control in public contexts; saving face important	Greater acceptance of emotional expression; individual feelings acknowledged	High-context: avoid causing embarrassment or strong negative emotions; low-context: can address problems more directly
Emotional Decision-Making	Collective emotional considerations; group harmony influences decisions	Individual emotional preferences; personal feelings drive choices	High-context: emphasize social proof and group benefits; low-context: focus on individual emotional satisfaction
Relationship Orientation	Emotions deeply embedded in long-term relationships; trust develops over time	Emotions can be engaged more quickly; transactional emotional appeals work	High-context: invest in relationship building before selling; low-context: can connect emotionally in shorter timeframes

genuinely felt by employees and authentically expressed in every customer interaction, not merely scripted in advertising messages.

Delivering on promises consistently over time builds the reliability component of trust, and EI contributes even here. Emotionally intelligent organizations recognize how unmet expectations generate negative emotions like disappointment, frustration, and betrayal. This recognition motivates more conservative, promising, and more aggressive delivery than competitors might practice. These companies also demonstrate EI in how they handle inevitable failures, acknowledging mistakes honestly, expressing genuine remorse, and taking meaningful corrective action rather than deflecting blame or offering hollow apologies. Brand loyalty emerges when emotional connections deepen beyond trust into genuine affection, identity alignment, or even love. The world's strongest brands have cultivated emotional bonds with customers that transcend rational evaluation. Apple users who feel their devices express their creativity and individuality, Harley-Davidson riders for whom the brand represents freedom and rebellion, and Patagonia customers who see the brand as an extension of their environmental values. These emotional brand relationships didn't emerge from superior product features alone but from emotionally intelligent brand building that created authentic emotional resonance with target audiences' identities, values, and aspirations.

Relationship marketing, the practice of creating long-term customer relationships rather than focusing exclusively on individual transactions, fundamentally depends on EI. Successful relationship marketing requires understanding how emotional bonds develop and strengthen over time. Like personal relationships, commercial relationships deepen through consistent positive experiences, authentic communication, demonstrated care during difficult times, and creation of shared meaning. Emotionally intelligent marketers design customer experiences with these relationship-building principles in mind, creating touchpoints that strengthen emotional connections rather than merely completing transactions. The digital transformation of marketing has not diminished the importance of EI; if anything, it has amplified it. While digital channels introduce efficiency and scale, they also create distance and reduce the emotional richness of human interaction. Successfully creating emotional connections through digital channels requires heightened EI to compensate for the missing interpersonal cues and interaction quality of face-to-face communication. Digital marketers must become skilled at conveying emotion through text, images, and video; at recognizing emotional states from digital behaviors and signals; and at designing digital experiences that feel personally relevant despite being delivered through technology.

2.4 INTEGRATION OF EMOTIONAL INTELLIGENCE WITH ARTIFICIAL INTELLIGENCE

EI and AI are two means of interaction with each other that are most interesting and significant and define the future of global marketing. These two types of intelligence are, in fact, rather complementary and mutually exclusive, as each one has its weaknesses and strengths that balance out the weaknesses of and enhance the advantages of the other. The ability to comprehend the role of integrating human EI with AI capabilities turned out to be a paramount skill to master among entrepreneurs and marketing executives. AI is particularly good at what humans find difficult or even impossible. AI is good at processing large amounts of information to extract patterns, being consistent at making millions of decisions, being able to work continuously, and being objective and free of emotional bias, and even at optimizing large systems full of interacting variables. All these AI advantages add lots of value to the marketing spheres that comprise the ability to personalize at scale, bid on an advertisement in real-time across thousands of keywords and placements, anticipate customer churn before it happens, and experiment with an unlimited number of message variations to find the best strategies [9].

The problem is, though, that AI systems do not possess even the EI that human beings introduce to marketing choices. The machines are incapable of experiencing feelings and having an intuitive grasp of the subtle emotional life of the consumers. Their problem is in context-related interpretation of emotions, that is, knowing that the same words or actions may convey a variety of emotions in different situations, cultures, or relationship histories. AI systems can struggle with the ethical issues that come with emotion-based marketing, like having persuasion techniques enter the arena of manipulation, or people who are vulnerable and prone to special treatment. The limitations of AI can be mitigated by human EI. Individuals come with knowledge of situations that can enable the right interpretation of emotional signals, given the circumstances. Human beings also have judgments that are ethical in the sense based on values and moral arguments, which are not limited to rule-following. We provide innovative thinking that produces new emotional appeals and brand stories that AI systems, which were conditioned to rely on past trends, would never independently produce. Authenticity of relationships is offered by human beings, the actual emotional attachment that customers cannot ignore, despite the growth of digital interactions [10].

This complementarity is acknowledged in the design of human-in-the-loop systems, which involve a human judgment on important decision-making points instead of full autonomy when it comes to AI systems. Human-in-the-loop designs help place AI systems in marketing scenarios so that they can do the analytical heavy lifting and leave human participation in making decisions that have a strong emotional or ethical component. As an illustration, an AI system could automatically examine the social media discussion to determine trends and patterns of sentiment, but the human would see variations in the pattern and determine how the brand should react in ways that reinforce and not harm emotional bonds with customers. Think about the use of this principle in the automation of customer service. A chatbot can be used to provide quick responses to a variety of frequent customer queries, as AI-powered chatbots are able to effectively manage numerous routine customer requests and lead customers through standardized procedures. This automation will add value by making the wait times shorter, and human agents will be able to engage in more complicated interactions. Yet, emotionally intelligent organizations realize when circumstances must be addressed by human hand, when clients are angry or aggravated, when it touches upon personal sensitive data or has a serious financial effect, or when an original resolution is necessary to reach an acceptable solution. The integration strategy channels such emotionally sensitive scenarios to be taken by human agents possessing EI to maneuver through them.

Sentiment analysis is another field of application where AI development and EI are integrated to produce better results. The latest natural language processing systems are able to process the text in a review of the customers, or in a post on a social media platform, or in a question on a survey, and classify the sentiment as positive, negative, or neutral responses. More advanced systems recognize individual emotions such as joy, anger, sadness, or fear. Such AI features allow businesses to track emotional reactions on thousands or millions of customer engagements, which cannot be analyzed with human abilities. Nevertheless, AI sentiment analysis is prone to serious limitations that can be fixed by human EI. The context has a significant influence on emotional meaning that is not easily explained by the existing AI. The meaning that would be determined solely by purely computational analysis may be totally inverted by sarcasm, irony, cultural idiom, and a context-specific reference. A review of the product that states "this product is so good I want to throw it out the window" could be treated as a negative review by AI systems that think in a literal way and interpret the words as a literal meaning of the throw out the window but in the emotional understanding of the human who is not so intelligent could see that this is a frustrated sarcasm that shows that the product is not working. The other challenge to AI sentiment analysis is cultural and emotional differences. The expression of emotions in different languages and different cultures differs in such a way that they cannot be perfectly reflected with the help of translation only. What is considered strong emotional language may also vary depending on the cultural background; what would be considered mild dissatisfaction in one culture may be a major case of upset in a different culture. Human reviewers, who are emotionally intelligent, and who are aware of these cultural subtleties, can tune the AI-produced scores on sentiment to the extent of the true emotional intensity in certain cultural contexts. Sentiment analysis is best done with a system that an AI is scaled with human interpretive power. AI scans all the available texts and generates patterns, trends in sentiment over time, and potentially meaningful emotion responses. Then, human analysts are left to review flagged material, make interpretations on ambiguous cases, detect emotional undertones that AI overlooked, and decide on how to act strategically. This combination enables organizations to be emotionally sensitive to their entire customer base and, at the same time, employ the use of human EI at its center of focus (Figure 2.1).

Emotion-aware marketing systems are the future of AI-EI integration, trying to establish artificial systems that can perceive and react to the emotional conditions of customers. These systems utilize different technologies such as facial expression, voice emotion, physiological signals (monitoring), and behavioral patterns to guess the emotional states. Theoretically, this kind of system could allow very reactive marketing responsive to the emotions of the customers, where presentations on the websites can change when a visitor appears confused, sales strategies can be modified when a visitor displays signs of indecisiveness, and extra support can be offered when a visitor becomes frustrated. Nonetheless, creating and launching emotion-sensitive AI systems present technical and ethical issues that involve human EI in order to address. Technical constraints imply that existing systems are able to recognize general emotional conditions but not subtleties, personal differences, and cultural diversity in expressing emotion. False positives and negatives are still prevalent; the system may perceive concentrated focus as confusion or miss some real frustration. At a deeper level, emotion-sensitive systems raise ethical issues regarding privacy, manipulation, and consent. Consumers might not be comfortable with the fact that their emotional conditions are being tracked and can be used to make them make a choice. It is not just a mere coincidence that a human salesman

FIGURE 2.1 The power of human-AI synergy in marketing.

can pick up on the emotional sign and react to it when an automated system is expected to identify the vulnerability and play upon it. Ethically sensitive organizations are aware of such ethical limits, and they develop emotion-sensitive systems with the right limitations, visibility, and control to the user instead of seeking maximum persuasion at whatever cost to the consumer.

The combination of emotional and AI in making global marketing decisions eventually needs a strategic framework that situates each of the intelligences in the areas where they generate the greatest value. The computer elements of AI must perform large-scale data analysis, optimization of systems with large numbers of aspects, consistency across high numbers of touchpoints, and proven methods at scale. The strategic direction that provides AI systems with purpose, interprets patterns that AI detects with an emotional meaning, makes high-stakes decisions with a strong emotional or ethical overlay, forms the authentic emotional relationship that generates long-term relationships with customers, and constantly develops emotional insights as cultures and markets vary should be guided by human EI. The entrepreneurs who are developing marketing organizations in the AI world have to develop both of these types of intelligence, and, more to the point, the organizational abilities to compound the two. This involves recruiting and training team workers with high EI, who will be able to collaborate with AI systems and not fear them. It requires technical infrastructure that enables AI tools to be made easily accessible to marketers but with proper human control. It requires an organizational culture that does not ignore either data-driven optimization or emotional wisdom, not taking either extreme of pure intuition versus pure algorithmic decision-making.

2.5 EMOTIONAL INTELLIGENCE AND ENTREPRENEURIAL PERFORMANCE

EI and its association with entrepreneurial success have increasingly come under research focus as researchers endeavor to ensure they comprehend why certain entrepreneurs develop successful businesses, whereas other entrepreneurs with seemingly the same attributes and prospects fail. Although aspects such as market conditions, technical capabilities, and financial resources are undoubtedly important, EI is found to be a key distinguishing factor that changes the results of entrepreneurship in various ways. The most direct relationship between EI and the performance of an entrepreneur may be leadership effectiveness. Entrepreneurs need to be the first ones to operate in unique, difficult situations that include having limited resources, having high uncertainty, influencing other team members when there is no guarantee of success, and a 24-hour effort in the face of unavoidable failures. These leadership issues require high levels of EI. Self-awareness helps entrepreneurs to understand when they are under stress, feeling fear, or being overconfident, and influence their judgment. Self-regulation helps them to remain calm and emanate confidence to their teams even in the face of immense adversity. Empathy helps entrepreneurs to know what drives various team members and stakeholders so that they can influence them better. Social skills make the relationship-building process and network establishment that open opportunities to resources, talent, and opportunities possible.

Findings have continuously shown correlations between EI and leadership effectiveness in different situations, and such connections are found to be even greater in the entrepreneurial environment, where the demands on a leader are extreme. With greater EI, entrepreneurs are better able to create stronger groups, establish more favorable organizational cultures, retain talent, and produce greater rates of employee commitment and engagement. These are the results of enabling psychological safety in which the team members feel an appreciation and no fear to share ideas, to acknowledge and capitalize on the input of individual employees in a meaningful manner, to handle conflict effectively, and make the team members committed to a shared vision that cannot be attributed solely to financial incentives. Opportunity identification – the skill of identifying and acting on the good business opportunities – is another area of EI influence on entrepreneurial performance. Conventional approaches to opportunity recognition focus on cognitive processes, such as pattern recognition, analytical assessment, and synthesizing creative processes. Nevertheless, EI helps in opportunity recognition in a number of ways. Empathy helps an entrepreneur recognize needs and frustrations that other people have encountered in their own lives, which is usually the source of a new venture idea. Emotional sensitivity to the market indicators assists businesspersons in feeling the shifts in consumer behaviors and the new trends anticipated in the market before those interested in analyzing it. The EI intrinsic motivation aspect facilitates the continued exploration and experimentation that may be required to change the first impressions into opportunities.

Take the example of the entrepreneur who created Airbnb. The first opportunity insight was based on a personal experience; the founders had to pay rent and observed that there were expensive hotels and a design conference that produced an accommodation shortage. Nonetheless, this personal experience, in order to be identified as a larger market opportunity, needed EI. They had to be empathetic in that their personal experience of frustration with overly expensive hotels and the need to experience the local life could give similar feelings to millions of other visitors. Their awareness of emotions was needed to realize the psychological obstacle that prevents people from living in the homes of strangers and how to handle these needs. They had to be socially intelligent so that they could create the trust mechanisms that the platform would operate on. The naked gift of analysis may never have discovered this opportunity, or known how to carry it out. Negotiation is one of the most essential entrepreneurial skills in which EI establishes tremendous performance benefits. Entrepreneurs are always negotiating with investors on valuations and terms, with potential customers on prices and contracts, with partners on collaboration structure, and with suppliers on costs and conditions. These negotiations are done within a set-up where the bargaining power of the entrepreneurs is usually low, and as such, the skill of negotiation becomes very essential. EI improves the negotiation results in various ways. Self-awareness enables entrepreneurs to understand their own emotional triggers and hot buttons so that they can be in control of them rather than being derailed by them when engaging in challenging conversations. Empathy will help the entrepreneurs to know the underlying interests and concerns of counterparties in relation to their stated positions, and in most cases, they may find innovative solutions that will satisfy the core needs of everyone involved. The social skills will help in the relationship development that builds goodwill and trust, which usually will achieve much better terms than solely adversarial methods would. Emotional leadership enables businesspeople to stay calm and strategic at the negotiation table without the emotional reactionary compromise or fixed stance that mostly comes to light in the face of pressure.

The studies concerning negotiation illustrate a consistent result, which is that people possessing strong EI are more successful, especially in complex negotiations where relationships are important and an inventive solution can be reached. To entrepreneurs, such negotiating benefits may have disproportionately large effects, such as obtaining funding on favorable terms or foregoing too much equity, winning a customer deal versus losing to competitors, and developing a partnership versus developing a controversial supplier relationship. Another mechanism by which EI influences the performance of an entrepreneur is conflict management capabilities. Conflicts are always unavoidable in the startup setting – co-founders on strategic direction, team members on priorities and responsibility, the venture, and the external stakeholder on expectations and deliverables. The manner in which these conflicts are managed has a significant implication on the outcomes of ventures. Positively handled conflicts may bring up vital matters, come up with innovative solutions, and build up relationships. Uncontrolled conflicts hurt the unity of the team, squander resources, and even end up destroying projects altogether. Entrepreneurs who have a high level of EI handle conflicts in a constructive manner compared to other entrepreneurs who have low levels of EI. They identify the symptoms of conflict in time before things deteriorate. They know that conflict is usually based on needs or concerns that are not met and not necessarily based on rational disagreements and hence they can deal with the underlying factors. They establish some conditions under which individuals feel comfortable airing out their differences. They spur constructive conflict talks that are preoccupied with stakes as opposed to positional issues. They mend relationships once conflicts are over, such that the end result of the process of resolving their disagreements would not make the team more disintegrated, but it would enhance its cohesiveness.

The engagement of stakeholders is more of EI as they have to deal with various constituencies at the same time. The investors desire growth and returns, and they tend to demand aggressive expansion. Employees require job security and meaningful work. Customers require value and good service. Couples want each other reciprocate. These groups of stakeholders have conflicting interests in most cases. The only way that emotionally intelligent entrepreneurs can handle these conflicting needs is by recognizing the emotional and rational interests of each group, managing to communicate in a manner appealing to various audiences, and by developing ingenious solutions that can suit the interests of various stakeholders instead of appeasing only one or the other. They need to balance investor expectations while simultaneously maintaining employee motivation. The bad news received by investors may put pressure on entrepreneurs to implement drastic changes, such as layoffs. When employees feel insecure, they require reassurance and an explanation. A business owner who has poor EI capability may just succumb to the pressure of the investor without bothering about employee implications or may not want to engage in uncomfortable discussions at all, and in this case rumor and anxiety may continue to brew. A highly sensitive entrepreneur will be able to see the justified interests of the investors and their need to communicate and feel secure psychologically. They design answers that acknowledge the difficulties without being deceptive but affirmative about the way to go, they negotiate with the investors to maintain the core members of the team but make the necessary changes, and they communicate with employees in a manner that does not cause panic.

These EI-performance relations are shown by case examples of successful global entrepreneurial ventures. Reed Hastings, the co-founder of Netflix, has a high EI in the way he approaches organizational culture. Hastings identified that in creative and fast-paced businesses, command and control management strangles innovation. Freedom and responsibility is a culture at Netflix that demonstrates an emotionally intelligent grasp of the need of talented individuals to be free and have trust rather than strict regulations. Radical transparency in the company concerning business performance is informed by the fact that individuals can deal with hard information rather than staying in the dark. The focus on direct feedback is informed by the fact that individuals desire to be better, and the ability to give feedback sincerely, albeit discomfort, is never harmful to relationships. It is these culturally intelligent emotions that have helped Netflix to have exceptional talent and dynamically adapt when the business transformed to integrate content production and streaming on the platform after starting with DVD rental. EI is an aspect of success in global entrepreneurial ventures that is usually evident in the path of transitioning during critical moments. Most technically genius founders have a hard time when their organizations grow to the size of businesses that need more advanced people leadership. The same skills, which helped them to develop novel products – analytical rigor, technical understanding, and product vision – are not adequate in leading organizations of hundreds or thousands of employees. The leaders who cultivate EI skills or leaders who introduce complementary leadership with a powerful EI are usually able to cross these transitions successfully. Companies that are unable to accomplish this EI jump tend to have their constraints limiting venture growth (Figure 2.2).

FIGURE 2.2 Impact of emotional intelligence on entrepreneurial performance.

2.6 DIGITAL EMOTIONAL INTELLIGENCE IN ONLINE CONSUMER ENVIRONMENTS

The process of digitalization of business and communication has completely changed the way emotions are used in a marketing setting. Face-to-face commercial interactions with traditional businesses were rich in emotions as facial expressions, voice tone, body language, and other interpersonal communications offered abundant information. Online space removes most of them, providing both challenges and possibilities to emotional marketing. To comprehend emotional processes in digital contexts, it is crucial to realize the way in which digital channels transform emotional experience and expression. Communication via text eliminates the probability of using tone of voice and facial expression, which makes it unclear regarding the meaning of emotions and makes misunderstandings more prevalent. As communication becomes asynchronous, emotional feedback loops are delayed, which would otherwise be utilized in face-to-face communication to control emotion. Anonymity felt in numerous online spaces can enhance the expressiveness of emotions – individuals tend to show greater emotions online as compared to offline. Digital communication is permanent. Therefore, the expressions of emotions can be re-read and reinterpreted many years after the event that has caused them.

Social media sites are one of the most complicated emotional environments that demand high levels of EI to operate in. The platforms enhance emotional contagion – the spreading of emotions by people over social networks as they see and reflect the emotional state of others. Positive feelings such as enthusiasm and joy can cause viral amplification when the content is emotional. Nonetheless, other negative emotions, such as outrage and anxiety, also go viral and occasionally cause reputational crises that run out of control. The digital emotional dynamics demand the ability to respond to such traits of emotionally intelligent social media marketing. Marketers should understand that social media users use the platforms to have emotional experiences, that is, to be entertained, inspired, affirmed, connected, and not to receive just pure information. Effective content must be emotional, which inspires sharing and participation. Nevertheless, when leaving to seek the emotional reaction without legitimate merit, it is backfiring because people are becoming aware of the manipulative nature of such material, and they are repelling it. To read emotional undercurrents in the social media discourse, digital emotional signs need to be interpreted. Emotions are clearly indicated with the help of emojis and emoticons, but they could be applied ironically. Capital letters and exclusion marks tend to indicate the intensity of emotions. Short answers that are delivered in quick succession can be a sign of high emotion. The pattern of dissemination of content, the number of people sharing it, and the speed of dissemination give hints regarding the ability to appeal to emotions. The emotional reactions of the audience are determined through the comment sentiment and toxicity levels. Emotionally intelligent marketers learn to read these online emotional cues instead of looking at the metrics that are easy to measure, such as likes or shares, that might not reflect emotional attachment.

The EI challenge and opportunity in e-commerce environments are different. Through online shopping, one is deprived of the emotional gratification of seeing or touching products, putting them on, or consulting experienced sales personnel. This poses anxiety and uncertainty that needs to be tackled by e-commerce that is emotionally intelligent on product details, customer reviews, open and liberal returns, and responsive customer care. The emotional aspects of reviews, ratings, and community signals have a role to play in e-commerce that is not limited to the informational benefit of the same. The positive reviews also reassure emotionally those who purchase the product that they will not be anxious about their purchases. The number of reviews indicates that other people have trusted the product, and this establishes a safety in numbers. Negative reviews, when managed well by companies, can in fact end up leading to more trust because of the authenticity and the way problems are addressed. The particular emotions conveyed in reviews, such as enthusiasm, disappointment, frustration, and delight, have a stronger effect on the emotional expectations and purchase intentions of the readers compared to the star ratings.

Intelligent e-commerce companies are aware that, when negative reviews are made, there is a chance to exhibit EI to the outside world. The character of companies in the light of how they react to criticism shows more about them than marketing claims do. Instead, defensive reaction and accusing customers or not resolving issues hurt credibility. Honestly accepting problems, showing real caring, and taking real corrective action are examples of EI that develop customer confidence. Intelligent companies understand that viewers observe such interactions and create perceptions of company values and customer care based on these interactions. Communities of user-generated content form emotional ecosystems that are cultivated or harmed by the brands in the manner in which they interact with them. The community is built around common interests, identities, or values, which establish emotional connections between the members and are not based on commercial relations with brands. The brands that are aware of the emotional texture of these communities – what matters to them, what rules do they have to follow, what can make them participate, etc. – can become welcome members of the community. Companies that consider communities as a marketing strategy and fail to respect the norms and emotional cultures of the community tend to be rejected or face backlash. The digital emotional responses to gender and culture have enormous implications for global digital marketing. Studies have shown that there are gender variations in the emotional expression and response in digital platforms, but more than as a result of socialization, these variables may be inherent. On average, women employ more emotionally expressive language in online communication, more emotional content, and react more to emotional appeals to specific types of products. Men might tend to show some kinds of emotions, such as anger or pride, and tend less to show others, such as vulnerability or sadness, to the world.

However, there are significant differences in these gender patterns within cultural contexts. In certain cultures, there is quite an equal emotional expression by both genders, while in others, there is a stronger division of gender. Global marketers who are emotionally intelligent do not embrace rigid gender stereotypes at the expense of acknowledging that gender socialization patterns can bring about certain patterns of responses in certain cultural markets. The trick is to get to know specific local cultural standards of conduct of gender and emotion instead of generalizing about

Western research. The digital expression of emotion tends to follow the cultural trend of expression of emotion, but with a few exaggerations or changes characteristic of the digital scenario. Cultures with traditional priorities on emotional restraint can exhibit a little more emotional expression on the Internet because of more anonymity and less face-saving influence. Nevertheless, there are still underlying cultural tendencies – what emotional forms are expected to be communicated, what level of emotion is acceptable, and in which situations the expression of emotions is encouraged or discouraged is a culturally diverse issue. EI is a combination of privacy issues in online marketing. Customers are becoming more anxious and frustrated with practices in data collection and targeting that seem to be intrusive. Organizations that have EI acknowledge such concerns as real, as opposed to them being seen as absurd fears or obstacles to be conquered. They adopt privacy policies that consider consumer emotional comfort; they offer transparent information on how data is used, meaningful control and opt-out; and they do not use any targeting method that makes them feel creepy or manipulated, despite their legality. The digital EI paradox is that the more the interactions are mediated by technology, the greater the requirement of human emotional wisdom, and which does not diminish. Online media builds a barrier, decreases the emotional depth, and can treat customers as objects more easily. By building empathetic designs that ensure digital experiences are familiar with the emotional state in mind of users, responding to digital interactions with emotional realism, and applying scale to digital connection to amplify and not to displace human connection, organizations can build sustainable competitive advantages in more and more digital markets.

2.7 ETHICAL AND PSYCHOLOGICAL DIMENSIONS OF EMOTIONAL INTELLIGENCE

When EI is applied to marketing, it is bound to create ethical dilemmas, which the entrepreneur and marketing experts can only take seriously. The ability to interpret emotions and know how to manipulate them turns out to be a power that can be applied in a responsible manner or in an unethical manner. The ethical implications of emotionally intelligent marketers are growing in relevance as the technology that detects emotion advances and the knowledge of the mechanism of emotional impact also advances. The worst possible use of EI in a marketing situation is emotional manipulation. Manipulation is when emotional influence methods are resorted to in the best interest of the person that is influencing, at the cost of the affected side and their free will to make decisions. In contrast to ethical persuasion, which acknowledges the existence of the agency of the individual and strives to achieve mutually beneficial results, manipulation addresses people as subjects to be manipulated and not participants to be involved. Some marketing techniques are evidently moving into the realm of manipulation. False scarcity is the creation of artificial urgency that is exploitative to create the sense of missing out without genuinely adding value. Manipulation is the use of emotional appeals to reach vulnerable groups of people, such as children, the elderly, and people with addiction problems or cognitive limitations, among others. Selective emotional framing, which is used to cover up the important negative aspects or dangers of products or services, uses emotional appeals. These feedback loops that target the psychological vulnerability to take advantage of them, as certain social media platforms and video games can be designed, are manipulative even when the user apparently agrees with it.

Organizations that have high levels of EI put limits on what is ethical emotional engagement and what is manipulation. This difference is guided by a number of principles. The disclosure of influence efforts gives informed consent – individuals need to know when they are being influenced and not being emotionally manipulated without their knowledge. Autonomy respect implies offering information and emotional background that allows making a true decision instead of feeling pressured or being overly judgmental. Mutual benefit will make the emotional influence meet the interests of both the company and the customer, instead of simply gleaning from the customers. Vulnerability protection is a form of special care that is created by working with people or groups with lower judgment capacities or higher levels of emotional susceptibility. The problem of consumer vulnerability is of particular interest since in this or that state of life, psychological state or demographic features precondition the increased vulnerability to emotional influence that should be considered by the representatives of the ethical marketing field. Financial hardship makes one susceptible to predatory types of loans or investment options that offer quick fixes. This vulnerability can expose individuals to exploitative funeral and estate service practices. Medical assertions are open to challenge due to health crises. Isolation predisposes one to manipulative social products or services. Adolescents and children have no proper judgment or emotional control abilities. Making emotionally intelligent marketers aware of such vulnerabilities will change their strategies, knowing that there are customer groups who will need extra protection at the expense of revenue in the short term. This could involve the refusal of business to those who cannot pay, the provision of more decision support and cooling-off time in the case of high-value purchases, the prevention of emotional manipulation of youthful audiences, or establishing special protection on products of potentially addictive value. The fast development of emotion-sensitive technologies brings up new ethical issues that should be taken into account. Emotional marketing is a formidable prospect due to the use of facial recognition systems, which interpret the emotional expressions of a face; voice analysis, which identifies emotions based on the voice; and behavioral tracking, which assumes the emotion based on online behavior. But these technologies also have the issue of surveillance, consent, and emotional privacy.

When the data collection is carried out in accordance with the law, many consumers are not ready to know that their emotional conditions are under surveillance and utilized in a commercial way. This unease is motivated by understandable fears of invasion of privacy, of unequal power imbalance that exists between companies learning more about the emotional circumstances of consumers than consumers themselves do, and about the potential abuse of emotional information. Organizations that use emotion-sensitive technologies should focus not only on the requirements of law but also on the requirements of emotion; that is, just because something can be done technically and legally, it does not mean it is also emotion-respecting and ethically correct.

There are a number of practices involved in the responsible use of emotion-aware technologies. The access to information regarding the collection and use of emotional data should enable informed consent. Purpose limitation is necessary to make sure that the emotional data is not utilized for other purposes that are not mentioned and do not just serve the good of the company. The process of data minimization removes all the emotional data more than that needed to serve the purpose. Security protection avoids emotional breaches of data that might lead to embarrassment or damage. The user control offers valuable opt-out features and deletion option. Periodic ethical assessment is used to determine the consistency of the emotional monitoring practices and organizational values and expectations of stakeholders. The psychological aspect of EI in marketing goes further to the psychological health of the marketing professionals themselves. The stress of working on the emotional impact on a daily basis may have its psychological effects. Marketers might develop the state of cognitive dissonance when the practice of the company contradicts personal values. Constant exposure to influence tactics may cynicize them on human emotion and motivation. There is a risk that they will get burned out due to the emotional strain of being enthusiastic and positive. Organizations that are aware of EI should take care of these effects on their own employees, and not only on the customers. Striking the right balance between persuasion and consumer welfare is a key conflict over marketing ethics. Every marketing is geared toward convincing, to change beliefs, attitudes, and behavior toward a direction that will be beneficial to the company. Convincing is not necessarily an unethical thing; it is only immoral when it enters into manipulation or when it is completely unacceptable to the interests of consumers to act in favor of the company. In terms of emotion-based marketing, the happy medium is in the persuasion communication, which is honest, respectful of autonomy, and seeks results that are mutually beneficial.

Such a middle ground can be different depending on the type of product and setting. In more discretionary buying of relatively low-stakes products or services, more aggressive emotional convincing might be acceptable since there are no high stakes and consumers can easily tune out. In cases where the number of alternatives available to the consumer is low, in case of high risks or long-term effects of a product or service, or in cases where services of products are provided to vulnerable groups, a higher ethical line should be applied and persuasion strategies more moderate. Corporate Social Responsibility (CSR) and ethical marketing are even treated by some as limitations to business performance or as a matter of mere reputation. Nevertheless, ethically smart companies acknowledge that ethical marketing is a manifestation of genuine values and interests of the business in the long term. When establishing a sustainable competitive advantage, companies that earn trust by acting ethically do so and do it in a sustainable way that tactical manipulation never brings about. Even though safeguarding the welfare of the consumer constrained the short-term revenue, those organizations that safeguard the consumer welfare create the loyalty and advocacy that lead to long-term success. Ethical leaders establish organizational cultures that tend to attract talented individuals who prefer to work in companies that they have confidence in. Ethical practice of EI will eventually involve continuous reflection and discourse, and not mere adherence to the rules. Ethical rules give guidelines, but certain circumstances will be characterized by trade-offs and ambiguities, which should be characterized by prudent judgment. Companies that embrace ethical EI establish platforms where dilemmas can be discussed, employees are given a chance to express their concerns without intimidation, and the habit of evaluating how practices are in conformity with proclaimed values. This continuous ethical involvement is integrated into the organizational culture and not pushed to the compliance functions.

2.8 MANAGERIAL IMPLICATIONS FOR ENTREPRENEURS AND MARKETERS

Knowledge in the theoretical and practical aspects of EI is only valuable when it is converted into practices in organizations that make marketing effective and entrepreneurial operations successful. The following section discusses the implications for practical managerial aspects of building emotionally intelligent marketing organizations and incorporating EI into AI-based marketing systems. The creation of emotionally intelligent marketing personnel starts with the hiring processes that determine the emotional capabilities of employees, in addition to the technical skills. Conventional marketing recruiting is mostly concerned with the ability to analyze, strategic thinking, creativity, and knowledge of the domain – valuable attributes. Nevertheless, other companies that embrace EI also evaluate the self-awareness of candidates, empathy, social skills, and emotional regulation used in the selection. Emotional competencies are well assessed through realistic simulation-based assessment centers. The ability of candidates to manage difficult interpersonal situations, such as dealing with an angry customer, resolving group conflict, adjusting communication to different cultures, and other situational exercises, demonstrates real EI competencies more accurately than either self-report questionnaires or assertions on the interview. Behavioral interviews that dwell on previous experiences in dealing with emotionally demanding situations give an indication of how the applicants have exhibited EI before. Multi-source reference checks involving former colleagues, subordinates, as well as supervisors, rather than just supervisors, indicate the manifestation of emotional competencies by the candidates in the real workplace relationships.

Nevertheless, employment based on EI does not imply that one should employ highly emotionally intelligent people. Emotional diversity is required in organizations; different people with different levels of EI can bring something different to the table. The most important thing here is to have adequate EI at the leadership levels and within the client-facing positions where EI has the most significant influence on performance and to have mechanisms in place that foster all employees to acquire emotional skills. EI development training structures must focus on both EI awareness and skills. Awareness training assists a person to be aware of the existing emotional patterns, the way emotions influence them in making decisions, and to identify personal emotional triggers, as well as shaping more advanced emotional vocabularies. Skill-building is aimed at the development of particular skills such as active listening, effective emotional regulation skills, effective feedback, and effective cross-cultural emotional navigation skills. There are a number of design principles that will be applied in effective EI training. Experiential education operating on role-plays, simulations, and practicing in reality is more effective than strictly didactic education. The continual support and development in terms of coaching, peer learning groups, and reinforcement by managers promote better improvement as compared to a single workshop. Individualized development plans based on the fact that different people have different levels of EI strengths and development requirements make learning more purposeful, as compared to regular programs. Combining with real working issues will guarantee the transfer of learning to real-life scenarios and not classroom knowledge.

Developing psychologically safe organizational cultures is perhaps the most significant managerial intervention in terms of the support of EI. Psychological safety, the collective assumption that risk-taking in interpersonal relationships is safe within a team, can make possible the honest emotional communication and vulnerable learning that the EI development demands. The psychologically unsafe environment results in individuals suppressing emotional struggles, evading difficult discussions, blaming others in situations of mistakes, and managing impressions instead of connecting with others. These defensive actions both inhibit personal EI growth as well as organizational EI. Psychological safety is established by the leaders in a number of practices. Vulnerability modeling can be influenced by admitting its mistakes and uncertainties, which implies that imperfection is not a problem. Punitive reaction instead of constructive reaction when people confront issues or confess mistakes is likely to foster honesty in communication. The very idea of asking side opinions and devil's advocate opinion explicitly indicates that one is not going to be punished in case of any disagreement. With the organization of inclusive processes where everyone is heard, there cannot be a situation of major personalities crowding out others during a discussion. Counting on the team members who have breached the psychological safety by blaming, dismissiveness, or ridicule shows that it is important that leaders create safe environments.

The EI of AI-based marketing systems must be strategically designed to place the human emotional wisdom in the areas where it is most valuable. There are a number of organizational models that have been effective in this integration. The oversight model makes AI systems largely autonomous but needs human intervention to review such decisions with strong emotional consequences. For example, AI will compose custom email messages automatically, and human review of messages to vulnerable client groups. The collaborative model is organized in a way that AI and human individuals do joint work on the tasks. AI designates the patterns of sentiment in customer feedback, and humans rate emotional backgrounds and formulate the strategy of response actions. In the human-primary model, human beings remain central in the decision process, with AI decision support offering relevant data analysis and optimization suggestions to human beings making the final marketing strategy decision. The decision to select any of these models will be based on a number of factors, such as the emotional impact of the decision, the cultural competency needed, the ethical delicacy involved, and the existence of human expertise. Tough decisions that are related to vulnerable groups or include a high level of ethical aspects must be more humanized. Human-primary approaches are advantageous in situations when complex cultural emotional perceptions are involved. It is safe to use more automated methods with human control as a result of routine optimizations that have well-understood emotional dynamics. Incentive systems and performance management must be able to reward the contribution of EI and not just those that are easily measurable. Conventionally used measures of marketing, such as conversion rates, customer acquisition costs, and revenue targets, are significant measurements of performance but might not capture the EI that produces success over time. Organizations can integrate EI into performance management in a number of ways.

EI contributions that remain unnoticed by quantitative measures are given by qualitative feedback collected through colleagues, customers, and other stakeholders in the 360-degree assessments that measure elements such as empathy, collaboration, conflict resolution, and relationship building. Measures of customer relationship quality, such as retention rates, referrals generated, and satisfaction scores, are measures that are impacted by EI. The study of the impact of emotional dynamics on team effectiveness in the scope of project retrospectives give insights into the influence of emotional intelligence.

Emotionally intelligent marketing has strategic guidelines that lay stress on a number of principles. Strategy must be customer-centric empathy, and the authentic emotional appreciation of customer experiences underlies positioning, messaging, and experience design. Genuine emotional connection needs to be based on matching marketing messages with real organizational values and employee experiences, and not creating emotional push-ups. Cultural EI requires one to adjust their strategy to suit the emotional norms of the country instead of relying on universal responses to emotions. Ethical boundaries create the context of avoiding emotional influence, which demonstrates respect for consumer autonomy and well-being. Long-term relationship focus puts more emphasis on long-term building of relationships rather than short-term conversion optimization.

Companies can enshrine these values in marketing policies, audit procedures, and strategic models that define the manner in which marketing judgments are reached. This makes EI institutionalized instead of having full dependence on individual capability.

2.9 FUTURE RESEARCH DIRECTIONS

The sphere of EI in international marketing settings is relatively recent, and there is still a lot of potential research that would enrich the theoretical background and convert the idea into practice. A number of research lines seem to be especially promising to the entrepreneurs and scholars who are interested in this intersection. Emotional AI and affective computing, an emerging type of technology that identifies, analyzes, and approximates emotions, is a fast-growing field of technology with extensive marketing implications. Existing systems can recognize primitive emotions based on facial expression, voice patterns, and physiological cues with reasonable accuracy under controlled conditions. Nonetheless, there are still major technical problems that are faced in the identification of subtle emotions, contextually relevant emotional meaning, and adaptation to individual and cultural differences in emotional expression.

A study into the possibility of creating emotional AI systems in a manner that can complement human EI could be an interesting endeavor. Some of the questions to explore are as follows: How can the output of emotional AI be made available to human decision-makers in such a way that it enhances their judgment instead of overwhelming it? Which kinds of emotional interpretation are better left to humans or should be left to AI? What makes systems understand their own limitations and elevate to human judgment in order to do so? Which training makes marketers work well with emotional AI tools? The study of emotional AI ethics and governance will gain significance as the technologies proceed. What is the way that organizations should consider consent to emotional monitoring? Are there any transparency requirements when it comes to emotional influence attempts? What ways can emotional AI be programmed to honor human dignity and autonomy? Which systems of governance are required to facilitate responsible innovation in emotional technology? Such questions demand an interdisciplinary approach between technologists, ethicists, psychologists, and marketing scholars in order to answer them. The EI measure of cross-cultural is facing persistent challenges that future studies should tackle. The majority of the EI tests were designed in Western culture and might fail to assess emotional competencies that are most appreciated in other cultures. What may seem to be seen as EI in individualistic cultures, such as assertive expression of emotions and directness, focus on individual emotions may be viewed as dissimilar to EI in collectivistic cultures that focus more on group harmony, indirect communication, and suppression of emotions. Culturally valid EI measures can only be developed by having knowledge of how the various cultural traditions define emotional competence. Certain cultures can place greater emphasis on emotional self-containment and submissiveness than on emotional expressions. Others can place more importance on group emotional integration, rather than on individual emotional integrity. The field would be taken a step ahead with research that develops culturally based EI models and does not use a simple alteration of the Western-developed instruments to new environments.

More serious research should be conducted on the correlation between EI and certain marketing performance. Correlational studies may positively indicate the relationship between marketer EI and different results, but cause-effect relationships are less understandable. Does EI bring a positive improvement in the performance of marketing, mainly because of improved customer understanding, enhanced relationship development, enhanced team leadership, and other channels? The knowledge of these mechanisms would lead to the development of emotional competencies to apply them more specifically to particular marketing work and situations. It would be interesting to conduct longitudinal research to monitor the development of entrepreneur EI and the extent to which the same is associated with venture performance. Are successful entrepreneurs able to gain greater EI out of their experiences, or are higher initial EI individuals more successful entrepreneurs? Are EI training interventions able to enhance entrepreneurial results, and does EI turn out to be so resistant to change? To what extent does founder EI influence or rely on critical events in venture development, such as funding rounds, new market expansion, and change of leadership?

The use of EI in digital and virtual environments is a comparatively understudied topic, even though these settings are becoming more and more significant. What is the influence of different digital modalities of communication on the needs of EI and its expression: text, video, asynchronous, synchronous? Which emotional competencies are most valuable in being a successful virtual team leader? What are some of the ways through which marketers can build and foster emotionally intelligent customer relationships in largely digital settings? What does training make effective EI on the virtual fronts? There is a need to have a systematic investigation on the application of EI and other individual difference variables, such as cultural intelligence, personality traits, and cognitive ability. These constructs are likely to interact in a complicated manner to affect the effectiveness of marketing. As an illustration, EI may partially substitute for the lack of cultural knowledge in marketing in diverse settings. There may be personality types that increase or restrict the ability of EI to convert into performance. The knowledge of these interactions would give more subtle direction when selecting and developing, and team building.

Studies that investigated the contextualities of the impacts of EI would shed more light on when and where EI is more relevant. Is there a situation in which EI does not provide much performance advantage? Could extreme EI occasionally be an obstacle? For example, can extreme empathy make sound strategic decisions that require hard trade-offs? Knowledge of positive and possibly negative outcomes of EI would offer more balanced information than the proposed unanimously positive outcomes. Emotionally intelligent marketing has ethical aspects that should be examined more through academic research. Studies may be conducted to find out how consumers perceive different emotional marketing techniques to determine what is respectful and what is manipulative. Research may explore the impact of varying strategies of emotion-sensitive marketing on consumer trust and quality of relationships in the long term. Researchers would be able to come up with ethical models of emotional marketing that can guide companies on how to deal with challenging choices. The most promising directions are interdisciplinary research based on the understanding of psychology, neuroscience, marketing, entrepreneurship, cultural studies, and technology. Neuroscience may help to clarify the biological processes through which EI could work and the ways to improve it. The topic of cultural studies can enhance insight into the issue of emotional diversity and its marketing implications. The patterns of human-AI collaboration can be researched by technology researchers. Theoretical predictions can be put to the test by marketing scholars in real-life market situations. This cross-disciplinary synthesis would move toward knowledge more rapidly than disciplinary silos would.

2.10 CONCLUSION

EI has also come out of the obscurity of corporate thinking into its proper niche as one of the key skills of business success and marketing performance in the global arena. This chapter has discussed the complex aspects of EI, covering the theoretical basis on which it is built, its use in the marketing environment, its involvement with AI, and finally its implications for entrepreneurs developing ventures at international levels. There are a few major contributions of EI to the global marketing decisions, and these are worth highlighting. First, EI allows the customer compassion that can be found between marketing that demonstrates customer-centricity in theory and marketing that has actual customer-centricity. In a world where products and services are becoming more and more similar in terms of functionality on functional levels, emotional attachment is the main distinguishing factor that produces sustained competitive advantage. Having an advanced level of EI, marketers are able to recognize the emotional forces behind consumer behavior and produce messages that produce genuine emotional responses that lead to loyalty and word-of-mouth promotion.

Second, EI gives the leadership skills needed to accomplish the individual challenges of entrepreneurship. It takes inspiration to develop something out of nothing when resources are limited, consistency when things are bound to go wrong, balancing the various stakeholders who will come bowing with different expectations and interests, and making a good decision despite the pressure and uncertainty. Highly emotionally intelligent founders make their teams more united, develop stronger, more effective relationships with investors and partners, and exhibit the ability to adapt when required by the situation.

Thirdly, EI facilitates cultural complexity management in international markets. The field of international business demands working in different cultural settings in which emotional norms, expressions, and interpretations differ considerably. Culturally and emotionally intelligent entrepreneurs and marketers are able to bend their approaches accordingly, as opposed to making inferences of universal emotional reactions. Such cultural flexibility forms genuine relationships within the domestic markets as opposed to the tone-deaf blunders most international expansion attempts make.

Fourth, EI gives the truly human abilities to supplement and direct AI systems. The unusual human abilities of dealing with emotional and social intelligence become less valuable as AI performs more and more analytical processing and operation execution. The wisdom of the human emotion comprehends the emotional texture that AI lacks, makes morally informed choices regarding the way to use emotional knowledge, develops the genuinely emotional bonds that customers desire, and offers the purpose and limitations that give AI systems their meaning and significance.

Fifth, EI assists in the ethical marketing practice in the era of ever-more influential technologies. The ability to read emotions and influence them brings a lot of power, and it should be stewarded in a responsible manner. The organizations that align with EI draw a distinction between ethical persuasion and manipulation, identify and defend the vulnerabilities of the consumers, deploy emotionally sensitive technologies with suitable levels of transparency and consent, and balance commercial interests with customer welfare. This is how EI is applied ethically, which creates the trust and reputation that can bring sustainable success.

To the entrepreneurs who want to capitalize on such insights, a number of practical suggestions can be made. To begin with, invest in building your own EI by engaging in purposeful practice, seeking feedback, and learning. It is possible to develop self-awareness, empathy, and relationship skills significantly, with the help of constant attention and practice. It should be considered hiring a coach or mentor who might give honest feedback on emotional blind spots and help to develop a particular competency.

Second, prioritize EI in recruitment and team building. Not only technical skills and experience, but also emotional competencies are determined when hiring. Develop training and organizational practices that will promote continuous EI growth. Cultures that appreciate psychological safety, honest communication, and moral emotional involvement should be established. Reward the use of EI by providing performance management systems.

Third, plan your marketing strategies as an organizing principle and not as an appendix, using EI as a key element in marketing. Start with true empathy for the emotional experiences, needs, and ambitions of target customers. Build positioning and messaging that builds genuine, emotive attachments in accordance with real organizational values. Create customer experiences that recognize and react to emotional aspects of customer experiences. Declare success in relation to quality and emotional connection, not in terms of transactions.

Fourth, integrate AI strategically, placing human EI where it brings the most value, and use AI to process data analytically and provide it with the scale of operations. Introduce human-in-the-loop designs that maintain human decision-making on matters that have strong emotional or ethical aspects. Instill in train team members the ability to cooperate with AI tools without losing their emotional wisdom. Periodically examine AI systems to make sure that they add value and do not reduce genuine emotional appeal to customers.

Fifth, create ethical boundaries that incorporate real respect for customer autonomy and well-being. Establish clear rules on what is considered acceptable emotional persuasion and what is considered manipulation. Develop special safeguards for vulnerable sets of customers. Use emotion-sensitive technologies with the required openness and agreement. Not just a marketing statement but actually a priority, ensure that the welfare of customers is both important and authentic because it is the trust that leads to success in the long term.

Sixth, cultivate cultural EI by engaging with a target market in an immersive manner, by working with local partners to gain cultural understanding, and by continually learning about emotional diversity across cultures. Learn not to make the assumption of emotional universality and merely adjust home market strategies only slightly. Learn the culture and not the stereotypes or cultural superficiality.

The future of global entrepreneurs is a combination of the most effective forces of EI and AI to the service of genuine value creation to society and customers. The markets are rewarding more organizations that take genuine concern about customer welfare, that instill trust as a result of sound practice, and that connect emotionally instead of maximizing conversion rates. This is achieved through EI that can help entrepreneurs to create such organizations – ventures that not only make it in business but also in ways that benefit human flourishing.

With markets that are increasingly global, increasingly digital, and increasingly mediated by AI, the primitive human skills of EI will become even more significant. It is entrepreneurs who cultivate effective EI both personally and in their companies, who view marketing as building valuable emotional relationships and not persuasion, who will combine human emotional wisdom with AI ability that will make the best and most sustainable companies of the next decades. The EI/global marketing overlap is not a minor or weak issue, but it is at the core of the entrepreneurial success of the twenty-first-century business environment.

REFERENCES

1. Petrides, K. V., & Furnham, A. (2001). Trait emotional intelligence: Psychometric investigation with reference to established trait taxonomies. *European Journal of Personality*, *15*(6), 425–448. DOI: 10.1002/per.416, Link: https://onlinelibrary.wiley.com/doi/10.1002/per.416
2. Mayer, J. D., Salovey, P., & Caruso, D. R. (2008). Emotional intelligence: New ability or eclectic traits? *American Psychologist*, *63*(6), 503–517. DOI: 10.1037/0003-066X.63.6.503. Link: https://psycnet.apa.org/doiLanding?doi=10.1037%2F0003-066X.63.6.503
3. Mayer, J. D., Salovey, P., & Caruso, D. R. (2002). Mayer-Salovey-Caruso emotional intelligence test (MSCEIT) user's manual. *Multi-Health Systems*. Link: https://www.psicothema.com/pdf/3273.pdf
4. Mayer, J. D., Salovey, P., Caruso, D. R., & Sitarenios, G. (2003). Measuring emotional intelligence with the MSCEIT V2.0. *Emotion*, *3*(1), 97–105. DOI: 10.1037/1528-3542.3.1.97. Link: https://psycnet.apa.org/doiLanding?doi=10.1037%2F1528-3542.3.1.97
5. Petrides, K. V. (2009). Trait emotional intelligence theory. *Industrial and Organizational Psychology*, *2*(1), 26–31. DOI: 10.1111/j.1754-9434.2010.01213.x. Link: https://www.cambridge.org/core/journals/industrial-and-organizational-psychology/article/trait-emotional-intelligence-theory/
6. Goleman, D. (1998). *Working with emotional intelligence*. Bantam Books. Link: https://www.penguinrandomhouse.com/books/83089/working-with-emotional-intelligence-by-daniel-goleman/
7. Goleman, D. (2006). *Emotional intelligence: Why it can matter more than IQ*. Bantam Books. (Updated edition). Link: https://www.penguinrandomhouse.com/books/35765/emotional-intelligence-by-daniel-goleman/
8. Locke, E. A. (2005). Why emotional intelligence is an invalid concept. *Journal of Organizational Behavior*, *26*(4), 425–431. DOI: 10.1002/job.318. Link: https://onlinelibrary.wiley.com/doi/10.1002/job.318
9. Tănase, G. C. (2024). The Integration of Emotional Intelligence into AI Marketing. *Revista de Management Comparat International*, *15*(1), 29–37. Link: https://ideas.repec.org/a/rdc/journl/v15y2024i1p29-37.html
10. Huang, M.-H., & Rust, R. T. (2021). A strategic framework for artificial emotional intelligence. *Journal of Service Research*, *24*(3), 273–288. DOI: 10.1177/1094670520902266. Link: https://journals.sagepub.com/doi/10.1177/1094670520975585

3 Navigating Challenges in Global Marketing

Aman Kumar and Anchal Singh

3.1 INTRODUCTION

When companies tap into new markets, they encounter many complex problems in creating effective global marketing strategies. For companies, this translates into strategically navigating these challenges by having a good grip on the subtleties of the local culture, competitive environment and consumer behaviour that characterise a potentially rich market among peers. These thematic issues can be resolved by addressing factors including psychic distance, self-reference criteria and standardisation versus adaptation within international marketing strategies [1]. The implications grow even bigger as organisations seek to preserve brand integrity while tailoring offerings to local desires. Cross-cultural marketing is, therefore, key to establishing brand awareness and loyalty across a variety of consumer markets. This informs Hua's commentary on how multinational companies tactically deploy culturally sensitive marketing strategies to manage the complexities of cross-cultural encounters [2]. These marketing strategies highlight the importance of creating localised approaches that respect culture while boosting brand visibility.

Also, the use of advanced technologies, big data and analytics in formulations enhances a company's international market strategy. Big data can be applied in the understanding of patterns of market development, and it supports risk management and decision-making to optimise international marketing [3]. With firms looking to expand into uncharted waters, comprehensive methodologies are needed to mitigate the unique compliance challenges presented by these varied international markets. In addition, the concept of glocalisation, which refers to the combination of global and local strategies, has emerged as a robust response to such challenges. It should be flexible and should reflect the global brand identity, which should be more or less similar but at the same time cater to the local preference or characteristics [4]. The implications of global consumer culture (GCC), in parallel with local consumer culture, highlight the need for brands to operate effectively in both contexts [5].

3.2 UNDERSTANDING THE GLOBAL MARKETING LANDSCAPE

In the 21st century, due to globalisation, the world has become smaller and the market a more complex place to navigate. As companies traverse through this terrain, understanding the dynamics impacting their marketing strategies and operational frameworks is key. The decreasing importance of geographical borders leads to

 DOI: 10.1201/9781003650775-3

increased competition, motivating companies to find new ways to do their marketing. Among the key challenges in formulating a global marketing strategy are cultural complexity, shifting consumer patterns and differing regulatory requirements shaped by trade agreements [6]. For businesses aspiring to achieve sustainable growth in this interconnected era, understanding this isn't just about knowing how to enter a new market but extends even deeper into shaping brand perception [7]. The tapestry of world markets does demand a deeper understanding of specific regional customs, values and shopper habits, which is imperative to multinational corporations (MNCs) that want to succeed on the international scene. This complexity is largely derived from cultural nuances that impact how consumers think, purchase and value products [8]. The finding that consumers' behaviour may often be derived from embedded cultural characteristics further emphasises the need to adapt marketing strategies to local tradition [9]. Global marketing management strategies, hence, have the challenge of balancing local perspective and broader company objectives to make markets more effective [10].

With the deepening of globalisation, consumers present the features of simultaneous embodiment of global cultural symbols and local identity. This double personality poses challenges to brands which try to strike a balance between global identity and local particularity. This concept, so-called GCC, suggests the existence of a worldwide, common consumer value system or value constellation which leads to greater consumer acceptance [11]. Therefore, MNCS need to embrace an adaptation approach to accommodate these differences to develop consumer retention [12, 13]. In addition, how urbanisation interacts with the global integration of markets adds another twist to consumer behaviour. With the rising urban living, the conventional buying pattern will change, and hence marketers will have to be friendly continuously to suit the changing needs of consumers to be in touch with them [14]. The examples of industrial and productive realities, including typical Tuscan wines, show that the regional substrate can condition the effectiveness of the marketing strategies and ultimately oppose the standardisation [15]. Therefore, navigating global markets successfully demands that firms not only focus on the logistical end of marketing but also on how to connect with various consumer bases more effectively by reaching out to them in a culturally sensitive and localised way [16].

In such an environment, knowledge of local cultures and mentalities is not a nice-to-have but a must-have to succeed in the long run. Brands that don't acknowledge these dimensions run the risk of losing the potential share of the cultural market, stressing the requirement of cultural knowledge as key cultural literacy, a global marketing concept [17, 18]. So, adopting a multi-faceted approach to market research, from quantitative to qualitative measurement of consumer behaviour, will result in a firm's greater ability to interact with different types of shopper demographics. Technology developments further complicate the global marketing environment, particularly in their use in data analytics and digital marketing. In international marketing, organisations have never been able to slice and dice global market trends, consumer behaviours and competitive dynamics on such a large scale with such powerful tools as they now can with what is being called big data. The use of big data in marketing departments enables firms to mitigate risk and develop more targeted marketing approaches across consumer segments [3]. This has special importance to companies that act globally, as it adds an element of flexibility to adapt to changing market dynamics.

Furthermore, as the business world rallies around global markets, the balance of competition and cooperation emphasises building solid marketing strategies. For export-oriented businesses, effective marketing strategies are essential because they provide access to international markets and enhance competitiveness [13]. When companies aim to expand their business and enhance their export potential, the main thing to do is to know the ropes about various markets and to customise the marketing efforts to suit those markets. In essence, the global marketing landscape is shaped by a multitude of factors that influence market dynamics and require marketers to adopt innovative strategies in response to globalisation, cultural diversity, technological advancements and other elements. And businesses that take a mindful approach to meeting these complexities and capitalise on these opportunities will continue to survive and thrive in the breeding ground of global trade. Nonetheless, the evolving nature of this landscape requires adaptive strategies and continuous research to orient oneself within the complexities of marketing on a global stage.

3.3 CULTURAL AND SOCIAL CHALLENGES IN GLOBAL MARKETING

Global marketing faces a few barriers, such as the cultural barrier and the social barrier. Cultural differences, consumer behaviours, social norms and technology's impact on marketing practices must all be considered to understand these challenges. When companies are growing in new markets, these barriers require more openness and planning than ever before.

Most global marketing problems are rooted in culture [18]. Culture has distinctive values, beliefs and social practices that lead to consumer behaviour and purchasing decisions. Hofstede's cultural dimensions theory succinctly explains how such dimensions as individualism versus collectivism, uncertainty avoidance and power distance influence marketing strategies [19]. For example, firms such as Jin et al. have been able to enter these markets successfully, as prior research shows that social media preferences differ significantly across countries [20]. There are no shortcuts here, and companies need to invest in understanding these dimensions because they determine how their branding, messaging and advertising are received by different groups of consumers. But social challenges, especially social media dynamics, tend to complicate bringing social products. For example, the recent turn towards influencer marketing is a prime example of how companies can navigate social media to connect with younger customers effectively. Although social media can supplement traditional marketing strategies, it should not completely supplant them [21, 22]. Additionally, the credibility and authenticity of influencers greatly influence consumers' perceptions of the brand [23]; thus, the effectiveness of influencer marketing reinforces the brand image, thereby influencing the intention to purchase. As a result, marketers need to walk the fine line between adapting to social media strategies and safeguarding the trustworthiness of their messaging.

In addition, consumer behaviour plays a role in exacerbating global marketing challenges, especially as it relates to complaint handling and brand loyalty.

In collectivist cultures, practices such as the preservation of "face" and the avoidance of direct confrontation are more prevalent, whereas individualistic cultures tend to exhibit more confrontational communication styles [24]. Understanding how these dynamics work will enable firms to better manage customer service and engage with their customers. Moreover, businesses are expected to adjust and align with cultural standards, requiring them to fine-tune product offerings and marketing messages towards the sensitivity of local customers [25].

3.4 ECONOMIC AND MARKET ENVIRONMENT CHALLENGES IN GLOBAL MARKETING

The economic and market environments are marked by shifting economic conditions, regulatory frameworks, competitive landscapes and diverse consumer behaviours across continents. Grasping and adapting to these intricacies are crucial for escalating the sales and adaptability of businesses operating in the worldwide market [26]. Globalisation has significantly impacted the economic sphere as it has brought both pros and cons to the business world. For example, firms seeking to access foreign markets must adapt their strategies to the various local economic environments they encounter; this includes a variation in local consumer tastes and conditions for regulations and market conditions. The growing complexity associated with globalisation requires firms to take local economic conditions into account when developing marketing strategies, and the resulting rise in competitiveness means that organisations must continually innovate their processes in order to remain relevant in the market [27].

A second major challenge lies in the differences in regulatory and compliance requirements between countries. Enterprises must contend with the inherent volatility of markets, which may arise from geopolitical conflict, economic downturns or policy shifts [28]. Such volatility necessitates businesses to develop adaptive and resilient marketing strategies. Insights into market demand and policy environments may require firms to adjust their pricing strategies or product offerings in response to shifts in economic conditions [29]. The ability to adapt is key to competing and succeeding in uncertain economic environments. Further, firms need to develop and incorporate unique marketing strategies to effectively combat these challenges. The interoperability of global marketing technologies can facilitate communication and connectivity across disparate markets, thereby strengthening organisational capability [30]. A strong technological infrastructure helps firms to adapt to emerging trends, spot market opportunities quickly and respond better to the economic scenario [31]. Additionally, small and medium enterprises (SMEs) have huge challenges in world markets. Competitive intensity in international markets presents distinct challenges for small and medium-sized enterprises, which often lack the financial resources and experience of larger firms [32, 33]. Overcoming these challenges could require that they adopt specialised marketing and utilise niche markets as they vertically integrate to create a clear competitive advantage to overcome their limitations of resources.

Overall, addressing the challenges posed by the economic and market environment in global marketing involves a combination of thorough research, strategic planning and adaptability. Organisations will need to stay ahead through local insights, regulatory adaptation and tech advances in building resiliency and competitiveness. Firms can build these capabilities to find themselves better-suited to act within the global marketplace.

3.5 LEGAL AND REGULATORY CHALLENGES IN GLOBAL MARKETING

Globalisation, surely, is creating increasingly competitive circumstances for nearly all businesses, which are constantly facing a combination of other legal and regulatory issues that can have a real effect on their operating model and market-entry strategy. These challenges are hand-in-hand with the internationalisation of trade, marketing practices and consumer protection regulations. Companies wanting to effectively manoeuvre through the global marketplace need a clear understanding of these legal landscapes. One of the key challenges is that countries have permitted different legal and regulatory frameworks. There are different laws in every country about the protection of the consumer, intellectual property, advertising and marketing standards. Cross-cutting and coherent legal frameworks are key to establishing and governing markets in environmental contexts, and the absence of such supporting legal mechanisms can create significant barriers to the effective operation of all facets of the marketing mix [34]. This can imply that companies may encounter unexpected legal challenges that complicate their business decisions in the absence of a strong legal framework.

Additionally, the diversity in regulations surrounding digital marketing practices adds another layer of complexity to the global marketing arena. Globalisation raises challenges related to the new global division of labour and compliance with labour laws, trade agreements and related regulatory frameworks [35]. Organisations must make sure that their policies comply with applicable domestic laws and international agreements facilitated by bodies such as the World Trade Organisation (WTO) [36]. As companies navigate this complex model of regulations, vigilance is required to ensure that their marketing strategies are compliant, while not stifling innovation. Also, global marketing strategies include financing as well. In modern times, since the world is a global village and money can be sent around the world in nanoseconds, strict measures must be in place to prevent financial relations from being used for careless purposes [37]. The foundation of a solid legal infrastructure to maintain stability and trust in the global economy depends on the creation of reliable cross-border financial transactions at international, national and sub-national levels. The business needs to handle the case well to build up investor confidence and get capital for marketing abroad.

The importance of data protection laws is also not to be ignored, as it affects digital marketing as well. Mone et al. stressed the developing discrepancies between such countries that already have forged more powerful data protection mechanisms, such as the EU privacy regulation General Data Protection Regulation (GDPR), and those with no broad legal privacy framework at all [38]. The resulting gap creates complications for any business operating across regional borders that often needs to adjust its marketing approach to comply with different degrees of data protection legislation, affecting the processes of data collection, advertising and consumer interaction practices.

Furthermore, with the advent of new trends in marketing like influencer marketing and digital advertising, the legal aspects regarding IP rights have become even more significant. Hence, the effects dedicated to the identification of the legal segmentation of labour law may need some additional detail when it comes to the perceptions of international intellectual property rights [39]. To avoid expensive litigation, the company must ensure its marketing activities do not infringe on existing intellectual property rights, which can differ widely from one jurisdiction to another.

3.6 TECHNOLOGICAL AND DIGITAL CHALLENGES IN GLOBAL MARKETING

Digital technologies have opened up new opportunities for businesses to connect with consumers around the world. Nevertheless, the incorporation of these technologies into marketing strategies presents immense challenges that companies need to address. They have to navigate everything from the skills gap in digital marketing to digital transformation complexities to maintain a competitive edge in the changing global playing field. The skills gap in digital marketing competencies is one of the main technological challenges for global marketers. Rapid technological change has meant that many marketers lack the fundamental knowledge and skills required to use digital strategies effectively [40]. However, digital marketing is still not very well documented and hence is often difficult, leading to an experimental approach towards the overall marketing strategy. Such a gap can confuse marketing strategy, resulting in the opportunity to take advantage of full potential through digital media, which could result in a loss of return on investment.

As a result, organisations are not immune to fitting all possible digital channels into one in a digital marketing strategy. SMEs are prone to following an unplanned approach to digital marketing practices, possibly due to a lack of coherent understanding of the bigger picture of the digital marketing framework [41]. As a result, SMEs must devise holistic plans that integrate data-driven approaches and make certain that they fully use digital platforms to connect with the appropriate target audience. However, the digital transformation of markets is also a move away from traditional marketing practices that have created complexities about how customers can be interacted with and engaged. The digital revolution has enabled a wide range of new forms of collaboration and the development of digital assets to address global challenges; however, firms often struggle to adapt traditional business models to these emerging opportunities [42].

Additionally, considering the developments within the digital economy, digital marketing strategies should emphasise the importance of analysing data and its impact on consumer behaviour through technology. Information from data analytics should be integrated into strategic management planning to support the implementation of digital marketing and to better understand market trends and consumer preferences [43]. Data privacy and compliance challenges persist for many organisations, especially when they operate across multiple jurisdictions, each with its own regulatory requirements. At the same time, the increase of digital marketing has also created challenges with competition and market saturation, making it harder to differentiate unique value propositions [44]. The pandemic accelerated digital adoption, compelling companies to rethink how they engage with customers and how they reach and convert customers in online environments [45]. Such a shift also highlights the need for companies to constantly evolve and innovate their marketing strategies to keep up with changing consumer behaviour and expectations.

3.7 LOGISTICAL AND OPERATIONAL CHALLENGES IN GLOBAL MARKETING

Global marketing comes with various logistical difficulties and operational issues that can seriously slow down a company from implementing efficient supply chain control and delivering its products around the world to its target markets. Globalisation has added layers of complexity that require a thorough understanding of logistics operations, infrastructure and geographical supply chain dynamics as organisations aim to satisfy consumer demands contained within cost targets with synchronised delivery. One such challenge is establishing and maintaining functional logistics networks. As globalisation advances, firms are required to adopt logistics capabilities that integrate domestic and international logistics networks in order to operate with greater agility and efficiency [46]. This encompasses both the domestic connections and warehousing and/or distribution, which can be challenging, especially in unrecognised environments.

Moreover, a multi-tiered supply chain that spans multiple countries further increases operational complexities. Volatile market conditions have created challenges for production scheduling, logistics distribution and cost control [47]. However, as supply chains become dispersed across geographies, interdependencies among suppliers, manufacturers and distributors must be managed effectively, and smooth operations require well-coordinated activities across all nodes in the supply chain. Many firms now use big data analytics to overcome operational challenges in logistics. Inefficiencies in logistics and supply chain management, such as late deliveries, rising fuel costs and unreliable suppliers, can be addressed through big data analytics, which enable firms to make better decisions, predict disruptions and optimise supply chain processes for greater operational efficiency [48].

Unforeseen events, for example, the COVID-19 pandemic, have shown the importance of supply chain resilience. Supply chain resilience is essential for organisations to absorb disruptions, maintain operations and continue delivering value [49]. It has also revealed vulnerabilities in the supply chain, leading companies to embrace agile operating models, broaden their sourcing and strengthen inventory management to protect against future disruptions. And the current climate makes that more difficult for the logistics of how our global supply chains function. Geopolitical uncertainties and cultural barriers represent major challenges in the development of strong supplier relationships [50]. Amidst this, businesses must enable collaboration between suppliers, align operational processes and negotiate terms of engagement. This can often mean new investments in supplier development as well as digital transformation initiatives aimed at improved communication and operational alignment throughout the supply chain. Logistics and supply chain strategy must also run the gauntlet of regulatory compliance. The large disparity between levels of local and global governance led to quite different legal and regulatory standards, which can lead to drastic consequences for organisations, particularly related to labour laws, safety standards or environmental regulation. Sodhi and Tang highlight the importance of transparency and compliance, which necessitate strong record-keeping and audit mechanisms [51]. That is a critical risk management failure and a major building block of the reputational wall that surrounds the business.

Overall, overcoming the logistical and operational hurdles of global marketing will prompt organisations to take more comprehensive approaches involving robust logistics systems, analytical data, and resilient compliance and supply networks. Logistical capabilities and operational efficiency can help businesses better serve the global marketplace, ensuring they remain at the forefront of this business world.

3.7.1 Strategic and Organisational Challenges in Global Marketing

Global marketing settings have been changing rapidly, which creates a lot of strategic and practical challenges for organisations. When a business goes international, it has to adjust not just for new markets but also for the different sociocultural, legal and technological configurations that characterise these markets. For firms wanting to achieve sustainable growth and operational efficiency in the global marketplace, acquiring clarity on such strategic and organisational problems is a must. One of the significant challenges involves aligning culture to strategy, which makes human resources management a key role in organisational productivity and efficiency [52]. As companies conduct business across borders, they face the need for a culture that embraces different ways of working, while also facilitating alignment with strategic objectives at a global level. A culture of organisational fallibility, for example, can increase employee performance and creativity, essential in fast-changing international markets. This alignment is important because it results in efficiencies and employee engagement, which can have positive effects on company performance [53–55].

Moreover, the deployment of Industry 4.0 technologies presents challenges for organisations, especially small and medium-sized enterprises (SMES). Organisational challenges in areas such as unavailability of skilled labour, policy failures and leadership vacancies hinder the smooth application of cutting-edge technologies for small and medium businesses (SMEs) [33, 56]. Many companies now implementing such technology need to progress their own people and organisational structure to further foster and sustain innovation. Failure to address these challenges could mean lost opportunities and a competitive disadvantage. These operational challenges are complicated by product innovativeness, particularly in emerging economies [57]. Strategic and organisational challenges in product development can hinder innovation in competitive environments; however, incorporating collaborative practices in the workplace enables employees to generate innovative ideas and new approaches by drawing on others' creativity and perspectives. In contrast, when collaboration is lacking, organisations may experience rising operational costs and reduced innovation performance [58]. This adheres to the need for seamless collaboration between the departments to ensure that product development meets market demand and is in line with the overall organisational capabilities as well.

Strategic challenges also arise from complex partnerships and collaborations. Organisations must manage the challenges associated with multiple cross-sector partnerships, including internal competition and tension, which can constrain collaboration and reduce the effective use of resources [59]. However, collaborative relationships are difficult to manage, meaning organisations are required to focus on high-quality communication and trust to utilise their opportunities collaboratively.

Each concept, therefore, opens the door to a world where navigating the global landscape over strategic agility is no longer a forced choice. Organisations are expected to be highly agile in terms of response to fast-changing market dynamics, consumer preferences and competitive pressure [60]. This has a particular bearing in uncertain times and can be improved through the encouragement of an innovation and learning culture [31]. A flexible strategic organisation is better equipped to respond to whatever situation arises in the external environment, the dynamics of the market, or even crisis challenges and organisations need to incorporate sustainability as part of their strategic frameworks as they grow to meet substantial environmental and social challenges. This process is supported by strategic agility, which acts as a key driver of environmental innovation within supply chains [61]. Increasingly, organisations today are held accountable not only for profitability but also for their environmental and social impact. So, it is most relevant to be viable and competitive to align the strategic objectives with sustainability.

3.8 MITIGATION STRATEGIES AND BEST PRACTICES IN GLOBAL MARKETING

Organisations seeking to improve operational efficiency, respond to compliance requirements and create the foundation for sustained competitive advantage have some strategic measures to consider, navigating the challenges of logistics, culture and legalities. Implementing robust risk management frameworks designed for the specific complexities of international marketing can also support effective mitigation efforts. The adoption of diverse risk-mitigation strategies can have a positive impact on firm performance, particularly in the context of small- and medium-sized enterprises (SMEs) [62]. This ensures a safe collaboration with local partners when it comes to risk mitigation in global marketing and accentuates the growing need to forge collaborative partnerships, and in particular to manage their expected complex projects, such as subsea production systems [63]. By working with local suppliers and stakeholders, organisations can leverage regional expertise, ensuring compliance with local rules and regulations and managing cultural and intercultural differences. Shared resources and knowledge foster collaboration among the supply chain players, leading to improved supply chain efficiency and overall success of the project. Using technology for better operational efficiency is another best practice that can prove to be critical. Digital twin and advanced data analytics can help businesses improve decision-making and risk identification, and operational planning. This approach makes a call for the implementation of advanced technology-assisted mitigation strategies in complex environments, highlighting the importance of advanced planning and simulation techniques [63]. Utilising technological tools helps organisations establish maximised processes, as communication is simplified for teams working in different parts of the world; improvement happens from all angles in effectiveness, reducing operational failures.

Also, laying a strong corporate culture focused on learning and adaptation is fundamental in building resilience. Organisations can manage the risks of change management by fostering a culture of organisational learning and strategic alignment with their environment [64, 65]. Organisations that engage in proactive learning can modify their policies quickly based on changes in the market, technology and consumer behaviour. Such training programmes, having relevance to the immediate challenges and work competencies of employees, go a long way towards improving an organisation's agility and overall preparedness. Good communication is another important factor to surpass global marketing problems. Effective communication of expectations and responsibilities across diverse teams helps to foster a culture of transparency and collaboration [66]. Open communication facilitates discussing ambiguities and negotiating solutions to problems faced in the supply chain management processes as it gets planned. Data can be powerful, but so, too, can the more human connection. Scenario planning and contingency strategies can strengthen institutional preparedness to deal with unforeseen challenges. Advanced planning and simulation techniques may help organisations to identify potential risks and plan actions for them. It is this kind of organisational culture that helps companies to adapt to changing market conditions and thrive in a dynamic global environment. These proactive strategies allow firms to quickly respond to environmental updates, industry disruptions or alterations in consumer behaviour.

Moreover, the integration of sustainability in strategic planning emerges as an opportunity and also as a best practice. Green supply chain management practices contribute to mitigating the environmental risk which organisations are exposed to and enhance the reputation of the organisation [66]. Through the diminishing of discrepancies between marketing strategies and sustainability goals, companies can both confront regulatory pressures, as well as fortify their market position in the eyes of consumers who are increasingly discerning eco-friendly attributes [21]. Hence, creative processes must be woven into the fabric of organisations as best practices that mitigate challenges that come with global marketing. Mapping innovative solutions is essential for addressing sustainability and operational challenges in the logistics and shipping industry, and organisations that fully embrace innovation and an innovation-oriented culture are better positioned to respond to changes in consumer demand, market forces and technological advances, enabling them to remain resilient and competitive [67]. Therefore, to address these global marketing challenges, firms require a holistic approach involving robust risk management, alliances, digital integration, communications, scenario planning, sustainability and innovation. Incorporating the above-mentioned strategies and best practices aids in enhancing organisational resilience and operational efficacy, as well as attaining a competitive advantage in the dynamic global business landscape.

3.9 IMPLICATIONS FOR GLOBAL MARKETERS

By the nature of global marketing, marketers must deal with multiple challenges and adopt strategies that consider the foreign markets. These trends highlight the importance of cultural adaptation, regulatory insight and creativity in their approaches if they are to keep pace with the evolving international marketplace. In an increasingly globalised marketplace, understanding consumer needs and competing across multiple markets presents challenges for firms, requiring the development of marketing strategies that are culturally sensitive while also complying with local regulatory requirements [27]. Given that products have such diverse connotations depending on cultural context, this requires marketers to not only honour local customs and laws but also understand economic conditions that impact those customs/laws, if they wish to engage global consumers meaningfully and inspire brand loyalty in different contexts.

Also, working efficiently with local partners can help marketers improve their operational capacity and cultural knowledge. As shown in the analysis of pharmaceutical strategies, the establishment of solid relationships with partners can facilitate access to markets and allow firms to position themselves favourably towards domestic competitors [68]. This course, by utilising familiarity and resources, aids organisations in operating in complex regulatory settings and aligns the organisation, including the consumption needs, appropriately. Recent disruptions, including the COVID-19 pandemic, have highlighted the need for marketers to adopt agile strategies and remain responsive to changing market dynamics [69]. Agile procurement and operational flexibility enable organisations to react and pivot effectively in periods of disruption and uncertainty [70]. And this flexibility allows for not only survival but also a foundation for innovation, since companies are rethinking their governance to drive consumer engagement and relational equity in challenging times [71].

Additionally, the rising demand for sustainable practices will drive marketers to include sustainability in their brand positioning. Green practices have also scaled in business development; organisations that connect these marketing solutions to green practices designed by regulatory frameworks automatically resonate with a growing population of consumers ready to sustain that shift [72]. Finally, ongoing learning and adaptation need to be a strategic focus of any global marketer. It will never be more important than being able to analyse market trends, consumer behaviours and competitive dynamics to drive strategies and find new opportunities. Marketers who incorporate insights drawn from existing case studies and market research will be in a better position to tackle new challenges and plan for the costs of going global.

3.10 CONCLUSION

Organisations need to consider various concepts of marketing on a global scale (including, but not limited to, cultural, legal, economic and technological, logistical and strategic challenges) in the complex world of international marketing. With constant changes brought about by globalisation, marketers need to take a strong and flexible approach to build strategies that work well for varying consumer bases while adhering to different regulatory provisions. For global marketers, the stakes are raised, and the reaction calls for a revised emphasis on cultural nimbleness, partnerships and best practices that increase operational effectiveness and engagement with consumers. Implementing best practices through risk management, technology implementation and sustainability-led efforts is a proven strategy to establish a robust and efficient system that increases brand equity and encourages long-term success. Also, it will help companies to capitalise on emerging markets and manage impediments by monitoring external market conditions in local contexts, powered by market forces despite the strategic misalignment of organisational goals. Marketing professionals can modify tactics based on continuous data collection regarding shifting consumer preferences and competitive pressures. This creates a framework that combines knowledge, capability and ethics to effectively navigate the complexities of global integration. Such commitment will not only help organisations deal with the complexities presented by most international markets but also establish them as leading figures within their domains, ensuring sustainability and growth in an age when international boundaries are shrinking at unprecedented rates.

REFERENCES

[1] Yinan, L. (2024). Strategic navigation in global markets: unveiling international marketing challenges. *Modern Economics & Management Forum*, 5(2), 152. https://doi.org/10.32629/memf.v5i2.1951

[2] Hua, S. (2024). Research on the relationship between cross-cultural marketing and brand recognition and loyalty. *Finance & Economics*, 1(9). https://doi.org/10.61173/da9qm268

[3] Li, L. (2023). The transformation of international marketing strategy under the background of big data. *Advances in Economics Management and Political Sciences*, 37(1), 107–111. https://doi.org/10.54254/2754-1169/37/20231848

[4] Visconti, L. M., Peñaloza, L., & Toulouse, N. (Eds.). (2013). *Marketing Management: A Cultural Perspective*, Routledge. https://doi.org/10.4324/9780203357262

[5] Steenkamp, J. (2019). Global versus local consumer culture: theory, measurement, and future research directions. *Journal of International Marketing*, 27(1), 1–19. https://doi.org/10.1177/1069031x18811289

[6] Hole, Y., Hole, S., & Bhaskar, M. (2019). Topic: global market challenges and their impact on businesses. *Restaurant Business*, 118(10), 519–531. https://doi.org/10.26643/rb.v118i10.9571

[7] Marcus, G. O., Oyenuga, M. O., & Ahungwa, A. I. (2020). Effects of sales promotion on consumer buying behaviour of food seasoning among Nigerian households: a case study of Nestle Maggi Naijapot. *Budapest International Research and Critics Institute Journal (BIRCI Journal)*, 3(1), 134–139. https://doi.org/10.33258/birci.v3i1.724

[8] Oyedele M. O., & Fredrick, E. (2023). Managing product features and customer satisfaction via product development, product branding, and product packaging: evidence from CWAY table water. *Marketing and Branding Research*, 10(1), 28–44. https://doi.org/10.32038/mbr.2023.10.01.03

[9] Zhou, L., Teng, L., & Poon, P. (2008). Susceptibility to global consumer culture: a three-dimensional scale. *Psychology and Marketing*, 25(4), 336–351. https://doi.org/10.1002/mar.20212

[10] Nim, N., Pedada, K., & Hewett, K. (2024). Digital marketing ecosystems and global market expansion: current state and future research agenda. *International Marketing Review*, 41(5), 872–885. https://doi.org/10.1108/imr-04-2024-0108

[11] Alden, D., Steenkamp, J., & Batra, R. (1999). Brand positioning through advertising in Asia, North America, and Europe: the role of global consumer culture. *Journal of Marketing*, 63(1), 75–87. https://doi.org/10.1177/002224299906300106

[12] Oyenuga, M. O., & Labiyi, O. (2024). Using marketing mix strategies to influence customer patronage in an indigenous restaurant. *Rowter Journal*. https://doi.org/10.33258/rowter.v3i1.1052

[13] Usmonova, D. (2024). The role of marketing strategies in improving the export potential of grape growing enterprises. *International Journal of Social Science Research and Review*, 7(5), 134–141. https://doi.org/10.47814/ijssrr.v7i5.2037

[14] Oyedele. (2024). https://blog.efmdglobal.org/2024/10/15/customer-centric-education-using-the-7ps-to-drive-student-satisfaction-in-higher-education/

[15] Vergamini, D., Bartolini, F., Prosperi, P., & Brunori, G. (2019). Explaining regional dynamics of marketing strategies: the experience of the Tuscan wine producers. *Journal of Rural Studies*, 72, 136–152. https://doi.org/10.1016/j.jrurstud.2019.10.006

[16] Özsomer, A., Simonin, B., & Mandler, T. (2023). Marketing agility in subsidiaries: market orientation and marketing program standardization as the "twin engines" of performance. *Journal of International Marketing*, 31(2), 6–24. https://doi.org/10.1177/1069031x221130740

[17] Mhlongo, N., Olatoye, F., Elufioye, O., Ibeh, C., Falaiye, T., & Daraojimba, A. (2024). Cross-cultural business development strategies: a review of USA and African. *International Journal of Science and Research Archive*, 11(1), 1408–1417. https://doi.org/10.30574/ijsra.2024.11.1.0233

[18] Oyenuga, M. O., & Akwen, P. I. (2025). Tourism and intercultural understanding in developing nations. *African Journal of Culture, History, Religion and Traditions*, 8(1), 1–14. https://doi.org/10.52589/ajchrt-okuxnmsq

[19] Matikiti, R., Mpinganjira, M., & Roberts-Lombard, M. (2018). Application of the technology acceptance model and the technology–organisation–environment model to examine social media marketing use in the South African tourism industry. *SA Journal of Information Management*, 20(1). https://doi.org/10.4102/sajim.v20i1.790

[20] Jin, S., Muqaddam, A., & Ryu, E. (2019). Instafamous and social media influencer marketing. *Marketing Intelligence & Planning*, 37(5), 567–579. https://doi.org/10.1108/mip-09-2018-0375

[21] Oyedele, M. O., Marcus, G. O., & Ahungwa, A. I. (2023). Do consumers care about green marketing practices? Insight from a developing nation. *Budapest International Research and Critics Institute Journal (BIRCI Journal)*, 6(3), 1424–1436. https://bircu-journal.com/index.php/birci/article/view/7665

[22] Schivinski, B., & Dąbrowski, D. (2014). The effect of social media communication on consumer perceptions of brands. *Journal of Marketing Communications*, 22(2), 189–214. https://doi.org/10.1080/13527266.2013.871323

[23] Hermanda, A., Sumarwan, U., & Tinaprillia, N. (2019). The effect of social media influencer on brand image, self-concept, and purchase intention. *Journal of Consumer Sciences*, 4(2), 76–89. https://doi.org/10.29244/jcs.4.2.76-89

[24] Liu, R. & McClure, P. (2001). Recognizing cross-cultural differences in consumer complaint behavior and intentions: an empirical examination. *Journal of Consumer Marketing*, 18(1), 54–75. https://doi.org/10.1108/07363760110365813

[25] Sharifonnasabi, Z., Bardhi, F., & Luedicke, M. (2019). How globalization affects consumers: insights from 30 years of CCT globalization research. *Marketing Theory*, 20(3), 273–298. https://doi.org/10.1177/1470593119887469

[26] Jafar, S. H., Oyedele, O. M., Nawaah, D., & Bolanle, A. S. (2025). Exploring leadership challenges for adoption of digital innovation and sustainability, in Singh, R., Corvello, V., Coniglio, I. M., & Khan, S. (Eds.) *Innovation Ecosystems and Sustainable Technologies*

(Emerald Studies in Sustainable Innovation Management), Emerald Publishing Limited, Leeds, pp. 253–269. https://doi.org/10.1108/978-1-83662-368-720251012

[27] Taochenyu, W. (2024). The impact of economic globalization on corporate marketing and countermeasures to cope with it. *Information Systems and Economics*, 5(1). https://doi.org/10.23977/infse.2024.050113

[28] Sudirjo, F. (2023). Marketing strategy in improving product competitiveness in the global market. *Journal of Contemporary Administration and Management (Adman)*, 1(2), 63–69. https://doi.org/10.61100/adman.v1i2.24

[29] Li, Z. (2024). Market demand, policy environment, and future trends: analysis of new energy vehicle industry in China. *Advances in Economics Management and Political Sciences*, 103(1), 25–32. https://doi.org/10.54254/2754-1169/103/2024bj0112

[30] Lawrence, D., & Mulaw, S. (2024). Global marketing management: challenges and opportunities in the international market. *Educational Administration: Theory and Practice*. https://doi.org/10.53555/kuey.v30i4.1594

[31] Oyedele, M. O., Sunday, A. O., & Abuh, A. I. (2024). Fostering technological-enhanced training and development for business survival and performance in the new normal. *Journal of Propulsion Technology*, 45(3) 1858–1869. https://propulsiontechjournal.com/index.php/journal/article/view/7479

[32] Latifah, L., Setiawan, D., Aryani, Y., & Rahmawati, R. (2020). Business strategy – msmes' performance relationship: innovation and accounting information system as mediators. *Journal of Small Business and Enterprise Development*, 28(1), 1–21. https://doi.org/10.1108/jsbed-04-2019-0116

[33] Omale, S. A., Oyenuga, M. O., Abdullahi, D., & Madu, I. (2024). Moderating role of entrepreneurial education on innovative work behaviour and resilience of SMEs. *Innovations*, 77(2), 1166–1185.

[34] Admasu, S., Yeshitela, K., & Argaw, M. (2024). Planning for ecosystem services compensation in the central highlands of Ethiopia. *Integrated Environmental Assessment and Management*, 20(4), 965–974. https://doi.org/10.1002/ieam.4832

[35] Ishmetova, S. (2024). Globalization and the international division of labor: legal challenges and perspectives. *International Journal of Law Justice and Jurisprudence*, 4(1), 14–17. https://doi.org/10.22271/2790-0673.2024.v4.i1a.89

[36] Ghezal, M., Hassan, R., & Lahsasna, A. (2022). Legal and regulatory approaches in ṣukūk issuance: a comparative analysis. *UUM Journal of Legal Studies*, 13(1), 249–281. https://doi.org/10.32890/uumjls2022.13.1.11

[37] Abdu-ALgafoor, M., & Herode, P. (2023). Legal protection of financial markets: a review. *Current Journal of Applied Science and Technology*, 42(17), 31–39. https://doi.org/10.9734/cjast/2023/v42i174135

[38] Mone, V., Abdulajonovich, S., Younas, A., & Petikam, S. (2024). Data warfare and creating a global legal and regulatory landscape: challenges and solutions. *International Journal of Legal Information*, 52(2), 124–134. https://doi.org/10.1017/jli.2024.22

[39] Dingeldey, I., Fechner, H., Gerlitz, J., Hahs, J., & Mückenberger, U. (2021). Worlds of labour: introducing the standard-setting, privileging and equalising typology as a measure of legal segmentation in labour law. *Industrial Law Journal*, 51(3), 560–597. https://doi.org/10.1093/indlaw/dwab016

[40] Royle, J., & Laing, A. (2014). The digital marketing skills gap: developing a digital marketer model for the communication industries. *International Journal of Information Management*, 34(2), 65–73. https://doi.org/10.1016/j.ijinfomgt.2013.11.008

[41] Taiminen, H., & Karjaluoto, H. (2015). The usage of digital marketing channels in SMES. *Journal of Small Business and Enterprise Development*, 22(4), 633–651. https://doi.org/10.1108/jsbed-05-2013-0073

[42] Yadykin, V., Barykin, S., Badenko, V., Bolshakov, N., Poza, E., & Fedotov, A. (2021). Global challenges of digital transformation of markets: collaboration and digital assets. *Sustainability*, 13(19), 10619. https://doi.org/10.3390/su131910619
[43] Saputra, A. (2024). The importance of digital marketing integration in strategic management planning. *Action Research Literate*, 8(5). https://doi.org/10.46799/arl.v8i5.340
[44] Meganingsih, F., Wisesa, A., & Fachira, I. (2024). Enhancing Nogi Living's brand awareness: a customer decision journey perspective through social media. *International Journal of Current Science Research and Review*, 7(6). https://doi.org/10.47191/ijcsrr/v7-i6-38
[45] Huang, Y. (2022). Responding to customer's decision-making intention in pandemic scenario: indicators for choosing the right marketing automation platform. *International Journal of Business Studies and Innovation*, 2(4), 1–9. https://doi.org/10.35745/ijbsi2022v02.04.0001
[46] Pamadi, M., & Sari, Y. (2022). Challenges of developing a logistics hub case study: Batu Ampar Port. *Jurnal Tataloka*, 24(3), 249–256. https://doi.org/10.14710/tataloka.24.3.249-256
[47] Xie, Q. (2024). Research on modeling and analysis of logistics business process based on petri net. https://doi.org/10.4108/eai.17-11-2023.2342825
[48] Wang, G., Gunasekaran, A., Ngai, E., & Παπαδόπουλος, Θ. (2016). Big data analytics in logistics and supply chain management: certain investigations for research and applications. *International Journal of Production Economics*, 176, 98–110. https://doi.org/10.1016/j.ijpe.2016.03.014
[49] Reynolds, S. (2024). Investigating the impact of information sharing on supply chain resilience. https://doi.org/10.20944/preprints202406.0557.v1
[50] Holloway, S. (2024). Exploring supplier relationships and inventory optimization in high-technology industries. https://doi.org/10.20944/preprints202407.0523.v1
[51] Sodhi, M., & Tang, C. (2019). Research opportunities in supply chain transparency. *Production and Operations Management*, 28(12), 2946–2959. https://doi.org/10.1111/poms.13115
[52] Mirzayi, M., & Motaghi, M. (2024). Relationship between strategic management of human resources and the culture of organizational fallibility with the mediating role of information technology. *Journal of Social Behavior and Community Health*. https://doi.org/10.18502/jsbch.v8i1.15678
[53] Nduji, R., Orji, M., Oyenuga, M, & Oriaku, C. (2023). Assessing e-business and organisational performance in Nigeria today: evidence from Jumia Ltd, Lagos. *Britain International of Humanities and Social Sciences Journal*, 5(2), 81–92. https://doi.org/10.33258/biohs.v5i2.897
[54] Omale, S. A., Oyenuga, M., & Gurin, I. M. (2023). Effects of COVID-19 pandemic on organizational transformation and employees' performance. *Journal of Management, Economics, and Industrial Organization*, 7(1), 16–33. https://doi.org/10.31039/jomeino.2023.7.1.2
[55] Oyenuga, M. O., Akhaine, M. E., & Omale, S. A. (2023). We need it: how digital marketing tactics influence the purchasing behaviour of Nigerian Millennials. *Konfrontasi Journal: Culture, Economy and Social Changes*, 10(2), 91–105 https://doi.org/10.33258/konfrontasi2.v10i2.275
[56] Alimohammadlou, M., & Sharifian, S. (2022). Industry 4.0 implementation challenges in small and medium size enterprises: a hybrid method of interval valued fuzzy bwm and dematel. https://doi.org/10.21203/rs.3.rs-1264244/v1
[57] Oyenuga, M. O., Andah, R. A., & Nduji, R. (2023). Employee participation and organisational performance in an emerging economy. *Konfrontasi Journal: Culture, Economy and Social Changes*, 10(2), 91–105 https://doi.org/10.33258/konfrontasi2.v10i3.281

[58] Ozer, M., & Dayan, M. (2015). Strategic, organizational and operational challenges of product innovation in emerging economies. *Journal of Global Scholars of Marketing Science*, 25(1), 5–16. https://doi.org/10.1080/21639159.2014.980040

[59] Babiak, K., & Thibault, L. (2007). Challenges in multiple cross-sector partnerships. *Nonprofit and Voluntary Sector Quarterly*, 38(1), 117–143. https://doi.org/10.1177/0899764008316054

[60] Villani, E. & Phillips, N. (2020). Formal organizations and interstitial spaces: catalysts, complexity, and the initiation of cross-field collaboration. *Strategic Organization*, 19(1), 5–36. https://doi.org/10.1177/1476127019897235

[61] Bouguerra, A., Hughes, M., Rodgers, P., Stokes, P., & Tatoğlu, E. (2023). Confronting the grand challenge of environmental sustainability within supply chains: how can organizational strategic agility drive environmental innovation?. *Journal of Product Innovation Management*, 41(2), 323–346. https://doi.org/10.1111/jpim.12692

[62] Yaakub, S., & Mustafa, H. (2015). Supply chain risk management for the SME's. *Academic Journal of Interdisciplinary Studies*. https://doi.org/10.5901/ajis.2015.v4n1s2p151

[63] Ochulor, O., Sofoluwe, O., Ukato, A., & Jambol, D. (2024). Challenges and strategic solutions in commissioning and start-up of subsea production systems. *Magna Scientia Advanced Research and Reviews*, 11(1), 031–039. https://doi.org/10.30574/msarr.2024.11.1.0072

[64] Omale, S. A., Yusuf, S. O., Oyenuga, M. O., Ikemefuna, M., Ojo, S. S., & Momodu, I. D. (2024). Organizational learning in the post-COVID-19 era: a prerequisite for stakeholder satisfactions. *Twist*, 19(3), 265–272. https://twistjournal.net/twist/article/view/339

[65] Percy, W., & Dow, K. (2021). The coaching black box: risk mitigation during change management. *Journal of Risk and Financial Management*, 14(8), 344. https://doi.org/10.3390/jrfm14080344

[66] Ibrahim, N., Sobry, S., Ismail, N., & Harahap, A. (2023). Supply chain risks, green supply chain management practices and organizational performance: a research direction. *Information Management and Business Review*, 15(3(SI)), 429–438. https://doi.org/10.22610/imbr.v15i3(si).3499

[67] Ogedengbe, D., Olatoye, F., Oladapo, J., Nwankwo, E., Soyombo, O., & Scholastica, U. (2024). Strategic HRM in the logistics and shipping sector: challenges and opportunities. *International Journal of Science and Research Archive*, 11(1), 2000–2011. https://doi.org/10.30574/ijsra.2024.11.1.0269

[68] Chao, C., Hu, H., Zhang, L., & Wu, J. (2016). Managing the challenges of pharmaceutical patent expiry: a case study of Lipitor. *Journal of Science and Technology Policy Management*, 7(3), 258–272. https://doi.org/10.1108/jstpm-12-2015-0040

[69] Omale, S. A., Oyenuga, M. O., & Oriaku, C. (2021). Effect of organizational culture on the performance of hospitality industry in COVID-19 era. *Abhigyan*, 39(3), 24–32. https://doi.org/10.56401/abhigyan/39.3.2021.24-32

[70] Cooper, M. (2024). Agile procurement in a changing marketplace: examining adaptability and responsiveness in supply chain management. https://doi.org/10.20944/preprints202407.0514.v1

[71] Niros, M., Niros, A., Pollalis, Y., & Ding, Q. (2022). Effective marketing strategies for global FMCG brands during the COVID-19 pandemic crisis. *International Marketing Review*, 40(5), 1012–1034. https://doi.org/10.1108/imr-11-2021-0327

[72] Zhao, R. (2024). Green trade barriers in global play: legal challenges and strategic opportunities for developing countries. *Journal of Education Humanities and Social Sciences*, 39, 48–55. https://doi.org/10.54097/kz926p47

4 Consumer Mind across Borders
A Global Analysis

Richa Rajshree and Yogita Bansal

4.1 INTRODUCTION

In the era of globalization, where the world has become a global village, understanding consumer behaviour across borders has become vital for organizations to establish themselves in the international market and achieve success. This has led to the emergence of new cultural frameworks that significantly impact consumer identities, motivations, choices and preferences. Although globalization has contributed towards the creation of homogenized global consumers, the persistence and intensity of local cultural values remain the same in shaping purchasing decisions of consumers. There is a complex and dynamic interconnection between global forces and local traditions that has given rise to a diverse body of literature to explore how consumers think, feel and act in international contexts.

4.2 LITERATURE REVIEW

Torelli and Stoner proposed a psychological framework which emphasized market expansion globally and psychological adoption by consumers. It focused on blending global consumer culture and individual consumer identity. It also highlighted the global-local identity tension, specifically in cosmopolitan consumers [1]. The study of Sharifonnasabi focused on three decades of Consumer Culture Theory (CCT) research. They explained the consumer diversity in the global market through homogenization (global convergence of tastes), glocalization (global products with local twists) and deterritorialization (transcending traditional cultural boundaries) [2]. De Mooij explained that consumer perception and behaviour are strongly determined by cultural values. She argued that without cultural adaptation, global marketing strategies will not work uniformly across countries at a global level [3]. Ritzer gave the concept of "McDonaldization" to explain cultural homogenization through efficient and standardized global brands. However, their opinion somehow ignored the cultural diversity, which significantly affects the consumer's perception regarding authenticity and uniqueness of the product [4]. Appadurai's theory of deterritorialization provided a cultural anthropological approach to consumer globalization, highlighting the uncertainty and instability of cultural identity in global consumption. It also emphasized the imagination and aspiration in consumer behaviour [5].

 DOI: 10.1201/9781003650775-4

Shimp and Sharma developed the Consumer Ethnocentric Tendencies Scale (CETSCALE) to measure consumer ethnocentrism. They found that nationalistic sentiments strongly influence the purchasing behaviour of consumers. Thus, they tend to prefer domestic goods over foreign goods, irrespective of their quality and price [6]. Netemeyer validated CETSCALE across different nations and supported the scale's popularity across the globe. Their study found that consumer ethnocentrism exists in varying degrees across nations, thus emphasizing that it is a global phenomenon [7]. Balabanis identified that cultural and demographic factors affect the degree of consumer ethnocentrism. The degree of preference towards domestic products varies, and it plays an important role in target marketing [8]. Acikdilli identified a strong link between patriotism and consumer ethnocentrism in Turkey. Their study highlighted the role of socio-political factors affecting consumer attitudes [9]. Vida and Dmitrovic examined psychological factors behind the ethnocentric attitude of global customers. Their study found that consumer attitudes are largely driven by emotional factors rather than rational factors [10]. Truong explored the role of gender and cultural factors in the era of digital consumption. This research found that men and women across cultures react differently to digital shopping environments [11]. Bradford and Sherry Jr. discussed consumer acculturation in their study and found that gender plays an important role in adaptation strategies. It has been found that women choose the socially accepted and followed paths to enter new shopping environments [12]. Price and Arnould studied how commercial friendships and consumer relationships influence loyalty and trust. They also identified the gender differences in shaping these relationships. It has been observed that women value relational aspects more, as compared to men [13]. Dong and Tian discussed that ethnocentric consumers use consumption habits and patterns to maintain their cultural identity. Their study found that women are playing the role of culture preservers in dispersed communities through influencing the purchase and consumption decisions of the family [14]. Oswald examined bicultural identity negotiation, especially among second-generation immigrants and found the internal conflict and creativity in consumer choices [15]. Alanezi analysed that culture affects the perceived value of available online reviews. As per their study, consumers belonging to collectivist culture value emotionally driven reviews, while consumers from individualist culture prefer analytical content [16]. Iyer and Shapiro examined that consumers from collectivist societies trust the online content if it is approved and positively reviewed by a larger community [17]. Chytkova found that the way reviews are made is also affected by the culture. Consumers belonging to Western culture give individual-centric reviews, while consumers from Eastern culture make reviews based on harmony and group consensus [18].

Kjeldgaard and Askegaard found in their study that global brands and symbols with local interpretations and meanings are adopted widely [19]. Üstüner and Holt performed the ethnographic study of Turkish women's consumption patterns and identified that global consumption is re-shaped through local habits and rituals, and social hierarchies [20]. Thelen investigated that in developed countries, consumer attitudes towards offshored services have been affected largely by the perception of economic threats and job displacement [21]. Klein worked on consumer animosity and explained that historical and political tensions between countries affect brand perception among consumers. Consumers may not prefer to purchase and use foreign brands due to past conflicts, irrespective of the product's quality and better price [22]. Sharma, Shimp and Shin explained in their study that consumers may avoid and neglect foreign brands because of the fear of economic dependency on foreign countries. They integrate consumer ethnocentrism with perceived economic threat [23]. Good and Huddleston found that mostly older, less educated and lower-income consumers have an ethnocentric attitude. These consumers tend to prefer domestic products over global brands [24]. Brodowsky explored that ethnocentrism also affects foreign car evaluations. As per his study, ethnocentric consumers still prefer domestic car brands over foreign cars regardless of their better performance [25]. The above analysis of literature on consumer behaviour across borders highlights the interconnection and interlinkage of culture, identity, emotions and politics in shaping consumer behaviour. From classical theories to modern digital research, it is proven that consumer behaviour around the globe is determined and shaped by a blend of local traditions and global influences. It is required for global businesses and brands to understand these factors to achieve success at a global level.

4.3 HISTORY

The evolution of consumer behaviour across borders took place centuries ago with an increase in global trade, immigration and cultural exchanges. Trade routes such as the Silk Road and colonial shipping networks initiated the exchanges of goods and services across borders, long before the modern concept of globalization. As per the study of Schultz and Pecotich, these exchanges significantly affected the consumption patterns, food, fashion and lifestyle preferences. The formation of General Agreement on Tariffs and Trade (GATT) and International Monetary Fund (IMF) after World War II, along with economic and industrial expansion globally, promoted international trade [26]. De Mooij, found that despite the Western-centric study of cultural consumer differences, the expansion of the multinational corporations introduced the global brands in different markets in the 1950s and 1960s [3].

In the 1980s, Hofstede's cultural dimension theory gave a strong basis for comparing different cultures and explained that values such as individualism, power distance and uncertainty avoidance affect consumer's decision-making [27]. At the same time, Levitt put forth the idea of standardized global marketing, which suggests that exposure to global media and products plays a significant role in shaping consumer choices and preferences [28]. Although this phenomenon was challenged by Mooij, who emphasized the significant role of deep-rooted cultural values and norms in shaping consumer choices and preferences [3]. Appadurai introduced the idea of *deterritorialization*, framing consumers as agents who interpret and reshape global cultural flows through imagination, aspiration and adaptation [5].

An important concept of consumer ethnocentrism emerged worldwide in the late 1980s and early 1990s, and consumers showed resistance to foreign goods. The CETSCALE was being used to measure the ethnocentric attitudes of consumers. Subsequently, researchers also explored phenomena such as consumer antagonism and country-of-origin effect among the consumers. They established a linkage between consumer choices and historical aspects and national identity. In the

2020s, new complexities in global consumer behaviour have emerged due to trade wars, economic nationalism, and the COVID-19 pandemic Oswald's research on Haitian immigrants and Üstüner and Holt's on Turkish women explain that a nation's identity, class and cultural values and norms significantly affect consumer behaviour in a global context [15, 20]. In the era of digitization, global consumer behaviour has been significantly influenced by online shopping platforms, digital payment systems, real-time connectivity between seller and buyer, and AI-based personalization. As explained by Alanezi, now consumers can search for the products in global or local markets based on the culture they belong to, the impact of influencers, user reviews, etc. [16]. The research of Truong and Iyer C. Shapiro suggests that digital consumer experiences are affected by the cultural values and norms, emotions, gender and community preferences [11, 17]. These factors influence the online shopping experiences of consumers. In the 2020s, new complexities have been observed in global consumer behaviour because of trade wars, economic nationalism and Covid-19. The phenomenon of ethnocentric buying behaviour is taking front seat again, and the global supply chain has been reevaluated. These shifts make it necessary for businesses to understand cultural factors while formulating and understanding global marketing strategies.

The historical analysis of global consumer behaviour identifies the nation's identities, cultural values and emotional frameworks that shape consumer behaviour across borders.

4.4 UNDERSTANDING CONSUMER BEHAVIOUR PATTERN ACROSS BORDERS

In the era of globalization where domestic economies have been integrated into one global economy and businesses have expanded in all parts of the world, it is the need of the hour to understand the consumer's behaviour across borders. The behaviour of the global consumer is shaped by a dynamic mix of factors such as cultural norms and values, economic development, technological advancement and historical experiences. To build a long-lasting relationship with consumers, businesses need to understand and analyse these factors. Businesses require an understanding of the cultural differences among consumers for the successful implementation of their marketing strategies. For example, emotions shape consumer choice and preferences and are expressed and interpreted in different ways across borders. De Run and others identified in their research that Japanese consumers often value emotional appeals and group harmony in advertisements, while vibrant and expressed messages with a personal touch in advertisements are valued by the Brazilian consumers. This illustration identifies that the same advertisements can be interpreted in different ways because of a distinctive emotional culture [29]. Luna and Gupta explained that the decision-making style also varies from culture to culture. For example, in Western countries, consumers' buying decisions are based on individual choices and preferences, speed and convenience. However, in Eastern cultures like India, consumers may first consult family or friends before making any buying decision, especially for the products of collective use. Thus, product reviews and social and community-based endorsements play an important role in these cultures [30]. Advancement and adoption of technology also impact cross-border differences in consumers' behaviour. For example, as explained by Donner and Tellez, in Western countries, the use of mobile platforms is focused mainly on speed and self-service, as compared to African or Southeast Asian countries, where mobile phones are used for shopping as well as community hubs and tools of financial inclusion. The use of WhatsApp and mobile money has influenced consumer behaviour significantly in Kenya's informal retail sector [31].

The perceived value of global brands also differs from country to country. As Zhou explained, in many countries like the United States and India, Apple is perceived as a symbol of status and innovation, while in some European countries it is seen with suspicion because of its labour practices and corporate taxes. In China, consumers associate Apple with a modern, luxurious lifestyle. Thus, apart from advertising, national disclosure, media and public sentiments shape consumer preferences and choice [32]. As discussed by Sheth, socioeconomic factors such as durability, value for money, aesthetic design, and sustainability features significantly influence consumer preferences [33]. For example, in rural India, refrigerators and other electric appliances are generally purchased based on their capacity to function with an unstable power supply. One more example can be from Germany, where products are purchased based on energy efficiency and eco-labelling.

4.5 CULTURAL IMPACT ON CONSUMER DECISION- MAKING

Culture of any society determines the values and beliefs, choices and priorities, interaction and communication styles, emotional reactions and responses, etc., of individuals. The cultural aspects affect individuals' definition of quality and satisfaction and guide consumers in pre-purchase decisions to post-purchase evaluation. Thus, consumer behaviour and decision-making are significantly affected by culture.

4.5.1 Individualism versus Collectivism

Consumer behaviour is significantly affected by the individualism versus collectivism dimensions of the culture of a society. Consumers belonging to an individualistic culture are basically motivated by personal needs and satisfaction, self-expression, independence in their decisions and choices, etc., as seen in the United States, Canada and the United Kingdom. For example, in such countries, if a consumer chooses a mobile phone, they tend to focus more on its unique features, brand recognition and the personal image associated with the product. The decision is made based on "what is best for me." On the other hand, in collectivist cultures like India, China and South Korea, purchase decisions are generally based on societal status, family expectations and priorities, group norms, etc. For instance, if in India a person wants to buy a car, the decision will be taken after consulting the family members to ensure harmony and respect. In purchase decisions, personal preferences matter, but societal image and status come first.

4.5.2 High-Context versus Low-Context Cultures

In high-context cultures, for example, Japan, Saudi Arabia and Korea, the consumers believe in implicit communication and their purchase decisions are often affected by brand trust, symbolic meaning and a long-lasting relationship with the sellers. For instance, a Japanese consumer may continue to buy electronic appliances of a particular brand or company out of trust and loyalty, and past reliability, even if the competitors are offering the same product with more new features and benefits. While in low context cultures like the United States, Germany, the weightage is given more to explicit communication and consumers in this culture rely more on transparency, reviews, price comparisons and logical reasoning behind the purchase. They tend to switch brands if better prices, features and utilities are offered by another seller. Their decisions are purely economic and rational.

4.5.3 Advertising and Message Appeal

Culture significantly impacts the meaning and interpretation drawn by the consumers of the messages conveyed by the advertisements. In countries where people give more importance to family and emotional values, advertisements invoking love, togetherness and warmth are more effective and successful. For example, in Latin America, Coca-Cola's family-centric holiday advertisement performed very well. In contrast, in the countries where individualism and rationalism are emphasized, advertisements with clarity and precision and showing functional benefits are more effective in affecting consumer's choices and preferences.

4.5.4 Ethical and Religious Frameworks

The religious and ethical framework of society also affects consumer choices and preferences. For example, in Muslim-majority countries, obtaining halal certification is necessary for food, cosmetics and even financial products. Many brands like Nestle and KFC obtained the halal certificate to serve these markets. As identified by Jamal and Shukor, in countries like India, religious festivals significantly affect the purchasing patterns, as at the time of festivals like Diwali and EID, the sale of gold, electronics, home decor and fashion products go up. Most Indian families tend to make large purchases on auspicious days and events [34].

4.5.5 Risk Aversion and Uncertainty Avoidance

Cultural factors also affect the consumers' risk taking and uncertainty-avoidance abilities while making purchasing decisions. In countries like Greece or Portugal, where high uncertainty-avoidance culture prevails, consumers tend to buy established products, which offer strong warranties and strong customer support. They do not try new or unfamiliar products until positive reviews and endorsements are received. In countries like the United States or Singapore with low uncertainty-avoidance cultures, consumers enjoy experimenting and experiencing new products, new technologies and new fashion trends. Hofstede identified that in these countries, consumers take risks in their buying decisions to discover new alternatives and opportunities. These factors positively impact the launch campaigns, trial strategies and marketing effectiveness [27].

4.6 EXPANSION OF DIGITIZATION AND TECHNOLOGY AND THE RISE OF GLOBAL CONSUMER TRENDS

The advent of new technology and increasing digitalization has brought a revolutionary impact on consumer behaviour. The ways consumers interact with products, services and global brands have changed remarkably. Now, consumers' access is not confined to geography or local retailers. They shape their choices and preferences based on global consumption trends through shared platforms and experiences. The increased digitization has changed the ways people buy and affected why, what and with whom they buy. All these have led to a transformation in global consumer consciousness.

4.6.1 Role of Social Media and the Convergence of Consumer Trends

The increasing use of social media platforms worldwide has contributed significantly to the rapid global circulation of trends and consumption patterns. For example, social media platforms like Facebook, Instagram, TikTok and YouTube disseminate the information, as well as enabling consumers to create new identities and follow the common influencers globally. As explained by Cova, youth of many countries follow the same beauty influencers, adopt similar makeup styles and follow the fashion choices of each other, creating a "digital tribe" as named by researchers [35]. For instance, the Korean skincare routine has been adopted globally, although its use and process may vary from country to country. Social media intensifies these trends by bringing the practices limited to certain areas into mainstream.

4.6.2 Growth of E-Commerce and Borderless Marketplace

The growth of e-commerce has ended the boundaries between the markets, and now consumers can have a global shopping experience from their smartphones. This has promoted the emergence of global brands and encouraged small businesses to expand globally from their inception. The credit goes to E-commerce platforms such as Amazon, Shopify and Etsy. As explored by Goldfarb and Tucker, nowadays consumers from any country can buy Korean cosmetics, Turkish tea and Scandinavian furniture from international sellers as conveniently as local ones [36].

4.6.3 The Role of AI and Cultural Personalization in Global Markets

The use of AI tools and data analytics enables global brands to provide highly personalized services to consumers across borders. This contributes to improving consumers' experiences and conversion rates. But it is also an important fact that global consumers respond to these personalized services as per their cultural values, norms and standards. For example, Netflix's recommendation engine may suggest a comedy show or movie in the United States but a romantic one to Indian consumers. One more example can be taken of Amazon, where personalized suggestions are based not only on consumers' behaviour but also on local shopping trends and seasonal festivals. Lobato suggested that AI recommendations should be culturally supported [37]. For example, if a brand recommendation is for pork products in Muslim-majority countries or revealing clothes in conservative cultures, it may create a challenge and damage the brand image.

4.6.4 Role of Cross-Border Influencers and Consumer Trust

In the global scenario where consumers are afraid of using new global brands, the role of influencers has become important in creating consumer trust. Consumers tend to follow the reviews and recommendations of relatable individuals. They do not rely on corporate advertisements and campaigns. Influencers have now become the trust intermediaries in the global markets. For example, an Indian influencer promoting Korean beauty products bridges the gap between the cultures of the two regions. These influences give a local touch to these products and enhance appeal to consumers. Abidin identified that in the era of digital consumerism, there is a shift from institutional trust to interpersonal trust. As influencers understand the domestic culture, speak in the local language and link personal stories with the product, consumers feel connected and find reliability and authenticity [38].

4.6.5 Digitization of Emerging Markets

The increased use of smartphones and digital payment systems in emerging markets has created a class of new global consumers on which global companies need to pay more attention. In many countries like India, Kenya, Nigeria and Indonesia, there has been a tremendous increase in the number of digital buyers. For example, mobile wallets like Paytm and UPI systems in India have democratized E-commerce, especially in rural areas. M-Pesa in Kenya has enabled consumers to transact online globally, even without a bank account. Donner explained that there is a shift in the cultural expectations, shopping habits and trust mechanism of the consumers. Global brands must integrate these changes in their delivery models, return policies and customer service strategies to connect and retain context-sensitive consumers [39].

4.7 THE DUAL FRAMEWORK OF CROSS-BORDER CONSUMER BEHAVIOUR – LOCAL VERSUS GLOBAL TRENDS

Local and global trends are different, particularly in their origin and impact on consumer behaviour. Local trends evolve from distinct cultures, regions or social contexts and are deeply linked to the traditions, values and daily lives of communities. Global trends extend across countries and are driven by technology, social media, multinational corporations and global impacts.

The first difference in local and global trends is the cultural differences. Local trends reveal the language. Customs, identification and inheritance of a particular group of people. For example, regional festivals, customs, language, clothing, local food habits and domestic crafts have roots in local culture and are transferred through many generations. Global trends often spin around universal themes such as style, innovation, sustainability and convenience. These involve plant-based diets, internet challenges, continuous services and trending fashion that surges worldwide irrespective of cultural background.

Another difference is based on consumer connection. As local trends reveal their identity, community and feeling of belonging, consumers tend to have a strong sense of attachment to local trends.

However, the global trends create a feeling of style, modernity, and connectedness because they are made on international platforms and by global movements.

The duration of global trends varies. While the local trends are long-lasting because of the deep cultural roots, the global trends are of short duration. Moreover, the local trends are run by community choices, local media and local influencers. In contrast, the global trends are propelled by global celebrities, viral contention social media platforms and international marketing drives.

For marketing, local trends need a local approach – products and promotion must be in accordance with the regional and cultural norms. Global trends go for bulk marketing, often with standardized branding and messaging that is well understood and accepted by the customers. Economically, local trends support local businessmen and artisans, encouraging sustainability and slower utilization patterns. Global trends aim for innovation and bend towards fast consumerism and keep benefiting multinational companies.

Despite these dissimilarities, there is interaction between both the trends. Sometimes, local trends motivate global awareness (like yoga from India or K-beauty from South Korea).

Global trends are sometimes modified locally to suit regional choices, which is known as "glocalization." Understanding the balance between these trends is the solution to succeed in a world that is culturally diverse and globally connected.

In today's connected world, local and global swings do not play alone, but they interact, clash and co-exist in many different manners. The buyers sail a world of global options refined by local views, thus making dual consumption trends that reveal both global desires and cultural rootedness. Interpreting this equilibrium is important in how a purchaser thinks and operates across borders.

4.7.1 Global Trends and Local Aspirations

World trends like sustainability and tech-driven lifestyles are gaining grip across many regions, but their implementation differs locally. For example, global sustainability drift may be seen in eco-friendly packaging in the United States, while in India and Kenya, sustainability may centre on plastic-free traditional substitutes such as cloth bags or banana leaf packaging – executed practically rather than ideologically.

Another example is the global "fast fashion" tide. Brands like Zara or HCM propel global styles, the local consumers in Indonesia or Morocco blend these items with traditional dresses like hijab or kaftan, making new fashion subcultures which are modern as well as culturally rich.

4.7.2 The Supremacy of Local Values in Consumption Patterns

Although global brands attract consumers, local traditions, festivals and rituals stay strong presenters of consumer identity. Brands that neglect the local modulation often break their connections with consumers deeply. For example, while Valentine's Day is a global celebration, local celebrations like Qixi in China or Karva Chauth in India have much stronger and deeper cultural and emotional importance, thus affecting product marketing, gift sections and shopping hike.

In food and beverage markets, McDonald's or Starbucks change menus to add local flavours like McAloo Tikki burgers in India and Matcha Lattes in Japan. These changes are not only cosmetics but show deep-rooted cultural choices that global brands must recognize to remain pertinent.

4.7.3 Glocal Influences around the Globe-Locals Are Getting Global

Local trends are affecting the global markets; this opposite flow is sometimes called "glocal influence," which shows growing accessibility to cultural diversity in global consumption. Indian wellness practices like yoga and Ayurveda, Japanese anime and Korean pop culture (K-pop) are no longer limited but are now having large worldwide followings.

African streetwear made by designers from Lagos and Johannesburg is acquiring global visibility, with celebrities and global retailers adopting local patterns. These are authentic exhibitions that change the global taste, showing that global styles are not Western influenced.

4.7.4 Identity Crisis among Local and Global

Today's consumers, especially youth, experience a dual recognition – desiring to adopt the global fashion along with maintaining their commitment to local values. A Brazilian youth may use global sneaker drops but still adhere to local music and cuisine. This duplexity leads to what is called "cultural code-switching," where purchasers easily make their choices based on features like wearing Western brands at the workplace but conventional attire at family events.

Such practices are also relevant in digital consumption: consumers can use global platforms like Netflix or TikTok but opt for content in their local language or focus attention on local composers, showing "glocal" involvement pattern.

4.7.5 Optimum Strategy – To Balance Global-Local Mix

Brands that master the "glocal" strategy grow internationally, balancing steadiness with cultural adaptations. For Example, Coca-Cola, while maintaining global branding, runs local vibrant campaigns during national festivals. Airbnb encourages global travel but exhibits local hosts and local experiences, revealing a blend of global access and local reliability.

On the other hand, brands that take no notice of sentiments may face repercussions. For example, huge consumer boycotts were initiated by Dolce and Gabbana's controversial 2018 ad in China, indicating how misreading local context damages global equity.

4.8 FACTORS AFFECTING GLOBAL CONSUMER CHOICES AND PREFERENCES

Consumer preferences in the global market are influenced by multiple interconnected factors, including individual psychology, social values, economic conditions, technological access, and cultural traditions. When markets are becoming more interconnected, it has become necessary for marketers, policymakers and businesses who want to operate worldwide to understand the choices made by consumers.

4.8.1 Cultural Frameworks and Value Systems

The culture has a significant role to play in consumers' choices, expectations and meaning of value. For example, in Japan and India, where collective culture exists, the buying decisions are made with group consonance or family benefit in mind. While in the United States or Germany, where individual culture exists, the consumers prioritize self-expression, convenience or personal preferences.

Example: A luxury car can be bought in China not solely for individual pleasure but to elevate the family status or meet social expectations in professional circles. However, in the United States, the car may be bought for performance or personal advantage.

4.8.2 The Economic Environment and Purchasing Power

The consumers' risk forbearance and purchasing behaviour are influenced by the economic environment, inflation, income levels and employment security. In developing nations, purchase depends on the needs and price sensitivity, while in developed nations, the emotional and desire factors play an important role.

In Brazil, a consumer may give priority to a smartphone with dual SIM features and long battery life, while a customer in France may go for lifestyle enhancement factors like camera quality or brand prestige.

4.8.3 Social Media Influence and Peer Networks

The consumer purchasing plan is influenced by the recommendations from family, friends, influencers and online communities. In digital mode, choices in fashion, technology and lifestyle sections swing by peer validation via reviews, ratings or social media engagement.

In many places in Africa where advertisements are less or limited, WhatsApp groups play an important role in finding products. While in Western countries, TikTok trends can lead to shortages because of viral demands.

4.8.4 Easy Accessibility and Availability of Technology and Digital Infrastructure

Digital reach influences the choice of consumers and how they find, research and connect with brands. In digitally advanced regions, consumers may use AI-powered suggestions, AI-try-ons and online shopping help, while consumers in emerging markets depend on mobile-friendly e-commerce platforms.

The consumers in South Korea often use AI-powered virtual try-ons for fashion and cosmetics. The rural areas in Indonesia frequently mediate with the local shops (warung) for ordering and delivery – which shows how access changes consumers' pathways.

4.8.5 Legal and Ethical Framework

Government regulations, import restrictions and branding needs define the availability of the product and shape the trust in countries; certifications or ethical labels such as "fair trade," "organic" or "eco certified" become a decisive element.

In the EU, uncompromising food labelling laws ensure that consumers are informed about the ingredient sourcing and may disapprove non-compliant foreign brands. While in Scandinavian countries, ethical consumerism gives importance to sustainable and cruelty-free products, which can be a slow concern in markets having price-sensitive purchasers.

4.8.6 Psychological Factors and Risk Orientation

The perception of consumers about risks and value varies – mostly in cross-border transactions. Choices of consumers are affected by their concerns about product genuineness, return policies, language barriers and payment security.

A US shopper may order electronics from China through AliExpress if the consumer protection policies and reviews are supportive. However, a buyer in Nigeria can choose to purchase at a higher price from a local platform like Jumia, because of more trust and easier conflict resolution.

The choices of buyers are not only dependent on a single factor but on an interplay of culture, context, access and psychology. Brands should make multidimensional strategies that consider these differences and identify common ground. Acknowledging the local factors within a global context is important to succeed in international markets.

4.9 SUSTAINABILITY AND ETHICAL CONCERNS IN CROSS-BORDER CONSUMER BEHAVIOUR

As globalization is augmenting, the collective responsibility of consumers regarding their impact on the environment and society is also developing. Sustainable and ethical utilization – the act of buying those goods that are produced, marketed and dumped without harming and providing maximum benefits to the consumers as well as the environment – has changed from a niche business to a global consumer shift.

4.9.1 Increased Awareness of Consumers towards Ethics

Today's younger generation consumers, like Millennials and Gen Z consumers, are aware of issues related to climate change, workers' exploitation, overproduction and animal brutality. A survey report by McKinsey in 2023 shows that 75% of Gen Z respondents were willing to pay more for sustainable products. This report shows that there is a shift in the values of consumers. Consumers not only buy the products, but they also buy environmental ethics and brand philosophies [40].

Brands like IKEA and HCM in Scandinavian countries have made huge investments in circular economic drive (e.g., buy-back and recycling schemes) that line up with the region's increasing awareness and regulatory backup for sustainable livelihood.

Consumers check the transparency and search for the eco-labels, cruelty-free certifications and carbon details before purchasing.

4.9.2 Cultural Orientation towards Sustainability

Consumers' backgrounds affect the perception and practice of ethical consumption. Sustainability mostly ties with one's identity, autonomy and consumer activism in Individualistic cultures. Consumers consider their purchases like votes for the world they like to live in. The same concepts are attached to tradition, community wellness and family ethics in collectivist societies. The sense of "mottainai" (it is a sense of regret over scrap) in Japan steers behaviours like diligent use of products, minimizing production and reuse.

Sustainable consumption in India is often a part of spiritual and economic care rather than an environmental attempt, for example, transferring clothes in families, reuse of containers, buying in bulk.

These culturally merged practices may not be tagged as "sustainable "but are associated with ethical consumption values.

4.9.3 Economic Disparity and Lack of Access to Sustainability in Developing Countries

The major barriers to the use of sustainability in emerging and developing economies are access and affordability. Due to production standards, the goods that are being produced ethically have higher price tags, which leads to exclusion of low- and middle-income consumers. Thus, the ethical intention often clashes with economic truth.

Example:

1. A consumer in Norway may pay $25 for a coffee that has been made ethically with certification and traceability
2. A consumer in Kenya, due to affordability issues, may depend on local markets, even when the beans are grown locally.

This shows that global ethical division happens where the ability to choose sustainable products depends on the purchasing power and the product availability.

4.9.4 Trust and Greenwashing across Borders

Consumers' doubt on "greenwashing" – wrong and overemphasized claims on sustainability – affects the consumers' decision differently based on trust in government and business. Consumers trust ethical claims in countries with high transparency standards, as compared to countries with less regulatory standards, where consumers trust their validity.

Example: In Europe, for verified environmental labelling, the brands must adhere to the EU Green Claims Directive, while in various parts of Southeast Asia or Latin America, Eco, vague, or natural labels may propagate without certification that cause confusion or distrust among consumers.

Hence, for the adoption of ethical consumption, a local regulatory system and consumer protection become important determinants.

4.9.5 Role of Digital Media and Activism

Technology, particularly social media, plays a reshaping role in escalating ethical consumption norms across borders. Mobile apps, influencer campaigns and viral hashtags enable consumers to access information about brand practices and share ethical concerns in actual times.

Example: Global demand for supply chain transparency was ignited by the Fashion Revolution campaign (#WhoMadeMyClothes) after the Rana Plaza Factory collapse in Bangladesh.

Various platforms like Buycott and Good on You allow users to scan products and talk about the product's environmental and ethical credentials – helping consumers to have informed choices.

Digital media acts as a global equalizer, helping the consumers of developed as well as developing countries to access the same ethical information, but variation in internet penetration and digital literacy persists.

4.9.6 Regional Implementation: Glocal Ethical Strategies

Now, global brands have adapted to cultural sensitivities and logistical truths in every market by adopting "glocal (global & local) approaches" and thus changing from a one-size-fits-all sustainability approach.

Example: Unilever launched personal care products for drought areas of Asia and South Africa, and hence dealt with the local needs while strengthening its global eco-brand name.

Nestle's Nespresso launched a capsule recycling scheme in Europe, but it realized that in Latin America it would require a community engagement approach to confirm success because of the variation in recycling infrastructure.

Ethical consumption and sustainability are not outlying trends, but they are core to consumer identification, brand trust and business success. Global policies must have a balance with the global ethical quality, along with cultural understanding, economic availability and local infrastructure.

Ethical consumption is not about telling every consumer what to buy – it is about creating environments where making the right choice is easy, affordable and meaningful, no matter where that consumer lives.

4.10 OUTLOOK OF CONSUMER BEHAVIOUR ACROSS BORDERS

The new era is being defined by hyper-connectivity, cultural diversity, ethical realization and digital personalization. The future of consumer behaviour across borders is a blend of local values, global experiences, digital interaction and not about converging into a single global mindset.

4.10.1 Rise of the "Glocal" Consumer

The partition between local consumption and global consumption is becoming narrower. Future consumers are probably to show dual loyalty to local trends as well as embracing global trends. The demand for the products will be driven by this "glocal identity" that has international standards with local aesthetics, ingredients or history.

Example: Indian consumers in future may favour those tech-savvy health apps (global trend) that are based on Ayurvedic propositions (local tradition).

Blockchain – based traceability for food (global tech) can be embraced by African consumers but anticipate supporting local farmers and domestic ingredients. This fusion will be crucial to product development and marketing in cross-border markets.

4.10.2 Acceleration of Digital-First Experiences

Future consumers are digitally native, depending on AI-curated shopping, Augmented Reality/Virtual Reality (AR/VR) tryouts and voice search. The various platforms like Amazon, Alibaba and regional businesses will help in expanding cross-border e-commerce but with emphasis on hyper-personalization.

The future predicted trends:

AI will envision preferences not only by purchase history but also by the cultural and emotional signals, and offerings to resemble regional values.

Real-time language translation, localized pricing and AR-based product visualization will augment cross-border shopping.

The global cross-border e-commerce sales are projected to reach $7.9 trillion by 2030, with outstanding growth in Southeast Asia, Africa and Latin America, according to Statista [41].

4.10.3 Sustainability as a Non-Negotiable Standard

Once, sustainability was a differentiator, but in the future, it will be anticipated. Consumers will be demanding sustainability in every product and service – not just marketed as an add-on. To prove ethical, brands will require transparent, blockchain-verified supply chains. Carbon labelling (such as nutrition facts) can become standard on packaging. Notwithstanding the environmental criteria, the companies may be disbarred from international platforms or fined by consumer rejection.

According to a projection by Deloitte in 2025, 71% worldwide consumers below age 35 will switch to brands that are based on environmental concerns [42].

4.10.4 Data Ethics and Trust Will Be Central

Future consumers will be highly concerned with data privacy and algorithmic bias at the time of cross-border shopping. These future consumers will be demanding transparency and personalization of their data, especially in areas with different privacy standards (e.g., US vs China vs EU).

Example: A Germany-based consumer (under GDPR) will be anticipating full data disclosure from a US-based company.

Due to transforming data policies, the Indian and Brazilian consumers will be demanding localization of data storage. The brands will be required to float international data ethics, providing opt-in/opt-out controls and an ethically framed recommendation system.

4.10.5 Identity-Driven and Activist Consumption

The future consumer will use investing power as a political act. Social values like gender equity, indigenous rights and racial justice will be directing the shopping across borders.

Example:

1. A brand may face international backlash and rejections on their silence on geopolitical issues like war, genocide and injustice.
2. Consumers are going to cross the boundaries virtually to favour the businesses that align with their values.

To stay aligned with growing moral expectations across borders, the social listening tools will be determining.

4.10.6 Behavioural Shifts Driven by Climate and Crisis

With the reshaping of global society by climatic changes, pandemics and geopolitical conflicts, there will be the emergence of important behavioural traits like consumer elasticity and adaptability.

Consumers may give more importance to the following:

1. Digital products and experiences over tangible goods
2. Durability and repairability instead of fast fashion
3. Regional sourcing in response to supply chain disruptions

Example:

After Covid, the demand for telehealth kits and home fitness increased – showing displacement towards blended living and self-reliance.

Climate-adaptable products such as water-retaining appliances and disaster kits are likely to control the consumption trend in flood and drought-liable areas.

4.11 CONCLUSION: FROM GLOBALIZATION TO FLUIDITY

Ethical consciousness, technological immersion and regional resilience will shape consumer behaviours across borders. Companies should accept the emerging mindset that is adaptive, informed and values-driven rather than moving behind the presumption of "emerging" versus "developed" markets.

To sustain success, future businesses must adopt ethical and localized strategies, invest responsibly in AI, and ensure that trust, privacy, and meaningful customer engagement evolve alongside operational efficiency.

REFERENCES

[1] Torelli, C. J., & Stoner, J. L. (2013). Global consumer culture and the psychological underpinnings of consumer behavior. *Journal of International Marketing*, 27(3), 3–13.

[2] Sharifonnasabi, M., Askegaard, S., & Linnet, J. T. (2020). Thirty years of consumer culture theory: A critical review and agenda for future research. Marketing Theory, 20(4), 423–435.

[3] De Mooij, M. (2013). *Consumer Behavior and Culture: Consequences for Global Marketing and Advertising* (3rd ed.). SAGE Publications.

[4] Ritzer, G. (1983). The McDonaldization of society. *Journal of American Culture*, 6(1), 100–107.

[5] Appadurai, A. (1990). Disjuncture and difference in the global cultural economy. *Theory, Culture & Society*, 7(2–3), 235–310.

[6] Shimp, T. A., & Sharma, S. (1987). Consumer ethnocentrism: Construction and validation of the CETSCALE. *Journal of Marketing Research*, 24(3), 280–283.

[7] Netemeyer, R. G., Durvasula, S., & Lichtenstein, D. R. (1991). A cross-national assessment of the reliability and validity of the CETSCALE. *Journal of Marketing Research*, 28(3), 320–327.

[8] Balabanis, G., Diamantopoulos, A., Mueller, R. D., & Melewar, T. C. (2001). The impact of nationalism, patriotism and internationalism on consumer ethnocentric tendencies. *Journal of International Business Studies*, 32(1), 157– 175.

[9] Acikdilli, G., Ziemnowicz, C., & Bahadir, S. C. (2017). Ethnocentrism in the global market: A study in Turkish consumers. *Journal of International Consumer Marketing*, 23(3), 173–187.

[10] Vida, I., & Dmitrovic, T. (2001). An empirical analysis of consumer purchasing behavior in the former Yugoslav markets. *Economic and Business Review*, 3(3), 131–207.

[11] Truong, V. H. (2025). Gendered and cultural emotions in digital consumer spaces: A cross-cultural UX analysis. *Journal of Interactive Marketing*. https://doi.org/10.48550/arXiv.2505.02852

[12] Bradford, T. W., & Sherry Jr., J. F. (2014). Orchestrating rituals through retail management: Lessons from consumer experience. *Journal of Retailing*, 30(3), 240–253.

[13] Price, L. L., & Arnould, E. J. (1999). Commercial friendships: Service provider– Client relationships in context. *Journal of Marketing*, 63(4), 38–56.

[14] Dong, L., & Tian, K. (2009). The use of western brands in asserting Chinese national identity. *Journal of Consumer Research*, 36(3), 504–523.

[15] Oswald, L. R. (1999). Culture swapping: Consumption and the ethnogenesis of middle-class Haitian immigrants. *Journal of Consumer Research*, 25(4), 303– 318.

[16] Alanezi, M. A., Alshurideh, M. T., & Kurdi, B. (2023). Cultural influences on online review helpfulness: A deep learning perspective. *Journal of Retailing and Consumer Services*, 71, 103156.
[17] Iyer, E. S., & Shapiro, J. M. (1999). Ethnic differences in the meaning and use of marketing signals. *Journal of Business Research*, 45(2), 103–112.
[18] Chytkova, Z. (2011). Consumer acculturation and narratives of self: The case of Russian-speaking immigrants in Germany. *Consumption Markets & Culture*, 14(3), 207–234.
[19] Kjeldgaard, D., & Askegaard, S. (2006). The globalization of youth culture: The global youth segment as structures of common difference. *Journal of Consumer Research*, 33(2), 231–247.
[20] Üstüner, T., & Holt, D. B. (2010). Toward a theory of status consumption in less industrialized countries. *Journal of Consumer Research*, 37(1), 37–55.
[21] Thelen, S. T., Yoo, B., & Magnini, V. P. (2011). Animosity, animosity toward international outsourcing, and foreign product purchase behavior. *Journal of International Consumer Marketing*, 23(2), 92–103.
[22] Klein, J. G. (2002). Us versus them, or us versus everyone? Delineating consumer aversion to foreign goods. *Journal of International Business Studies*, 33(2), 345–363.
[23] Sharma, S., Shimp, T. A., & Shin, J. (1995). Consumer ethnocentrism: A test of antecedents and moderators. *Journal of the Academy of Marketing Science*, 23(1), 26–37.
[24] Good, L. K., & Huddleston, P. (1995). Ethnocentrism of Polish and Russian consumers: Are feelings and intentions related? *International Marketing Review*, 12(5), 35–48.
[25] Brodowsky, G. H. (1998). The effects of country of design and country of assembly on evaluative beliefs about automobiles and attitudes toward buying them. *Journal of International Consumer Marketing*, 10(3), 85–113.
[26] Schultz, C. J., & Pecotich, A. (1997). Marketing and development: Macromarketing perspectives. *Journal of Macromarketing*, 17(1), 4–10.
[27] Hofstede, G. (1980). *Culture's Consequences: International Differences in Work Related Values*. Sage Publications.
[28] Levitt, T. (1983). The globalization of markets. *Harvard Business Review*, 61(3), 92–102.
[29] de Run, E. C., Butt, M. M., Fam, K.-S., & Jong, H. Y. (2010). Attitudes towards offensive advertising: Malaysian Muslims' views. *Journal of Islamic Marketing*, 1(1), 25–36.
[30] Luna, D., & Gupta, S. F. (2001). An integrative framework for cross-cultural consumer behavior. *International Marketing Review*, 18(1), 45–63.
[31] Donner, J., & Tellez, C. A. (2008). Mobile banking and economic development: Linking adoption, impact, and use. *Asian Journal of Communication*, 18(4), 318–332.
[32] Zhou, L., & Wong, A. (2008). Exploring the influence of product conspicuousness and social compliance on status-seeking consumption in China. *Journal of Consumer Behaviour*, 7(4–5), 263–271.
[33] Sheth, J. N. (2011). Impact of emerging markets on marketing: Rethinking existing perspectives and practices. *Journal of Marketing*, 75(4), 166–182.
[34] Jamal, A., & Shukor, S. A. (2014). Religion and consumer behaviour: A conceptual overview. *International Journal of Islamic Marketing and Branding*, 1(1), 58–75.
[35] Cova, B., Kozinets, R. V., & Shankar, A. (2012). Consumer Tribes. Routledge.
[36] Goldfarb, A., & Tucker, C. (2019). Digital economics. *Journal of Economic Literature*, 57(1), 3–43.
[37] Lobato, R. (2019). *Netflix Nations: The Geography of Digital Distribution*. NYU Press.

[38] Abidin, C. (2016). "Aren't these just young, rich women doing vain things online?": Influencer selfies as subversive frivolity. *Social Media + Society*, 2(2), 1–17.
[39] Donner, J. (2022). *After Access: Inclusion, Development, and a More Mobile Internet*. MIT Press.
[40] McKinsey & Company. (2023). The state of fashion 2023: Resilience in the face of uncertainty. Retrieved from https://www.mckinsey.com
[41] Statista. (2024). Forecast on cross-border e-commerce revenue worldwide 2023–2030. Retrieved from https://www.statista.com
[42] Deloitte Insights. (2025). Global consumer trends: The rise of the responsible buyer. Retrieved from https://www.deloitte.com

5 Reviewing the Role of Artificial Intelligence in Modern Business

Anitha Mani and Geetha Manoharan

5.1 INTRODUCTION

Artificial intelligence (AI) is drastically changing the field of business in modern society [1]. From a conceptual innovation to a fundamental enabler of strategic business transformation [2, 3], advanced machine learning (ML) algorithms, natural language processing (NLP), and automation capabilities have driven AI. Businesses in various sectors are using AI [4, 5] so that there is a chance to simplify operations, make better decisions, and strengthen customer relationships. McKinsey & Company's 2024 report on companies that have embraced AI in at least one function shows a 10–15% increase in productivity, most notably in operations, customer service, and marketing [6]. AI is being applied not only to automate repetitive tasks but also to create real-time insights, improve predictive accuracy, and enable hyper-personalisation of services in sectors, including retail, healthcare, finance, logistics, and manufacturing [7, 8]. The way AI manages big data, fraud detection, supply chain optimisation, and flawless customer experiences, usually generated by tools which also include chatbots and recommendation engines, highlights even more its relevance in business [9–11].

This article intends to investigate the what's and uses, along with the impact of AI in contemporary corporate operations. It looks at how AI has been included in several operational spheres, including supply chain management, human resources, marketing, and finance. With the means of emotion-based sentiment analysis and also customised recommendations, the article has also examined the changing potential of AI in seeking to improve the experience of the customers. It also examines the moral quandaries AI presents, particularly those affecting data privacy, algorithmic discrimination, and legislative changes regulating its use. In the current study, the investigator has additionally aimed to take into account all the commercial prospects that are offered in the digital world, as well as the developing relevance of corporate models motivated by AI. Another crucial issue is how AI is influencing employment, particularly how automation and intelligent systems are redefining job positions, generating demand for new skill sets, and inspiring organisational restructuring. With the extensive research of current literature, made studies, using the secondary data sources, this paper offers a composite image of AI in corporate life by 2025.

DOI: 10.1201/9781003650775-5

The study aims to provide a broad picture of AI applications and issues across numerous sectors, even if it is limited to the range of easily available secondary data and recorded case studies. It thus rules out primary empirical findings or data collection. Moreover, considering the rapid advancement of AI technology, some fresh innovations or geographically specialised applications might not be well reflected in this review. The major objective of this study is to present a thorough view of the function of AI in changing corporate structures, therefore comprehending both the potential it gives and the challenges it presents to modern firms.

5.2 UNDERSTANDING ARTIFICIAL INTELLIGENCE IN BUSINESS

Artificial intelligence refers to the simulation of human intelligence in machines designed to learn, understand, and perform tasks similar to human intelligence [12–14]. Without explicit programming for every scenario, these systems can handle chores including problem-solving, pattern recognition, language interpretation, and decision-making [15–17]. The pillars like Alan Turing and John McCarthy have made the investigation into the idea of introducing the new intelligent robots [18, 19], hence introducing AI in the 1950s. Since then, particularly in the recent two decades with the rise of big data, increased computer power, and cloud technologies [20, 21], AI has advanced dramatically. From theoretical models to useful applications in business, the evolution of ML, where computers learn from data, and deep learning, where neural networks replicate human cognition, has signalled a turning point in AI's path. Figure 5.1 [22] provides the details on the application of AI in business, where points like business implication, human implications, social applications, predictive methods, industrial applications, and recognition methods are mapped.

Several AI technologies are becoming rather popular in the modern corporate environment [23]. Predictive analytics in sales, finance, and inventory management depends much on ML, which lets systems grow from experience and past data without explicitly programming [24, 25]. NLP involves guiding machines to comprehend and respond to human language in the core of chatbots, virtual assistants,

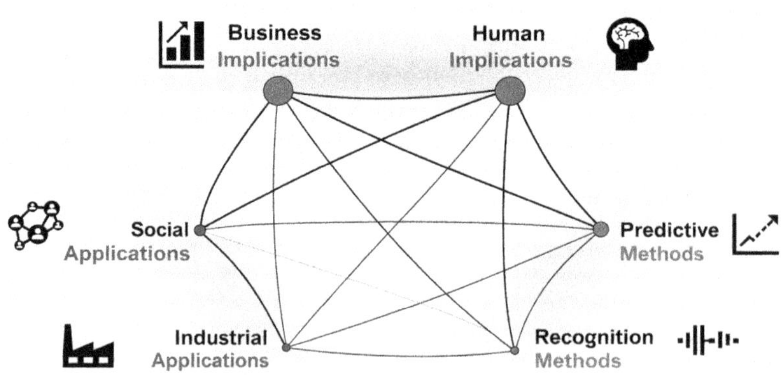

FIGURE 5.1 AI in business: what's hot in the latest research.

and sentiment analysis tools [26]. Robotic process automation (RPA) is applied especially in sectors like banking and insurance [27] and to automate repetitive, rule-based tasks, therefore enhancing the efficiency of operations [28]. Another field of AI, computer vision, allows robots to interpret visual input; this finds great use in factory quality control, retail monitoring, and even customer involvement via augmented reality systems. Gartner highlights the degree of AI's impact in the business sector since over 75% of organisations have already implemented one or more AI technologies into their major operations as of 2024.

As the corporate climate in today's world is very competitive in nature, the acceptance of AI has found a growth which is ever more vital [29, 30]. Though there are many differences, one of the main differences in a digital-first economy is the capacity which has to react fast to real-time insights, predict consumer requirements, and provide customised services. AI helps businesses to get a strategic edge by improving decision-making accuracy, cutting operating expenses, and raising agility in reacting to market developments [31, 32]. For instance, whereas supply networks driven by AI can identify disruptions and automatically change logistical plans, AI–driven analytics enable businesses to identify consumer trends and maximise marketing campaigns. By allowing the development of hitherto unthinkable new business models and products, AI also stimulates creativity [33, 34]. Companies that ignore AI run behind in a fast-changing global market since consumer expectations, operational complexity, and the speed of technical change keep accelerating [35].

5.3 INTEGRATION OF AI IN BUSINESS FUNCTIONS

Often referred to as artificial intelligence, or AI, artificial intelligence has proven to be beneficial for significant business activities [36]. This has drastically altered how businesses interact with their stakeholders, run, and choose their strategic direction. By adding this technology to a wide spectrum of departments, beginning with operations, and finishing with finance, companies have been able to accomplish their ideal performance goals, boosting responsiveness, and hence producing more value by means of intelligent systems. With regard to operations and supply chain management, AI is revolutionising traditional manufacturing and logistics by way of automation and enhanced visibility [37]. For speed picking, packaging, and shipping, for example, companies such as DHL and Amazon have set AI-powered robots and predictive algorithms in their warehouses. Wolnika (2024) highlighted that demand forecasting uses predictive analytics to estimate future needs based on historical sales data, market trends, and external factors such as weather and economic conditions. With little human involvement, automated systems driven by AI can today manage challenging logistical chores, including route planning, inventory control, and quality inspection [38]. Reducing overstocking and stock-outs for companies will help to raise customer satisfaction and efficiency. IoT (Internet of Things) technologies improved real-time tracking systems that give end-to-end supply chain visibility, enabling dynamic rerouting and proactive issue resolving, especially during occurrences like the COVID-19 epidemic [39]. SmartTec solutions [40] have provided the details on the ways in which the business owners use AI for

FIGURE 5.2 Ways business owners use AI.

successfully running a business, where the majority have started customer service, cybersecurity/fraud management, as shown in Figure 5.2.

AI-driven data customization and targeted advertising strategies have significantly enhanced marketing effectiveness and customer engagement. By way of personalised content and customer data analysis, AI technologies increase engagement and conversion rates, therefore reflecting preferences [41]. About AI, it has been adopted by well-known websites like Google and Meta, which seek more advertisement placements as well as improved return on investment for advertising. Digital marketing rates people, assesses campaign performance, and recommends the optimal messaging and platforms [42] using ML algorithms. NLP-enabled sentiment analysis lets companies understand consumer impressions by means of social media posts, reviews, and comments [43]. This real-time information improves consumer communications and brand planning ability. Moreover, chatbots and virtual assistants have become essential instruments in the sales process since they provide fast responses, answers to questions, and help consumers through 24/7 buying decisions. Two AI technologies among many helping sales teams to lead score and customer journey optimisation are Salesforce and HubSpot.

AI has made significant strides in human resource management by accelerating hiring practices, improving workforce analytics, and promoting employee engagement [44]. AI techniques are applied in talent acquisition using facial recognition and speech analysis technology [45] to scan resumes, shortlist candidates, and even conduct first video interviews. This not only slows down the hiring process but also reduces early recruitment stage prejudice. Platforms like HireVue and Pymetrics use AI to assess candidates depending on skills and behavioural qualities, therefore transcending simple resumes [46]. AI systems tracking feedback, performance metrics, and interaction patterns, once used to pinpoint burnout or discontent, can track employee engagement [47]. By means of organisational trends and external labour market conditions, predictive analytics is also applied in workforce planning to assist HR teams in forecasting staff needs, retention issues, and training needs [48]. These revelations inspire a proactive attitude to people management and help to simplify decisions.

In financial management, AI mostly supports investment analysis, fraud detection, and automatic repetitive financial process automation [49]. AI helps fintech companies and financial institutions rapidly find fraud activities by spotting odd spending patterns and behavioural abnormalities. Developed by companies such as Mastercard and PayPal, AI-based fraud detection systems continuously learn from new data to increase accuracy [50]. AI also aids forecasting and investment planning through the means of analysis of great volumes of financial data, market trends, and economic indicators to provide strategic recommendations. Robo-advisors employ AI to create customised investment portfolios depending on risk tolerance and preferences, like those used by Betterment and Wealthfront. RPA is therefore widely used by financial firms to manage regular processes such as invoice processing, reconciliation, and reporting; so, manual labour and mistake rates are much reduced [51]. Apart from raising production, this promises improved accuracy and compliance in financial processes. Table 5.1 shows the business function and application of AI for the operation of a successful business.

AI improves customer experiences by allowing companies to forecast needs, modify interactions, and provide real-time support. AI consumer applications like customised recommendation systems are obvious. AI algorithms suggest products based on browsing histories, purchasing patterns, and preferences of Amazon and Flipkart users [52]. Netflix and Spotify change streaming content using ML, therefore increasing consumer satisfaction. These ideas represent prior behaviour and

TABLE 5.1
Business Function and AI Application

Business Function	AI Application	Impact
Operations and Supply Chain	Predictive analytics, real-time tracking	Improved efficiency, cost reduction
Marketing and Sales	Personalisation, chatbots, sentiment analysis	Increased engagement, customer satisfaction
Human Resources	AI recruitment tools, performance tracking	Faster recruitment, better employee management
Financial Management	Fraud detection, investment analysis	Risk reduction, more accurate predictions
Customer Experience	Personalised recommendations, emotion recognition	Enhanced customer satisfaction and loyalty
Product Development	Generative design, AI-driven testing	Reduced time-to-market, innovative product features

Author Source

change with guest interaction with the site, therefore offering a simple but transforming experience [53].

New instrument makers also apply emotional recognition and sentiment analysis to alter consumer emotions. AI may find faint emotional cues in consumer comments, social media posts, and video conversations by methods of facial recognition and NLP [54]. This helps businesses change reactions, clarifies consumer knowledge, and enhances offerings. Sentiment analysis lets companies track public sentiment during crises or new product releases to enable quick reaction. Businesses employing IBM sentiment analysis rose by 20% in 2023, and customer satisfaction with AI demonstrates its growing relevance in the creation of brand reputation. Moreover, changing consumer service automation and corporate interactions are virtual assistants and AI-powered chatbots. These intelligent systems save human involvement by controlling order status, product specs, and 24/7 troubleshooting. Using AI chatbots, HDFC Bank, Swiggy, and Zomato answer hundreds of client questions, hence improving response times and service. Advanced chatbots can learn from conversations, pick context, and escalate difficult situations to people [55]. This strategy combines efficiency with human touch when called for. More fascinating, responsive, customised consumer experiences produced by AI help companies by themselves boost digital loyalty and competitiveness.

5.4 ETHICAL AND REGULATORY CONCERNS

Particularly in connection to data privacy, algorithmic bias, and legal compliance, important ethical and legal issues have surfaced as AI is swiftly adopted into corporate activities. Data privacy and protection rank among the main issues modern society faces. Massive volumes of personal and behavioural data are required if AI systems are to operate as expected, especially in purposes including consumer analytics, tailored marketing, and workforce monitoring. But gathering and using this kind of data begs serious questions about authorisation, openness, and misuse. Public awareness raised by well-documented data breaches and incidents like Facebook–Cambridge Analytica one leads to more stringent policies. The European Union proposed an AI Act upgrading the General Data Protection Regulation (GDPR) and demanding openness, responsibility, and risk assessments for high-risk AI applications in 2023, establishing a worldwide baseline for data governance. Still another crucial question is whether automated decision-making systems and AI algorithms are biased. AI systems taught on historical or unbalanced data could accidentally duplicate or exaggerate already existing societal and cultural biases. This is most evident in employment algorithms, credit scoring systems, and facial recognition technologies, where biases in training data can lead to unfair or discriminatory outcomes against certain groups. Studies have discovered, for example, that some AI-powered employment systems favoured men depending on biased training data. These issues also highlight significant issues of justice, equity, and responsibility, especially in circumstances when AI decisions limit people's access to fundamental products or livelihoods [56]. Dealing with this challenge requires the implementation of ethical AI design concepts inside businesses, in addition to technical solutions incorporating numerous data sets and algorithm auditing inside other entities.

Moreover, the fast-growing nature of AI leaves legal and regulatory gaps. Although some countries have developed advanced AI control, many businesses still operate free from rules or a clean moral environment. Standardised global guidelines enable one to ensure continuous ethical compliance and accountability, by means of which one can reassure others. For instance, many underdeveloped countries are still in early stages of developing legal structures to manage technology, even if the EU and Canada have developed comprehensive AI rules. Companies must thus manage a challenging and shifting regulatory terrain, frequently balancing compliance aims with creativity [56]. Companies have to create robust corporate governance structures, do regular risk assessments, and include legislators to help to build moral AI guidelines. Ensuring ethical implementation and legal accountability as it develops will surely help to raise public confidence and preserve AI relevance in the direction of industry.

5.5 AI-DRIVEN BUSINESS MODELS AND ENTREPRENEURSHIP

Apart from disturbing contemporary corporate operations, the evolution of AI has produced whole new business models and entrepreneurial activities based on AI as the main agent of value generation [57]. Starting AI-centric companies in industries including finance, healthcare, education, and logistics reveals the rising conviction that AI might upend already established sectors. CB Insights projects global AI start-up investment of $75 billion by 2024; areas most in demand are generative AI, AI-driven medical breakthroughs, and autonomous systems. Start-ups such as OpenAI, UiPath, and Synthesia have demonstrated how rapidly ideas sparked by AI could flourish by filling in-demand markets with innovative technology addressing sector shortages. By use of cloud infrastructure and data assets, these agile enterprises offer businesses scalable, intelligent solutions.

AI has also led a new wave of corporate model innovation by altering the development, supplied, and documented value. Companies are adding AI into key products to offer special, predictive, adaptable, and tailored solutions. AI is providing dynamic pricing models in e-commerce, whereby pricing fluctuates in real time depending on demand, user activity, and outside variables for ride-hailing companies such as Amazon and Uber. Driven by AI algorithms tracking user activity and preferences, sites such as Grammarly and Netflix [58] routinely display subscription-based and premium models. Customising experiences and up-selling relevant knowledge helps businesses to extract more profit, hence improving customer retention. Furthermore, AI is driving the shift from product-based companies to service-oriented platforms where continuous learning and optimisation offer always appreciated consumer value.

Notable modern AI-driven entrepreneurship is the building of platform-based ecosystems allowing data exchange, cooperation, and profitability. Sometimes firms, developers, and customers co-create value running under AI markets. For instance, Salesforce's Einstein tool compiles AI into customer relationship management (CRM) systems so businesses may project consumer behaviour, simplify processes, and enhance service delivery [59]. Likewise, Google Cloud's AI Hub and Amazon's SageMaker give companies and developers the tools and infrastructure needed to develop, educate, and apply AI solutions [60, 61]. These types of technologies occasionally include paid toolkits for corporate use, data-as-a-service models, and Application Programming Interface (API) access fees used in monetising systems. Originally a research tool and developing into a commercial platform with a subscription-based revenue model and enterprise API services, OpenAI's ChatGPT is an incredible case study, generating over $1.3 billion just in 2023 alone [62]. All things considered, putting AI into entrepreneurial tactics and business models is producing a dynamic and creative economy. As AI capacities keep growing, future corporate performance will depend more and more on the capacity to employ not only as a technology but also as a strategic enabler of scalable, sustainable, customer-centric solutions.

5.6 IMPACT OF AI ON THE WORKFORCE

The introduction of AI into corporate operations has resulted in a complicated discussion on how technology could impact the workforce, especially with regard to the harmony between job displacement and employment generation. Some job categories, especially those needing consistent or rule-based work, are disappearing as artificial systems and technologies get ever more adept at performing tasks once done by humans. India most certainly displays such a shift already. For instance, Wipro noted in 2023 that frequent testing combined with AI-based automation solutions let over 300 employees off from back-end operations. ICICI Bank also included AI technologies to speed approvals and fraud detection, therefore minimising the human loan distribution personnel in the banking sector. These images, especially in middle-skill employment vulnerable to automation, highlight the rising trend of labour displacement. Still, AI is redefining current employment as well as generating new ones. Demand particularly is for AI ethicists, data scientists, ML engineers, cybersecurity analysts, and AI trainers.

Based on significant hiring across IT hubs, including Bengaluru, Hyderabad, and Pune, following a NASSCOM study from late 2023, AI-related employment in India surged by over 45% year over year [63]. Sometimes these sectors require more domain-specific knowledge and cognitive ability, which emphasises the requirement of concentrated re-skilling and up-skilling programmes. Government initiatives aimed to prepare the workforce for the AI-driven future coexist with business alliances, including TCS's "Ignite My Future" and Infosys's "lex." These projects seek to provide staff members with analytical and digital tools required for relevance in numerous sectors. Table 5.2 discusses the impact of the workforce on AI.

Along with the changes that are made in the number of employees, the nature of the employment, which is undergoing a shift, has an increasing emphasis on the hybrid human AI collaboration. Other than fully replacing the human workforce, the AI is designed in a way that there is a hybrid between the AI collaboration involving human decision-making in various sectors. In the case of healthcare, AI has assisted doctors in analysing the complex data of diagnostics, whereas in the case of agriculture there are many tools which are helping the farmers make data-driven decisions regarding the information on irrigation and crop rotation that is needed to get maximum agricultural production. There is a role for a blended technical

TABLE 5.2
AI Impact on Workforce

AI Impact Example in India (2022–2024)	Sector	Nature of Impact	Outcome
Wipro's AI-based automation deployment	IT/Software Services	Job Displacement	Over 300 manual QA/testing roles automated using AI
ICICI Bank's AI in credit processing	Banking	Job Restructuring	Reduction in processing staff; AI-based fraud detection adopted
Tata Steel's AI in predictive maintenance	Manufacturing	Job Creation & Role Change	Created new roles in AI maintenance teams; reduced unplanned downtime
Apollo Hospitals' AI diagnostics	Healthcare	Human-AI Collaboration	Doctors supported by AI in diagnostics; improved patient outcomes
NASSCOM & IBM Skills Build Program	Cross-industry	Reskilling/ Upskilling	Over 2 lakh learners trained in AI, cloud, and cybersecurity

Author Source

understanding and also domain expertise, which emphasises the need for having interdisciplinary education and also results in lifelong learning. The future of employment will not be marked by machines replacing humans, but it is about how effectively humans and the intelligent system can collaborate. Thus, it will build a workforce which is not only technologically benefited but also can adapt innovative techniques, which is crucial for having full potential for AI and creates a resonating workplace.

5.7 CHALLENGES AND OPPORTUNITIES AHEAD

AI is continuing to shape of the landscape for modern business, which can have several problems, like organisations must navigate the full leverage potential. One of the main barriers to AI adoption is the resistance to change within organisations. Many companies, especially traditional ones, particularly resistant to employing AI [64], could have cost concerns, disturbance of current operations, or lack of technological understanding. Acceptance of AI into corporate processes is further hampered by employee's fear of job loss and ambiguity over the long-term advantages of technology. Companies also often struggle to match AI projects with more general strategy objectives and gaining CEO buy-in for changes motivated by AI. Table 5.3 provides the details on the challenges and opportunities ahead with business models and AI applications.

Further complicating acceptance of AI are scalability and infrastructure issues. If AI systems are to run well, they need strong IT infrastructure, big datasets, and great processing capabilities. For many companies, especially small- to

TABLE 5.3
Challenges and Opportunities Ahead

Business Model	Company Example	AI Application	Monetisation Strategy
Subscription-Based Model	Netflix, Spotify	Personalisation, content recommendation	Monthly/annual subscription fees
Freemium Model	Grammarly, LinkedIn	AI-driven writing suggestions, networking	Premium subscriptions for advanced features
Platform Ecosystem Model	Salesforce, Amazon Web Services	AI tools for CRM, cloud services	API usage fees, cloud service subscription
Data-as-a-Service (DaaS)	Palantir, ZoomInfo	Data analytics, market insights	Pay-per-use or subscription model
API-Based Model	OpenAI, Twilio	Natural language processing, automation	Pay-per-use for API calls

Author Source

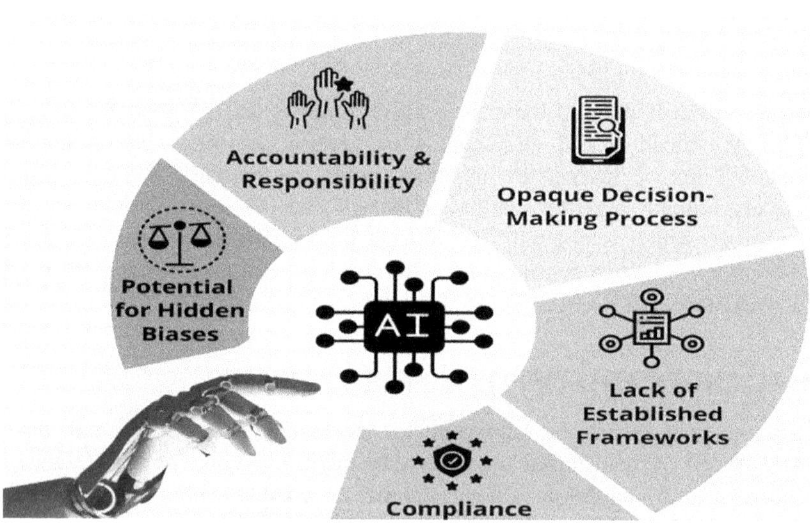

FIGURE 5.3 Ethical challenges in AI integration.

medium-sized ones, installing and maintaining AI systems running can be costly. Moreover, the need for constant data collecting and management, as well as the fast speed of technological development, inspires companies to be flexible in changing AI capacity. This is especially true in industries like healthcare, where legal restrictions and data privacy issues add even more degrees of complexity when expanding AI solutions over vast networks or several nations. Figure 5.3 brings out the details on the ethical challenges in AI integration.

Still, AI has great and expanding possibilities despite these obstacles. As AI develops, it presents huge creative opportunities in many different sectors. Companies that can surpass first adoption challenges will be in a great position for major benefits in terms of cash generation, customer satisfaction, and efficiency. As was already noted, the emergence of AI-driven business models creates new opportunities for entrepreneurial activity, particularly in fields including predictive analytics, automated supply chains, and tailored services. Moreover, the democratisation of AI presents interesting opportunities for general AI integration since more companies of all kinds can access more easily available technology and platforms. Taken together, appropriate infrastructure, ability, and strategic planning will give companies hitherto unheard-of chances for future growth.

5.8 CONCLUSION

Ultimately, AI has obviously evolved into a transforming tool in modern businesses, changing sectors, increasing efficiency, and improving customer experiences by means of change. From operations and marketing to human resources and finance, the integration of AI across many corporate activities has already proven demonstrable benefits, including improved decision-making, optimal supply chains, and tailored services. Adoption of AI does, however, not come without difficulties, including data privacy issues, algorithm bias, scalability problems, and organisational opposition. These problems have to be aggressively addressed via ethical frameworks, ongoing education, deliberate technology, and staff investments.

The ramifications are obvious for politicians and corporate leaders: AI is a strategic tool rather than only a technical one that might change the competitive situation. Leaders should give AI top priority and careful application so that technology enhances human-centric values, including justice, transparency, and responsibility. This underlines not only technical capacity but also the necessity of building inside companies a creative and flexible culture. Conversely, legislators have to aim for clear, flexible regulations that allow AI innovation while safeguarding public interest, particularly in sectors like data privacy and workforce displacement by means of adaptation.

Encouragement of cooperation between people and AI systems will help us to balance the adoption of AI with human-centric values ahead. Unlike replacement, AI can improve human ability. Stressing on increasing productivity, creativity, and decision-making, companies must thus see AI as an amplifier of human potential, ensuring that its adoption is inclusive and fair. With the appropriate approach, AI will continue to propel social development, creativity, and business growth.

REFERENCES

[1] Mossavar-Rahmani, F., & Zohuri, B. (2024). Artificial intelligence at work: Transforming industries and redefining the workforce landscape. *Journal of Economics & Management Research*, 5(2), 2–4.

[2] Rane, N. L., Paramesha, M., Choudhary, S. P., & Rane, J. (2024). Artificial intelligence, machine learning, and deep learning for advanced business strategies: A review. *Partners Universal International Innovation Journal*, 2(3), 147–171.

[3] Islam, M. A., Hasan, M. A. R., Juthi, S., & Haque, S. (2025). A systematic review of business strategy transformation using AI, machine learning, and deep learning. *Innovatech Engineering Journal*, 2(01), 31–46.
[4] Aldoseri, A., Al-Khalifa, K. N., & Hamouda, A. M. (2024). AI-powered innovation in digital transformation: Key pillars and industry impact. *Sustainability*, 16(5), 1790.
[5] Selvakumar, P., Shanthi, M., Pitchiah, R., Sharma, M., Dahake, P. S., & Manjunath, T. C. (2025). The role of artificial intelligence in business model innovation: Overview of AI technologies. In *AI-Driven Business Model Innovation* (pp. 219–246). IGI Global. https://doi.org/10.4018/979-8-3693-9571-4.ch009
[6] Kochkina, N., Andriushchenko, I., & Gatto, G. (2024, October). Strategic AI adoption: Economic impact, case studies from handy AI, and industry readiness. In *2024 IEEE International Conference on Artificial Intelligence & Green Energy (ICAIGE)* (pp. 1–6). IEEE. https://doi.org/10.1109/ICAIGE62696.2024
[7] Venkatesh, V., Thong, J. Y. L., & Xu, X. (2012). Consumer acceptance and use of information technology: Extending the unified theory of acceptance and use of technology. *MIS Quarterly*, 36(1), 157–178. https://doi.org/10.2307/41410412
[8] Frank, A. G., Dalenogare, L. S., & Ayala, N. F. (2019). Industry 4.0 technologies: Implementation patterns in manufacturing companies. *International Journal of Production Economics*, 210, 15–26. https://doi.org/10.1016/j.ijpe.2019.01.004
[9] Paramesha, M., Rane, N. L., & Rane, J. (2024). Big data analytics, artificial intelligence, machine learning, internet of things, and blockchain for enhanced business intelligence. *Partners Universal Multidisciplinary Research Journal*, 1(2), 110–133.
[10] Sarma, W., Nagavalli, S. P., & Sresth, V. (2020). Leveraging AI-driven algorithms to address real-world challenges in E-commerce: Enhancing user experience, fraud detection, and operational efficiency. *International Journal of Research and Analytical Reviews*, 7, 2348–1269.
[11] Ahmed, F., Ahmed, M. R., Kabir, M. A., & Islam, M. M. (2025). Revolutionizing business analytics: The impact of artificial intelligence and machine learning. *American Journal of Advanced Technology and Engineering Solutions*, 1(01), 147–173.
[12] Korteling, J. H., van de Boer-Visschedijk, G. C., Blankendaal, R. A., Boonekamp, R. C., & Eikelboom, A. R. (2021). Human-versus artificial intelligence. *Frontiers in Artificial Intelligence*, 4, 622364.
[13] Haenlein, M., & Kaplan, A. (2019). A brief history of artificial intelligence: On the past, present, and future of artificial intelligence. *California Management Review*, 61(4), 5–14. https://doi.org/10.1177/0008125619864925
[14] Ruggeri, F., Banks, D., Cleveland, W. S., Fisher, N. I., Escobar-Anel, M., Giudici, P., . . . & Zhang, Z. (2025). Is there a future for stochastic modeling in business and industry in the era of machine learning and artificial intelligence?. *Applied Stochastic Models in Business and Industry*, 41(2), e70004.
[15] Sarker, I. H. (2022). AI-based modeling: Techniques, applications and research issues towards automation, intelligent and smart systems. *SN Computer Science*, 3(2), 158.
[16] Eppe, M., Gumbsch, C., Kerzel, M., Nguyen, P. D., Butz, M. V., & Wermter, S. (2022). Intelligent problem-solving as integrated hierarchical reinforcement learning. *Nature Machine Intelligence*, 4(1), 11–20.
[17] Musayeva, M. (2025). Models and algorithms for building a knowledge base for decision support systems in primary healthcare. *International Journal of Medical Sciences*, 1(1), 118–124.
[18] Haenlein, M., & Kaplan, A. (2019). A brief history of artificial intelligence: On the past, present, and future of artificial intelligence. *California Management Review*, 61(4), 5–14. https://doi.org/10.1177/0008125619864925

[19] Haenlein, M., & Kaplan, A. (2019). A brief history of artificial intelligence: On the past, present, and future of artificial intelligence. *California Management Review*, 61(4), 5–14. https://doi.org/10.1177/0008125619864925
[20] Gill, S. S., Tuli, S., Xu, M., Singh, I., Singh, K. V., Lindsay, D., . . . & Garraghan, P. (2019). Transformative effects of IoT, Blockchain and Artificial Intelligence on cloud computing: Evolution, vision, trends and open challenges. *Internet of Things*, 8, 100118.
[21] Siripurapu, S., Darimireddy, N. K., Chehri, A., Sridhar, B., & Paramkusam, A. V. (2023). Technological advancements and elucidation gadgets for Healthcare applications: An exhaustive methodological review-part-I (AI, big data, block chain, open-source technologies, and cloud Computing). *Electronics*, 12(3), 750.
[22] Soni, N., Sharma, E. K., Singh, N., & Kapoor, A. (2019). *Impact of artificial intelligence on businesses: From research, innovation, market deployment to future shifts in business models*. arXiv. https://arxiv.org/abs/1905.02092
[23] Benbya, H., Davenport, T. H., & Pachidi, S. (2020). Artificial intelligence in organizations: Current state and future opportunities. *MIS Quarterly Executive*, 19(4), 9–21. https://doi.org/10.17705/2msqe.00003
[24] Adam, M. B. (2018). *Improving Complex Sale Cycles and Performance by Using Machine Learning and Predictive Analytics to Understand the Customer Journey* (Doctoral dissertation, Massachusetts Institute of Technology).
[25] Wamba, S. F., Gunasekaran, A., Akter, S., Ren, S. J.-F., Dubey, R., & Childe, S. J. (2017). Big data analytics and firm performance: Effects of dynamic capabilities. *Journal of Business Research*, 70, 356–365. https://doi.org/10.1016/j.jbusres.2016.08.009
[26] Young, T., Hazarika, D., Poria, S., & Cambria, E. (2018). Recent trends in deep learning based natural language processing. *IEEE Computational Intelligence Magazine*, 13(3), 55–75. https://doi.org/10.1109/MCI.2018.2840738
[27] Pramod, D. (2022). Robotic process automation for industry: Adoption status, benefits, challenges and research agenda. *Benchmarking: An International Journal*, 29(5), 1562–1586.
[28] Kitsantas, T., Vazakidis, A., & Chytis, E. (2024). Integrating robotic process automation with artificial intelligence for business process optimization. *Journal of System and Management Sciences*, 14(7), 217–242. https://doi.org/10.33168/JSMS.2024.0712
[29] Horowitz, M. C., Allen, G. C., Kania, E. B., & Scharre, P. (2022). *Strategic Competition in an Era of Artificial Intelligence*. Center for a New American Security.
[30] Fousiani, K., Michelakis, G., Minnigh, P. A., & De Jonge, K. M. (2024). Competitive organizational climate and artificial intelligence (AI) acceptance: The moderating role of leaders' power construal. *Frontiers in Psychology*, 15, 1359164.
[31] Alghamdi, O. A., & Agag, G. (2023). Boosting innovation performance through big data analytics powered by artificial intelligence use: An empirical exploration of the role of strategic agility and market turbulence. *Sustainability*, 15(19), 14296.
[32] Wamba, S. F. (2022). Impact of artificial intelligence assimilation on firm performance: The mediating effects of organizational agility and customer agility. *International Journal of Information Management*, 67, 102544.
[33] Pagani, M., & Champion, R. (Eds.). (2023). *Artificial Intelligence for Business Creativity*. Taylor & Francis.
[34] Uctu, R., Tuluce, N. S. H., & Aykac, M. (2024). Creative destruction and artificial intelligence: The transformation of industries during the sixth wave. *Journal of Economy and Technology*, 2, 296–309.
[35] Tariq, M. U., Poulin, M., & Abonamah, A. A. (2021). Achieving operational excellence through artificial intelligence: Driving forces and barriers. *Frontiers in Psychology*, 12, 686624.

[36] Rajagopal, N. K., Qureshi, N. I., Durga, S., Ramirez Asis, E. H., Huerta Soto, R. M., Gupta, S. K., & Deepak, S. (2022). Future of business culture: An artificial intelligence-driven digital framework for organization decision-making process. *Complexity*, 2022 (1), 7796507.

[37] Adesoga, T. O., Ajibaye, T. O., Nwafor, K. C., Imam-Lawal, U. T., Ikekwere, E. A., & Ikechukwu, D. (2024). The rise of the 'smart' supply chain: How AI and automation are revolutionizing logistics. *International Journal of Science and Research Archive*, 12(2), 790–798.

[38] Onukwulu, E. C., Agho, M. O., Eyo-Udo, N. L., Sule, A. K., & Azubuike, C. (2024). Advances in automation and AI for enhancing supply chain productivity in oil and gas. *International Journal of Research and Innovation in Applied Science*, 9(12), 654–687.

[39] Dolgui, A., & Ivanov, D. (2022). 5G in digital supply chain and operations management: Fostering flexibility, end-to-end connectivity and real-time visibility through internet-of-everything. *International Journal of Production Research*, 60(2), 442–451.

[40] SmartTek Solutions. (2025). 8 key benefits of using artificial intelligence for business. https://smarttek.solutions/blog/benefits-of-using-ai-for-business/

[41] Kumar, V., Ashraf, A. R., & Nadeem, W. (2024). AI-powered marketing: What, where, and how?. *International Journal of Information Management*, 77, 102783.

[42] Lee, J., Suh, T., Roy, D., & Baucus, M. (2019). Emerging technology and business model innovation: The case of artificial intelligence. *Journal of Open Innovation: Technology, Market, and Complexity*, 5(3), 44. https://doi.org/10.3390/joitmc5030044

[43] Ranjan, M., Tiwari, S., Sattar, A. M., & Tatkar, N. S. (2024). A new approach for carrying out sentiment analysis of social media comments using natural language processing. *Engineering Proceedings*, 59(1), 181.

[44] Sundari, S., Silalahi, V. A. J. M., Wardani, F. P., Siahaan, R. S., Sacha, S., Krismayanti, Y., & Anjarsari, N. (2024). Artificial intelligence (AI) and automation in human resources: Shifting the focus from routine tasks to strategic initiatives for improved employee engagement. *East Asian Journal of Multidisciplinary Research*, 3(10), 4983–4996.

[45] Tambe, P., Cappelli, P., & Yakubovich, V. (2019). Artificial intelligence in human resources management: Challenges and a path forward. *California Management Review*, 61(4), 15–42. https://doi.org/10.1177/0008125619867910

[46] Tambe, P., Cappelli, P., & Yakubovich, V. (2019). Artificial intelligence in human resources management: Challenges and a path forward. *California Management Review*, 61(4), 15–42. https://doi.org/10.1177/0008125619867910

[47] Kuznetsov, M., Kuznetsova, S., Artemova, E., & Lydia, E. L. (2024, January). An analysis concerning how artificial intelligence is affecting human resource management techniques. In *Proceedings of Eighth International Conference on Information System Design and Intelligent Applications* (pp. 347–355). Springer Nature Singapore.

[48] Ramu, M., Ilakkiya, T., Venkatesh, P., Anantharajan, R. S., & Senthilnathan, C. R. (2024, October). Understanding the scope of artificial intelligence in hr technology E-recruitment–A theoretical perspective. In *2024 International Conference on Power, Energy, Control and Transmission Systems (ICPECTS)* (pp. 1–5). IEEE.

[49] Maota, T., & Naidoo, V. (2025). The impact of artificial intelligence on human resource management: Barriers and benefits. In *Sustainable Management Practices for Employee Retention and Recruitment* (pp. 311–342). IGI Global Scientific Publishing.

[50] Budhwar, P., Chowdhury, S., Wood, G., Aguinis, H., Bamber, G. J., Beltran, J. R., . . . & Varma, A. (2023). Human resource management in the age of generative artificial intelligence: Perspectives and research directions on ChatGPT. *Human Resource Management Journal*, 33(3), 606–659.

[51] Menzies, J., Sabert, B., Hassan, R., & Mensah, P. K. (2024). Artificial intelligence for international business: Its use, challenges, and suggestions for future research and practice. *Thunderbird International Business Review*, 66(2), 185–200.

[52] Huang, M.-H., & Rust, R. T. (2021). A strategic framework for artificial intelligence in marketing. *Journal of the Academy of Marketing Science*, *49*(1), 30–50. https://doi.org/10.1007/s11747-020-00749-9
[53] Sajeev, S. (2024). *A Study on the Role of Artificial Intelligence Tools in Shaping Consumer Demand in E-Commerce with Special Reference to Ernakulam City* (Doctoral dissertation, St. Teresa's College (autonomous) Ernakulam).
[54] Dong, J. (2024). Natural language processing pretraining language model for computer intelligent recognition technology. *ACM Transactions on Asian and Low-Resource Language Information Processing*, 23(8), 1–12.
[55] Sood, P., Tanwar, H., Singh, J., Ruhela, A. K., Gupta, N., & Kumar, R. (2024, November). Revolutionizing customer service: An AI-powered chatbot approach using advanced NLP techniques. In *2024 3rd Edition of IEEE Delhi Section Flagship Conference (DELCON)* (pp. 1–5). IEEE.
[56] Walter, Y. (2024). Managing the race to the moon: Global policy and governance in artificial intelligence regulation—A contemporary overview and an analysis of socio-economic consequences. *Discover Artificial Intelligence*, 4(1), 14.
[57] Shollo, A., Hopf, K., Thiess, T., & Müller, O. (2022). Shifting ML value creation mechanisms: A process model of ML value creation. *Journal of Strategic Information Systems*, 31(3), 101734. https://doi.org/10.1016/j.jsis.2022.101734
[58] Verhoef, P. C., Broekhuizen, T., Bart, Y., Bhattacharya, A., Dong, J. Q., Fabian, N., & Haenlein, M. (2021). Digital transformation: A multidisciplinary reflection and research agenda. *Journal of Business Research*, 122, 889–901. https://doi.org/10.1016/j.jbusres.2019.09.022
[59] Nishat, A. (2024). AI innovations in salesforce CRM: Unlocking smarter customer relationships. *Aitoz Multidisciplinary Review*, 3(1), 117–125.
[60] Google Cloud. (2023). AI hub: Share and discover AI assets. https://cloud.google.com/ai-hub
[61] Amazon Web Services. (2023). Amazon SageMaker - Build, train, and deploy machine learning models. https://aws.amazon.com/sagemaker/
[62] OpenAI. (2024). OpenAI annual report 2023: AI adoption and revenue insights. https://openai.com/reports/annual-2023
[63] Tambe, P., Cappelli, P., & Yakubovich, V. (2019). Artificial intelligence in human resources management: Challenges and a path forward. *California Management Review*, 61(4), 15–42. https://doi.org/10.1177/0008125619867910
[64] Dwivedi, Y. K., Hughes, L., Ismagilova, E., et al. (2021). Artificial intelligence (AI): Multidisciplinary perspectives on emerging challenges, opportunities, and agenda for research, practice and policy. *International Journal of Information Management*, 57, 101994. https://doi.org/10.1016/j.ijinfomgt.2019.08.002

6 Transforming Entrepreneurship through Artificial Intelligence

Opportunities, Challenges, and the Road Ahead

Hemachandran Kannan and Manjeet Rege

6.1 INTRODUCTION

6.1.1 The meeting of AI and Global Entrepreneurship

The entrepreneurial environment is facing a radical shift caused by the blistering development of artificial intelligence (AI) technologies and their democratization. The previously monopolized field of technology giants and research laboratories with large financing is now available to startups and small businesses all over the world. The competitive landscape of the global markets is being redefined as a result of this democratization of AI capabilities, and now entrepreneurs can use advanced analytical tools, automation systems, and predictive models, which were unimaginable only a decade ago. The merging of AI and entrepreneurship is not a technological change but a paradigm shift, a change in how businesses formulate opportunities, interact with customers, streamline operations, and increase global reach. The contemporary entrepreneurs are playing in an environment where data is more available, computational power is greater, and algorithms are more sophisticated than ever. These circumstances present unprecedented opportunities and complicated challenges that demand new patterns of perceiving and acting.

By definition, global entrepreneurship places one in the context of different markets, cultural settings, regulatory systems, and competitive landscapes. Highly intelligent automation, pattern detection, and learning algorithms available in AI technologies are a potent set of tools that entrepreneurs can use to build a more flexible and dynamic system to handle this complexity. It is fitting that AI can be the backbone of contemporary entrepreneurial activities aiming to go global as it is based on natural language processing (NLP), which allows reaching customers with various languages, as well as machine learning algorithms that can predict market trends across geographies.

 DOI: 10.1201/9781003650775-6

6.1.2 Development of Self-Directed Entrepreneurial Models by Evolution

The development of entrepreneurial marketing has been full of various stages, which were defined by the prevailing technologies and the communication paradigms of the time. The pre-digital world was dependent on old-fashioned advertising, word of mouth, and physical distribution. With the advent of the internet and digital technologies occurring in the 1990s and the early 2000s, there are new opportunities to engage customers directly, to do targeted advertising, and to create an e-commerce platform. This new age, however, is an advancement. The scale of consumer behavior analysis, predicting purchasing patterns with incomparable accuracy, real-time content and recommendation customization, and automatic optimization of marketing campaigns on a cross-channel and geographic scale can now be performed by AI-powered marketing systems. These abilities make marketing less of a creative and intuitive field of study and more of a data-intensive science, using human creativity and machine intelligence. Modern entrepreneurial ventures are being formed on AI-first business models as AI is no longer a supporting tool but is the value proposition. The example of Netflix, Spotify, and Amazon has shown that AI-based personalization and recommendation systems can enable companies to generate sustainable competitive advantages and transform whole industries. To the modern entrepreneur who has ventured into the global markets, the need to know and use AI effectively in marketing strategies is no longer a choice but a survival and growth clue (Figure 6.1).

6.1.3 Chapter Objectives and Chapter Structure

The chapter is designed to give a detailed analysis of the way in which AI is revolutionizing entrepreneurship as part of global marketing. The analysis has been organized in a manner that aims to answer three main questions: What opportunities does AI present to entrepreneurs who work in the global markets? What are the

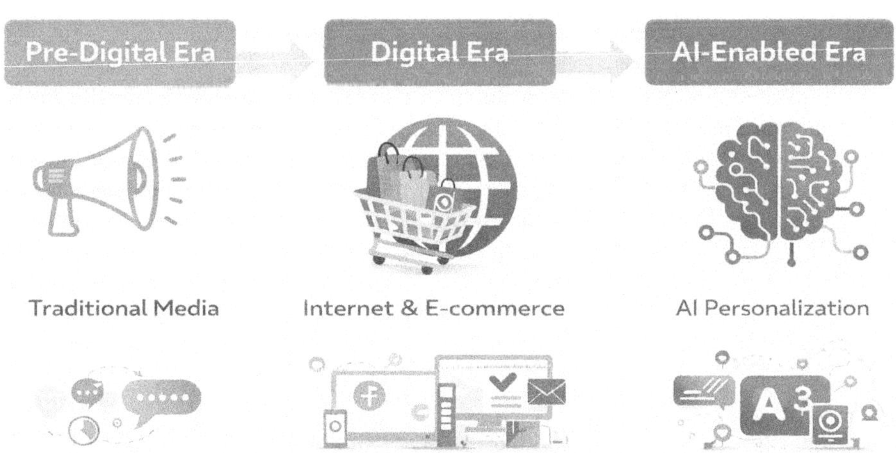

FIGURE 6.1 Evolution of marketing-driven entrepreneurial models.

opportunities that should be seized, and what are the challenges and barriers that should be overcome? And what is the future of AI-powered entrepreneurship?

The chapter is organized into a number of parts. Our starting point is the role of AI in entrepreneurial innovation, and the detailed consideration of the associated technologies that are transforming the venture concept and its startup. Then we examine AI-based marketing plans throughout the world, and how entrepreneurs can exploit smart systems to engage customers, enter the market, and build their brands in different geographical locations. The further chapters discuss how entrepreneurial decision-making should be transformed by data-based solutions, the opportunities and challenges of using AI peculiar to entrepreneurs, and the most important ethical and governance issues that should inform responsible AI use. The practical examples of the successful AI-based businesses are presented in real-life case scenarios, and the final chapters present the future-oriented insights related to new trends and the future of AI-based entrepreneurship on a global scale.

6.2 AI AS A CATALYST FOR ENTREPRENEURIAL INNOVATION

6.2.1 Artificial Intelligence Technologies for the Future of Ventures

The ecosystem of AI comprises a wide range of technologies that provide a variety of opportunities in terms of applying them to entrepreneurship innovations [1]. The modern AI systems are based on machine learning, which allows computers to learn based on the data they get and improve their functioning without specific programming. The potential of this development on entrepreneurs is immense since they have the ability to develop dynamic processes that will improve with time as they obtain customer data and market intelligence. A subfield of machine learning, deep learning uses artificial neural networks; it has transformed pattern recognition in text, speech, and images. Deep learning is being used to identify products and images, as well as detect defects and diagnose diseases, by entrepreneurs [2]. NLP technologies allow machines to read, comprehend, and write human language, and these technologies create opportunities for chatbots, sentiment analysis, automated content creation, and multilingual customer service.

Computer vision technologies enable machines to comprehend visual data in the world and have been used in autonomous vehicles, retail analytics, and manufacturing quality control, as well as augmented reality experiences [3]. Physical manufacturing, logistics, service delivery, and agriculture operations are also changing and being automated using robotics and automation systems that are increasingly powered by AI. All these technologies are part of a toolkit that can be used by entrepreneurs to be innovative in the integration when it comes to addressing the needs of the market to produce new value propositions [4]. The cloud computing revolution has played a major role in democratizing access to these AI technologies. Cloud services such as Amazon Web Services, Google Cloud, and Microsoft Azure provide pretrained AI models, development systems, and scalable infrastructure, which reduce the costs involved in adopting AI by startups and small enterprises by orders of magnitude. This model of infrastructure-as-a-service enables business people to test their ferocious AI potential without colossal investments in hardware and expert skills.

6.2.2 Machine Learning, NLP, and Automation Application in Startups

Machine learning is the base technology of the startups that strive to create intelligent and adaptive systems. Machine learning algorithms in customer relationship management are used to forecast customer lifetime value, churn likelihood, and the best engagement strategies based on their interaction patterns. Machine learning can be used in developing products with fast prototyping and testing based on simulation and predictive modeling, which lowers the cost and time to market. Machine-learning-based recommendation systems are now ubiquitous in e-commerce systems, media, and service platforms. These systems examine the user behavior, preferences, and context to recommend individualized products, content, or services to the user. In the case of entrepreneurs, effective recommendation systems may contribute greatly to customer interaction and conversion rates and revenue per user, and generally enhance the user experience.

6.2.3 Restructuring Product Development and Market Discovery

AI is completely transforming the way businesspeople think of developing products and ensuring they have the market. The conventional product development has been a linear approach in the sense that an idea was developed into a product in the marketplace and in most cases took a lot of investments before getting customer feedback. With AI-driven solutions, it is possible to experiment quickly, undergo continuous learning, and refine the development process in an adaptive way. Generative design systems take advantage of AI algorithms to search a huge space of solutions and generate sets of design alternatives optimized by a set of criteria, including cost, performance, or manufacturability. This method hastens innovation because it enhances human creativity with computer exploration. AI-assisted code generators assist software development by providing entrepreneurs with suggestions and enhancements when developing a product through code completion, bug detection, and code documentation.

AI-driven analytics has transformed market discovery, the process of determining the viability of customer segments and value propositions. Now, entrepreneurs have a chance to analyze the active large data sets of social media, search patterns, e-commerce, and other Internet sources to determine the new needs, learn the competitive dynamics, and forecast the market trends. Predictive analytics models are used to predict demand trends, so that the entrepreneurs can make intelligent decisions regarding the product features, price, and the time to enter the market. AI-driven A/B testing and experimentation systems help entrepreneurs to quickly test their hypotheses regarding customer preferences, effectiveness of messaging, and product features. Adaptive testing, such as multi-armed bandit algorithms, is an automatic optimization of experiments, and it directs more traffic to higher-performing variations at each iteration as the process of trying alternatives. This would significantly help in speeding up the rate of learning, and it would also help in minimizing the chances of making a decision on the basis of inadequate or misleading information.

6.3 ARTIFICIAL INTELLIGENCE–BASED INTERNATIONAL MARKETING

6.3.1 Smart Customer Segmentation and Hyper-Personalization

The classical methods of customer segmentation were based on demographic category, geographical area, and general psychography. Although helpful, these methods tended to end up producing fairly rough categories that overlooked significant individual characteristics and behavioral peculiarities. The concept of AI-powered segmentation is based on entirely different principles: based on machine learning, the patterns in customer data that a person analyst can miss during traditional analysis are recognized. Clustering optimizations take into consideration several customer behavior dimensions at once and create segments based on purchase behavior, exploring behavior, content behavior, response frequency, and marketing message reaction. These algorithmically generated segments tend to reflect upon customer groups that do not fall into traditional categories and yet have coherent beliefs and preferences. This is especially beneficial to global entrepreneurs, who can determine cross-cultural segments that have common needs even though they might be separated due to geographical or demographic factors. Hyper-personalization is the development of segmentation to individual-level customization. Instead of thinking of customers as part of segments, AI systems form dynamic individual profiles, which keep on changing according to new interactions and behaviors. In real-time decisions on what content to see, what products to recommend, what offers to present, and how to communicate with any customer, these profiles are informed.

Hyper-personalization is not limited to the marketing aspect but to the customer experience in general. The AI of e-commerce platforms personalizes product discovery interfaces to every visitor. Not only are recommendations personalized by content platforms but also page layouts, navigation structures, and editorial features. Communication channels adjust the timing of messages, channels to be used, and content according to personal preferences and behaviors. To entrepreneurs venturing into foreign markets, hyper-personalization will provide a way of competing favorably with the already established players. Through the provision of highly sentient experiences to every customer, startups have the ability to create loyalty and interaction that surpasses the resource benefits of bigger contenders. Nonetheless, the process of personalization must be done well in consideration of privacy issues and cultural sensitivities, especially when it is carried out in different international markets.

6.3.2 International Market Entry Predictive Analytics

Expanding into foreign markets has always been full of uncertainties and risks. Entrepreneurs have to face new competitive conditions, regulatory sectors, cultural values, and consumer demand with limited local expertise and assets. AI-driven predictive analytics are highly effective in giving entrepreneurs more visibility to minimise uncertainty and make better decisions when entering the market. Machine learning models are applied in market demand forecasting to predict future demand trends on the basis of historical trends, economic trends, seasonal trends, and emerging trends. These models can be used by an entrepreneur who is looking to expand internationally to determine the size of their market in other geographies, the best time to do so, and predict the growth of revenue in different situations. The sophisticated models are using external factors, including regulatory changes, competitive action, and macroeconomic conditions, to give stronger predictions. The AI-driven competitive intelligence systems are designed to monitor the actions of competitors in the various markets continuously, as they track the price variations, product releases, marketing efforts, user reviews, and the sentiments of people on social media. This live intelligence can assist business persons in detecting the gaps in the market, making comparisons with their products, and predicting how they will respond to their venturing strategies. NLP allows examining the content and messages of competitors in other languages and understanding how they position themselves in other markets.

Cultural adaptation modeling is an AI tool that examines the local preferences, behaviors, and cultural norms, which assists business people in modifying goods, messages, and business models to align with the local culture. Visual content preferences between cultures can be analyzed by computer vision systems, and language patterns, sentiment expression, and styles of communication can be analyzed by NLP systems. Such understandings guide localization policies that extend beyond mere translation to include cultural adjustment that is significant. Risk assessment models are complex models that are set up by integrating various sources of data to determine the risk involved when entering a particular market. These are models that take into account political stability, complexity of regulations, and protection of intellectual property, currency volatility, and maturity of the market. These tools have the benefit of enabling business people to make more balanced decisions regarding where to grow and how to organize their international activities by quantifying risks in a variety of dimensions [5].

6.3.3 Artificial Intelligence-Based Content Creation and Optimization of Engagement

The art of content marketing has been the new core of entrepreneurial marketing tactics though producing content that is of high quality and relevant extensively across various markets and languages poses a great challenge. Intelligent content generation applications are changing this reality by automating different content creation processes and, at the same time, producing quality and relevant content. Natural language generation systems have the capability of producing written materials such as product descriptions and email messages, blogs, and social media updates. These systems compare the current high-performing content, learn styles and patterns, and create new content that conforms to brand voice and preferences of the audience. In the case of global businessmen, being able to produce content in various languages without necessarily making native speakers available in each market is made possible by the concept of multilingual generation. Generative AI systems, which have the ability to generate images, graphics, and videos in response to a text description or design parameters, are radically changing the creation of visual content. The tools allow entrepreneurs to create visual resources quickly to use in marketing campaigns, product mockups, and social media content without having to use a significant amount of design resources. Style transfer algorithms have the ability to localize visual media to the cultural requirements of various markets without losing any brand uniformity.

The content optimization systems employ AI as a tool to evaluate the performance data and keep on enhancing the content effectiveness. These systems test the difference in headlines, images, calls-to-action, and content structure, and they learn which ones create the most engagement and conversion. Dynamic content assembly systems are systems that automatically tailor content to either individual users or segments, and they draw upon libraries of components to generate optimized experiences. The concept of engagement optimization is more than content since it involves the customer journey using all channels. AI systems can be used to understand customer movement across touchpoints and point out the best routes to conversion and areas of friction or abandonment. Machine-learning-driven attribution modeling brings in more precise insights into the contribution made by various activities in marketing to the outcome, which allows making more resource allocation decisions. The social media management platforms take advantage of AI to post optimally, trending topics, recommend content, and interact with audiences at a mass level. Sentiment analysis is used to track brand mentions and customer reactions on all platforms, notifying the entrepreneur about the problems or potential. The algorithms of influencer identification can assist an entrepreneur in identifying and assessing prospective partners within influencer marketing activities in various countries.

6.4 DECISION-MAKING TRANSFORMATION IN ENTREPRENEURSHIP

6.4.1 Opportunity Identification Based on Data

Traditional methods of identifying opportunities within entrepreneurship were strongly dependent on personal experiences, observations in the market, and pattern recognition [6]. These are still useful, but AI-based analytics allows us to take a more systematic and comprehensive way to find out about entrepreneurial possibilities. AI systems can recognize the patterns, trends, and gaps that may be invisible to a human being because of processing large quantities of data of various types [7].

The trend analysis systems track various data feeds such as search patterns, social media discussions, news alerts, patent applications, and e-commerce transactions to chart the emergent customer demands and market changes. Time-series analysis and anomaly detection are part of these systems, so the entrepreneur can be able to identify accelerating trends at an early stage, allowing them to be in a better position than market trends. In the case of international businesspeople, multi-market trend analysis allows for determining the patterns that are local and those that are also international [8]. Gap analysis tools employ AI in order to determine untapped customer needs and market niches. These systems discover patterns of customer complaints, customer reviews, forum discussions, support tickets, and social media complaints, after which these patterns are examined in order to identify common pain points and unmet needs. Competitive gap analysis compares products in one market to those in another to determine what features, services, or market segments are well offered in certain markets and not others and indicates that cross-market innovation transfer may be possible [9].

Technology scouting systems are used to track scientific publications, patents, startup ecosystems, and technology platforms in order to identify emerging technologies that may support new business models or product innovations. Synthesis tools are AI-based applications that assist entrepreneurs to know what is going on in the technical world beyond the scope of their expertise and to envision what it can be used to do. This would be especially useful in science-based businesses and technology entrepreneurs who are looking to commercialize innovations [10]. Customer insight mining is an NLP and machine learning–based approach to mining actionable insights on unstructured customer data. With these systems, the interactions of customer services, transcripts of sales calls, responses to surveys, and social media discussions are analyzed to help determine common themes, emerging preferences, and unmet needs. These insights guide product development focus, marketing communication, and service enhancement efforts for entrepreneurs.

6.4.2 AI in Pricing, Demand Forecasting, and Risk Management

The pricing policy has a strong influence on revenues and positioning, but the optimal pricing is not easy to determine, especially in the dynamic global markets that have different economic factors and business rivalry. Dynamic pricing systems that use AI keep prices continually updated according to real-time aspects such as demand trends, inventory, competitor prices, customer groups, and external forces such as the weather or events. The machine learning in demand forecasting models is more accurate in predicting future demand as compared to traditional statistical forecasting models. These models have many variables such as historical sales, seasonality, promotional calendar, economic, weather, and emerging trends. In the case of businesses that depend on inventory, proper demand forecasting will decrease the stockouts and surplus stock that directly affect profitability. In the case of service businesses, demand forecasting enhances capacity management and planning of resources. Price optimization algorithms help define the price points that maximize profits to be received by the products or services based on the analysis of the demand elasticity to price variations in each type of customer, time frame, and competitive environment. Such systems can conduct advanced simulations to test the pricing strategies prior to implementation to minimize the chances of making pricing errors. Purchasing power, competition intensity, and sensitivity of prices to customers vary; therefore, localized pricing optimization is used in the global markets. There are several dimensions of risk management in entrepreneurship, which are market risk, operational risk, financial risk, and strategic risk. The AI systems offer the entrepreneur more advanced risk assessment and reduction software. Credit risk models assess the probability of a customer defaulting on payment, which is used to make a decision concerning payment terms and credit limits. Detection systems detect fraud or suspicious transactions or activities that may be a security breach or fraud.

AI-driven scenario planning tools can help business starters to change the possible outcomes (several possible futures) and create contingency plans. These systems provide the simulation of the influence that can be provided by different external factors, such as economic conditions, regulatory changes, or competitive actions, on business performance. Probabilistic approaches, such as Monte Carlo simulations, compute uncertainties and assist entrepreneurs in making decisions that are resilient under a variety of possible circumstances. The models of supply chain risk assessment detect weaknesses in the procurement, logistics, and distribution networks. Such systems take into account the reliability of suppliers, the risks of geopolitics, the possibility of natural disasters, and some logistical complications in order to advise diversification processes and backup strategies. These tools are essential sources of intelligence to global entrepreneurs whose business activities must operate sustainably because of their complex international supply chains.

6.4.3 Human-Artificial Intelligence Cooperation on Strategic Planning

Human judgment and AI in strategic decision-making are essentially not substitutional but collaborative. The solution to this entrepreneurial strategy involves the fusion of the pattern recognition, analysis power, and relentless processing of AI, and the contextual knowledge, ethical judgment, creative intuition, and stakeholder management abilities that, nevertheless, are uniquely human.

Decision support systems learn to combine human judgment with the AI-generated insights without overriding the former. These systems provide pertinent data, emphasize tendencies and the occurrence of aberration, propose alternatives, and measure the amount of uncertainty but leave the ultimate decision-making to the human decision-makers. Decision support is effective because it maintains the balance between the richness and cognitive manageability of information and expresses insights in a manner that will enrich, not overload, human judgment. The augmented analytics platforms allow entrepreneurs to query data and experiment with hypotheses using natural language interfaces. Instead of complex analytical abilities, the platforms enable business people to pose plain language questions and obtain visualizations, statistical analysis, as well as narrative explanations. This makes analytics more democratic so that more members of the team become involved in making decisions based on data and also promotes a culture of analytical information in the organization.

Human judgment and local knowledge are integrated in collaborative forecasting systems, which make use of algorithmic predictions. It is always found that pure algorithmic or pure human forecasting is inferior to hybrid techniques because each technique is used to and compensates for the other's shortcomings. Algorithms can be used to offer uniformity and handle large amounts of data, and human beings add contextual aspects, recent trends, and the qualitative knowledge that may not be represented in history. Explainable AI systems are used to solve the black box issue of using complex machine learning models, as they are transparent in explaining how conclusions are drawn. In the case of entrepreneurial decision-making, explainability is essential in that it allows decision-makers to evaluate the position of AI recommendations against strategic goals, counteract possible biases or mistakes, and build trust in AI-recommended decisions. LIME (Local Interpretable Model-Agnostic explanations) or SHAP (SHapley Additive explanations) can give an insight into the factors that impact the AI prediction most of all. Strategic foresight platforms

TABLE 6.1
Core AI Technologies and Their Applications in Entrepreneurial Marketing

Technology	Primary Capabilities	Marketing Applications	Entrepreneurial Benefits
Machine Learning	Pattern recognition, prediction, classification	Customer segmentation, churn prediction, lead scoring, demand forecasting	Improved targeting accuracy, reduced customer acquisition costs, optimized resource allocation
Natural Language Processing	Text analysis, sentiment detection, language generation	Chatbots, sentiment analysis, content creation, social listening	24/7 customer engagement, multilingual support, scalable content production
Computer Vision	Image recognition, object detection, visual search	Visual product search, user-generated content analysis, retail analytics	Enhanced product discovery, improved customer insights, automated quality control
Predictive Analytics	Trend forecasting, scenario modeling, risk assessment	Market opportunity identification, campaign optimization, customer lifetime value prediction	Data-driven decision-making, reduced market entry risks, improved ROI
Recommendation Systems	Personalization, preference modeling, collaborative filtering	Product recommendations, content curation, personalized offers	Increased conversion rates, higher average order values, improved customer satisfaction
Marketing Automation	Workflow automation, trigger-based actions, multi-channel orchestration	Email campaigns, social media management, lead nurturing	Operational efficiency, consistent customer experiences, scalability

apply AI to scan the external environment to pick weak signals of possible changes that may affect strategic planning. These systems are used to track news, social media, and technical publications, among others, in order to detect nascent trends, potential disruptions, and strategic opportunities or threats. By increasing traditional strategic planning with AI-based environmental scanning, entrepreneurs will be able to create more attentive and progressive strategies (Table 6.1).

6.5 OPPORTUNITIES FOR ENTREPRENEURS IN THE AI ERA

6.5.1 Accelerated Innovation Processes and Lean Experiments

The increase in the speed of the innovation cycle is one of the greatest opportunities that AI offers to entrepreneurs. The classical product development and market validation took a long period of time and resources before getting market feedback. AI facilitates fast prototyping, testing, and iteration with simulation, predictive, and automated experimentation systems. Digital twin technologies are based on AI to create virtual models of processes, products, or systems, which can be tested and refined without the need to do any physical prototyping. Business owners can consider many possibilities in terms of design, experiment with the performance in different scenarios, and tune the settings before investing in the actual manufacturing. This approach significantly reduces development costs and shortens time-to-market while improving final product quality. Quick experimentation solutions based on AI allow entrepreneurs to experiment with business model variants, pricing approaches, and marketing tactics in a very fast and efficient way. Automated A/B testing systems are systems that run experiments continuously on digital channels, automatically testing new alternatives and allocating resources to the more effective variation. Multi-armed bandit algorithms are used to maximize exploration-exploitation trade-off, maximize learning, and minimize opportunity cost.

Validation is based on simulations that enable entrepreneurs to run business ideas in virtual settings before entering the market. The agent-based modeling predicts customer behavior, reaction to the competition, and the market dynamics, which are essential in determining how a business model may perform in different situations. Simulations may expose the various unintended consequences, vulnerabilities, and propose changes before being utilized in the real world. The AI-powered analytics that determine the features that are vital to the initial market validation and those that can be postponed improve the development of minimum viable products. Through the analysis of user behavior data of comparable products or platforms, AI systems are able to forecast which of the features will lead to adoption and engagement, enabling entrepreneurs to direct limited resources to capabilities with the greatest impact.

6.5.2 Advanced Marketing Intelligence Democratization

In the past, advanced marketing analytics and customer intelligence systems could be enjoyed only by big organizations with huge budgets and dedicated teams. AI is currently democratizing these features, making them accessible to the small outfits and startups that could not access such tools and insights previously. With this democratization, the playing field in the competition is even-handed, and the entrepreneur with limited resources can fight better. Cloud-based AI services offer ready-made models and machine learning services that ease the deployment of AI solutions manifold by minimizing the skills needed to deploy AI solutions. Cloud computing providers such as Google Cloud AutoML, Amazon SageMaker, and Microsoft Azure AI enable business people to create personalized models without any advanced technical expertise. Such platforms prepare data, train models, and deploy AI to non-experts. The marketing intelligence platforms take data from various sources and deliver cohesive analytics, campaign administration, and client engagement services. Such platforms are powered by AI-based tools like predictive lead scoring and content optimization, as well as intelligent attribution modeling. In the case of entrepreneurs, such unified platforms do not require the development of tailored analytics infrastructure, even though they offer the capabilities characteristic of enterprises.

OpenAI products and systems have established an open-source community of resources. TensorFlow, PyTorch, and others offer strong features for creating custom AI applications. Ready-made frameworks to perform common tasks, such as image classification, language translation, and sentiment analysis, are free, and that means that an entrepreneur does not have to create a framework but can work on the existing one. Community support and educational resources have become widespread around AI technologies, and it has become much easier to allow entrepreneurs to acquire AI literacy and capabilities. Connections are made available through online courses, tutorials, documentation, and community forums. This educational ecosystem will allow entrepreneurs to skill up their staff, so that they do not have to depend on the limited and expensive AI specialists.

6.5.3 AI-Based Business Model Scalability

The unique scalability benefits of the AI-based business models can make it possible to experience rapid growth without many extra resources. Also, unlike in the context of the traditional business, where scaling might need corresponding expansion of the workforce, physical facilities, or inventory, AI-enabled enterprises can be scaled with a mainly digital infrastructure investment. AI-driven Software-as-a-Service can be used to deliver service to more customers at low marginal costs after the core capabilities have been built. One customer recommendation system, personalization engine, or analytical system can tend to have thousands or millions of customers with similar infrastructure. The cost structure allows the entrepreneur to gain profitability at a smaller scale and increase returns as they scale. AI is implemented in marketplace and platform companies to match supply and demand, price optimization, and quality throughout their ecosystems. The advantages of these platforms are network effects, where the value-added benefits increase the more participants join. These dynamics are advanced through AI that will make matching more efficient, so that transactions are less frictious, and quality remains a central concern as the platform expands on a global scale.

Automation of customer support and customer service with the help of AI-powered chatbots and virtual assistants allows entrepreneurs to deliver responsive customer experiences without corresponding staff growth. Such systems process more routine queries, transactions, and troubleshooting and redirect complicated problems to human agents. This is because with an increased number of customers AI systems become more competent with the learning process, thus creating a virtuous cycle that enhances the quality of the services. The compounding benefits of AI-driven ventures are provided by data network effects. The more user information these businesses store, the more accurate and able their AI systems become, developing superior user experiences that bring more users into their systems and more data as a result. This dynamic generates defensible competitive positions and natural moats that only get stronger. Automated localization and adaptation capabilities enhance the ability of AI-based entrepreneurs to reach every corner of the world. Language translation systems facilitate the interaction between languages. Cultural adaptation algorithms can be used to optimize the products and experiences based on local tastes. These functions enable the small teams to be used in a variety of international markets at the same time.

6.6 OBSTACLES AND DILEMMAS TO ADOPTION

6.6.1 Information Quality, Technology, and Expertise Deficits

Although AI has tremendous opportunities, it cannot be stated that the benefits are achievable with minimal challenges. The quality of data is one of the underlying challenges to most entrepreneurs who aspire to use AI solutions. The quality of data used to train machine learning models is all that matters, and bad data produces untrustworthy or biased results. The infrastructure of data, governance processes, and quality controls needed to sustain high-quality datasets is not present in many startups. Another issue is the availability of the data, especially when dealing with new startups. The training data needed to achieve successful machine learning are usually large quantities, and novel ventures frequently do not have sufficient historical data. Cold start is an issue in recommendation systems, personalization engines, and predictive models in case there is not enough data to make accurate assumptions. The AI systems require entrepreneurs to establish mechanisms for obtaining or creating training information before they can provide value. Startups and other small-sized ventures may have a burden in terms of infrastructure needs to implement and operate AI systems. Even though cloud services have lowered entry barriers in infrastructure, the costs may continue to rise as the quantity of data and the complexity of computation increase. Complex deep learning applications can be trained on specialized hardware such as GPUs, which can be very costly for model training. Entrepreneurs have to be attentive to whether the utility of AI solutions is worth investing in infrastructure.

Entrepreneurs are the ones who experience the impact of the AI talent shortage more than others. The market for skilled data scientists, machine learning engineers, and AI experts is also very competitive, and the large technological companies and well-financed projects attract compensation packages that the startups cannot afford. The creation of internal AI needs either competing in this talent market or investing in training programs to create skills in existing teams. The implementation of AI systems requires integration issues in terms of integrating into the technical infrastructure and business operations. The old systems might not have the Application Programming Interfaces or access to the data needed by AI. The organizational procedures might have to be redesigned heavily to support AI-based workflow. Such integration endeavors may take huge amounts of time and knowledge before the fruits of AI are realized. An obstacle that exists notwithstanding the democratization of AI tools is the technical complexity. The choice of algorithms, the data preparation, the optimization of model parameters, and the results interpretation still involve a lot of experience. None of the non-technical entrepreneurs might be able to judge AI solutions, judge vendor assertions, or make wise judgments regarding AI investments. Such a knowledge gap poses the risks of implementing unsuitable solutions or ensuring that the available value is not harnessed.

6.6.2 Transparency Problems and Algorithmic Bias

The issue of algorithmic bias has become a pressing one as AI systems continue to participate more profoundly in the process of making decisions that would impact the lives and opportunities of people. Machine learning models that have been trained on biased historical data will reproduce such biases and, in some cases, increase them. To entrepreneurs, unbalanced AI systems may cause unfair treatment of customers, discrimination, and loss of reputation, as well as legal liability. Training data bias is when the set of data to train AI models does not reflect the diversity of the target population or scenarios that it will confront in practice. The historical data could be biased or discriminatory toward minorities. Indicatively, facial recognition systems, which are trained mostly on light-skinned face photos, do not perform well on dark-skinned faces. Gender stereotypes in product recommendation through the use of customer preference models trained on the basis of past purchase data are possible. The design of algorithms may also add or alleviate bias. Selection of features used in models, weighting of data, and optimization goals all have effects. Even when demographic traits are not explicitly modeled to drive AI systems, entrepreneurs must pay close attention to whether such systems will be associated with inconsistent effects on the various demographic groups. Measurement bias occurs when the phenomena that AI systems are measuring do not exactly measure the underlying constructs of interest. As an example, the use of arrest records in place of crime does not explain variations in the pattern of enforcement across communities. The extent of engagement is not always a good indicator of the quality of content. Entrepreneurs should be able to consider critically whether the AI systems are measuring what they want their systems to measure.

The complexity of such AI systems is problematic in terms of the way they explain and are transparent in how they reach their decision-making. Deep neural networks are also black boxes in which even their developers cannot completely explain the reasons as to why certain outputs are produced when specific inputs are supplied. This loss of transparency poses issues to debugging systems, biases detection, and user trust, and satisfies regulations of explainability. The responsibility is complicated with the involvement of AI systems in making decisions or contributing significantly to them. In situations where there are errors and damaged consequences, the question of who should be held accountable among the system designers, data providers, implementing organizations, and individual operators is highly ambiguous. Business people who implement AI systems should have effective accountability structures and management systems. Biases may increase over time in AI systems that learn to generate their own feedback. It is possible that recommendation systems can form filter bubbles that restrict exposure to different content. Predictive policing can cause police to target the high-crime neighborhoods, with more arrests in those areas, which lead to the predictions being reinforced. Entrepreneurs need to carefully keep an eye on deployed AI systems on such dynamics and put protective measures in place.

6.6.3 Risks in Cybersecurity and Intellectual Property

AI creates new cybersecurity risks that entrepreneurs will have to deal with. Adversarial attack is a technique that can be used to impair AI models with well-calculated inputs with the intention of generating false results. Such attacks may deceive image recognition systems, manipulate language models, or circumvent fraud detection systems. The vulnerabilities pose a great threat to the business model of entrepreneurs who require the reliability of AI in their business model. On data poisoning attacks, the AI systems are affected in the training phase as the training data is corrupted. Attackers input false labels or malicious examples, which make models pick up wrong patterns. These attacks are especially worrying to AI systems that never stop learning through user-generated information because a malicious user may be able to manipulate the workings of the models on purpose. Model theft is another kind of intellectual property risk in which assailants steal proprietary AI models by repeatedly querying and analyzing them. Competitors with ample resources or malicious actors are capable of creating costly AI models without investing in data acquisition, labeling, and training. Entrepreneurs need to take precautions on the intellectual property of their AI and, at the same time, be open to engaging customers.

The dangers to privacy increase as AI systems process more and more personal data. Machine learning models may also accidentally learn and expose sensitive information in training data. Aggregate models can be inferred to produce information at the individual level. These risks pose legal liability due to the privacy laws and jeopardize customer confidence in the entrepreneurs who manage data related to their customers. Vulnerabilities to the supply chain are created during the process of AI development with the assistance of third-party data, pretrained models, open-source libraries, and cloud infrastructure. Any vulnerabilities in the AI systems could be brought about by compromises at any point in this supply chain. Business people need to consider the security measures of the vendors and apply verification measures to the components they integrate.

6.7 GOVERNANCE AND ETHICAL CONSIDERATIONS

Figure 6.2 highlights Ethical and governance considerations.

FIGURE 6.2 Ethical and governance considerations.

6.7.1 Conscientious AI in Entrepreneurial Marketing

The ethical applications of AI in the marketing setting involve balancing the business interests with the respect of the customer autonomy, privacy, and wellbeing of the customers. Entrepreneurs are tempted to apply AI power to manipulative, customer-exploiting, or psychologically vulnerable uses. Having a responsible AI practice acknowledges that the success of any business cannot be sustained without customer trust and being in line with societal norms and expectations. The concept of transparency in AI use refers to the ability to notify customers about the presence of an AI system and the purpose behind using their data. Automated marketing products must not make customers think that they are being treated with human concern when their interaction is triggered by an algorithm. The algorithmic nature of the products would need to be considered when using the product recommendation, such that it does not come out as neutral information. By adopting transparency, the entrepreneurs are likely to have stronger customer relations even though it may affect conversion in the short run. Mechanisms of consent and control provide the customers with meaningful options regarding data collection and AI-based personalization. Granular privacy controls, opt-in strategies, and data portability reflect adherence to customer autonomy. Even though extensive controls can decrease the data accessibility to AI systems, they are consistent with the developing privacy laws and consumer demands.

The knowledge of behavioral economics demonstrates the ability of AI systems to take advantage of cognitive biases and shortcuts in decision-making. Although these methods may propel short-term interest and conversion, they present a question of ethical concerns regarding manipulation. Conscientious entrepreneurs will weigh whether their AI is used to assist customers to make informed choices that act in their best interests or take advantage of their vulnerabilities to make commercial profits. Wellbeing is the aspect that deals with the possibility of AI-induced marketing efforts resulting in bad habits or consequences. The process of addictive engagement optimization, marketing products to unhealthy risk groups, or encouraging unrealistic social comparisons can all be ethically questionable. Entrepreneurs need to consider the effectiveness of AI applications and also their potential effects on society. An inclusive design makes AI systems useful to the various populations instead of causing their performance to favor the majority population at the expense of the minority. This should involve training data of all kinds, mixed design teams, and clear-cut testing among groups of people. The inclusive design embraced by the entrepreneurs increases their markets and expresses social responsibility.

6.7.2 Meeting Global Data Protection Regulations

Regulations governing data privacy, as well as AI, have been growing ever more difficult as governments across the world enact detailed models. The General Data Protection Regulation (GDPR) by the European Union has brought about formidable precedents on the right of individuals, consent, and accountable duties. Other such rules have materialized in California (CCPA), Brazil (LGPD), China, and many locations. The principles of data minimization entail the gathering of data required to fulfill the outlined purposes and keeping it no longer than necessary. In the case of AI applications, this principle clashes with the general principle that the larger the amount of data, the better the performance of the model. Entrepreneurs have to create a balance between these considerations by explicitly stating the purposes of data collection and applying data lifecycle management. Purpose limitation limits the application of data collected to the purposes that were disclosed to individuals during collection. To process this principle without consent, it may be illegal to use customer data gathered to make transactions to train AI models to make marketing decisions. Entrepreneurs need to have clear connections between the point of data collection and its real use. Legal basis requirements are requirements concerning legitimate grounds or reasons why personal data should be processed, such as consent, fulfilling a contract, legal requirements, and legitimate interests. The use of legitimate interests would necessitate weighing between the needs of business and personal rights and freedoms. The business people should take special caution to identify legitimate grounds for their data processing operations.

The rights of individuals under contemporary privacy laws are the right to access personal data, right to correction of inaccuracies, deletion in special cases, and data portability. The AI systems should be tailored in order to respect such rights and allow extracting, deleting, and correcting data without impairing the functionality of the systems. Automated decision-making rights directly relate to AI, in which human review options must be taken in decisions that have major impacts. Various jurisdictions impose limits on cross-border transfer of data in their respective countries that mandate sufficient protection of the data. To entrepreneurs who are internationally operating, the challenge of compliance with such requirements can be sustained by adopting standard contractual provisions, adhering to adequacy ruling, or resorting to other acceptable options. The transfer restrictions should be considered in cloud infrastructure options and data localization options. The accountability requirements have the organizations show compliance with them by documentation, privacy impact assessment, and governance frameworks. Regular audits, privacy-by-design methods, and data protection officers aid in creating accountability. These practices should be instilled in the operations of entrepreneurs at the onset of their operations and not later on to comply with them.

6.7.3 Increasing Consumer Trust by Explainable AI

Trust is a vital resource to an entrepreneurial enterprise, especially those that are consumer facing. Explainability is necessary to foster trust as AI systems continue to mediate relationships with customers and make critical decisions. The customers wish to know why they were given specific recommendations, what factors were used to make decisions that impacted them, and how their information is utilized. An expoundable model structure gives emphasis to design transparency. Linear models, decision trees, and rule-based systems are inherently interpretable, whereas complex neural networks are not. In the cases where it is suitable for the application, simpler models are preferred over more complex models due to their benefits of transparency, despite being slightly less predictive. In a lot of marketing tasks, interpretable models are enough, and not within the repertoire of complex deep learning methods. The techniques of post-hoc explanation help to obtain insights about complex models after training. LIME produces local model-behavior approximations on a case-by-case basis. SHAP adopts an importance value to features using the principles of game theory. Neural networks have attention mechanisms that indicate the most significant inputs in terms of their impact on the outputs. Those methods enable an entrepreneur to describe particular decisions to the customers or regulators, even in complex models.

A counterfactual explanation provides details on what must be different to achieve a different outcome, and provides customers with insight into how to get the desired effects. As an example, when an AI system rejects a loan application, a counterfactual explanation could suggest that a small increase or decrease in income or debt-to-income ratio would have led to approval. These descriptions enable clients with practical knowledge. Natural language generation converts technical AI into understandable clarifications. These systems do not provide raw model scores or feature importance values but instead produce narrative explanations, which are comprehensible by the non-technical user. The accuracy-accessibility balance must be designed so that it does not simplify the data too much, but at the same time it should not be too difficult to understand. Interactive explanation interfaces enable a customer to gain insight into AI decision-making by tweaking inputs and seeing outputs. These interfaces turn the explanations that are presented in the form of a fixed presentation into a learning interaction. The customers gain intuitive knowledge about the behavior of AI systems through experimentation.

Processes in explanation governance define the policies according to which and when the explanations are made. All AI-made decisions do not need to be explained in more detail, yet major decisions that impact customer opportunities or experiences should be transparent. To communicate AI decision-making, entrepreneurs need to come up with clear standards for providing explanations and training employees.

6.8 CASE STUDY OF INTERNATIONAL STARTUPS

6.8.1 Artificial Intelligence Customer Acquisition in New Economies

Emerging markets are not only extraordinary in terms of opportunities but also pose major challenges to the entrepreneur. High populations, the rising levels of the middle classes, and the rising levels of digital uptake present significant market opportunities. There are, however, poorly developed infrastructure, credit histories, and cultural backgrounds that make customer acquisition difficult. AI is helping businesspeople to sail through these hurdles and establish thriving businesses in the emerging economies. An example case would be a fintech company that is active in Southeast Asia, which is offering microloans to the previously unbanked communities. Conventional credit rating systems do not work in such markets, as there are few formal credit histories. The startup has come up with AI models that evaluate creditworthiness based on alternative data such as mobile phone usage history, social network attributes, online behavior, and psychometric tests. The machine learning algorithms determine trends that are associated with repayment behavior without referring to the conventional credit bureaus. Users who lack any form of credit history and have a stable phone use, consistent work-related signals, and financial accountability can receive credit based on the presence of digital transactions. The AI system gets more and more accurate as it learns through the results of repayments.

The acquisition of customers is based on AI-assisted targeting via social media and mobile. NLP is used to analyze the local language usage patterns to find potential customers who are talking about financial needs. Lookalike model finds people like successful borrowers. Customized messages that are designed to suit the local dialect and cultural values will enhance interaction and conversion. The business has accomplished an impressive massive scale with millions of customers in various countries and has a default rate that is similar to that of conventional lenders. The AI-based solution has allowed the entry of the market with a minimum of capital because the infrastructure of the physical branches and human underwriters has been minimized. The success shows that AI can bring financial services to a larger customer base democratically and at the same time establish lucrative enterprises within the emerging markets.

6.8.2 AI-Based Platform-Based Entrepreneurship

Platform business models add value by bringing consumers and producers together to generate and exploit network effects as well as cut transaction costs. The matching efficiency, quality, and pricing optimization have become the core of platform success using AI. A number of entrepreneurial businesses have developed their own successful platforms in the world through the successful use of AI. Online education platforms link students all over the world to tutors who provide instructions in various subjects and languages. The platform will succeed on the basis of pairing students with the right tutors according to their learning requirements, languages, compatibility of schedule, and preferences for teaching styles. Recommendation systems based on AI processes historical matching data, student feedback, learning outcomes, and interactional patterns to recommend the best matches. NLP allows the platform to work with dozens of languages without having every tutor know many languages. Real-time translation helps in communication and speech recognition, and generation develops accessible learning. The services have now been extended to serve more than 100 countries, and AI has allowed the platform to reach the world with matching which would otherwise have been impossible without human mediation.

Quality assurance is an AI-based method that monitors the interactions during a lesson, and factors that can include student engagement, signs of learning, and signs of satisfaction analyze this. The system recognizes tutors who persistently achieve good results and raises alarming trends to be examined by humans. This is an automated quality check that ensures standards and grows very fast. Dynamic pricing algorithms optimize their prices according to demand trends, availability of tutors, sensitivity of prices to students, and the competitive activity. Individualized pricing packages denote personal readiness to pay and sustain fairness. The pricing model achieves the maximum transaction volume and platform revenue and makes the tutors and students feel valued. The platform has been profitable and able to serve millions of students worldwide. The founders attributed the platform's success to

AI-driven matching, quality assurance, and pricing optimization features that enabled rapid global scalability. The case demonstrates that AI may be facilitating technology for platform-based global entrepreneurship.

6.8.3 Lessons Learned in Successful AI Ventures

1. A review of successful AI-based entrepreneurship shows that a number of trends and lessons are common to them. To begin with, the entrepreneurial successes of successful entrepreneurs are often about clear issues with customers and their resolution through AI in itself. Technology is also a mode of creating value, not an end. This customer-focus approach makes sure that AI investments focus on actual needs.
2. More successful projects tend to have narrow scopes of AI usage initially instead of trying to completely automate it in the first place. They determine certain processes in which AI can provide evident value and early wins that can prove value and create momentum. After initial applications are successful, it continues to use AI on a limited basis.
3. Effective AI entrepreneurs make early investments in data infrastructure because they understand that the quality and availability of data are the determinants of AI effectiveness. They also deploy data collection, cleaning, storage, and governance systems at an early stage instead of adding such capabilities as an afterthought. This base allows for unending AI enhancement.
4. Successful ventures are using AI capabilities with human judgment and expertise instead of going fully automated. They acknowledge the abilities of AI to process data and predict patterns without eliminating human functions of interpreting contexts, making ethical decisions, and managing relationships. This is a more effective method compared to humans and AI.
5. Effective AI entrepreneurs have unrealistic expectations of what AI can achieve and the time frame of value creation. They will not go through the hype cycle and become disappointed when AI fails to bring about transformative outcomes. Tenacity through patience in investing in AI capabilities will pay off in large proportions in the long run.
6. Effective ventures put their customers in the first place by promoting trust and transparency in the use of AI. They tell it straightforwardly regarding the functionality of the AI systems, the data collected, and its utilization. This openness instills confidence in their customers and stands out from other competitors who shroud AI practices in secrecy.

6.9 FUTURE OUTLOOK: THE ROAD AHEAD

6.9.1 New Waves in AI-Based Entrepreneurship

The AI environment is ever-changing and has lately witnessed several new-fangled trendy areas that will influence entrepreneurship prospects and difficulties over the next few years. Generative AI is possibly the most notable innovation in the recent past, and models can both generate original text, images, and code, as well as music and other content. Entrepreneurs are already creating businesses based on generative AI features, including content creation services, design software, or custom entertainment. Multimodal AI systems that analyze and generate data of various types at the same time are getting more advanced. Multi-modality systems with vision, language, and audio comprehension models allow richer applications compared to single-modality systems. To entrepreneurs, multimodal AI opens access to such opportunities as virtual assistants, immersiveness, accessibility technology, and creative uses. Another frontier is autonomous AI agents, which are capable of pursuing complex objectives with weak human control. These agents are able to deconstruct high-level goals into sub-tasks, operate on tools and APIs, collect information, and act on goals. The use of entrepreneurs is in virtual employees, automated research assistants, and automated complex business processes.

Edge AI – models that execute on devices, instead of cloud servers – overcomes the problem of latency, privacy, and connectivity constraints of cloud-based AI. With increasing edge processing capacity and efficiency of models, entrepreneurs will be able to develop applications that run offline, keep privacy by local processing, and provide real-time responses. The uses include smart devices, autopilot cars, and industrial systems. Federated learning allows training a model by collaborating with distributed datasets without data centralization. This method resolves the problem of privacy because the data remains locally, and yet it is possible to learn based on aggregate patterns. One way that entrepreneurs can use federated learning to create AI systems that enjoy the benefits of network effects without violating privacy and regulation is encouragement of network effects. The process of AI democratization will carry on accelerating as more tools will be made more accessible and easy to use. Non-technical entrepreneurs can use powerful features provided by no-code and low-code AI platforms. Fine-tuning pretrained foundation models can be reduced to specific applications, which lower the data and computation needs in designing custom AI. The entrepreneurial environment in the future will be greatly influenced by the regulation and governance of AI. New global laws and regulations are being created that cover the safety of AI, fairness, transparency, and accountability. It is the duty of the entrepreneurs to operate in this changing regulatory environment with a view to future requirements. Individuals who adopt responsible AI practices will be in the right position to succeed in the long term.

6.9.2 The Generative AI and Autonomous Agents Role

The GenAI has gained much popularity because of its impressive features and universal nature. Emergent capabilities, such as high-level reasoning, synthetic creativity, and the ability to follow instructions, can be shown by large language models such as GPT-4. To entrepreneurs, these capabilities allow them to do things that would have been considered just a dream a few years ago. An undeniably clear area of application of generative AI lies in content creation. Automated content generation is becoming a business for entrepreneurs to market, journalize, educate, and entertain. Nevertheless, the most effective uses are those that use AI generation and machine editing, plus creative direction, in conjunction with humans instead of trying to fully automate. The best results are achieved when hybrid workflows, which use AI to develop quick drafts and explore, are used with human judgment applied to the final outputs. Generative design refers to an AI tool that searches through a large number of solutions in engineering, architecture, and product design. These tools enable entrepreneurs in design-intensive industries to quickly prototype, optimize on various criteria, and find non-obvious solutions. AI combined with human insight and discovery boosts the speed of innovation. Large language models have transformed conversational AI. Chatbots and virtual assistants are now able to converse in very natural, context-responsive, and useful conversations. The entrepreneurs are implementing such systems to provide customer service, sales, education, health coaching, and many more. The major success factor is in the cautious scoping of applications to domains, where the existing capabilities are adequate, and taking relevant protection measures.

Large language models turned into autonomous agents are a new frontier with an enormous potential for impact. Such agents are able to break down complicated goals, seek out information, use tools, write and execute code, and modify their methods repeatedly through feedback. Previous entrepreneurial uses are automated research, automated data analysis, automated workflow, and software development support. Nevertheless, autonomous agents also pose significant questions in reliability, security, and alignment. These systems are free to act in unanticipated ways, commit errors with high stakes, or aim to achieve an objective that may not support the intention of the user. Every entrepreneur using autonomous agents should introduce rigorous overseeing and validation of systems to allow safe and trustworthy functioning. Generative AI and autonomous agents have economic ramifications that are highly debatable. Optimists also see a blossom of creativity and productivity, since the AI does the routine tasks and multiplies human abilities. The pessimists fear the replacement of knowledge workers and the accumulation of economic benefits. The truth of the matter on the part of the entrepreneur will probably entail not only artistic prospects but also rivalry with AI becoming more accessible (Table 6.2).

6.9.3 Training the Next Generation of Entrepreneurs to Work in AI-Based Markets

With the growing role of AI in the world of entrepreneurship, universities, and accelerators, support organizations need to change their methods of training entrepreneurial leaders. The classic entrepreneurship education that focuses on business planning, financial management, and marketing basics is still of importance but not enough. The competencies required in AI-driven markets are new and required by future entrepreneurs. To be technologically literate, an entrepreneur does not have to become a machine learning engineer, but they must have adequate knowledge to make wise decisions regarding AI opportunities and applications. The entrepreneurship coursework needs to offer the foundational principles of data science and machine learning concepts and practical use of an AI tool. This technical background allows entrepreneurs to consider AI solutions, effectively interact with technical teams, and find good uses. Data thinking is a cognitive change between the intuitive

TABLE 6.2
Preparing Entrepreneurs for AI-Driven Markets – Key Competencies and Development Strategies

Competency Area	Core Skills	Development Approaches	Strategic Importance
Technical Literacy	Understanding of AI capabilities and limitations, data fundamentals, ML concepts	Online courses, certifications, hands-on experimentation with AI tools	Essential for evaluating AI opportunities, selecting appropriate solutions, and managing technical teams
Data Management	Data collection, cleaning, governance, privacy protection, infrastructure design	Formal training in data science, mentorship from experts, implementing projects	Foundation for all AI applications; determines quality and reliability of AI systems
Strategic Thinking	Identifying AI opportunities, evaluating ROI, integrating AI into business models	Business strategy courses, case study analysis, consulting with AI strategists	Critical for aligning AI investments with business objectives and competitive positioning
Ethical Judgment	Recognizing AI risks, implementing responsible AI practices, navigating ethical dilemmas	Ethics courses, participation in ethics reviews, learning from case studies	Increasingly important for maintaining trust, regulatory compliance, and social license to operate
Change Management	Leading AI transformation, managing organizational resistance, redesigning processes	Leadership development programs, change management training, organizational psychology	Necessary for successful AI adoption; technical capabilities mean little without organizational alignment
Cross-functional Collaboration	Working across technical and business functions, communicating with diverse stakeholders	Team projects, interdisciplinary education, facilitation skills development	AI success requires collaboration between technical experts and business leaders
Continuous Learning	Staying current with rapidly evolving AI technologies, adapting to new capabilities	Following research developments, attending conferences, participating in communities	Essentially, given the rapid pace of AI advancement, yesterday's cutting-edge quickly becomes outdated

thinking toward pure intuition and evidence-based decision-making with the help of analytical tools. Entrepreneurs of the future will have to learn to feel comfortable with data, statistical arguments, and experimental methods. They must study how to devise hypotheses, experiment design, results interpretation, and integrate information in the data with the judgment of the context. The ability to work interdisciplinarily is becoming more significant because successful AI projects need to be able to cross technical and business boundaries. Entrepreneurs should have the ability to put together and direct groups that integrate the proficiency of AI with area insight, entrepreneurial aptitude, and user-oriented design. The education programs are to establish opportunities for interdisciplinary collaboration between business, engineering, and design students in terms of ventures.

The ethical reasoning concerning AI applications should be part of entrepreneurship education. The next generation of entrepreneurs will have to make a complicated choice regarding the privacy of the data, fairness of algorithms, transparency, and the social effects of their AI. The judgment necessary to practice responsible innovation can be developed by case-based learning about ethical dilemmas in AI entrepreneurship. It is necessary to have a global perspective because AI has the ability to facilitate global entrepreneurship. The entrepreneurial leaders in the future must have knowledge of various markets, cultures, regulatory frameworks, and ethical standards in different locations. Entrepreneurship education should focus on international experiences, cross-cultural projects, and case studies from around the globe. The most critical ones are perhaps an adaptive mindset and a continuous learning orientation due to the rapid development of AI. AI capabilities, competitive dynamics, and best practices are going to keep evolving, and entrepreneurs need to anticipate them. The education programs must promote ambivalence, a passion to learn, and the ability to face changes. The ecosystems of entrepreneurial support should also develop. The accelerators and incubators are to be able to access AI expertise with the help of advisors, workshops, and collaborations with AI researchers and companies. The funding organizations should build the capacity to assess AI ventures and offer suitable capital frameworks. The policymakers must look at ways in which regulations may facilitate responsible AI innovation and safeguard the interests of the people.

6.10 CONCLUSION

6.10.1 Summary of Key Insights

1. In this chapter, the revolutionary nature of AI on entrepreneurship with regard to global marketing has been explored. A number of central insights can be made out of this analysis. To begin with, AI is not merely a technology that entrepreneurial organizations may adopt or neglect: it is being used to completely transform the competitive landscape, customer demands, and functional needs to succeed as an entrepreneur. The entrepreneurs who do not become AI literate and are not able to utilize it face the risk of being phased out of the market in favor of competitors who are more technologically advanced.
2. AI presents entrepreneurs with numerous opportunities in a significant and multidimensional way. The benefits of AI include the ability to innovate and target customers more efficiently, provide data-driven decisions, and build scalable business models. The democratization of AI using cloud technology and open-source software has the effect of making these capabilities more and more available to ventures of every scope. Such opportunities, however,

do not come easily, and the implementation of AI technologies is not enough. AI requires careful consideration in the business models, processes, and strategies to achieve success.

3. AI opportunities are associated with serious challenges. Barriers to adoption are the data quality and availability issues, technical complexity, talent constraints, and infrastructure requirements. The algorithmic bias, the transparency, and the privacy are ethical issues that should be taken seriously. The protection of intellectual property and cybersecurity threats requires effective protection. Entrepreneurs need to work with these obstacles as they develop their enterprises with few resources and knowledge.
4. Responsible AI implementation is not an ethical requirement but a strategic necessity. Enterprises that value transparency, fairness, privacy protection, and explainability establish a better customer relationship and set themselves on a path to success in the long term. On the other hand, the ones who utilize AI capabilities in manipulative or malevolent means are reputed to lose integrity, regulatory reprimand, and disbelief by the customer. The most successful entrepreneurs who apply AI take both the technical sophistication and the ethical basis.
5. Rapid technological change, the shift in regulations, and the transformation in society will determine the future of AI-powered entrepreneurship. New possibilities and new concerns are emerging with new capabilities such as generative AI, autonomous agents, and so forth. To survive in this dynamic environment, entrepreneurs need to develop adaptive mindsets and orientations toward continuous learning.

6.10.2 Global Marketing and Entrepreneur Strategic Implications

1. This analysis has a number of strategic implications for entrepreneurs and marketers based in a global setting. To begin with, the capabilities of AI must not be considered as an addition to the business model design but rather should be factored into the business model development process. The questions that must be posed by entrepreneurs are how AI can assist in adding value to their proposal, enhancing customer experiences, and making operations more effective, or developing competitive advantages. It is much easier to start with AI-native architectures and add retrofitting capabilities subsequently.
2. The data strategy should be given high importance in the planning of an entrepreneurship. The effectiveness of the AI systems will be highly dependent on the quality and quantity of the data that they have. Business entrepreneurs are well advised to invest in data infrastructure, governance procedures, and data collection procedures at an early stage. They must also think about the role of the network effects and data accumulation in building defensible competitive positions in the long term.
3. In AI-driven markets, partnership and ecosystem approaches gain greater significance. Not many ventures already have all the required capabilities of AI internally, especially at the initial stage of their creation. Capability can

be developed faster through strategic collaboration with providers of AI platforms, sources of data, technology consultants, and academic institutions. Innovation ecosystems also offer talent, knowledge, and access to collaborative opportunities.

4. Talent strategy should take care of the AI skills gap. Entrepreneurs have to make hard decisions on whether to develop internal AI by hiring and training or get it by partnering, through consultants, and external services. The integration of fundamental internal strengths and strategic alliances with other companies is usually the best approach. The establishment of learning cultures in which members of the team constantly master AI literacy aids organizations to keep up with technological changes.
5. Risk management systems should deal with the unique issues of AI systems. Conventional methods of risk assessment might not fully address algorithmic bias, adversarial attacks, or other unintended effects of AI decision-making. The entrepreneurial sector should engage in governance procedures that involve various views in the design of AI, frequent audits of system performance within demographics and systems of problem identification, and solutions.
6. The customer communication regarding AI must be based on transparency and empowerment. Instead of hiding the application of AI, the successful entrepreneurs explicitly explain how AI can improve the customer experiences, the data collected, and the reasons and how the customers can manage their interactions with AI systems. This disclosure creates trust and differentiation in markets where most rivals conceal their AI practices.
7. International entrepreneurs have to struggle with different regulations, cultures, and morals in different markets. The AI governance strategies must be crafted to support the most demanding needs of the entrepreneurs, as opposed to the least challenging market. This high-watermark technique will make operations easier and less risky in terms of regulatory breaches or loss of reputation.

6.10.3 Future Research and Practice Guidelines

Although significant gains have been achieved regarding the influence of AI on entrepreneurship, many significant questions still exist. More studies should be conducted in a number of areas. A longitudinal study of AI-embracing ventures as they progress could help in understanding AI capabilities and implementation strategies that work, as well as how AI influences both the performance and rate of survival of long-term ventures. A cross-industry, cross-geography, and cross-stage of venture cross-research would shed light on the ways the entrepreneurial effects of AI differ in each situation. Do other sectors offer the same opportunities and challenges as AI? What are the cultural context influences and effects on AI adoption? Are there AI advantages and expenses associated with early-stage and growth-stage ventures? The study of responsible AI practice in the business context would guide both the ethics and implementation principles. Which forms of governance are the best for startups? What should resource-constrained ventures do to ensure the existence of sufficient fairness testing and bias mitigation? What are some examples of business models that have been successful at integrating profitability and responsible AI practices?

Research into the role of AI in the labor market concerning entrepreneurial ventures and the ecosystems more generally would help answer the essential questions concerning workforce changes. What is the effect of AI-adopting ventures on their talent needs? What positions are being invented, changed, or removed? What can be done to have workers successfully adapt to AI-augmented positions? Research on AI entrepreneurship in developing and emerging markets would help to define how AI influences inclusive economic development. Will AI assist resource-starved entrepreneurs to break the barriers of the past? What are the infrastructure constraints and lack of data in these areas with respect to AI adoption? Which policies and programs can be effective in enhancing AI entrepreneurship in the developing economies? To practice, some priorities are formed. Schools and colleges ought to keep on developing entrepreneurship programs to incorporate AI literacy, data thinking, and ethical reasoning. The support organization of entrepreneurs must devise special programs that will serve AI venture requirements. Industry associations ought to establish platforms for information in terms of sharing best practices and emerging issues. Entrepreneurs might be able to find their way in the confusing world of AI tools, services, and vendors with the aid of standards and certification programs. Evaluation of autonomy in AI platforms, comparison of functionality, and confirmation of ethical processes would minimize information asymmetries to the disadvantage of resource-constrained entrepreneurs.

The policymakers ought to look into the consideration of the middle ground that would allow responsible AI innovation but not at the expense of the people. Clear regulations, AI support and development, investments in digital infrastructures, and schemes that ensure the development of AI skills are all beneficial to healthy entrepreneurial ecosystems. AI is only at the initial stages of transformation of entrepreneurship. New innovation, disruption, and evolution will continue to be witnessed in the coming years, with AI capabilities enhancing and adoption increasing. Those entrepreneurs who are mindful enough to integrate technical savvy with moral underpinning, who will take into consideration both the opportunities and obligations, will create novel, competitive, and sustainable businesses that will characterize the coming generation of global business. The future progress requires boldness, inquisitiveness, and dedication to making sure that AI will be used for human prosperity and general prosperity.

REFERENCES

1. C. Schade, T. Burmistrov, and M. Hund, "Predicting entrepreneurial activity using machine learning," *Electron. Commer. Res. Appl.*, vol. 55, p. 101195, Sep. 2023, doi: 10.1016/j.elerap.2022.101195. [Online]. Available: https://www.sciencedirect.com/science/article/abs/pii/S2352673422000555
2. "AI implications for entrepreneurship," *Int. J. Entrepreneur. Behav. Res.*, vol. 28, no. 7, pp. 816–837, 2022, doi: 10.1108/IJEBR-05-2021-0426. [Online]. Available: https://www.emerald.com/insight/content/doi/10.1108/IJEBR-05-2021-0426/full/pdf

3. Y. Yuan et al., "The impact of deep learning based-psychological capital on entrepreneurial intention," *Sci. Rep.*, vol. 14, p. 18216, Aug. 2024, doi: 10.1038/s41598-024-68997-1. [Online]. Available: https://www.nature.com/articles/s41598-024-68997-1
4. "The democratization of deep learning through cloud computing platforms," *Int. J. Comput. Eng.*, vol. 13, no. 2, pp. 45–56, Jul. 2025. [Online]. Available: https://carijournals.org/journals/IJCE/article/view/3004
5. Innominds, "How NLP-based cognitive capabilities of AI chatbots increase business interactivity," *Innominds Blog*, May 19, 2021. [Online]. Available: https://www.innominds.com/blog/how-nlp-based-cognitive-capabilities-of-ai-chatbots-increase-business-interactivity
6. A. Schöneseiffen, "A new opportunity for opportunity recognition? AI and entrepreneurship," in *Proceedings Academy of Management Annual Meeting*, 2024, doi: 10.5465/AMPROC.2024.17172abstract. [Online]. Available: https://journals.aom.org/doi/10.5465/AMPROC.2024.17172abstract
7. "Using AI and big data analytics to support entrepreneurial decision-making," *PMC*, p. PMC12546928, Oct. 2025. [Online]. Available: https://pmc.ncbi.nlm.nih.gov/articles/PMC12546928/
8. M. Verma et al., "Artificial intelligence in patent and market intelligence: A new paradigm for technology scouting," *arXiv:2507.20322*, Jul. 2025. [Online]. Available: https://arxiv.org/abs/2507.20322
9. "Customer feedback analysis using NLP," *Indian J. Entrepreneurship*, Feb. 2021. [Online]. Available: https://www.indianjournalofentrepreneurship.com/index.php/tcsj/article/view/158186
10. "The role of natural language processing in enhancing customer insight marketing effectiveness," *SPAST Abstracts*, 2023. [Online]. Available: https://spast.org/index.php/sgshm/article/download/5343/740/11071

7 The Rise of the AI-Powered Marketer

Redefining Global Strategy with Intelligence and Empathy

Sneha Polaki

7.1 INTRODUCTION

Marketing is undergoing a revolutionary shift in the current very competitive and globalized world market. A field that was, formerly mainly a creative and communicative activity is quickly turning into a data-driven science of exactness. There is an evolution that is taking place as artificial intelligence (AI) and emotional intelligence (EI) come together and are transforming how businesses think, carry out, and evaluate their marketing campaigns. As businesses are no longer limited to the old silos of customer engagement, they are utilizing hi-tech technologies to reach out to customers in a more interactive, personalized form with more effective use of emotions.

AI plays a major role in efficiency in marketing [1]. AI helps marketers analyze huge volumes of data in real time through tools like machine learning, natural language processing (NLP), and predictive analytics tools. The technologies enable a greater understanding of consumer behavior, and business organizations can engage in greater content and offerings, and communicate with greater accuracy than ever before. Chatbots that can give 24/7 customer support to algorithms that can recommend the appropriate product depending on your browsing history, AI assists marketers to deliver the right message at the right time to the right audience. Such a degree of personalization greatly ups customer satisfaction and retention [2]. Nevertheless, even though AI is fast and scalable, it fails to elicit the emotional sensitivity needed to develop meaningful human relationships. Here, EI comes as an indispensable supplement. EI in marketing can be defined as recognizing, sympathizing, and acting on the needs of customers regarding feelings and cultural situations [3]. It makes sure that the robotized and data-based interactions are without the feeling of being mechanical or impersonal. For example, in emotive marketing, tone, sentiment, and context are considered in communications to ensure that the communications are respectful, inclusive, and relevant. This combination of technology and human empathy is essential for building trust and fostering long-term brand loyalty.

 DOI: 10.1201/9781003650775-7

The combination of AI and EI poses challenges and opportunities to entrepreneurs, especially businesspersons dealing with culturally diversified and international markets [4]. On the one side, AI allows startups and small companies to expand their business and compete with the bigger ones efficiently by automating the campaign management and customer segmentation process or performing the analysis of their performance. On the one hand, EI grants them the capability to develop brand stories that would echo among various and even across the same demographic and geographical/cultural lines. The information about the local culture, the peculiarities of the language, and the triggers of specific emotions is essential in targeting global customers, and emotionally intelligent strategies would help to avoid a misunderstanding and a cultural blunder. Furthermore, the digital age means that moral considerations are playing an increasingly larger role in marketing decisions. Emotionally intelligent governance should come side by side with responsible use of AI so that the process of managing customer data is not used unfavorably toward the customers. The companies that neglect to be ethical are likely to lose their consumer base, as this is a very important asset in any market [5].

Therefore, the blending between AI and EI is rewriting the future of marketing. By effectively exploiting both of the capabilities, entrepreneurs will be able to develop customer-responsive, agile thinking, which is effective not only in its eco-friendly nature but is also ethically correct and emotionally appealing. When data and emotion are both strong forms of currency in the world, this combination of the two provides the proper sustaining point of competitive advantage.

7.2 THE EVOLUTION OF MARKETING: FROM BROADCAST TO INTELLIGENCE-DRIVEN ENGAGEMENT

Marketing has been changing consistently along with the technological developments, experiencing massive shifts with the passage of the span of history. Since the advent of the print media to the emergence of broadcast communication and the eventual take-off of digital platforms, each wave of technology has completely reinvented the communication process between brands and their audiences. The print age was characterized by unrestricted delivery of mass communication by a few facilities without much differentiation. It was replaced by the broadcasting era, television and radio, which enabled marketers to serve more people with more appealing and audio-visual content. But it is the digital revolution that has brought the most radical changes, as it has given us the opportunity to communicate in real time and real interactivity, as well as hyper-targeting through available tools. The current digitalization process has been driven by strong digital innovations in the fields of data analytics, machine learning, and algorithms based on AI. These innovations are allowing businesses to get past words much of the time and rather provide individualized experiences that engage the particular preferences, behaviors, and purchasing trends of particular individuals [6]. AI systems are currently able to consume huge amounts of raw customer information, including clickstreams and search queries, social media activity, and transactional data, to create descriptive and predictive insights about customers [7]. Such insights can determine not only the product suggestions but also when, how, and in what referential mode they are delivered, which lets the brands target the customers much more accurately than ever. With all these possibilities of technology, there comes a major threat of data-centric marketing that is associated with losing a real human connection. The more brands tend to use AI to automate and personalize contacts, the more they are likely to develop cold transactions, or even creepy experience, which can prove efficient but not heartwarming. It is a vital differentiating factor in the current complex digital environment, overwhelmed by information and promotional messages, where the connection that brands make to consumers on an emotional level is everything. When this is done, the consumer will feel more inclined to memorize the brand, take initiatives to use it, and be loyal to the brand, which probably knows their feelings, beliefs, and cultural exportation.

This is the point when EI comes to play in contemporary strategies of marketing [8]. According to Goleman [9], EI is hence the ability to identify feelings and deal with them – together with feeling knowledge of other people. When applied in marketing, EI is the ability of brands to talk about themselves in a manner that is emotionally sensitive, contextually, and culturally pertinent. It concerns hearing the voice of the customer in the sense that it concerns hearing it not only through the numbers but also through the lens of understanding that there is a person behind the numbers. AI and EI form synergetic relations [10]. AI brings accuracy, flexibility, and real-time responsiveness, while EI introduces empathy, ethical sensitivity, and cultural awareness. The combination of the two can produce some highly human and effective marketing strategies. An example is that a brand can utilize AI to segment customers based on their purchase behavior and what they browse but use EI to create messages that would resonate with the current emotional state or situation of the customers, such as a festive communication during festivals or a soft touch during a disaster.

Such a two-fold strategy is especially crucial to brands with a presence in various international markets. Depending on geographies, the level of cultural sensitivity, emotional touch, and local context changes drastically. A marketing campaign that may sound good in one culture may miss or even turn bad in another culture in case it lacks EI. Hence, the marketers should not only focus on data-driven segmentation techniques, but they should also introduce cultural empathy into their marketing. For example, understanding that some regions prioritize community values and reserved communication, while others respond more strongly to individualism and innovation, helps marketers create authentic and culturally appropriate messaging. In addition, the aspect of emotionally intelligent marketing is also important in driving the entire experience of customers. It also enables the brands to move beyond the concept of transaction but to rather have two-way conversations with their audiences [11].

This comprises giving attention when customers give their feedback, giving priority to complaints by putting themselves in the customers' shoes, and updating brand communication to suit how the target community feels. This responsiveness creates a trusting clientele and allows the brand to be seen not only as responsive but also attentive to various consumer identities. In the modern environment, where the values of trust, brand responsibility, and ethical behavior of the customers are becoming more conscious, emotionally sensitive communication emerges as the foundation of brand loyalty. EI in marketing is particularly relevant during sensitive situations, e.g., acute political unrest, health crisis, natural disasters, when any tone or timing misstep might have a consequence on reputation. Brands that are aware of emotions during such moments have the chance to strengthen the relationship with their consumers by being solidaristic, compassionate, and relevant. On the other hand, insensitivity, even toward steering based on correct facts, may look tone-deaf. Therefore, emotion-driven marketing will make sure to keep the data-based approaches closer to a real-world social and emotional framework.

EI embedded in the marketing schemes offers a comparative advantage to the entrepreneurs and startups. As AI gives them a scale and automation available to enterprises only a few years ago, EI allows them to be adaptable, friendly, and human-oriented. Trust and authenticity are some of the common methods created by startups to attract the first batch of customers, and EI goes in this direction because narrowing the gap between brand identity and the emotional fears and desires of customers helps in attracting them. Furthermore, with marketing getting more natural-sounding and conversational via social media, messaging systems, and interactive platforms, EI is key in terms of creating stories that sound organic, welcoming, and custom. Brands using emotionally intelligent methods, such as adaptive customer service bots or culturally sensitive advertising narratives, can make digital experiences feel more human.

7.3 THE ROLE OF ARTIFICIAL INTELLIGENCE IN GLOBAL MARKETING

7.3.1 Data-Driven Decision Making

In this modern age of digital marketing, information has turned out to be the most precious resource as far as tactical planning and implementation are concerned. Companies are becoming less dependent on the use of intuition in making decisions, instead becoming more focused on the views of empirical evidence and forecasting. AI becomes the core element of this transformation as it allows marketers to make accurate decisions based on data. AI systems have the power to extract value in the form of actionable intelligence, based on the processing of huge amounts of structured and unstructured data through modeling and machine learning algorithms, and through neural networks [12].

Among the key advantages of AI-based data analysis, there is the ability to trace the patterns that would be expected to go unnoticed when conducted manually. Unstructured data (social media posts, customer reviews, and sentiment analysis) can be combined with the structured data (purchase histories, clicks on websites, and customer demographics). Machine learning algorithms keep learning from this information over time, and they improve their accuracy, thus over time identifying consumer preferences, churn prediction, and better audience segmentation. Neural networks, especially, are worthwhile because of their capability to identify nonlinear connections in exotic data sets, which is precisely what is required of a more demanding task like image identification in advertising or NLP in a conversational marketing tool.

Predictive modeling also helps to improve the process of making decisions since the marketers would be able to predict customer behavior and market trends. Whether the leads are most likely to convert, when to expect the customers to engage in repeat purchases, or what campaigns to stir interest in particular audiences, algorithms could predict all that. Such insights enable dynamic distribution of the marketing resources so that when several assets are being used, they are used in areas where there is maximum probability of generating good outcomes. It is especially imperative in circumstances where marketing expenses have to be maximized through diverse channels, namely, email, social media, search, and e-commerce sites. In addition, decision-support systems built on AI-driven dashboards have decentralized analytics usage within an organization. The marketer no longer needs to depend on IT sections or data scientists to explain the facts. Teams not accustomed to working in the technical field can engage with insights and make strategy changes in real time through user-friendly interfaces and actual reports. That develops an attitude of agility and responsiveness that allows campaigns to be tested, altered, and amplified swiftly by using quantifiable performance parameters. Nonetheless, one must remember that data-driven decision-making does not come without its problems. The nature of data quality, algorithm bias, and consumer data use are important aspects of consideration. Although it is true that AI can be used to analyze immense sets of data, the input and the design of the models and algorithms themselves are only as good as the output. Thus, organizations should invest in data governance, transparency, and interdisciplinary cooperation to make sure the insights implemented in AI systems are precise, equitable, and correspond to business interests and consumer attitudes. The advocacy of AI, in reality, runs deeper than automation of the marketing process and applies equally to intelligent decision-making. When applied efficiently, AI can turn marketing into a proactive process by turning it into an insight-driven field able to predict any changes in the market and respond to them in real time [12].

7.3.2 Hyper-Personalization

The engagement with the customer is being redefined through the use of AI, which makes it possible to personalize the experience and carry out intelligent recommendation systems in real time. With more customers in the digital age demanding a high level of personalization and personal satisfaction through a streamlined experience, companies are now resorting to AI as a way of providing tailored content, products, and services that fit the exact set of needs and preferences of any individual customer. Real-time personalization means dynamically adapting content and offering on a real-time basis with AI-driven algorithms based on immediate behavior, context, and past experience of a user. Such systems reach far beyond simple segmentation to provide a form of responsiveness and relevance that offers greater customer satisfaction as well as boosted business performance.

Real-time personalization is one of the capabilities of AI that allows analyzing both structured and unstructured data in real time. These AI algorithms merge information gathered in various ways, including browsing history, buying habits, search patterns, and social media, and use the latest approaches, including machine learning and NLP, to produce valuable data. The data is then used to make dynamic user profiles, which change each time a user interacts with them. Consequently, the brands can personalize not only the homepage banners, content in emails but also the push notifications and the chats in the chatbots in real time so that the message comes out relevant to the distinct experience of every user. One of the main uses of AI to personalize experiences, which helps to boost involvement and purchases, is recommendation engines. These systems use collaborative filtering, content-based filtering, or hybrid approaches to recommend products, services, or content relevant to users. Collaborative filtering involves discovering the similarity between the behaviors of the individual users to suggest things to them, whereas content-based filtering suggests things with the corresponding characteristics that the individual has already interacted with. The hybrid models take the best out of both to enhance recommendation accuracy. As an example, the Netflix, Spotify, and Amazon platforms employ such systems to create user interface personalization to maximize user retention and result in repeat consumption.

Digital advertising and customer communication are also changing because of real-time personalization. Programmatic advertising platforms employ AI in the sense that they display ads that are well targeted, contextually dependent, and location-based, allowing optimization by use of real-time bidding and segmentation. In the same way, email marketing platforms that rely on AI scale subject lines, content blocks, and send times according to interactions with the recipient, which massively increases the open and conversion rate [13]. Besides, AI can make the larger digital experience more personal by adjusting the interface and interactions in response to user behavior. As an example, websites have the possibility to restructure the navigation menus or prompt the next steps depending on the real-time signals. Even such tools of conversational AI as chatbots, or virtual assistants, can change the tone and conversation according to the sentiments defined based on the message the user writes, consuming more emotional engagement.

To justify the advantages of real-time personalization, which are positive engagement, increased customer retention, and increased Return on Investment, a marketer should consider ethical challenges pertaining to data privacy and algorithmic transparency. In this way, it is crucial to ensure that personalization initiatives are effective, as they do not infringe on the autonomy of users.

7.3.3 Programmatic Advertising

Advances in AI have completely changed the response of digital advertising, especially in the aspects of ad placement that have become based on real-time bidding (RTB) and the segmentation of the audience. Media buying in traditional advertising was also manual, and time-consuming, with wide demographic standards. Modern AI also allows advertisers to obtain more accurate data-driven scheduling of where, when, and to whom the ads need to be displayed, which leads to higher utilization of resources, less waste, and better performance of the campaigns [14]. At the crux of the ad placement through AI resides real-time bidding, where a flow of digital ad inventory is sold and purchased on an impression level via programmatic advertisement systems.

In just a few milliseconds, the rated factors may include the behavior of a user, the type of device, location, and contextual information to see whether a specific user is a good match with the ad. In that case, a bid, which is automatic, is made on the impression. In this procedure, brands are able to tune up their messages to the hilt and guarantee that funding is utilized on high-opportunity viewers as opposed to unselective exposure. Segmentation driven by AI, in addition to RTB, assists in the greater specificity of the targeting. Instead of using the static and slow-changing customer segments, AI continuously examines the data flow in various channels, including web usage, mobile app use, and behavior in a purchase channel, as well as social activity, to create dynamic, real-time audience profiles. These profiles help marketers group users according to their intent, behavior, or stage in the customer journey, being able to deliver highly relevant adverts that appeal to the individual's needs. Such granularity enhances the click-through-rate (CTR) and the return on ad spend (ROAS) so that campaigns become effective and less expensive.

Moreover, AI streamlines the distribution of media across several media. It checks the performance indicators in real time and automatically reinvests advertising spending in the most successful channels, whether in search, display, video, or social media. An example is that when a specific campaign becomes unsuccessful in one platform, the system could assign the funds to another channel that is showing a better performance in terms of engagement or conversion. Such flexibility will guarantee that the investments that are placed in marketing are always linked to performance returns.

The AI is also involved in the optimization of creativity [15]. Using A/B testing to optimize various ad versions, it sees which pictures, titles, or calls to action work better, and makes adjustments to those changes, AI makes sure that the creative resources are made relevant to the audience. This not only increases the ad impact but also saves time and cost normally spent seeking to accomplish the test and revision task of the manual process. In spite of all the benefits that accompany the automation of ad placement, there are transparency and brand safety issues associated with it. Advertisers have to make sure their advertisements will be placed in relevant contexts, and they should not be associated with dangerous or non-relevant stuff. Moreover, the issues of privacy, data utilization, and algorithmic fairness have to be solved with strong governance and ethical control.

To recap, AI changes media buying from a stagnant and reactive procedure to a dynamic and optimized role. Using real-time bidding, sophisticated division, and cross-channel insight, marketing professionals can place ad investments more proficiently and make great enhancements in the performance of the campaign results [14].

7.3.4 Chatbots and Virtual Assistants

AI is bringing about a paradigm shift in the redesign of customer support and sales functions. The second most widely used application is the implementation of AI-powered chatbots, that is, automated and conversational applications that imitate human-like dialogue. Such systems can offer customer service through the day, have great capacity to accept thousands of queries at the same time, and offer multi-lingual customer support, which further helps to increase customer satisfaction and operational efficiency [16]. Chatbots are no longer simple scripted bots. By using innovations in NLP and machine learning, new chatbots can determine the intent of users and the sentiments they portray, in addition to providing contextual responses. They are currently embedded into websites, messaging apps, and e-commerce sites, and they help customers to navigate through services, troubleshooting, and even the purchasing choice. This 24/7 support can shave off the response time tremendously and allow a better user experience, eliminating the wait and the possibility of relying on other human agents outside working hours.

Chatbots are digital assistants in sales, communicating with potential customers, suggesting products to them according to their tastes, and bringing them into the purchase funnel. They access and examine customer data on the spot, and that fact contributes to making the response more individualized and to raising conversion rates. As an example, a chatbot on a shopping site can suggest products based on browsing history or inform users about available offers, tasks that were previously handled manually by human agents.

Operational: AI chatbots will decrease overheads because they will automate regular requests and can liberate human agents to work with complicated, high-value agents. This not only reduces the cost of labor but also guarantees scalability, especially in international business with high customer engagement. Despite their shortcomings, such as dealing with subtle or emotional discussions, AI-based chatbots are in a continuous state of development with respect to the input of the user and repeated training. According to Preece and Shneiderman [16], properly designed interactive systems may address the needs (i.e., fallback functional and emotional) and, therefore, chatbots should become an inseparable component of the contemporary customer engagement approach.

7.3.5 Predictive Customer Insights

Another era of forecast analytics has been opened up by AI, enabling firms to take action ahead of consumer tendencies by means of a wide array of information, such as online trails, trade histories, mobility, and response models. This forecasting prerequisite has been identified as a life cycle selling and churn management backbone that brands can use to make proactive and therefore efficient decisions that culminate in improved customer engagement, loyalty, and profitability [7].

With the machine learning algorithms, the AI platforms will be capable of detecting minor behavioral patterns and usage trends that indicate which part of the journey a customer is at (discovery, first purchase or maintenance, or disengagement), and they will then find themselves being utilized when it comes to the use of AI in learning a customer's journey better. The tendencies identified with the models could be the diminishing activity or the frequency of purchases or a lower percentage of attendance to marketing material, which in many cases serve as precedents to churn. This vision will allow the marketers to rightly interfere in the customer lifecycle at the right time, creating personal relevance by offering incentives, offering, or sending a message in order to recover the customer and extend the customer lifecycle. Applying AI in the lifecycle marketing will enable the brands to tailor the messaging to the levels of customers: acquisition, onboarding, engagement, retention, and reactivation. Taking a case scenario, one can conduct a friendly series of letters at the onboarding stage, which could be built on AI based on the user's interest or interaction. With already established clients, predictive models can offer an opportunity for upsell or cross-sell that comes along with the past purchases, as well as the current exploration of the client. The current that such level of personalization brings to the fore increases the satisfaction index of the customers and consequently the chances of making a repeat purchase.

Furthermore, dynamic content recommendations are a major element in all the mentioned industries, which rely on predictive analytics. It is possible to use AI to make timely and customized recommendations depending on real-time behavior, e.g., how long a user dwells on a specific product page, categories they view, or content they read twice. These insights allow the marketers to pass the right message, product, or content at the best time, thus offering a highly receptive and interactive customer experience. Predictive tools such as Netflix or Spotify allow recommending entertainment services according to the history of watching or listening, current mood, or consumption patterns. Equally in e-learning spaces, AI can inform learners of the risk of dropout by analyzing the frequency of logging in, their performance in assignments, and course navigation patterns to administer prompts or assistance measures. Predictive analytics in retail assists in demand forecasting, inventory management, and customer-specific discounting schemes based on expected behavior. Another field that is advanced by predictive AI is the customer lifetime value (CLV) modeling. By approximating the lifetime value that a customer brings to the organization, companies can divide their databases so that they have high- and low-value customers, and accordingly adjust the marketing investments. The retention strategies can be customized according to customers who appear to pose a risk of churn and also have a high revenue potential.

The usage of AI-driven predictive tools is more critical than ever since new marketers have to work within the constraints of a highly competitive and fast-moving digital world [7]. Applied with a sense of ethical and intelligent responsibility, these technologies are not only able to lessen churn but also to increase every aspect of the customer experience through real-time synchronization of marketing with user interest and action.

7.3.6 AI Agents: The Interface of Intelligence and Empathy

The use of AI agents is one more major step in marketing technology, which allows perfectly uniting of automation and emotional reactivity. Such intelligent systems cover chatbots, voice assistants, recommendation engines, and self-thinking decision-making tools, and their purpose is to communicate directly with customers in real time on multiple types of digital platforms. Although the previous generations of AI agents were exclusively task-oriented and script-based, the current systems have found a way of doing the same but with the knowledge and understanding of how the user would like to be engaged, which is more intuitive, empathetic, and aware of the situations at hand [12] (Figure 7.1).

Modern AI agents are highly complex and cannot only be compared to the mechanisms of static dialogue management or keyword detection. Using the cutting edge of NLP, sentiment analysis, and deep learning, they can interpret any emotional overtones of a conversation i.e., frustration, curiosity, enthusiasm, hesitation, and change their behavior in a corresponding manner. The functionality not only

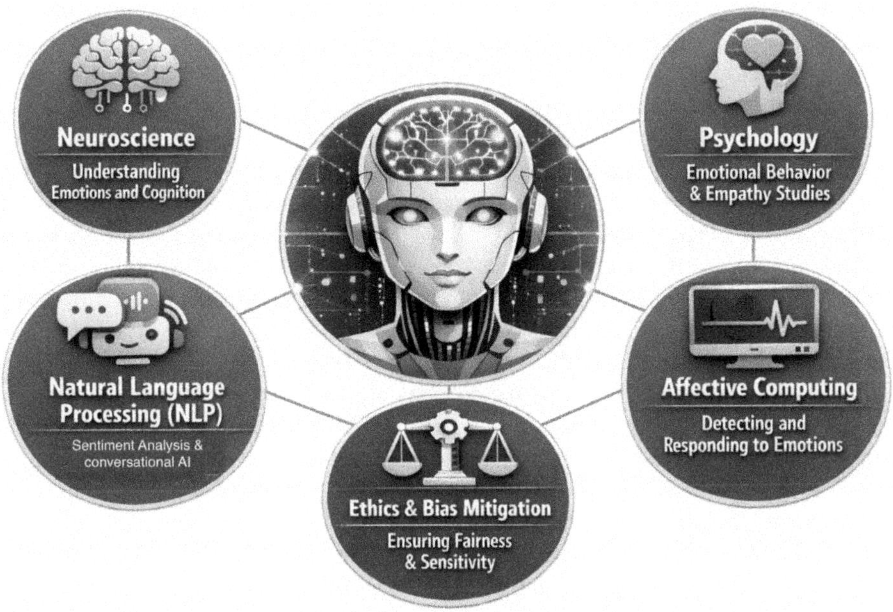

FIGURE 7.1 Key contributors enhancing emotional intelligence in AI agents.

improves the interaction itself but also makes the customer experience more personal and evocative. In an example, an AI-controlled chat assistant that reads indicators of customer frustration would change its tone to sound more reassuring, provide simplified solutions, or escalate the question to a human agent without being told to do so explicitly by the user. Some of the most evident and influential retail uses of emotionally intelligent AI agents include these. As an example, Sephora offers its virtual artist, which is enabled via computer vision and machine learning: users can simulate cosmetic items on their faces using augmented reality. Meanwhile, it personalizes product offers according to facial aspects, likes, and style of interaction. In a similar fashion, H&M uses the Kik chatbot, which communicates with their customers by engaging them in the dressing and advising their purchase and providing guidance in a conversational manner, causing a user to interact with the bot in a manner that is reminiscent of human communication. These are examples of the emotionally intelligent AI agents that lead to conversions by helping to build low-friction, seamless, and emotionally fulfilling experiences.

7.4 EMOTIONAL INTELLIGENCE IN MARKETING: THE HUMAN ELEMENT

7.4.1 Understanding Consumer Emotion

The concept concerning EI is a vibrant element in contemporary marketing since it helps a brand with accessibility to communicate with the consumer at a much more profound and personal level. Based on the capability to identify, comprehend, and properly react to feelings both of oneself and others, EI enables marketers to construct messages that will harmonize with the psychological and emotional conditions of target groups. According to the definition given by Goleman [9], EI comprises self-awareness, self-control, motivation, and empathy, as well as social skills, all of which are required in crafting emotionally appealing communicative strategies.

Marketing-wise, EI enables brands to get out of staying transactional and get into storytelling and inspiring consumers through the values, needs, and aspirations of the consumer. The current consumers do not want to purchase products or services but instead are in search of experiences, sense, and identity with what fits in their personal identity. Emotionally intelligent marketing helps to make use of it by using messages that will render feelings of trust, happiness, hope, or urgency according to the goal of the campaign and the target segment.

To give an example, when a storm or another incident of uncertainty hits the place, emotionally intelligent campaigns are more likely to sound humane, supportive, and encouraging rather than aggressive and hard-selling. Conversely, feeling happy, proud, or goal-oriented on special occasions or motivational inspirations, brands are capable of relating the messages to such moods. Such emotional alignment increases interest, memorability, and builds long-term brand loyalty. In addition, EI is not only an issue of external messaging, but it also influences internal marketing processes. Emotionally intelligent teams are in a better position to cooperate, learn more about each other, and positively respond to criticism, which all ensure more inclusive and successful campaigns. The necessity to be more emotionally aware and selective in brand relationships entails consumers, as well as their selectiveness when it comes to brand relationships, and, therefore, one of the vital tools in developing trust and authenticity in the digital era is EI as a competitive edge.

7.4.2 Empathetic Messaging

Empathy is the process of brand communication through the way of understanding and reacting to the emotions, values, and experiences of the audience. When empathy is incorporated in marketing campaigns, it becomes indicative that a brand not only establishes its sensitivity toward the consumer needs but also a reflection on its understanding of the macro society and culture. This emphatic attitude also promotes trust, genuineness, and emotional commitment – mainly becoming more critical in a world where buyers necessitate deeper relationships with companies they pursue. Empathy-guided communication consists of recognizing social problems, cultural identities, and personal difficulties, and avoids making money out of it. As an example, we can take the brands that refer to the importance of mental health or that advocate inclusion: they show that they care about the causes that are close to their audiences. This will create long-term rationality and affect, and the consumers will promote the brand and stick around with it. Moreover, empathy will prevent tone-deaf messaging, particularly in moments of crisis or when cultural sensitivity should be maintained.

Advertising, which can be perceived as a concern and a show of solidarity, will have better performance and positive brand associations. Finally, empathy will help brands go beyond transactional relationships to create emotionally intelligent and culturally respectful relationships found across global markets.

7.4.3 Ethical Brand Positioning

EI is very important in the development of marketing messages that are socially responsible, inclusive, and respectful. As consumers become more discerning about authenticity, ethical actions, brands are being forced to go beyond transactional messages and create brand communications that factor in the various identities, lived experiences, and cultural sensitivities. Marketers can move through these nuances using EI by appealing to the markets without being alienating, stereotypical, and exploitative in the messaging [12]. Marketing teams that are emotionally intelligent are ones that understand the cues created by the audience reactions and social trends hidden beneath their surface and can change their tone, imagery, and narratives in a manner that creates a sense of belonging and being respected. Emotional awareness appears in campaigns, including the promotion of body positivity, gender inclusiveness, or environmental responsibility, which are more likely to establish a more powerful engagement and beneficial brand sentiment. By contrast, tone-deaf or exclusionary ads may incite a negative reaction, undermine credibility, and destroy brand equity.

Marketers do not damage their reputation by simply including EI in planning campaigns and communicating their brands; they also achieve long-term loyalty. The potential of responsible messaging based on an emotional understanding is that it makes the brand sound responsible and culturally sensitive, which are qualities that are becoming decisive to consumers when deciding which brand to patronize.

7.4.4 Crisis Communication

Situations like the pandemic of COVID-19 put lots of pressure on companies to speak not only clearly but also be compassionate. The rational confidence in the adequacy of their brand was tested by the brands of EI during the times of confusion, fear, and upheaval, and showed empathy, transparency, and solidarity as paramount in their communications. Instead of making all the possible efforts to drive revenue, those brands moved toward human-centric communication, as they understood the effects that the crisis had on their audiences, both emotionally and psychologically [7]. Responsibly emotional actions comprised messages of assurance, flexible policy (extended returns or skip a payment), and information on health and safety measures. Brands such as Airbnb, Nike, and Dove, to mention a few, put on hold the promotional messages and instead provided support to the healthcare workers, promoted responsible attitudes, or highlighted the stories of resilience. These steps spoke a lot to the consumers, as many of them needed to feel stable, treated kindly, and have a sense of belonging in the middle of a world emergency.

There was also a more open operation of the business in terms of free communication of supply chain delays or operational issues, which assisted in developing trust, in that the customers valued honesty as much as corporate rhetoric. Brands that recognized the common human experience but never tried to use it to their advantage were trusted with more loyalty and long-term affection. Putting into practice emotionally intelligent marketing in times of registration is not just ethical but also an effective business strategy, as Kumar and Ramachandran [7] propose. Brands stand to benefit in terms of emotional connection, something that in most cases translates into improved retention and positive brand equity long after the crisis is past and forgotten, due to the degree of care and understanding they show.

7.5 SYNERGIZING AI AND EI IN MARKETING STRATEGY

AI and EI are bringing a complete future-visible marketing strategy in place. AI is efficient in the processing of enormous amounts of data, the discovery of behavioral patterns, as well as the dynamic scale-based engagement that AI facilitates. EI, however, makes sure that it makes these interactions emotionally intelligent, respectful, as well as in line with human values. When used in combination, they facilitate such a marketing environment that is not only effective and flexible but also culturally and ethnically sound.

There is a synergy that exists in various aspects.

- **Personalized storytelling:** Individualized storytelling goes to a new level as AI provides real-time information on what customers like and EI creates an exclusive story according to the current emotions and cognitive triggers.
- **Adaptive experiences:** The efficiency of the adaptive experiences increases when people are identified as having changed their behavior by AI, and the subsequent changes should be both empathetic and non-obtrusive, ensured by EI.
- **Inclusive targeting:** The power of AI is to give Inclusive targeting precision in the segmentation of the market, whereas EI protects against the ability to make a tone-deaf message; context adaptation. This combined approach is especially effective in international marketing, where the same sensitivity and cultural awareness are especially important to ensure relation and adoption. With the help of this technology that enables emotional and social participation, according to Preece and Shneiderman [16], user satisfaction and long-term loyalty will be maximized, and therefore, it is crucial, especially in marketing, to rely on AI-EI synergy when it comes to being more human-oriented.

7.6 ENTREPRENEURIAL APPLICATIONS AND COMPETITIVE ADVANTAGES

AI and EI can become a potent strategic tool available to entrepreneurs working in the emerging markets. AI can be used to achieve operational efficiency through automation of routine and repetitive tasks, distribution of resources in an optimal manner, as well as through analysis of large volumes of data that allow market trends to be uncovered. This assists in cutting down on the expenditure and expanding business on a large scale without large overheads. Meanwhile, EI guarantees that the communication and engagement tactics of the brand would stay sensitive, inclusive, and culturally broad-minded pinch on the portfolio, which is important in the markets where consumers are diverse, and expectations are changing [9]. In combination with

AI, EI enables business owners to determine which consumer needs have not been met using predictive analysis and create emotionally powerful messages that lead to brand loyalty.

These two abilities enable startups to develop purpose-driven brands that establish trust and stand out from the crowd or price competition. This synergy specifically promotes scalable and emotionally smart development in areas where its digital infrastructure is increasing at a fast rate, which is attractive to both the rational and emotional aspects of consumer judgment.

7.7 CASE STUDIES

7.7.1 Spotify

The Wrapped campaign on Spotify uses AI to optimize the personal data of listeners of the app and generate end-of-year summaries. It comes in colorful, mime, sharable formats that make readers nostalgic and emotional. The campaign personalizes emails and promotes the emotional connection with the user, complemented with artistically written messages and illustrations, which build additional attachment to the brand.

7.7.2 Nike

Nike combines data analytics in real time and emotional storytelling to create campaigns that resonate throughout the world. The unification of the data revelation with the subjects of cultural empathy, persistence, and social importance allows Nike to present powerful stories touching on the hearts of a variety of audiences. This emotionally intelligent philosophy boosts brand loyalty and restates its character as a purposeful brand.

7.7.3 Netflix

Netflix uses AI prerequisites and suggestions in content and audience adaptation. Its success consists of a combination of such capabilities in favor of emotionally appealing programming that corresponds to the variety of users' preferences [12].

7.8 CHALLENGES AND ETHICAL CONSIDERATIONS

- **Data Privacy:** With the increased data gathering of the AI systems, the cases of surveillance and its misuse have become a more concerning issue. EI assists in the framing of respectful data practices.
- **AI Bias:** Biases in the past could be transmitted with the help of algorithms. Being human-in-the-loop guarantees justice.
- **Emotional Exploitation:** Brands cannot afford to exploit emotions for personal gain.
- **Transparency:** The consumers must know when they are dealing with AI systems.

7.9 FUTURE OUTLOOK

Global marketing in the future will be determined by an effective and smart combination of AI and human emotional understanding. With digital ecosystems changing faster than ever before, AI has recently shifted to a front-end decision-making force, which is helping to shape customer experience in real time. But to maintain such technological advancement in the long run interest of brand equity and customer trust, there has to be a human touch in the form of EI.

Among the most revolutionary changes in this field was the Emotion AI, AI that was built to identify and analyze human feelings by detecting facial recognition, intonation of our voices, gestures, and even behavioral patterns. It is now installing emotion AI technology in advertising platforms, virtual assistants, customer-care bots, as well as retail spaces. Such systems are able to read nuanced emotional cues and implement those changes in the responses, thus achieving the identification of an angry customer by tone and changing the message in order to look more understanding. Although Emotion AI might provide potent features to make personalization and emotional appeal more engaging, the use of Emotion AI also brings up ethical, cultural, and psychological questions. Marketers have to be very careful in the mouth usage of such tools, more so in the globalized markets where the demonstration of emotions is shaped by cultural norms. What an emotional cue means in a Western setting would be a completely different meaning in an Eastern or Aboriginal system. Thus, the success of the Emotion AI depends on both the technical accuracy and cultural smartness and emotional morale. Privacy and consent are another dimension of great significance. Emotion AI tends to use biometric information, which is very sensitive, e.g., facial scans, voice recording. With circular laws changing, such as the EU GDPR, or India DPDP Act, marketers will have to make sure that the application of such technology is open, consensual, and in line with local data standards. Responsible uses of Emotion AI, highlighted by the promotion of user autonomy and the absence of abuse, manipulation, or exploitation on an emotional level, require a strong framework of governance. Irrespective of these concerns, Emotion AI has even greater potential in providing strategically important applications. With the brands that learn to responsibly use their power, this has the potential to deliver those deeply personalized experiences to an individual, which are emotionally intelligent experiences that can both drive engagement and contribute to long-term loyalty. As a case in point, an online learning platform with access to webcam information would recognize when a learner was getting frustrated and be able to spontaneously provide simplified material or a tutor. Equally, a chatbot could detect the reluctance of buyers and act to console them or suggest an action. The future belongs to the brands that are able to sell not numbers but people; the brands whose marketing has become immersive and highly human-centered will become the winning ones; and the winning brands will be those that manage to merge the computational power of AI with the emotive understanding of EI. This does not just mean technical implementation but also alignment on the organizational level, i.e. the marketing teams, data scientists, and ethicists must work together to create emotionally intelligent campaigns and make them inclusive, respectful, and ethically compatible.

To conclude, the AI is not the only way marketing in the future will be formed; rather, it is the AI with the ethical sensitivity and empathetic understanding of a human being. Emotion AI is an extremely effective technology, but it is like all strong technology; in order to be effective, it has to be used responsibly. The marketers who can accept its possibilities and the shortfalls will be the most successful in a new digital engagement era.

7.10 CONCLUSION

The new era of global marketing is not a field of AI against EI, but the synergies of assets that, when used strategically, brand communications and connections once again become a world of possibilities. AI is extremely precise, fast, and scalable. It manipulates big data, forecasts customer behavior, automates decision-making, and offers real-time personalization. Yet when done entirely on a machine level, AI solutions can lack human understanding, leaving them rather insensitive, culturally insensitive, or emotionless. Here is when the EI comes in. EI brings the necessary human element: empathy, context, ethical sensitivity, and social sensitivity. It makes sure that advertising is not disrespectful, insensitive, and lacks emotion. In combination, AI and EI allow the brands not only to figure out what their customers want but also how they feel and why they choose to do it. These two levels of awareness enable marketers to come up with campaigns that can be easily implemented but significant in implication. The AI-EI combination is and can be a strategic differentiator for entrepreneurs, even in developing or highly competitive markets. It enables them to automate the operations, but at the same time, they are able to develop real customer relationships. Target messaging, emotionally astute interaction, and inference-based innovation combined can create a more equal playing field on which small and developing companies may compete with larger ones. In this era of a sea of choices, the differentiator that enables consumers to make long-term decisions is the emotional connection they have with the brand (along with being smart).

Going further, the best marketing activities will be those that combine technological progress with human values. The more immersive the digital experiences, and the more embedded our daily interactions with AI, the higher the demand for emotionally intelligent design. Marketing should not only be clever but also caring, more wholesome, and ethical. The idea, in other words, is not that a future forward marketing strategy will automatically be the one that embraces the latest tools, but rather, it will be one that has integrated those tools with the eternal truths about people. A combination of AI analytical capabilities and EI empathetic understanding will help marketers create a better connection, foster brand loyalty, and help the brands embrace a future that is not only intelligent but also connecting at an all-new level of humanity.

REFERENCES

[1] Rust, R. T., & Huang, M.-H. (2021). Artificial intelligence in service. *Journal of Service Research*, *24*(1), 3–22. https://doi.org/10.1177/1094670520902266

[2] Lemon, K. N., & Verhoef, P. C. (2016). Understanding customer experience throughout the customer journey. *Journal of Marketing*, *80*(6), 69–96. https://doi.org/10.1509/jm.15.0420

[3] McStay, A. (2018). *Emotional AI: The rise of empathic media*. SAGE Publications.

[4] Van Doorn, J., Mende, M., Noble, S. M., Hulland, J., Ostrom, A. L., Grewal, D., & Petersen, J. A. (2017). Customer engagement behavior: Theoretical foundations and research directions. *Journal of Service Research*, *20*(3), 245–259. https://doi.org/10.1177/1094670516679272
[5] Wired Staff. (2021, March 5). Facial recognition and emotion-detection software are creating a dystopia of surveillance. *WIRED*. https://www.wired.com/story/artificial-intelligence-empathy/theguardian.com+7wired.com+7wired.com+7
[6] Kaplan, A. M., & Haenlein, M. (2019). Siri, Siri, in my hand: Who's the fairest in the land? On the interpretations, illustrations, and implications of artificial intelligence. *Business Horizons*, *62*(1), 15–25. https://doi.org/10.1016/j.bushor.2018.08.004
[7] Kumar, V., & Ramachandran, D. (2021). Evolution of marketing as a discipline: What has happened and what to look out for. *Journal of Marketing*, *85*(1), 1–20. https://journals.sagepub.com/doi/10.1509/jm.79.1.1
[8] Belk, R. (2013). Extended self in a digital world. *Journal of Consumer Research*, *40*(3), 477–500. https://doi.org/10.1086/671052
[9] Goleman, D. (1995). *Emotional intelligence: Why it can matter more than IQ*. Bantam Books. https://www.scirp.org/reference/referencespapers?referenceid=773626
[10] Mikalef, P., Krogstie, J., Pappas, I. O., & Pavlou, P. A. (2021). Investigating the effects of big data analytics capabilities on firm performance: The mediating role of dynamic capabilities. *Information & Management*, *58*(2), 103434. https://doi.org/10.1016/j.im.2019.05.004
[11] Araujo, T (2018). Living up to the chatbot hype: The influence of anthropomorphic design cues and communicative agency framing on conversational agent and company perceptions.
[12] Davenport, T. H., Guha, A., Grewal, D., & Bressgott, T. (2020). How artificial intelligence will change the future of marketing. *Journal of the Academy of Marketing Science*, *48*(1), 24–42. https://link.springer.com/article/10.1007/s11747-019-00696-0
[13] Kietzmann, J., Paschen, J., & Treen, E. (2018). Artificial intelligence in advertising: How marketers can leverage artificial intelligence along the consumer journey. *Journal of Advertising Research*, *58*(3), 263–267. https://doi.org/10.2501/JAR-2018-035
[14] Davenport, T. H., & Ronanki, R. (2018). Artificial intelligence for the real world. *Harvard Business Review*, *96*(1), 108–116. https://hbr.org/2018/01/artificial-intelligence-for-the-real-world
[15] Grewal, D., Roggeveen, A. L., & Nordfält, J. (2017). The future of retailing. *Journal of Retailing*, *93*(1), 1–6. https://doi.org/10.1016/j.jretai.2016.12.008
[16] Preece, J., & Shneiderman, B. (2009). The reader-to-leader framework: Motivating technology-mediated social participation. *AIS Transactions on Human-Computer Interaction*, *1*(1), 13–32. https://aisel.aisnet.org/thci/vol1/iss1/5/

8 Data-Driven Marketing Strategies

Solomon Jeresa, Abhinav Sinha, and Michael Oyedele Oyenuga

8.1 INTRODUCTION

In today's hyper-connected market, characterised by an abundance of information, marketing has transformed from an area largely dedicated to creativity into one grounded in analytics, algorithms, and results. Data-driven marketing entails the use of customer and market data to inform decisions across the whole marketing life cycle, from segmentation and targeting to personalisation and performance optimisation [1]. Thus, it is not simply another tactical add-on to the mainstream marketing process; it is a core restructuring of how organisations create, deliver, and measure value. Data is increasingly relevant across fields and is especially important in marketing strategy.

The evolution of data-driven marketing strategies is rooted in the meteoric rise of digital touchpoints and the availability of consumer data. Information is now collected from various sources such as transactional databases, web analytics, mobile applications, social media, and Internet of Things (IoT) devices. This information or data forms the basis for very detailed insights into customer behaviour, preferences, and intentions, enabling firms to offer precise experiences that foster engagement and loyalty [2, 3]. Hence, data-driven strategies have become essential competitive advantages across sectors ranging from retail and finance to healthcare and entertainment.

This change is further fuelled by the emergence of machine learning (ML), artificial intelligence (AI), and advanced analytics tools aided by these developments, enabling marketers to accurately predict customer behaviour, automate campaign management, and optimise content delivery in real time [4]. Nevertheless, causing the data-centric marketing transition would, and already is, create hurdles: from ensuring data quality to complying with complex regulations, including the European General Data Protection Regulation (GDPR) and the California Consumer Privacy Act (CCPA), to tackling heightened consumer concerns regarding privacy and algorithmic transparency.

Data-driven marketing strategies are more likely to succeed when supported by organisational capabilities such as data literacy, cross-departmental collaboration, and a mindset oriented towards experimentation [5]. On the other hand, even the most advanced equipment would falter in providing long-term value if guided by the absence of a well-thought-out strategic vision and ethical governance of data.

DOI: 10.1201/9781003650775-8

Thus, a thorough grounding in the principal foundations of data-driven marketing theory, technology, applications, and limitations is of prime importance to marketing scholars and practitioners alike. The section to follow goes into all these foundational aspects in considerable depth with a comprehensive view of the strategic frameworks and meanings that shape modern marketing.

8.2 FOUNDATIONS OF DATA-DRIVEN MARKETING

8.2.1 Key Concepts of Customer Data and Behavioural Insights

At the heart of data-centric marketing is the capacity to collect, manage, and analyse various forms of customer data. This data is largely first-party (owned data direct to customers), second-party (shared with other partner organisations), and third-party data (collected by external aggregators) [6]. First-party data, such as the purchase record and website behaviour, is considered the most reliable and most valuable because it is highly accurate and exclusive.

Furthermore, behavioural data makes a record of how the audience interacts with content, platforms, and digital services. This data helps marketers understand how prospective customers make decisions. Behavioural metrics like click-through rates (CTRs), bounce rates, and heatmap analytics allow marketers to develop methods and talk online with their target customers in real time [7].

Understanding the conceptual differences between structured data (characteristics like age, location, and size of transactions) and unstructured data (characteristics like text reviews, social media posts, videos, etc.) is critical. Although structured data can facilitate quantitative analysis and automation, unstructured data, assessed using natural language processing (NLP) and sentiment analysis, also infuses a great deal of context into customer profiles [4].

8.2.2 Enabling Technologies and Platforms

For data-driven strategies, the technological backbone is the very essence of their execution. No data can be effectively utilised without the use of technology. Customer relationship management (CRM) systems, customer data points (CDPs), and data management platforms (DMPs) are technological processes that can aggregate and centralise data from various sources for further segmentation and targeting. More sophisticated systems use AI and ML for building predictive models and for generating automated recommendations.

Marketing automation platforms like HubSpot, Marketo, and Salesforce enable the launching of campaigns based on user behaviour and life cycle stages, integrated with CRM databases. Trigger-based communication will provide a direct response to the action performed by a customer in real time, for example, cart abandonment or product page views. In turn, integration with data analytics platforms such as Google Analytics or Tableau enables marketers to visualise performance in a cross-channel manner with attribution for the results to individual touchpoints [1].

Through the integration of big data analytics, firms have been able to make the shift from descriptive analysis (what has happened) to predictive analysis (what will happen) towards prescriptive analytics (what to do). This evolution has been at the core of dynamic pricing, prediction, customer lifetime value (CLV) forecasting, and content optimisation, and leaders in the organisation must explore this evolution irrespective of the numerous challenges [8].

8.2.3 Strategic Frameworks: Segmentation, Targeting, and Personalisation

Segmentation has always served as one of the primary pillars of marketing, with data, of course, adding sophistication and tangibility to its application. Behavioural and psychographic segmentation has replaced traditional demographic or firmographic segmentation techniques; these define micro-targets of niche customer segments [9]. Clustering algorithms are used on e-commerce sites to create lookalike audiences based on browsing behaviour, purchasing trajectories, and engagement metrics.

Effective targeting means offering the right product to the right segment with the right message, which is usually aided by predictive modelling and propensity scoring. Personalisation takes the invitations a step further by creating custom experiences for an individual. These could include email subject lines that are personalised to dynamic content on a website based on user profile information [10].

A classic example of large-scale personalisation would be Amazon's recommendation engine [11]. By predicting future purchases via a complex analysis of user behaviour across categories, time, and frequency, it then suggests items pertinent to the predicted purchase, thus enhancing average order values while retaining users. This ability is being increasingly adopted in areas such as streaming, finance, and digital health, in which real-time personalisation translates to user satisfaction and competitive differentiation.

8.2.4 Customer Journey Mapping and Experience Design

Customer journey mapping constitutes one of the most crucial applications of data in marketing strategy. It outlines the entire path from awareness to conversion to engagement after purchase, detailing different touchpoints for interaction. It is data-informed journey mapping that points out pain points, drop-off areas, and high-conversion triggers, hence helping marketing teams allocate resources effectively and determine a content strategy [10].

Leveraging advanced technologies makes it possible for marketers to analyse customer behaviour that transcends devices and channels. For example, a user might become aware of the brand through Instagram, then browse its website on a desktop, and finally purchase or redeem an offer through a mobile app. The seamless interconnection of these experiences guarantees omnichannel consistency, which is paramount to trustworthiness and coherence for users and brands alike.

Experience design that draws from journey data organises the micro-interactions (from the loading time of a button to the clarity of a message thanking for a purchase) that form an aggregated perception about an entity. Data could tell when a user has left, when they had doubts, or what would push them to convert. This is how organisations can now create experiences that are not just reactive but even foresightful [12].

8.2.5 Real-Time Decision Making and Predictive Analytics

Modern-day marketing relies heavily on data but is defined by speed and anticipation [13]. Real-time analytics are platforms that allow companies to act immediately on user signals, and this is vital in sectors such as e-commerce and fintech, where the scope of engagement is often in seconds. For example, if users hang on the pricing page or abandon their carts, automated interventions like chat pop-ups or discount offers could be initiated to pull back the conversion.

Predictive analytics helps a firm anticipate future customer actions based on patterns noted in past data. This covers churn prediction, propensity to purchase models, and the next-best-offer model. For example, Netflix uses its viewers' data to recommend shows and to decide which original content to produce depending on expected audience demand [4].

The use of machine-learning algorithms in predictive marketing centres on the training of models on labelled data, recognising distinct patterns, and determining actions. These models become adaptive with time, improving accuracy as they experience large volumes of data, thereby rendering personalised solutions scalable to campaign optimisation.

8.3 SOURCES AND TYPES OF MARKETING DATA

At the dawn of data-driven marketing, businesses are depending on an unprecedented range and quantity of sources and types of marketing data to help shape strategy, optimise customer interactions, and, perhaps most importantly, take them to the next level and begin to grow. The digital age has birthed a new era of data availability, enabling marketers' power to leverage anything from traditional demographic data to new and complex, behavioural, branding and sentiment analysis. There are many datasets that marketers use to derive insights, and it is important to know what they are and what they look like to use insights to impact your campaigns.

8.3.1 Primary Data Sources

Primary data contains primary facts, that is, the facts that are gathered directly from the horses' mouths to cater for the specific research needs of an organisation. This data can be gathered through conducting surveys, interviews, focus group discussions and observations, which are direct approaches that aid in deepening knowledge in consumers' behaviour, attitudes, and perceptions [14]. Finally, marketers can simply ask consumers what influencing and non-influencing factors influence their purchasing or non-purchasing behaviour.

For instance, one of the more well-known applications of raw data is product testing, where companies seek feedback for new concepts from potential users. This instant feedback can help develop the product, the way the product is packaged and the way the product is marketed, even before it is available to the larger market. It allows marketers to iterate on their products aggressively to meet consumer expectations because they get a direct line to consumers.

8.3.2 Secondary Data Sources

The second type of sources is often referred to as secondary data. This is computed using the data available from other sources. Secondary sources include market research reports, academic studies, government publications, and third-party analytical companies. The benefit of secondary data is that it is typically cheaper, involves less time, and can prove less difficult to obtain than primary data collection [15]. Marketers scan the landscape for trends and competition, and measure success in entering a target industry by consuming such data. Additionally, major sources of secondary data are offered on digital platforms and social sites, where data on consumer behaviour, attitudes, and brand discussions can be found.

8.4 BIG DATA AND ITS INTEGRATION

The advent of big data is a quantum leap in the possible consumer data accessible to marketers. Big data is a large dataset originating from multiple online and offline sources such as social media interactions, web clicks, transaction logs and sensor data. Companies can use big data for marketing research and to build consumer projections and predictions in real time, such as behavioural insights [16]. This understanding enables better targeting, allowing marketers to match consumer demands more closely to their campaigns.

With the ongoing ascendancy of AI technologies, organisations are increasingly using AI tools to crunch their big data. AI-based algorithms will allow marketers to find hidden patterns and relationships from very large data sets that would have been impossible to recognise with the naked eye, a development which will then foster more accurate targeting and segmentation methods. Such insights from a data perspective can be the backbone of marketing initiatives by informing and even setting the tone for a more aggressive approach to data-influenced marketing.

8.4.1 Emerging Data Sources

With the explosion of information in the digital age, new sources of data and analysis became available, including things like social media analytics and Internet-of-Things (IoT) devices [17]. Real-time data, such as trends, social media, and data aggregation sites, offer marketers immediate glimpses of consumer behaviour and preferences, helping them assess public sentiment and refine their strategies accordingly. New data sources applicable to labour market analysis can provide marketers with insights into emerging consumer trends and opportunities [18].

In addition, in the evolving e-commerce era, companies are using consumer-generated data such as that being generated by reviews, social media conversations, and online forums. Such user-generated insights can be informed by using this data to tailor and optimise innovative approaches to both product development and marketing that draw from the trends observed in actual consumer experiences with a company's offerings.

Therefore, knowing where and what types of data for marketing exist proves important for organisations developing a marketing strategy. With primary data, secondary data, analyses of big data, and new digital sources available, marketers can build campaigns that are in tune with consumer needs. The evolution of data standards would enable marketers to build more comprehensive customer insights, which could be critical to successful marketing strategies in the future.

8.5 DATA COLLECTION, INTEGRATION, AND MANAGEMENT

Data is collected by many organisations, and with all of this varied data stored, it must be integrated, managed, and used effectively for insights that translate into informed decisions and ultimately better customer interaction and satisfaction [19]. As digital channels proliferate and the volume of consumer data expands, the capacity to gather, analyse, and integrate actionable data has repercussions far beyond traditional marketing modes. Additionally, with a data-driven approach being fundamental to business performance and strategy, understanding the frameworks and methodologies for data collection and management for agencies and organisations to stay competitive is key for businesses looking to thrive in such a transforming market.

The most basic thing that needs to be addressed when collecting data is picking the right way to collect data. To accumulate thorough insights, organisations usually use a combination of qualitative and quantitative strategies. Data collection methods, such as surveys, interviews and observational techniques, are important [20]. This leads to a well-organised and sound marketing research process, as it is shown by a systematic review that utilises methodological pluralism, understanding would ensue on how to use multiple research methods for collecting the knowledge about the consumers and their preferences.

It should be noted that the information collected may be acquired with the assistance of automated devices and techniques that enable a person to save time and money. Automated data collection solutions offer organisations a way to collect the same information from multiple sources simultaneously, reducing the burden of manual data entry and analysis [21]. However, this approach is also dependent on the quality of raw data and the sufficiency of the representativeness of the sampling, for insights to be trustworthy.

Collecting the data is one thing, but integrating and managing that data is equally important and is critical when it comes to transforming that raw data into actionable insights. It becomes critical for organisations to have the best data management systems that manage the data at one location, from different sources, and provide the interpretation in one go. Working with data from different tools increases overall reliability for insights and allows organisations to take a holistic view of their marketing strategies [20]. By articulating the capacity to throw big data analytics on both of these types of insights, it shows how organisations will want to stay nimble and responsive to changing consumer demands.

Additionally, as organisations collect sensitive consumer information, it is critical to ensure the integrity and security of data during collection and management processes. From a consumer and privacy perspective, it is paramount to maintain data integrity with regard to personal data so that there is little to no risk of data breaches or misuse of information. Therefore, organisations should have clear policies, and appropriate methodologies should be put in place to guide how data is used, processed, and shared across the organisation [22]. Ethical practices should become a part of the data management background so that, in case of a data breach or sensitive data sharing, customers are aware of their data and hence develop a long-lasting relationship based on transparency and trust.

Sophisticated technologies like AI and ML can take data analysis to the next level. Using these technologies, organisations can identify patterns and insights that are not readily available through traditional analysis methods. An example of big data applications in portfolio management demonstrates AI optimisation in decision-making processes, resulting in superior marketing strategies and better resource allocation [23].

If collected, combined, and stewarded correctly, marketing data provides the ultimate design for developing successful strategies and communicating with people. The integration of both quantitative and qualitative approaches in optimised real-time automated processes, improving data quality with the use of advanced analytical methods, will allow companies to gain knowledge from data.

8.5.1 Analytics and Insights for Marketing Strategy

In a world that sees ongoing international and global market shifts, data is crucial to generate marketing tactics that align with what consumers want and need. The power of analytics is now put to use in a marketer's routine marketing activities, which enables organisations to know their customers better and customise offerings according to their customers. Marketers can utilise advanced analytics to understand how consumers behave, how to structure marketing campaigns and how to optimise business performance.

Among other reasons, one of the major benefits of using analytics in marketing is that it allows firms to find customer segments more efficiently. Through customer data such as demographics, purchase history, and online behaviour, marketers can create segments in which they want to serve audiences with the products or services that the company offers. Aligning consumer needs with marketing messaging represents a superior approach, as it is centred on stronger consumer interest and promotes increased loyalty to the brand [24]. By categorising consumers based on interest or behaviour, businesses can create more targeted campaigns with messages that are tailored to the specific wants and needs of particular consumer segments, driving improved engagement and conversion rates.

There is also the use of predictive analytics as a stronger tool for marketers to be able to anticipate consumer behaviours and market trends. This would enable businesses to anticipate any changes in consumer tastes and adjust their planning based on such changes via ML algorithms and statistical models. Data-driven approaches have become a dominant trend in the marketing field, as companies that adopt data-driven strategies achieve stronger customer engagement and higher returns on investment [25]. Taking an approach such as this means that a business is ahead of the game in knowing what is happening in their market and how their target consumer base is evolving. Active marketing strategies are also made possible by real-time analytics. It lets organisations monitor the performance of a campaign in real time, so that they can adjust on the fly with actual data. For example, if businesses are evaluating the effectiveness of their marketing channels, analytics can help show which channels give off the highest level of engagement [26]. This agility at scale means that marketers can pivot quickly based on changing market dynamics and customer feedback. This demonstrates that analytics and big data in marketing support smoother strategic decision-making and enable the development of personalised marketing approaches aligned with consumer preferences [27].

In addition, advanced analytics tools such as AI-enabled CRM enhance customer engagement initiatives [28]. These create agile organisations that synthesise data across a multitude of touchpoints to deliver personalised experiences and predictive customer service. Leveraging analytics not only increases the effectiveness of marketing campaigns but also enhances customer loyalty by predicting customers' needs based on past interactions [29]. These insights transform a basic customer journey into a more enriching one, leading to long-term associations between brands and consumers.

There is no doubt that analytics does work to a certain extent in marketing, but companies should also know that there are some challenges regarding the same, such as those relating to consumer privacy, as well as the attribution model that needs to be followed to ensure that the data which is processed is done properly by an experienced workforce. So, it is only when marketing teams adopt data literacy, along with ongoing training in advanced analytics, that marketers will unlock the full potential of analytics [30]. Data-focused companies can use insights without having their customers lose faith in them. But ultimately, analytics and insights have solidified themselves as a driving factor in shaping marketing strategy for organisations, giving them an edge in understanding consumer behaviour and maximising the effectiveness of their initiatives. This insight into analytics is not only vital but will serve as a significant driver for continued market success as brands navigate through their consumer engagement complexities.

8.6 PERSONALISATION AND CUSTOMER EXPERIENCE

The desire for personalisation in customer experience has been a popular term among marketers for several years now. It's this movement from broad, generic, "spray and pray" style advertising campaigns to increasingly relevant or customised communications to individuals that is starting to change the way brands market themselves to consumers. Due to huge technological advances and the usefulness of data analytics and AI, marketing has become a more personalised process from the viewpoint of marketers, allowing them to offer a better personalised experience to the customer.

Personalisation is the process of tailoring a message, content, or service to the preferences and behaviours of an individual. This is enabled due to the abundance of customer data, such as purchasing history, digital engagement habits, and demographic information. The experiential value generated by personalised marketing can lead to increased customer satisfaction and loyalty, which in turn contributes to greater profitability and positively impacts business performance [31]. The continued evolution of AI and ML technologies has changed the ways that brands can incorporate personalisation strategies into their business models, and these data-driven insights allow businesses to create more relevant and targeted marketing messaging, leading to much higher levels of customer engagement and Return on Investment (ROI) [25]. Such algorithms have the potential to harness the power of big data to interpret how consumer habits are affected, when marketers and researchers know what consumers not just currently want, but even before the consumer themselves are aware of it and hence tailor marketing strategies to align closely with consumer expectations. It is vital for organisations as well to be ahead of their competition and in an ever-paced and responsive world of business [32].

In industries such as beauty, lifestyle, and fashion, where the customer experience is highly important to shoppers, personalised content is especially crucial in creating brand loyalty. This emphasises the need for organisations to focus on delivering outstanding customer experiences that foster long-term relationships and loyalty [33, 34]. In this age of big data, the importance of gathering and analysing consumer insights cannot be overstated. Customised marketing plans based on an in-depth understanding of consumer behaviour can contribute to organisational success [35]. By employing data mining techniques to divide audiences and tailor marketing messages, organisations can create more focused marketing campaigns that resonate with specific customer groups. Brands that shift their emphasis from mass marketing to personal experiences will be in a position to benefit not only consumers but also take advantage of market opportunities [36].

However, it is crucial to note that personalisation should be done with caution, as there is a risk of unavoidable issues. This excessive use of personalisation or invasive marketing practices makes the user uncomfortable, which will automatically reduce the trust of the consumer. Achieving the right balance between delivering a personalised experience and protecting consumer privacy is crucial, as any damage to a brand's image can be irreparable [37].

8.7 CAMPAIGN PLANNING AND OPTIMISATION

The conduct of marketing campaign planning and optimisation processes is one of the key aspects of effective marketing strategies, as this aids an organisation to undertake targeted efforts that maximise impact and engagement. With the marketing landscape constantly evolving, it is crucial to utilise sophisticated strategies, such as data analytics, consumer insights, and cutting-edge technologies, to make campaign goals a reality.

Any successful marketing campaign is based on planning. By clearly establishing objectives and identifying target audiences, effective phases of campaign planning are created. To create campaigns that resonate, organisations need to know their consumers' needs, wants, and pain points [38]. Well-designed marketing campaigns recognise that customers engage across multiple channels along a continuous marketing journey; therefore, integrated online and offline approaches should be used to create a consistent and cohesive customer experience [39]. In the modern digital environment, this may include social media, email marketing, content marketing, and traditional advertising to effectively communicate with customers.

However, marketing campaigns require continuous tracking and modification to sustain their effectiveness. Firms need to establish key performance indicators (KPIs) that help them track progress and measure their results. Monitoring detailed performance metrics – such as CTRs, conversion rates, and levels of audience engagement – helps organisations identify potential areas for improvement and informs data-driven decision-making [40]. So, if a social media marketing campaign generates high engagement but low conversion rates, marketers will be able to assess the messaging or landing page experience to optimise the campaign and deliver even better performance.

Campaign optimisation also benefits significantly from predictive analytics. AI and ML algorithms can also analyse campaign data from the past, recognising patterns and predicting future performance for other marketers. It's also more specific in targeting and allocation of resources. Subsequent feedback loops are also important in the optimisation of the campaign. When it comes to real-time feedback, firms can get it very quickly by doing surveys or looking at engagement metrics. Feedback is a key mechanism for maintaining the relevance of the campaign and can help to be in tune with the needs of the audience, which, if achieved, can also have important consequences for the success of campaigns [41]. This helps contribute to a culture of innovation in stakeholder organisations, enabling them to flex more effectively in the economic market cycle. An idea campaign also should involve well-orchestrated efforts across other department levels, sales, service operations, and marketing [42]. This helps organisations leverage a solid understanding of consumer preferences, data-driven insight, and feedback-driven continuous improvement to up the ante of their campaigns for maximum effectiveness.

8.8 EMERGING TECHNOLOGIES AND TRENDS IN DATA-DRIVEN MARKETING STRATEGIES

From marketing techniques to data analysis, the advancement of technology has changed the face of marketing, with the new technologies paving the way for organisations to interact with the audience. Consequently, the future of marketing strategies will continue to involve granular and data science-based analysis of the consumers that can progressively offer personalised, more adapted, predictive, and influential communication and interaction with a certain targeted audience through innovative mediums such as AI, ML, and big data analytics. As they do, their success will hinge almost entirely on data, the most quantifiable asset of our time. Real-time analytics of consumer preference and behaviour is becoming affordable for a lot of organisations as advanced analytics is being used to mine data for insights [34]. AI and ML techniques provide actionable insights into consumer preferences and tendencies by enhancing marketing effectiveness [29]. This leads to a more forward-looking approach that adjusts marketing strategies based on live data, keeping organisations aligned to changing consumer expectations.

Moreover, the adoption of big data analytics in consumer segmentation and targeting is increasing. Li (2023) explains how organisations can sift through this data to identify custom segments that can tailor their marketing strategy to suit special needs and preferences, among others. This level of detail enables marketers to create campaigns that actually appeal to specific sectors or individuals, which makes for improved enthusiasm and conversion.

Another major trend that is driven by the ability to analyse consumers' online behaviours and preferences is personalised marketing, which laid the groundwork for marketers to tailor messages and recommendations to cater to individual customers, therefore enhancing the overall customer experience and satisfaction. Brands that take advantage of personalised marketing strategies are capable of generating significantly higher engagement, since individual communication makes consumers feel a bond with the company. The reason is that this dynamic cultivates loyalty and also yields a higher lifetime value of a customer, which is a crucial aspect of establishing and running a successful business [43].

One more trend quickly gaining momentum that is ending the status quo of consumer engagement is the integration of IoT tech into marketing strategies. As an illustration, using interactions in the connected environment based on Internet of Things (IoT) technology and data-driven marketing, brands can retrieve data on the consumer in real time based on consumer behaviour from embedded devices, resulting in better profiles of the consumer and integrated and contextually relevant experiences [44]. By combining these elements, marketers can create campaigns that respond to the specific needs of their audience, such as triggering an optimised version of a retargeting ad based on certain behaviours and preferences.

As businesses implement these systems to propel their marketing strategies into the future, ethical issues surrounding data privacy and consumer consent should be at the forefront. The increasing quantity of data being generated raises questions as to how this data is collected, stored, and used. Companies must be equipped with policies and practices that establish consumer privacy protection and compliance with relevant legislation [45]. This creates trust and credibility, and that is crucial in building and maintaining positive customer relationships in a world where security and privacy concerns reign [3].

Hence, the prospect of data-driven marketing strategies is associated with the introduction of smart technologies that assist businesses in utilising data more effectively to enhance customer interaction. AI, big data analytics, and IoT create levels of personalisation, segmentation, and dynamic interaction that all enhance marketing effectiveness and business results. By using these technologies responsibly, businesses can position themselves for success in an increasingly competitive landscape while building lasting connections with customers.

8.9 CHALLENGES, STRATEGIC CONSIDERATIONS, AND IMPLICATIONS OF DATA-DRIVEN MARKETING STRATEGIES

The first struggle of data-driven marketing is the difficulty in gathering and managing data. Companies, rather, struggle to keep up with the amount of data that can be processed and analysed to help them make better decisions. In addition, organisations must have deep systems for collecting, assimilating, and analysing data. Big data, AI, and digital marketing analytics play a critical role in enabling marketers to align consumer needs with marketing messaging, thereby increasing consumer interest and strengthening brand loyalty [24]. But translating this abundant information into action likely becomes difficult without the correct data management tools and frameworks in place.

Another issue in data-driven marketing is the quality and accuracy of data, which is a major challenge. Data is the foundation for making informed decisions; however, when data quality is poor, strategies can be misguided and resources wasted. Using predictive analytics to identify patterns in market tendencies and consumer behaviours involves extensive data cleansing and validation processes before marketing decisions can be made based on accurate insights [46]. To maximise the value they derive from analytics initiatives, organisations need to invest in full-circle data governance to tackle data accuracy and integrity issues and enhance them.

Ethics plays a very significant role in determining the way and processes of data shifting, which involves protecting data from the character of customers, who should be protected as well, to use them in marketing. As data breaches and the potential misuse of consumer information become increasingly concerning, organisations should amend their data collection practices to have more transparency while upholding regulations like the GDPR. Therefore, being able to find a middle ground between data-driven decision-making and moral boundaries is imperative, or else, as Li points out, brand reputation and trust can be diluted [47]. Ethical data usage, where consumers are informed about what data is being collected and how it is used, is now essential for organisations to build positive consumer relationships.

The other component is making sure marketing teams have the right skills to make data-led strategies work. For many organisations, a digital skills gap is still an obstacle; employees might not know how to interpret complex data sets and derive actionable insights, and in such a situation, even the most sophisticated solutions might fail. Enhancing employees' skills in data analytics and AI technologies is essential for organisations to effectively leverage data in their marketing activities [48]. Investing in outfit training and ongoing education programmes to close the skills gap will also help upskill their people to be able to leverage data-led insights into strategic decisions.

It is equally strategic and imperative in successfully executing data-driven tactics. It requires a culture of data literacy within the organisation, where one team collaborates with other departments to extract insights from data. If marketing teams do not align with data analysts, data-driven strategies may not be implemented effectively. Building cross-functional teams helps organisations develop more effective marketing strategies based on consumer insights while ensuring a holistic alignment between marketing goals and overall business objectives.

Parsing through the data complexities of marketing strategies poses a conundrum most organisations have yet to solve and carries significant implications for their operations and success. When data is used effectively, it helps brands understand consumers better to create targeted marketing campaigns that effectively reach their audience. Using the type of data that only proper ML can get, this focused effort leads to higher marketing ROI and increased sales growth. Akter et al. emphasise this by acknowledging that data-driven strategies give organisations the ability to utilise customer data for long-term competitive advantage in the global marketplace [49].

8.10 ETHICAL AND REGULATORY CONSIDERATIONS

As marketing increasingly makes use of consumer data, the ethical aspects of this practice raise important issues. The GDPR in the European Union and the CCPA in California have introduced stricter standards around consent, data access, transparency, and user rights. [6]. These new forms of regulation transform how organisations adopt, store, and use personal information.

Beyond compliance, ethical data governance has now taken on a brand imperative. Consumers have more awareness about their data rights and will take brands to task if they misuse their data or keep them in the dark about the status of their data. Some of these reputational costs range from algorithmic bias, dark patterns, and data breaches.

A fair treatment of data-driven marketing involves transparency, data minimisation, and informed consent. For example, the likes of Apple have made some show of public commitment to privacy in recent iOS updates, a move which has merely served to further destabilise the increasingly paranoid ecosystem in which surveillance capitalism operates.

Finally, marketers should also look into fairness and explainability, analysing the outputs of AI systems. The answer is no. Using data/datasets from the produced AI to train it may lead to erroneous classification and discrimination.

8.11 CONCLUSION

Data-driven marketing is the leading strategy to survive in the present marketing efforts for organisations to create dynamic engagements with consumers and continuously adapt to prevailing and rising market forces. By harnessing data analytics, they can build a rich view of their customers' behaviour, preferences, and trends, to deliver highly tailored marketing experiences that speak directly to their target consumers.

Data-driven approaches are being embraced by organisations around the world; however, ethics and privacy must be taken into consideration. Through transparent stewardship of data and consumer consent-driven practices, brands can strengthen trust as the reason to believe for long-lasting relationships.

The rapid pace of data technologies now also presents an opportunity for marketers to retool their approach. Real-time analytics, ML, and AI-driven insights for marketing are what will provide the necessary checks and balances to ensure that companies such as these stay on track and are ready and able to pivot as new trends are observed and changing consumer behaviours are exposed. Creating competitive advantage and increasing the likelihood of successful adaptation in a volatile marketplace are possible for a company that fosters a culture of data-informed decisions. Through the use of data-driven marketing, every organisation can evolve and create meaningful engagements that resonate with consumers, which can enable sustained growth in the fast-moving digital economy. Therefore, great organisations are those which apply data strategically to inform and mould marketing efforts, as analytics and insights progress through time.

REFERENCES

[1] Chaffey, D., & Ellis-Chadwick, F. (2019). *Digital marketing* (7th ed.). Pearson Education.

[2] Oyenuga, M. O., Ahungwa, A. I., & Onoja, E. (2021). Effect of brand equity on consumer behaviour among students of Veritas University, Nigeria: a study of Apple smartphones. *Marketing and Branding Research 8*, 48–64 https://doi.org/10.33844/mbr.2021.60329

[3] Rosário, A. T., & Dias, J. C. (2023). How has data-driven marketing evolved: challenges and opportunities with emerging technologies. *International Journal of Information Management Data Insights*, *3*(2), 100203. https://doi.org/10.1016/j.jjimei.2023.100203

[4] Davenport, T. H., Guha, A., Grewal, D., & Bressgott, T. (2020). How artificial intelligence will change the future of marketing. *Journal of the Academy of Marketing Science*, *48*(1), 24–42. https://doi.org/10.1007/s11747-019-00696-0

[5] Wedel, M., & Kannan, P. K. (2016). Marketing analytics for data-rich environments. *Journal of Marketing*, *80*(6), 97–121. https://doi.org/10.1509/jm.15.0413

[6] Martin, K. D., & Murphy, P. E. (2017). The role of data privacy in marketing. *Journal of the Academy of Marketing Science*, *45*, 135–155. https://doi.org/10.1007/s11747-016-0495-4

[7] Gabelaia, I. (2022). The applicability of artificial intelligence marketing for creating data-driven marketing strategies. *Journal of Marketing Research and Case Studies*, 2022, 466404.

[8] Jafar, S. H., Oyedele, O. M., Nawaah, D., & Bolanle, A. S. (2025). Exploring leadership challenges for adoption of digital innovation and sustainability, in Singh, R., Corvello, V., Coniglio, I. M., & Khan, S. (Ed.) *Innovation ecosystems and sustainable technologies (Emerald studies in sustainable innovation management)*, Emerald Publishing Limited, Leeds, pp. 253–269. https://doi.org/10.1108/978-1-83662-368-720251012

[9] Xu, K., Zhou, H., Zheng, H., Zhu, M., & Xin, Q. (2024). Intelligent classification and personalized recommendation of e-commerce products based on machine learning. arXiv (Cornell University). https://doi.org/10.48550/arxiv.2403.19345

[10] Lemon, K. N., & Verhoef, P. C. (2016). Understanding customer experience throughout the customer journey. *Journal of Marketing*, *80*(6), 69–96. https://doi.org/10.1509/jm.15.0420

[11] Zhang, Z. (2024). Market segmentation and personalized marketing strategy optimization driven by big data analysis. *Disruptive Human Resource Management: Proceedings of the 1st International Conference (ICDHRM 2024)*, Bhubaneswar, India. https://doi.org/10.3233/atde240434

[12] Alam, M. N., Turi, J. A., Bhuiyan, A. B., Kharusi, S. A., Oyenuga, M., Zulkifli, N., & Iqbal, J. (2024). Factors influencing intention for reusing virtual reality (VR) at theme parks: the mediating role of visitors' satisfaction. *Cogent Social Sciences*, *10*(1). https://doi.org/10.1080/23311886.2023.2298898

[13] Rosário, A. T., Cruz, R., Moniz, L., & Figueiredo, J. (2024). Introduction to data-driven marketing. In A. T. Rosário, R. Cruz, & L. Moniz (Eds.), *Data-driven marketing for strategic success* (pp. 1–36). IGI Global. https://doi.org/10.4018/979-8-3693-3455-3.ch001

[14] Oyenuga, M. O., Akhaine, M. E., & Omale, S. A. (2023). We need it: how digital marketing tactics influence the purchasing behaviour of Nigerian Millennials. *Konfrontasi Journal: Culture, Economy and Social Changes*, *10*(2), 91–105 https://doi.org/10.33258/konfrontasi2.v10i2.275

[15] Nunan, D., & Domenico, M. (2018). Rethinking the market research curriculum. *International Journal of Market Research*, *61*(1), 22–32. https://doi.org/10.1177/1470785318805294

[16] Shi, Z., Xia, J., & Wen, Z. (2022). Big data usage in marketing research. *Frontiers in Business Economics and Management*, *5*(3), 242–248. https://doi.org/10.54097/fbem.v5i3.2029

[17] Apata, A. O., Oyenuga, M. O., Abeoba, M., & Ugom, A. (2024). Internet of Things (IoT) solutions for smart transportation infrastructure and fleet management. *Journal of Propulsion Technology*, *45*(4), 1492–1505. https://propulsiontechjournal.com/index.php/journal/article/view/8325

[18] Harkness, T. (2021). The history of the data economy: part ii: analytics arrives. *Significance, 18*(4), 16–19. https://doi.org/10.1111/1740-9713.01547
[19] Oyenuga, M. O., & Fredrick, E. (2023). Managing product features and customer satisfaction via product development, product branding, and product packaging: evidence from CWAY table water. *Marketing and Branding Research, 10*(1), 28–44. https://doi.org/10.32038/mbr.2023.10.01.03
[20] Tawfik, G., Dila, K., Mohamed, M., Tam, D., Kien, N., Ahmed, A., ... & Huy, N. (2019). A step by step guide for conducting a systematic review and meta-analysis with simulation data. Tropical *Medicine and Health, 47*(1). https://doi.org/10.1186/s41182-019-0165-6
[21] Ali, S., Foreman, J., Capasso, A., Jones, A., Tozan, Y., & DiClemente, R. (2020). Social media as a recruitment platform for a nationwide online survey of covid-19 knowledge, beliefs, and practices in the United States: methodology and feasibility analysis. *BMC Medical Research Methodology, 20*(1). https://doi.org/10.1186/s12874-020-01011-0
[22] Risser, H., Morford, A., Fernandez, F., Moskowitz, K., Doheny, M., Yang, Y., ... & Lattie, E. (2024). Best practices for online and virtual data collection methods to ensure data integrity. *Translational Issues in Psychological Science, 10*(2), 150–161. https://doi.org/10.1037/tps0000410
[23] Odeyemi, O., Mhlongo, N., Nwankwo, E., Scholatica, U., & Okoye, C. (2024). Big data applications in portfolio management: a review of techniques and strategies. *International Journal of Science and Research Archive, 11*(1), 1984–1999. https://doi.org/10.30574/ijsra.2024.11.1.0268
[24] Mahi, R., Alam, F., & Hasan, M. (2024). Exploring the confluence of big data, artificial intelligence, and digital marketing analytics: a comprehensive review. *GMJ, 3*(3), 1–12.
[25] Hermayanto, R. (2023). Effective marketing strategies in business: trends and best practices in the digital age. *Jurnal Ad Ministrare, 10*(1), 61. https://doi.org/10.26858/ja.v10i1.45101
[26] Harrigan, P., & Hulbert, B. (2011). How can marketing academics serve marketing practice? the new marketing DNA as a model for marketing education. *Journal of Marketing Education, 33*(3), 253–272. https://doi.org/10.1177/0273475311420234
[27] Appiah, A. K. (2026). Quality assurance metrics and lean management interventions for reducing errors in high-volume hospital blood culture processing. *Magna Scientia Advanced Research and Reviews, 16*(2), 228–236. https://doi.org/10.30574/msarr.2026.16.2.0058
[28] Oyenuga, M. O., Andah, R. A., Marcus, G. O., & Agabi, A. U. (2019). Effects of customer relationship management on product innovation in Nigeria. A case study of xerox HS Nigeria Limited. *American Journal of Theoretical and Applied Business, 5*(4), 113–126. https://doi.org/10.11648/j.ajtab.20190504.15
[29] Johnson, O., Brown, W., & Wilson, G. (2024). Examining the impact of technology adoption on marketing strategies in retail. https://doi.org/10.20944/preprints202407.1215.v1
[30] Gnizy, I. (2020). Applying big data to guide firms' future industrial marketing strategies. *Journal of Business and Industrial Marketing, 35*(7), 1221–1235. https://doi.org/10.1108/jbim-06-2019-0318
[31] Shah, I., Rajper, Z., Ghumro, I., & Mahar, S. (2019). Experiential value mediates relationship between experiential marketing and customer satisfaction. *Sukkur IBA Journal of Management and Business, 5*(2), 45–61. https://doi.org/10.30537/sijmb.v5i2.315
[32] Παπουτσόγλου, M., Ampatzoglou, A., Mittas, N., & Angelis, L. (2019). Extracting knowledge from on-line sources for software engineering labor market: a mapping study. *IEEE Access, 7*, 157595–157613. https://doi.org/10.1109/access.2019.2949905

[33] Oyenuga, M. O., & Labiyi, O. (2024). Using marketing mix strategies to influence customer patronage in an indigenous restaurant. *Rowter Journal*. https://doi.org/10.33258/rowter.v3i1.1052

[34] Rosdiana, R., Arini, R., & Gomies, S. (2024). The role of content marketing and customer experience in increasing customer loyalty in the beauty industry in Jakarta. *WSSHS*, *2*(07), 1203–1211. https://doi.org/10.58812/wsshs.v2i07.1080

[35] Peng, Z. (2021). Application of mining algorithm in personalized internet marketing strategy in massive data environment. https://doi.org/10.21203/rs.3.rs-181097/v1

[36] Marcus, G. O., Oyenuga, M. O., & Ahungwa, A. I. (2020). Effects of sales promotion on consumer buying behaviour of food seasoning among Nigerian households: a case study of Nestle Maggi Naijapot. *Budapest International Research and Critics Institute Journal (BIRCIJournal)*, *3*(1), 134–139. https://doi.org/10.33258/birci.v3i1.724

[37] Hegiarto, A. & Sapitri, R. (2024). Implementation of personal selling and direct marketing in increasing sales turnover at agency centre HNI Cianjur. *International Journal of Education Social Studies and Management (IJESSM)*, *4*(2), 334–340. https://doi.org/10.52121/ijessm.v4i2.253

[38] Sharmila, E., Ramesh, V., Jayaprakash, R., Karthika, S., & Shankar, P. (2024). Effectiveness of 2 different campaigning methods in reaching the public: conventional pamphlet campaign vs social media campaign - a pilot study. *The Journal of Community Health Management*, *10*(4), 137–140. https://doi.org/10.18231/j.jchm.2023.031

[39] Kite, J., Chan, L., MacKay, K., Corbett, L., Reyes-Marcelino, G., Nguyen, B., . . . & Freeman, B. (2023). A model of social media effects in public health communication campaigns: systematic review. *Journal of Medical Internet Research*, *25*, e46345.

[40] Thomson, K., Hillier-Brown, F., Todd, A., McNamara, C., Huijts, T., & Bambra, C. (2018). The effects of public health policies on health inequalities in high-income countries: an umbrella review. *BMC Public Health*, *18*(1). https://doi.org/10.1186/s12889-018-5677-1

[41] Smidt, C. (2019). A uniter and a divider: American presidential campaigns and partisan perceptions of the national economy. *American Politics Research*, *48*(2), 329–340. https://doi.org/10.1177/1532673x19875712

[42] Ramesh, V., Jayaprakash, R., Karthika, S., & Shankar, P. (2023). Effectiveness of two different campaigning methods in reaching the public: conventional pamphlet campaign versus social media campaign: a pilot study. *International Journal of Community Medicine and Public Health*, *10* (11), 4411–4414. https://doi.org/10.18203/2394-6040.ijcmph20233486

[43] Joel, O., & Oguanobi, V. (2024). Data-driven strategies for business expansion: utilizing predictive analytics for enhanced profitability and opportunity identification. *International Journal of Frontiers in Engineering and Technology Research*, *6*(2), 071–081. https://doi.org/10.53294/ijfetr.2024.6.2.0035

[44] Zhou, T. (2023). Harnessing the power of social media marketing to boost e-marketplace performance: a paradigm shift. *Journal of Digitainability Realism & Mastery (Dream)*, *2*(04), 50–54. https://doi.org/10.56982/dream.v2i04.117

[45] Chowdhury, S. (2024). Navigating the challenges and opportunities of digital marketing adoption in the multinational FMCG sector. https://doi.org/10.20944/preprints202407.0948.v1

[46] Rolando, B., & Mulyono, H. (2024). Unlocking the power of data: effective data-driven marketing strategies to engage millennial consumers. *Transekonomika Akuntansi Bisnis Dan Keuangan*, *4*(3), 303–321. https://doi.org/10.55047/transekonomika.v4i3.662

[47] Li, L. (2023). The transformation of international marketing strategy under the background of big data. *Advances in Economics Management and Political Sciences*, *37*(1), 107–111. https://doi.org/10.54254/2754-1169/37/20231848

[48] Su, Y., Backlund, P., Engström, H., & Strand, M. (2021). Data-driven method for mobile game publishing marketing promotion. *2021 IEEE International Conference on e-Business Engineering (ICEBE)*, pp. 35–42. https://doi.org/10.1109/icebe52470.2021.00016

[49] Pandey, N., Nayal, P., & Rathore, A. (2020). Digital marketing for b2b organizations: structured literature review and future research directions. *Journal of Business and Industrial Marketing*, *35*(7), 1191–1204. https://doi.org/10.1108/jbim-06-2019-0283

9 The AI Gold Rush
Transforming Finance across the Globe and in India

Mushtaq Ahmad Shah

9.1 INTRODUCTION

The use of Artificial Intelligence (AI) is no longer a futuristic idea but a robust technological tool that is already transforming the financial services ecosystem in the modern world [1]. Currently estimated at US$35 billion in financial services in 2023, spending on AI is expected to almost triple to US$97 billion by 2027 across industry verticals such as banking, insurance, capital markets, and payment processing. Financial services companies are the highest AI system investors; the technology has the potential of automating up to 39% of customer-facing activities in banks and 33–37% in capital markets and insurance using large language models (LLMs) and other generative AI systems [2]. The Indian context is also significant. The Reserve Bank of India (RBI) and NASSCOM claim that the country's fintech hub has been significantly pushed onto a path by AI. The innovation and investment have seen massive growth, making India one of the top three fintech ecosystems in the world. The Indian financial sector is rapidly entering into the use of AI-based solutions (Figure 9.1) for credit scoring, detection of fraud, personalized customer interaction, and adherence to regulatory requirements.

Indian banks and non-banking financial companies are using and exploring AI tools to improve their business efficiency, lower non-performing assets, and provide ultra-personalized services to their customers. India AI and the downloadable regulation sandpile of the RBI still serve as further evidence of the desire of the country to emerge with a strong and accessible financial system with the base of AI. This is being employed broadly in front-end and back-end applications, including chatbots and robo-advisors, underwriting systems, compliance systems, and fraud-prevention systems. AI agents and Retrieval-Augmented Generation (RAG) models are currently being tested to provide real-time analysis and risk assessments, and new technology (such as quantum computing) may enable drastic increases in fraud detection and high-frequency trading. With the mounting access privileges that AI systems have to sensitive financial information, data privacy and algorithmic bias, cybersecurity, and deepfake fraud risks have become the principal concerns [3].

According to the World Economic Forum's Global Risk Report 2024, "misinformation and disinformation," largely driven by AI, is now ranked as the most severe short-term global risk, surpassing even geopolitical conflicts and climate events.

DOI: 10.1201/9781003650775-9

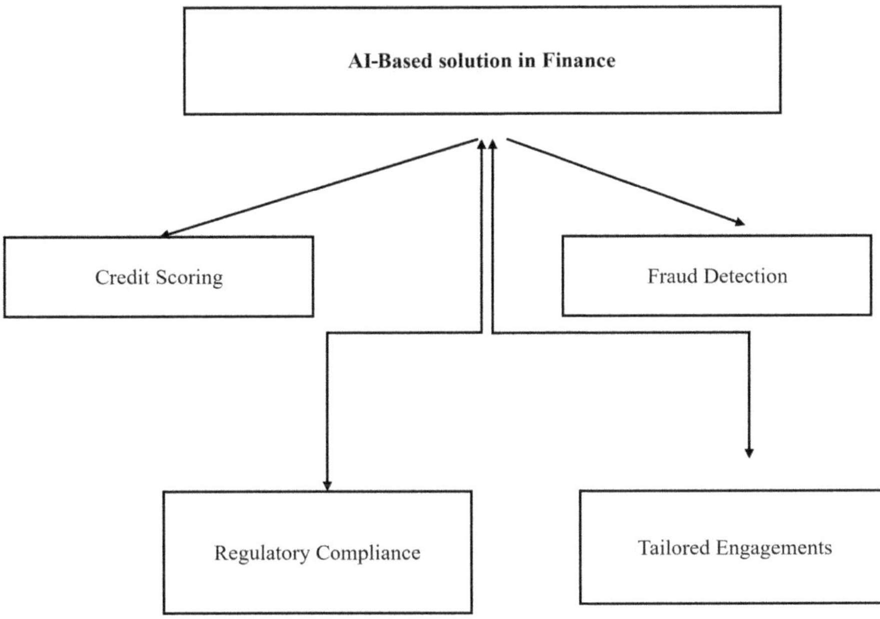

FIGURE 9.1 AI use in financial system.

(Source: Author.)

Additionally, AI's opaque decision-making (often referred to as the "black box" problem) challenges regulatory oversight, especially in developing economies like India, where digital literacy and data governance are still maturing [4]. Moreover, as the financial sector undergoes this AI-driven shift, the impact on employment, reskilling, and organizational culture cannot be ignored. A recent Accenture survey reported that 90% of financial services leaders believe their organizations need to undergo significant talent transformation to align with AI strategies.

9.1.1 Growing Role of Artificial Intelligence

AI is swiftly transforming the financial services industry across the world, which is now acting as a center in all areas of operation, customer interaction, and risk mitigation. As the world investment in AI in banking is expected to rise over US$97 billion by 2027, AI integration will change the way of identifying fraud, credit scoring, and personalized financial services. Speedy AI adoption is being made possible by the thorough digital infrastructure and regulatory policies in India involving the sandbox in RBI and the India AI mission. But this giga-step in technology does not come without complicated challenges, such as the risks to privacy of data, algorithmic opacity, the risk of cyberattacks, and certain ethical considerations. Innovation and accountable governance should coexist in a financially oriented sector where trust and transparency prevail. The global regulatory landscape remains fragmented, with differing approaches across the European Union (EU AI Act), the United States (AI Executive Order), and regional frameworks such as those by the Monetary Authority of Singapore (MAS). In India, while the Digital Personal Data Protection Act, 2023, marks progress, comprehensive AI regulation specifically for the financial sector remains in its infancy. Against this backdrop, this chapter aims to offer a comprehensive exploration of the opportunities, risks, and regulatory challenges associated with AI in financial services. It analyses global trends, examines India's trajectory in AI adoption, and proposes a roadmap for responsible AI integration that safeguards systemic stability, consumer trust, and inclusive innovation.

9.2 REVIEW OF LITERATURE

The use of AI tools such as Robotic Process Automation (RPA), intelligent Software as a Service (iSaaS), and AI bots in core banking operations is under consideration [5]. Sharma and Gupta [5] point out that customer service, loan processing, and fraud detection are the areas most significantly improved through AI. Reference [6] presents a bibliometric investigation of fintech applications in banking from 2016 to 2022, focusing on AI, Machine Learning (ML), and blockchain technologies. Their findings point to the increased academic production after 2019 and indicate the supremacy of research by China and the USA, especially in the digital payment and crowdfunding circles. Reference [7] evaluates the compatibility between AI and Islamic finance using expert opinions collected from 12 countries. They come to a conclusion that there is a strong possibility that AI can contribute to the use of Islamic banking principles, especially in such spheres as risk assessment and profiling of customers without undermining Shariah compliance. This finding is further supported by [8], who mapped the evolution of AI research in Islamic banking using the VOSviewer tool, noting that the number of research articles produced by Southeast Asian and Gulf nations is steadily increasing. AI is causing a huge revolution in the field of finance as it provides not only brand-new opportunities but also intricate problems.

Reference [9] state that AI is rescripting the paradigms, services, and models in FinTech by including advanced ML into economy and financial systems to design smarter and more personalized financial mechanics. As financial systems became more dependent on such technologies, the demand for transparency has become a necessity, as [10] points to explainable AI (XAI) methods such as Shapley values as the key to trust and compliance with regulations. When it comes to personal finance, reference [11] discusses the transformative impact of AI-assisted budgeting applications and robo-advisors on personal financial planning and decision-making, whereas reference [12] argues that AI-based algorithms may introduce bias and therefore require strong governance frameworks to ensure fair and sustainable implementation. All these studies discussed above prove that AI will revolutionize the field of finance both on the institutional and individual level, but its success will have to be supported by the principles of transparency, fairness, and considerate integration. The analysis offered in this literature review shows how interesting the idea of introducing AI into mainstream and Islamic banking, fintech, and model governance is, and predicts the advent of clearer, more efficient, and inclusive financial frameworks in the future.

9.3 GLOBAL TRENDS IN AI IN FINANCE

The worldwide financial services sector is experiencing a tectonic shift driven by the blistering pace of business innovation, hybridization, and convergence of AI, more so generative AI and ML. The spread of AI in financial institutions around the world continues to grow in abundance to make operations more efficient, cut overhead costs, offer the best decisions, and hyper-personalization of customer experiences. Financial services are one of the most AI-intensive sectors in the world; as per industry estimations, spending on AI in financial services reached $35 billion in 2023 and is expected to rise to $97 billion consumption in 2027. Small applications of AI are currently being deployed in capital markets and insurance, and in payments and retail banking to automate processes, manage risk, and get a competitive edge.

The Global AI in Finance Market is experiencing substantial growth, as evidenced by projections from 2023 to 2033. The market, which stood at $12.4 billion in 2023, is forecasted to reach $73.6 billion by 2033, demonstrating a robust compound annual growth rate of 19.5% (Table 9.1).

This growth is prompted by both the component of the Solution and the component of the Service, and the former one always takes the bigger chunk of the market, which points toward the high level of demand for AI-enabled platforms and software in the financial market. Although the segment of the Solution has a leading position in terms of its absolute size, the fact of the "Service" segment growth reflects the necessity for professional help in the stages of AI technologies implementation and maintenance. All these tendencies point to the importance and the long-lasting AI adoption in the financial sphere, as the technological breakthroughs, as well as the supportive construction, contribute to the further evolution of this environment. The facts and figures are more probably found in a market research report conducted by Market.us, and reveal the enticing outlook of the use of AI in finance in the following

TABLE 9.1
Global AI in Finance Market for Each Year from 2023 to 2033

Year	Solution (USD Billion)	Service (USD Billion)	Total Market Size (USD Billion)
2023	8.5	3.9	12.4
2024	10.1	4.7	14.8
2025	12.2	5.5	17.7
2026	14.6	6.6	21.2
2027	17.4	7.9	25.3
2028	20.8	9.4	30.2
2029	24.9	11.2	36.1
2030	29.8	13.4	43.2
2031	35.7	15.9	51.6
2032	42.8	18.8	61.6
2033	51.5	22.1	73.6

Source: Author.

decade. Another revolutionary trend is the acceptance of LLMs, and they represent a new era of generative AI features. Such models, which process unstructured data and provide human-like responses, are transforming different financial processes. They are being deployed to automate the customer service processes, produce financial reports, drive robo-advisors, and even help in creating dynamic portfolio management. Banks and insurers use LLMs to create an analysis of large data, detect market trends, and provide client queries in real-time, streamlining operations and simultaneously improving service quality [13]. Although developers were entirely preoccupied with the efficiency and cost-cutting potential of first-wave applications of AI in finance, the financial institutions across the world today are shifting their focus to revenue generation and product innovation. About 7 in 10 executives in the world in the financial industry reckon that AI will play a direct role in increasing revenues in the next several years. GenAI is making it possible to build new products on underserved market segments, including mass-affluent customers, and generate new revenues based on predictive analytics, customized lending propositions, and real-time investment information. This is a transformation of process mechanization to strategic differentiation. At the same time, the stack of AI technology itself is changing. Financial companies are already relying on small language models (SLMs) controlled in specific tasks, AI agents that can make decisions independently, and even investigate the way to incorporate quantum computing to accelerate high-frequency trade and detect fraud. The technologies are increasing the capacity of the sector to handle the data-intensive operations in a quicker and more accurate way, redefining the global finance competition.

AI is transforming the financial workforce of the world as well. Instead of causing mass layoff, AI is changing occupations and professional skills. There are new roles like AI auditors, prompt engineers, data governance experts, and so on. Also, the traditional roles are changing to collaborate with an intelligent system. The leaders in the financial sector around the world 90% as revealed by an Accenture survey feel that their organizations need to redesign reskilling and talent strategy to keep in line with the future of work precipitated by AI. Synchronous with the opportunities are the risks, which are increasing. The advent of synthetic media and deepfake technologies has brought into question cybersecurity in areas that have high stakes, such as the finance sector. There is an increase in AI-assisted fraud, scams, and misinformation, which forces companies to consider investing in powerful detection tools, real-time detection, and digital forensics. With misinformation spurred by AI now the greatest short-term global risk, as established in the Global Risk Report 2024 published by the World Economic Forum, the risks associated with geopolitical threats and environmental threats have taken a back seat. Finally, open innovation and collaboration are gaining more and more ground in financial institutions. The collaboration between banks, fintech, Big Tech, and regulatory bodies aims at the speedy advance toward AI, protocol standardization, and best practices sharing. This group action is resulting in an increased pace of innovation and also reducing fragmentation and risk.

To sum up, the field of fintech is experiencing a new era of change – with intelligence, speed, personalization, and complexity. Such are the enormous advantages, but leaving them without some form of ethical governance, accountable innovation, and international harmonization of regulation would be irrational and imprudent when it comes to sustainable development.

9.4 RISKS AND CHALLENGES OF AI IN FINANCE

Although the ever-increasing pace and the introduction of AI in the financial industry is already bringing about tangible improvements in efficiency and innovation, it also provides a highly complicated assemblage of threats and concerns that are likely to become a threat to the sector in the event they are not dealt with in a significant manner. With the more widespread use of AI-based systems in central financial functions, which are used to handle everything, including fraud analysis and credit scoring, customer support, and algorithm trading, the consequences of failure, bias, or malevolence become exacerbated. These risks do not only exist theoretically, but they have already started manifesting themselves in institutions around the world.

An algorithm bias is one of the most urgent issues. The fact that an AI model is trained with historical or incomplete data sets does suggest that it might reinstate and enhance the already existing socio-economic inequalities. Within the scope of lending, e.g., the AI-based credit scoring mechanisms can have a systematic bias against members of certain demographics and can automatically fail to approve their loans or suggest unfavorable terms. The results are sometimes challenging to comprehend or dispute because many of these types of models are black-box, i.e., have hidden steps of decision-making within. This inability to be transparent may destroy trust and bring up grave ethical and legal dilemmas, especially in regulated settings where justice and responsibility prevail. This is closely connected with the problem of data privacy and security. The AI systems need enormous amounts of data to operate efficiently, which usually toys with sensitive information regarding finances and personal details. That poses a twofold threat: on the one hand, it is possible to breach consumer data and in large numbers due to potential data breaches or even cyberattacks; on the other hand, weak data governance practices can result in unwarranted surveillance, profiling, or even discriminatory treatment. This risk has been further increased with the advent of generative AI since it is much easier to produce deepfakes, synthetic identities, and even fraudulent documents, which can be utilized by ill actors to abuse the loopholes that are present in the financial system. As an example, a worker in the finance department of one of the largest corporations in the world recently wired 25 million dollars after being tricked by a deepfake video showing his boss as the CFO of this corporation – this is one of the most obvious examples of how dangerous and advanced such attacks may become.

The second very important problem is the issue of distortion and disinformation, which was found by the World Economic Forum as the leading short-time global risk in 2024. In financial markets, AI can be used to create false information that will create market manipulation, panic selling, or reputational damage. The AI models themselves are not error-free, and they are prone to hallucinating data, offering inaccurate or outdated suggestions, as well as interpreting inputs in a manner that the algorithms were not intended to do. Such mistakes in situations where stakes are high, e.g., in trading or when acting as a financial advisor, may lead to huge financial losses, breach of regulations, or legal implications. Besides, AI-generated content, when it is impossible to differentiate between such production and the work of humans, also generates problems with checking the validity of the information available, which only complicates the process of making decisions within the financial field. Operationally, excessive and blind faith in AI systems may result in systemic risks when no one oversees these systems. Automation carried out too vigorously by financial institutions could indirectly weaken inter-checks and balances. Should AI systems go down or become corrupted, whole lines of operations, including processing of transactions or customer services, may be disrupted. This risk is particularly important in those institutions that have to work in the jurisdiction where digital maturity or IT infrastructure is weak, which is why the fallback schemes are barely designed or not established at all. Also, a concern of vendor dependence and third-party risk is increasingly on the rise, especially as most financial institutions outsource their AI parts to third-party providers. Regulatory compliance, transparency, and resilience along complex supply chains are proving to be a harder task. The regulatory environment is yet another challenge. Although the global world, including the European Union (via its AI Act), the United States, and Singapore, has tried to establish regulatory systems, the world lacks unanimity regarding the regulation of AI in the finance sector. Such variance is a point of confusion and uncertainty, especially for cross-border financial entities that have to meet various legal requirements. In India, the RBI and other regulators have already taken some promising first steps, such as regulatory sandbox and data protection regulations, but the path ahead is a long one in relation to AI-specific regulation, ethical standards, and risk classification models that are specific to the Indian socio-economic environment.

Finally, the problem of transformation of the workforce cannot be overlooked. Since AI is reducing the manual effort in more and more tasks, there is also an escalating fear of displacement of work, disproportionate skills, and duplicative work. In case AI is mathematics and treating new opportunities, there will always be a need to fill in new roles with highly advanced knowledge, which cannot be found among the existing employees, including AI governance, compliance analytics, and prompt engineering. Without proper planning, reskilling and change management planning can eventually culminate in cases of employee resistance, talent loss in organizations, and lack of organizational culture. The inclusion of talent development, conscientious AI awareness, and inclusive innovation, therefore, should be some of the possible ways of behavior taken on board by leaders to improve their digital transformation plans.

9.5 INDIA-SPECIFIC TRENDS IN AI IN FINANCE

India is fast developing as a key player in the world financial technology system, and the UK is quickly catching up on the use of AI in its financial system. As an emerging market with an expanding fintech ecosystem that is worth $50 billion and a high extent of smartphone penetration, as well as a younger generation of web-savvy minds, India is an ideal place to adopt AI. Spreading all the way through the financial institutions, starting with nationalized state banks and working its way up to small fintech startups, AI is finding its uses in the country in increasing the experiences of its customers as well as the way it handles its operations and moves toward a more financially secure sector (Figure 9.2). India is one of the three largest fintech ecosystems in the world, with more than 2,100 fintech startups, with many companies developing AI-based financial services and products, according to a report

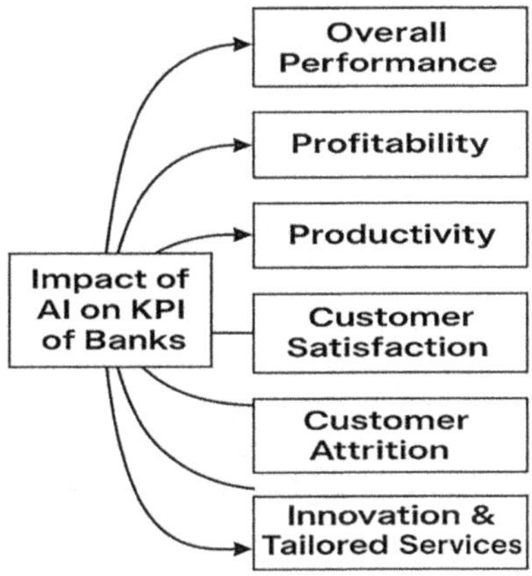

FIGURE 9.2 Impact of AI on banks.

(Source: Author.)

released by NASSCOM. One of the reasons behind this growth is the digital public infrastructure of India, especially the popularity of the Unified Payments Interface (UPI), Aadhaar-based eKYC, and the India stack. Such platforms have established a powerful base for large-scale application of AI. AI is also extensively used in digital lending platforms to enable real-time credit decisions based on alternative data sources such as mobile usage, utility bill payments, and social media footprints. Through this, fintech companies and non-banking financial corporations (NBFCs) have been in a position to provide microloans and credit lines to the underserved and rural communities, thus enhancing financial inclusion.

The banking system is becoming one of the spheres where AI is also applied extensively; banks, including governmental ones, use AI to detect and prevent fraud, model risk, and provide customers with chatbots, as well as ensure compliance with regulations (Figure 9.2). In India, major banks such as HDFC, ICICI, SBI, and Axis Bank have introduced intelligent digital assistants powered by AI, which can be used to find answers to thousands of questions raised by customers, which increase service efficiency and scales accordingly. Meanwhile, the AI is used in the back end, such as to monitor transactions, verify documents, KYC (Know Your Customer), and AML (Anti-Money Laundering) compliance, which has resulted in cost savings and operational resilience.

The second notable trend is that Indian regulatory authorities actively contribute to the implementation of responsible AI. The RBI has developed AI and ML regulatory sandboxes focused on financial services, allowing tentative experiments with new technologies. Simultaneously, the Digital Personal Data Protection Act, 2023, has also been established as the foundation of controlling the privacy of data, which is an essential requirement in the ethical use of AI. Moreover, the Securities and Exchange Board of India (SEBI) has prompted players in the market to look at the possibility of AI-based solutions in trade monitoring and market prediction.

The regulatory trends point to the increasing acceptance of the potential of AI and the readiness to contribute to its safe and inclusive integration.

The use of AI in reshaping the process of customer acquisition, underwriting, and portfolio management capabilities is also evident in India due to the emergence of Insurtech and WealthTech platforms. Companies such as Policybazaar, Zerodha, and Groww have introduced AI to personalize insurance advisory, automate claims, and create algorithm-based investment advice. More so, in the world of payments and wallets (Paytm and PhonePe) that receive billions of real-time transactions across India, AI is being instrumental in payment gateway and wallet fraud analytics.

Nonetheless, there are also peculiar issues arising in the Indian context. Poor quality of data, infrastructural constraints, poor digital literacy, and linguistic diversity within specific regions are formidable factors that hinder the blooming of AI. As Tier 1 cities are rapidly being digitized, financial institutions in rural and semi-urban regions are struggling to implement AI tools because of the interfering nature of internet connectivity, small dataset, and resistance to culture. Also, most companies urgently need specialized professionals in the field of AI ethics, data science, and XAI, as those would play a vital role in scrupulous and fair use of AI in the monetary world.

Nevertheless, India is disciplined in its mission of becoming a hub of AI in the global market. The IndiaAI mission launched by the government, in collaboration with the Ministry of Electronics and Information Technology (MeitY), aims to advance a nationwide AI ecosystem. Multiple Indian higher educational establishments and research organizations also collaborate with banks and fintech companies to create locally specific AI models that could operate within the complicated Indian market.

9.6 FUTURE OUTLOOK AND POLICY RECOMMENDATIONS

With the development of AI, the future of finance will become more standardized through the successful and responsible inclusion of AI technologies in business models, regulatory systems, and customer systems. World over, AI is likely to make preparations to move to a highly combined interceptive and intelligent application with partial autonomy to make dynamic decisions. Within the financial sector, the shift will transform fundamental operations – not only real-time risk management/predictive analytics but also conversational banking and decentralized finance (DeFi) advice – along the way. Within the next ten years, there is a good chance that AI will not only be built into operational processes but also into strategic decisions made, governance at the boardroom level, and in public financial systems.

In India, AI can truly transform the lives of Indians by virtue of converging with the digital public infrastructure in the country and the growing ecosystem of fintech. Nevertheless, the key that opens this potential in a sustainable way is the necessity of a forward-looking and humanistic approach of both private and public stakeholders. The emergence of GenAI, AI agents, and quantum-enabled technologies necessitates dynamic interoperable frameworks to scale with the newer technologies. This is a positive direction in which India is taking initiatives, with investments being made ever since in the area of AI R&D and recent developments of AI-hubs and

AI-centered skilling programs under the IndiaAI mission. However, the problem is how to translate pilot projects to large-scale, real-life impact and guarantee equity, transparency, and accountability.

To this effect, various policy recommendations can be made to the financial institutions, regulators, and government institutions at the global and Indian levels. To begin with, what is pressing is the need to develop clear regulatory frameworks that are specific to AI in the finance sector. They ought to cover algorithmic responsibility and interpretation, oversight and integrity, innovation by means of regulatory sandboxes and controlled experimentation. Since finance is cross-border, there needs to be a global cooperation of regulators, like those that existed in Basel Committee or G20, to harmonize regulations, especially on model risk management, sovereignty of data, and cybersecurity. No less importance should be given to the data infrastructure and quality. High-performance AI depends on structured, representative, and well-governed data.

In India, a lack of coherent data could be fragmented or skewed toward the urbanized due to socio-economic inequality, and, thus, financial support of quality data custodianship and data partnerships between the government and businesses is vital. Efforts like the National Data Governance Framework Policy need to be put into action in order to develop secure, anonymized, and freely accessible data ecosystems in which AI innovation can be made. Additionally, it is necessary to educate people about AI so that they endear it to them. The trust gap between consumers and the institutions can be closed with the help of outreach programs explaining the use of AI in financial products, mitigating fears of surveillance or discrimination, and insisting on the right to personal data protection. In India, community-based and vernacular-language educational campaigns can play a significant role in improving digital and financial literacy for AI-based services.

9.7 CONCLUSION

The use of AI in the financial services industry is a turning point in the history of finance in the world. AI is no longer an exotic add-on; it is emerging as a central enabler of strategic change, operational effectiveness, and customer experience personalization. Financial institutions are investing demographically in AI systems to boost competitive predictive analytics and automation of advanced processes and to discover new sources of revenue worldwide. The underrated digital public infrastructure, the promoting atmosphere of fintech in India, and regulatory openness to experimentation and innovation are quickening this change in India. All these global and local trends are intertwining to position a future environment in which AI is used to carry out and redefine the way financial services are designed, delivered, and regulated.

Nevertheless, with the maturity of the technology and deeper technological application in crucial financial processes comes another parallel set of perils of the more complex risks. The aspects of algorithmic biases, black box decision-making, deepfake scam, data privacy, and job replacement are critical problems for developed and developing economies. These risks are more evident in such industry domains as financial services, where trust, transparency, and stability are pillars. The unregulated use of AI would only heighten the system's weaknesses, push people away, and enlarge disparities in gaining access to financial services. In the future, not only is technological prowess going to determine the success of AI in finance, but institutional accountability and shared governance are going to be key factors. It is incumbent on policymakers to act with haste to put in place adaptive risk-sensitive policies that will enhance innovation and guard the interests of the people. It is necessary that financial institutions have a strategy with responsible AI practices in addition to fairness, accountability, and transparency. Meanwhile, governments and players within the industry should collaborate to create inclusive data ecosystems, reskill workers, and create confidence among the population in AI-powered systems. It is still a chance to be a leading example in the area of ethical, inclusive, and scalable AI innovation in India that fits its socio-economic realities. The world needs to embrace a common goal of AI, the one that fosters efficiency with justice, growth with regulation, and innovation with fairness. In such a way, AI will be not only a technological disruptor but also an ecosystem enabler of the more resilient, transparent, and inclusive financial future.

REFERENCES

[1] H. Arslanian and F. Fischer, *The Future of Finance: The Impact of FinTech, AI, and Crypto on Financial Services*. 2019. doi:10.1007/978-3-030-14533-0

[2] S. S. Dubey, V. Astvansh, and P. K. Kopalle, "Generative AI Solutions to Empower Financial Firms," Dec. 10, 2024, *Social Science Research Network, Rochester, NY*: 5050951. doi:10.2139/ssrn.5050951

[3] M. A. Shah and F. Uddin, "Exploring Security and Privacy Challenges for Banks in the Evolving Landscape of the Metaverse," in *Metaverse Security Paradigms*, IGI Global Scientific Publishing, 2024, pp. 280–303. doi:10.4018/979-8-3693-3824-7.ch011

[4] M. A. Shah, "The Impact of FinTech on Entrepreneurial Intentions Among Young Indian Entrepreneurs Using Crowdfunding, Blockchain, and Mobile Payments," in *Models, Strategies, and Tools for Competitive SMEs*, IGI Global Scientific Publishing, 2025, pp. 325–340. doi:10.4018/979-8-3693-4046-2.ch015

[5] A. Srivastava and A. Kumar, "Reshaping Banking with Digital Technologies," in *Fintech and Cryptocurrency*, 2023, pp. 35–57. doi:10.1002/9781119905028.ch3

[6] M. A. Chowdhury, M. Sahabuddin, M. U. Miyan, M. Sozon, and M. T. Miah, "Assessing the Evolution of Fintech Adoption in Traditional Banking: A Bibliometric Analysis Using R," *J. Manag. Econ. Stud.*, vol. 5, no. 3, Art. no. 3, Dec. 2023, doi:10.26677/TR1010.2023.1349

[7] K. Abbas and M. Hafeez, "Will Artificial Intelligence Rejuvenate Islamic Finance? A Version of World Academia," *Hitit İlahiyat Derg.*, vol. 20, no. 3, Art. no. 3, Dec. 2021, doi:10.14395/hid.931401

[8] R. B. Abdallah, T. Brahimi, Y. Essafi, and R. B. Abdallah, "Analysis and Visualization of Scientific Research on Islamic Banking and Artificial Intelligence," Dec. 06, 2022, *Preprints*: 2022110554. doi:10.20944/preprints202211.0554.v2

[9] Y. Cao and J. Zhai, "A Survey of AI in Finance," *J. Chin. Econ. Bus. Stud.*, vol. 20, no. 2, pp. 125–137, Apr. 2022, doi:10.1080/14765284.2022.2077632

[10] B. Quinn, "Explaining AI in Finance: Past, Present, Prospects," Jun. 05, 2023, *arXiv*: arXiv:2306.02773. doi:10.48550/arXiv.2306.02773

[11] A. Fauzi, "AI Unleashed Transforming Personal Finance with Artificial Intelligence," Apr. 07, 2024, Social Science Research Network, Rochester, NY: 4884500. doi:10.2139/ssrn.4884500
[12] D. K. Riyazahmed, "Algorithmic Trading Models, Aversion, and the Indian Scenario," Apr. 05, 2024, Social Science Research Network, Rochester, NY: 4817578. Accessed: Jul. 11, 2025. [Online]. Available: https://papers.ssrn.com/abstract=4817578
[13] S. Bhoyar, P. Bhoyar, and M. Shah, "A Machine Learning-Based Predictive Approach in Evaluating Consumer Behavior," *J. Stat. Manag. Syst.*, vol. 26, pp. 1955–1963, Jan. 2023, doi:10.47974/JSMS-1131

10 Unveiling Emotional Intelligence

The Key to Entrepreneurial Success in a Tech-Driven Global Market

Sarita Peddi and Geetha Manoharan

10.1 INTRODUCTION

Entrepreneurs are dealing with a hybrid landscape of rapid technological progress and changing customer habits in a continuously interdependent world economy. Triumph in such a scenario relies on the marriage of Emotional Intelligence (EI) and Artificial Intelligence (AI), which holds great promise for improved decision-making as well as marketing effectiveness.

10.1.1 Emotional Intelligence

EI is the capacity to empathize with others and recognize one's own and other people's feelings and manage emotions [1]. EI is a primary ability with five key domains: self-awareness, self-regulation, motivation, empathy, and interpersonal skills. In more recent times, research has shown that EI can affect organizational relationships and leadership actions significantly [2]. The higher EI leaders would be more apt to establish stronger, more conducive organizational environments, facilitating creativity, energy, and cooperation. EI allows for a deeper connection with team members and consumers, thus yielding better organizational performance overall. Emotional intelligence plays a significant role in entrepreneurship by improving interpersonal relationships, leadership effectiveness, and decision-making abilities.

10.1.2 Literature Tends to Recognize the Involvement of EI in Entrepreneurship

Entrepreneurs have to work in high-stakes environments in which emotional considerations often influence their choices. High EI has been associated with improved conflict resolution and negotiation abilities—two of the key building blocks of entrepreneurial success [3]. Higher levels of EI among entrepreneurs indicated

DOI: 10.1201/9781003650775-10

greater problem-solving ability and greater ability to adapt to sophisticated market behavior than their less emotionally intelligent counterparts. They also establish stronger networks, which are precisely crucial for entrepreneurship due to its highly relationship-oriented nature [4]. For business persons who desire to succeed in the long term, however, EI is as much a corporate requirement as a personal talent.

10.1.3 Global Marketing's Artificial Intelligence in Review

With its ability to enable businesses to review meaningful data and generate authentic insights, AI revolutionizes global marketing. AI technologies like machine learning (ML), natural language processing (NLP), and predictive analytics assist companies in personalizing customer experiences, anticipating consumer needs, and optimizing marketing [5]. A seminal piece in Business Research posits that AI solutions possess the ability to radically boost customers' satisfaction and engagement levels for brands that adopt them. AI also provides real-time data analysis, enabling marketers to adapt quickly to changing consumer trends and preferences [6]. Their impact on marketing effectiveness as well as sway on consumer engagement rises as they move forward.

10.1.4 Interconnection between Marketing Success, Artificial Intelligence, and Emotional Intelligence

EI and AI together provide a staggering amount of creativity in marketing strategy. AI gives data-driven insights needed to understand consumer preferences, and EI enables business owners to read and react to these numbers with empathy. Studies have shown that in marketing performance, a union of data analytics with emotionally intelligent know-how about consumer behavior is much more effective. For example, businesses that incorporate emotional aspects into their AI-based marketing efforts enjoy higher customer involvement and brand commitment [7]. In an intensely competitive world, industries such as Brawny Synergy not only boost short-term sales but produce long-term buyer relationships as well. Lastly, with an technology-driven global economy worldwide, the convergence of EI and AI provides an entrepreneurial strategic potential. Enhanced decision-making is guaranteed with this two-way approach as it guarantees enhanced relationships with buyers, ultimately guaranteeing entrepreneurial success in the long run. With a proper understanding of all these problems, this chapter discusses how the entrepreneurs will be able to make proper use of EI and AI in order to develop sustainable marketing strategies with an aggressive style.

10.2 THE ROLE OF EMOTIONAL INTELLIGENCE IN ENTREPRENEURSHIP

There cannot be a greater emphasis on the necessity of EI in the increasingly competitive and dynamic entrepreneurial world. It is essential to have a set of competencies for entrepreneurs to perform better in people relationships, make more informed choices, and create successful organizational cultures.

10.2.1 Understanding Emotional Intelligence

10.2.1.1 Components of EI

EI is defined by five core components:

- **Self-awareness** entails acknowledging one's strengths, weaknesses, values, and emotions, which leads to the correct self-judgment. Self-awareness enables entrepreneurs to make sound judgments, as proposed by [8], by building stronger relationships with their employees and customers.
- **Self-regulation** is the capacity to effectively manage one's emotions and impulses. This skill enables entrepreneurs to keep their cool when faced with pressure and deal with setbacks positively. Studies point out that self-regulated entrepreneurs are more capable of coping with changes in their business environments [2].
- **Motivation** involves the aspiration to attain goals for personal motives in addition to external compensation. Strong motivational skills are owned by successful entrepreneurs and make them more resistant and determined when confronted with problems [9]. Such entrepreneurs create a vision and lead others along it.
- **Empathy** is the capacity to share and understand other people's feelings, which is very important in creating effective relationships with employees and customers. The importance of empathy in increasing customer engagement and satisfaction.
- **Social skills** encompass the capacity to manage relationships and motivate others, which is critical for teamwork and leadership effectiveness. High EI improves communication, collaboration, and conflict resolution, allowing leaders to build a unified work environment.

10.2.1.2 Importance of EI in Leadership

The leadership function of EI is imperative. Leaders who are high in EI perform better in managing a positive corporate culture, thus impacting employee happiness and productivity positively. Leaders demonstrating high EI capabilities are able to drive teamwork relationships, generating higher performance and innovation. Finally, EI improves change management: leaders who demonstrate empathetic communication perform better when navigating their organization through change [8].

10.2.2 Emotional Intelligence and Decision Making

10.2.2.1 Impact on Strategic Decisions

EI plays a significant role in decision-making, especially strategic decision-making [10]. Entrepreneurs are frequently required to make high-stakes decisions that are subject to the influence of emotion. By tapping into EI, they can keep emotions at bay and be objective and rational, thereby reducing the dangers of hasty responses. Entrepreneurs with high EI are able to assess risks and opportunities more efficiently and integrate emotional awareness into strategy planning.

In addition, EI assists in providing cooperative decision-making. Managers with EI usually establish teams that can carry out useful arguments, thereby making a place where various opinions are promoted [7]. Such cooperation generally leads to higher innovation and creativity in organizations.

10.2.2.2 Examples of Successful Entrepreneurs

Effective entrepreneurs demonstrate the possibilities of EI when making decisions. Howard Schultz, the former Starbucks CEO, is a case in point. He is famous for his empathetic leadership style. Schultz, through his ability to relate to his employees and customers, could make strategic decisions that considered employee well-being and customer satisfaction, which translated to the success of Starbucks globally [8].

Equally, Microsoft CEO Satya Nadella revolutionized the company's culture based on a powerful focus on empathy and teamwork. His commitment to knowing employees' and customers' needs has reoriented Microsoft's innovation and strategic planning [11]. Such instances demonstrate how EI-informed decision-making not only affects the success of individual entrepreneurs but also promotes sustainable business operations.

10.2.3 Building an Emotionally Intelligent Organization

10.2.3.1 Promoting EI in Company Culture

Developing an emotionally intelligent organization needs to have a conscious focus on EI in the culture of a company. Leaders need to role-model emotionally intelligent behavior and develop values that foster openness, empathy, and collaboration. Organizations that have an EI culture have fewer cases of employee turnover and more job satisfaction.

In addition, fostering EI in the organization includes acknowledging and rewarding emotionally intelligent behaviors. Adopting policies that give value to emotional competence—for instance, employee feedback systems that value interpersonal relationships—can create an environment in which EI flourishes. Periodic evaluations of emotional intelligence at the organizational level can help identify areas for improvement and assess the effectiveness of EI development initiatives.

10.2.3.2 Training and Development Programs

Successful training sessions to develop EI skills are essential in order to develop EI within a company. Successful training must emphasize the improvement of self-awareness, emotional management, and communication and interpersonal skills. According to research conducted by [12], it was observed that those companies that had invested in EI training exhibited enhanced employee engagement and performance.

These may include group training, mentoring, and coaching in order to foster a culture of ongoing learning. Moreover, establishing an emotionally intelligent pipeline of leaders through specialized training will help ensure future organizational leaders possess these vital competencies [13].

Briefly, the use of EI in business goes beyond personal ability; it guides decision-making, influences organizational culture, and ultimately decides success in a competitive market. By investing in EI building and creating an emotional awareness-based culture, entrepreneurs can propel their organizations toward sustained growth and innovation.

10.3 THE INFLUENCE OF AI ON GLOBAL MARKETING STRATEGIES

AI in global marketing has changed how businesses connect, customize offerings, and engage with customers. Because AI technologies are progressing so fast, marketers can now use data to gain strategic insights, enhance customer experiences, and react to market pressures faster than ever before.

10.3.1 Overview of AI Technologies in Marketing

10.3.1.1 Machine Learning

One of the areas of AI employing algorithms for data analysis, learning, and predictive models is ML. Marketing applications of ML include consumer segmentation, trend forecasting, and forecasting. For instance, firms employ ML algorithms to identify consumer behaviors of product utilization, where they are able to target their promotional messages effectively [8].

The efficiency of ML in assisting with marketing success is attested to by existing research. Businesses that utilized ML in marketing optimized campaign performance by 30% through targeted advertising. Furthermore, ML allows businesses to achieve maximum return on investment by allowing them to optimize campaigns in real time based on performance metrics.

10.3.1.2 Predictive Analytics

Predictive analytics is the use of past data to forecast future outcomes. It uses statistical techniques and ML to analyze trends and predict the behavior of customers. Marketing professionals use predictive analytics for consumer segmentation, lowering attrition rates, and informing product innovation. The importance of predictive analytics in worldwide marketing is critical. Aberdeen Group's study in 2022 identified that firms that used predictive analytics experienced a 36% improvement in the client retention rate compared to companies that did not apply predictive analytics [14]. As a result, predictive analytics allows companies to anticipate client needs, which leads to improved customer satisfaction and loyalty.

10.3.1.3 Chatbots and Customer Engagement Tools

Chatbots are computer programs utilizing AI to mimic interactions with customers, thus increasing customer interaction and service. They provide real-time responses to questions asked by clients, enable lead generation, and operate around the clock, thus maximizing customer interaction.

Current research highlights the importance of chatbots to facilitate improved customer experience. According to a PwC [15] study, 77% of customers have had positive experiences with chatbots and virtual assistants, leading to greater engagement and higher conversion rates. As businesses expand globally, chatbots can be programmed to speak multiple languages and respond to multicultural settings appropriately, thus improving consumer relationships [6].

10.3.2 The Global Marketing Landscape

10.3.2.1 Trends and Challenges in International Markets

Since businesses operate in many foreign markets, they have to contend with several different cultural, economic, and regulatory environments. The trend in the present day revolves around the imperatives of localization and cultural awareness. Reports show that consumers favor brands that recognize and express their cultural values.

But there are challenges. Businesses are confronted with the complexity of data security and privacy legislation, including the General Data Protection Regulation (GDPR) in the EU and comparable legislation increasingly applied globally. The legislation can discourage the application of data-driven marketing practices [16]. Marketers need to navigate sensitively, avoiding safety risks but not losing the value offered by AI technology.

10.3.2.2 Personalization and Customer Experience

Personalization is a key driver in present-day marketing strategies, as customers demand personalized experiences based on their own interests. AI technologies enable marketers to learn from customer data through the development of tailored content that resonates.

It has been found through research that personalization works for customer satisfaction and loyalty. According to research by [17], companies that implement AI-driven personalization programs have a 20% increase in conversion rates. With AI, businesses can create personalized messages for marketing that resonate with the consumer, supporting customer retention and advocacy [18]. Besides, AI enhances customers' experience through the prediction of customers' needs and offering anticipatory solutions. Based on customers' history of buying behavior, AI can offer product or service suggestions that align with a customer's interests and thus simplify the purchasing process.

10.3.3 Modern Examples of AI in Successful Global Marketing Programs

Several companies have been able to use AI technologies to enhance their global marketing campaigns, which demonstrate the strong impact of AI on marketing strategy.

Coca-Cola has successfully leveraged AI with its Freestyle vending machines, which gather consumer taste data to provide personalized beverage recommendations, increasing customer satisfaction and sales. Netflix employs sophisticated ML algorithms to look at viewing history and recommend specific videos based on individual tastes, greatly improving subscriber retention; roughly 80% of what customers watch is the result of these recommendations. Amazon utilizes predictive analytics to quantify customer demand and offer personalized product suggestions in accordance with shopping behavior, which has proved very effective. During 2022, the personalized recommendations created nearly 35% of Amazon's total revenues, reflecting the power of AI in enhancing customer experience [8]. AI technologies impact global marketing strategies holistically. Through the application of ML, predictive analytics, and chatbots, businesses can optimize campaigns and deliver tailored customer experiences, ensuring long-term success in evolving markets.

10.4 INTEGRATING ARTIFICIAL INTELLIGENCE WITH EMOTIONAL INTELLIGENCE IN INTERNATIONAL MARKETING

10.4.1 The Synergy between Emotional Intelligence and Artificial Intelligence

10.4.1.1 Enhancing Customer Relationships by Data-Driven Insights

The integration of AI and EI in recent years has transformed advertising practices to a large degree by enabling businesses to create stronger relationships with their clients. EI is the ability to recognize, comprehend, and manage one's and others' emotions. With AI, businesses can potentially utilize evidence-based facts to make client relationships stronger.

AI technologies read large volumes of customer data in order to identify emotions and trends. ML algorithms are employed by brands to quantify consumer activities, comments, and conversations to test emotional responses. The method not only makes decision-making easier but also raises marketing personalization. Predictive analytics helps businesses forecast client tastes and needs, and so make emotionally relevant one-to-one communication.

Recent research has shown that businesses using AI-based EI [10] in their marketing campaign have seen incredible increases in customer loyalty and satisfaction. It allows brands to transform from being transactional to being relationship-based in reality, hence increasing long-term engagement and trust.

10.4.1.2 Tailoring Marketing Strategies through Emotional Intelligence

Organizations that use EI in combination with AI are able to craft more compelling narratives that resonate with the emotional hot buttons of their listeners. Adaptability is needed in the global market, driven by cognitive and behavioral cultural differences. With the emotions revealed in customer feedback, social media conversations, and ratings, AI allows organizations to craft ads that specifically speak to various demographic groups.

Companies using emotion-based advertising techniques attained better engagement than those adopting conventional techniques. By realizing some emotional drivers—for example, happiness, concern, or nostalgia—marketing teams can craft customized content directly appealing to customers' emotions and intentions. Additionally, emotional segmentation enables the identification of certain emotional segments within a target market and tailoring communication and product offerings to suit. This increases customer experience and conversion rates as emotionally stimulating communications are more relatable to customers.

10.4.2 Tools and Techniques

10.4.2.1 Emotional Analytics Tools

To effectively complement cooperative activities between EI and AI, organizations are increasingly using emotional analytics solutions that are specifically designed to detect and react to customer feelings and sentiments. These solutions monitor social media, reviews, and surveys to measure emotional responses and sentiments toward a brand or product.

These tools are IBM Watson Tone Analyzer, Clarabridge, and Affinio, and they help business organizations measure real-time emotional tone and sentiment and consequently make necessary changes in their marketing approach in a timely manner. The latest research [16] states that organizations using these tools have achieved higher customer satisfaction levels due to more emotionally engaging and personalized promotional messages.

Moreover, the arrival of NLP also backs emotional analytics with even better sentiment analysis. NLP helps brands build an even fuller image of customer emotions, translating into more informed marketing decisions.

10.4.2.2 AI-Driven Customer Feedback Loops

AI-enriched feedback loops are one of the central means of mixing EI with AI in marketing. The feedback loops enable companies to collect, read, and react to consumers' emotions on the fly incessantly, that is, there can be an interactive dialogue between businesses and shoppers in real time dynamically.

Customer feedback data collection and analysis can be scanned by AI to detect emotional sentiment and trends over time. For instance, sites like Qualtrics and SurveyMonkey use AI to decode answers and create actionable recommendations. Businesses that applied these feedback loops were able to have a response time to customers that was 40% more rapid, effectively raising customer retention rates.

The iterative processes of these feedback loops also allow firms to try out emotional marketing approaches, optimizing campaigns rapidly as they gauge responses from customers and sentiment shifts. Such responsiveness is vital in today's rapid-paced digital marketing era, where consumers can suddenly change tastes.

10.4.3 Real-World Applications

10.4.3.1 Examples of Brands Successfully Merging EI with AI

Several brands have proven the success of combining EI and AI, highlighting creative methods that improve customer relationships and marketing effectiveness.

- **Coca-Cola:** Through the use of AI analysis to recognize consumer sentiment during their ad campaigns, Coca-Cola has successfully developed commercials that appeal to nostalgic sentiment and common cultural moments. Emotionally appealing marketing tactics have resulted in large increases in brand engagement and customer loyalty.
- **Unilever:** Unilever utilized AI-powered emotional analysis tools to analyze the reactions of consumers toward their campaigns in various geographies. With these insights, Unilever was able to better align its messages with more culturally relevant emotions, leading to expanded market share within multicultural markets globally [19].

10.4.3.2 Lessons Learned from Failures

While many brands have effectively tapped into the synergies of EI and AI, others have run into issues of value as lessons. One such example is GAP, which drew criticism for an ad campaign that overlooked the emotional aspects of its customers. The campaign came across as tone-deaf, resulting in a huge decline in customer interaction and criticism on social media. This failure emphasized the need for emotional sensitivity in branding and the dangers of misreading consumer attitudes [20].

Pepsi is another example, whose ad employed social justice imagery, which was subjected to harsh criticism for not being emotionally considerate. The backlash highlighted the urgent need for businesses to genuinely connect with the emotional spaces of their consumers.

Examples here indicate that though the blending of EI and AI can bring about revolutionary positive results, an in-depth knowledge of EI is necessary to steer clear of pitfalls. Brands must become aware of a genuine empathy for the audience in order to design campaign communications that communicate well. The intersection of AI and EI in global marketing is a high-potential area for companies to build deeper relationships with their customers, tailor marketing efforts, and create better emotional connections with their audience. With emotional analytics tools and AI-based feedback loops, brands are able to create data-backed insights that resonate with consumer sentiment and drive engagement.

As illustrated through effective case studies and validated through the learning of failures, businesses will need to go into this integration with an honest appreciation of emotional dynamics to allow their marketing efforts to connect with their consumers in a favorable manner. In doing so, they not only improve their perception of the brand but also create long-term loyalty within the increasingly competitive global market.

10.5 DECODING CONSUMER BEHAVIOR THROUGH EI AND AI

10.5.1 Understanding Consumer Emotions

10.5.1.1 The Psychology of Consumer Behavior

Consumer behavior is inherently influenced by a multifaceted interaction of psychological elements, including perceptions, motivations, beliefs, and emotions. Emotions are central to influencing consumer choices and preferences. Consumers' emotional reactions can powerfully change the way they perceive brands and products, driving them toward or away from a purchase.

Psychologically, the emotion can be explained through a number of models, such as the Affect Transfer Model, which posits that the feelings of consumers toward a brand can determine their intention to purchase. Further, the Behavior Influence Model stresses how emotional cues can create impulse buying tendencies, illustrating how emotions can dominate rational thinking in the decision to buy. Emotional appeals in advertisements frequently influence purchasing decisions more so than rational appeals [17].

10.5.1.2 How Emotions Influence Buying Decisions

Emotions are an essential part of the decision-making process, serving as a driving force that motivates consumer behavior. In contrast to earlier models of consumer behavior—largely based on rationality—current research emphasizes that emotions tend to influence purchasing decisions more deeply than rational thinking [7].

Various emotions may result in certain consumer actions. For example, happiness might increase the appeal of the product, leading to impulse buying, while fear or worry might lead to avoidance coping behavior during shopping conditions. The influence of happiness relating to a product, as that enhances brand allegiance, while disagreeable emotions against a product do not inspire repetitive buying.

Consumer behavior theory of EI cannot be underestimated. Consumers with high EI are better at recognizing their own and other individuals' emotional conditions that drive their buying behaviors. Companies that recognize and respond to such emotional forces have the ability to develop advertising efforts that move consumers more deeply through emotional fears and needs.

10.5.2 Leveraging AI for Emotion Recognition

10.5.2.1 Techniques for Analyzing Customer Sentiments

AI technologies have been capable of jumping by leaps in sentiment analysis and facilitating brands to understand consumer sentiments appropriately. Various advanced techniques make it possible, and organizations are enabled to understand how emotions influence consumer behavior.

NLP is among the most important technologies that are used in sentiment analysis of customer opinions in words—for example, customer feedback, social media, and survey comments. Algorithms are able to make estimates of emotional tones by keeping an eye on words and phrases that are associated with different feelings. IBM Watson Natural Language Understanding and Google Cloud Natural Language APIs are some of the tools that apply advanced NLP techniques in analyzing large volumes of data at high speeds, identifying predominant sentiment patterns.

Another promising method is facial recognition technology, which deciphers human emotions from facial expressions. Analyzing micro-expressions, companies can learn about instantaneous emotional reactions toward advertisements or product experiences. Research shows that AI-based emotion recognition using facial analysis can make marketing more than 25% effective, as marketers can make precise adjustments in messages based on people's responses.

Also, voice analysis technology examines the tone, pitch, and speech rate to measure emotions. This method has become especially significant in customer care environments, where the emotional status of the customers can be used to shape the manner in which the service representatives engage.

10.5.2.2 Examples of Successful Sentiment Analysis

A number of firms have been able to effectively use AI-based sentiment analysis to better understand consumer behavior and emotions.

Netflix has used sentiment analysis to create personalized content recommendations according to the emotions of viewers. Through the analysis of social media sentiments and review information, Netflix can modify its marketing strategies and tailor user experiences, leading to an improvement in viewer retention [19].

Nike utilized sentiment analysis in a large-scale advertising campaign, using AI to measure consumer response in real time. By making rapid adjustments to their messaging based on positive or negative sentiment feedback, Nike was able to boost engagement rates on social media dramatically, as well as record a significant sales boost during the campaign duration [19].

These examples reflect the disruptive capability of sentiment analysis for brands, which reveals how AI offers deeper insights into consumer sentiment and subsequent purchasing behaviors.

10.5.3 Creating Emotionally Intelligent Marketing Campaigns

10.5.3.1 Creating Campaigns that Connect Emotionally

Creating campaigns that emotionally connect with consumers relies on an intimate understanding of the emotional landscape that they live in. Placing EI at the center of campaign creation results in more genuine and authentic messaging.

The initial step is to uncover the emotional hot buttons unique to the target segment. Brands can leverage emotional analytics software to further understand customer feelings and tastes, allowing them to develop campaigns that appeal directly to consumer values. One key framework applied in this effort is emotional storytelling, which plays on emotions of happiness, nostalgia, or empathy [21]. Effective campaigns tend to use poignant stories that resonate with consumers at an emotional level, focusing on authenticity and genuine insight. For example, when it ran its "Real Beauty" campaign, Dove featured actual women telling their stories, building an emotional bond that resonated with many consumers and ultimately fostering brand loyalty [17].

10.5.3.2 Measuring the Impact of Emotionally Targeted Campaigns

In order to gauge the effectiveness of emotionally intelligent campaigns, brands need to install strong metrics to measure impact. Quantitative and qualitative metrics exist by which consumer emotional reactions toward campaigns may be evaluated.

Key Performance Indicators (KPIs) should incorporate metrics such as engagement rates, conversion rates, and customer opinion analysis before and after the launch. Social Listening Platforms (e.g., Sprout Social, Hootsuite) can measure changes in consumer sentiment on social media and provide insight into emotional acceptance of the marketing.

Previous research suggests that emotionally intelligent campaigns have yielded better Return on Investment (ROI), where revenue effects of 20–30% are associated with higher consumer engagement [18]. Furthermore, qualitative measures such as surveys and focus groups can uncover consumers' emotional response and sentiment and enable brands to make adjustments incrementally.

Breaking down consumer action in the field of EI and AI provides additional detail about emotional purchase drivers. By grasping the psychological underpinnings behind consumer emotions, employing AI processes for sentiment monitoring, and constructing emotionally engaging ad campaigns, the brand is enabled to engage in a more emotional relationship with consumers.

The successful examples give us understanding that the cumulative effect of these techniques can create powerful emotional bonds leading to brand allegiance and increased sales. Businesses applying EI to marketing are better positioned to prosper in an increasingly competitive and emotionally charged market environment.

10.6 STRATEGIES FOR ENTREPRENEURS TO DEVELOP EI AND LEVERAGE AI

Entrepreneurs have the dual responsibility of navigating through intricate market trends and competing with others. Two support beams essential to fulfilling this role are EI and AI. This article presents how entrepreneurs can leverage their EI, implement AI in business operations, and leverage the synergy of these two powerful tools.

10.6.1 Building Emotional Intelligence Skills

10.6.1.1 Self-Assessment and Continuous Learning

Entrepreneurs need EI because it enhances their interpersonal and self-management skills. Self-awareness is the initial step toward developing EI. Entrepreneurs have many tools and models at their disposal to assess their emotional abilities. One such technique is the Emotional Quotient Inventory (EQ-i), which assesses functions of EI such as self-knowledge, empathy, and interpersonal skills.

Through continuous learning, entrepreneurs can develop their emotional skills in harmony with their personal and professional aspirations. This can be achieved by reading books, attending workshops, and taking online courses on EI. According to reference [22] participation in continuous learning programs can improve leadership performance and job satisfaction.

10.6.1.2 Coaching and Mentoring

Investment in mentoring and coaching programs can greatly develop an entrepreneur's EI. A mentor can offer precious information and constructive comments to enable entrepreneurs to identify their emotional strengths and weaknesses. Reference [23] reported that mentoring relationships enhance emotional competency, resulting in improved decision-making and interpersonal effectiveness in entrepreneurial settings.

Coaching schemes, especially EI training programs, enable entrepreneurs to learn skills like emotional regulation and empathy in applied contexts. Training programs tend to feature role-plays and feedback sessions to improve an individual's emotional reactions while confronting adversity. Developing these capabilities helps entrepreneurs boost employee, customer, and stakeholder interactions toward a more coherent and engaged working environment.

10.6.2 Implementing AI in Business Operations

10.6.2.1 Choosing the Right AI Tools

For business owners, choosing the appropriate AI tools is important to automate processes and improve decision-making. There are different AI applications, such as customer relationship management (CRM), data analytics, and marketing automation. Business owners need to evaluate their individual business requirements to identify which AI tools will yield the greatest impact.

Software like Salesforce Einstein and HubSpot leverage AI to improve customer insights and marketing automation. Reference [24] underscores the importance of selecting AI tools that align with organizational goals. The study confirms that companies employing optimally aligned AI software have recorded a 35% increase in productivity and 40% improved customer satisfaction. Also, entrepreneurs need to consider how scalable, user-friendly, and integrable the tools are into existing systems. By selecting tools that meet their particular requirements, entrepreneurs can automate business processes and optimize performance.

10.6.2.2 Building an AI-Driven Marketing Strategy

Adequate utilization of a good marketing strategy supported by AI will greatly enhance the reach and connectivity of an entrepreneur. Several strategies are available to utilize AI for targeting and personalization. Entrepreneurs may employ algorithms in AI to learn about consumer habits, segment an audience, and design targeted campaigns that appeal to specific segments.

Aside from that, advertisements using AI to access social media as well as for content marketing is gaining wider acceptance. HubSpot and Hootsuite are programs employed with AI capabilities in posting every once in a while, watching the engagement habits, and even in creating the content in tandem with the interest received. A whole marketing campaign leveraging an AI can not only fetch the customers but also create loyalty through tailored interaction.

10.6.3 Best Practices for Integrating EI and AI

10.6.3.1 Collaborating with AI Experts

AI business application needs proper knowledge of the technology and its implications. Partnering with AI experts can help entrepreneurs gain the required knowledge to use AI effectively. It can be achieved by hiring in-house data scientists, consulting AI companies, or attending AI technology workshops and webinars.

By employing professionals, entrepreneurs have more opportunities to optimize the usage of AI and implement it in their own context. Based on a research report, "Building AI Competence in Small Businesses," with the implementation of mentorship and working alongside AI professionals, the learning process can be quickened, and an even better implementation process can result. This helps entrepreneurs to manage technological advancements and maximize the utilization of AI.

10.6.3.2 Continuous Evaluation and Adaptation

For the harmonious integration of AI and EI, there is a need for continuous evaluation and alignment. Entrepreneurs must regularly evaluate the effectiveness of their EI programs and AI technologies to see if they are aligned with organizational objectives and expectations.

Feedback loops may be employed to instill this process of evaluation. Employee surveys, customer feedback, and performance measures assist in marking areas for improvement and to guide future decision-making. Reference [25] confirms that organizations that continuously evaluate and adapt their strategies achieve higher success rates in meeting organizational objectives.

Moreover, keeping updated with the recent advancements in EI and AI fields enables entrepreneurs to refine their strategies on an ongoing basis. Network meetings with business leaders and conferences related to their industry can acquaint entrepreneurs with newer practices and developing technologies, leading to a culture of continuous enhancement.

For entrepreneurs, the cultivation of EI and the successful utilization of AI are critical keys to success in the competitive world of today. By developing EI competencies through self-awareness, life-long learning, mentoring, and coaching, entrepreneurs can enhance interpersonal competence, which creates better team working and customer relations. Implementing AI in business operations enables entrepreneurs to improve operational efficiency, customer engagement, and strategic decision-making. So, the convergence of these two fields demands working in collaboration with AI specialists and continual review to guarantee that businesses are agile and highly responsive to shifting market dynamics. Through adopting these measures, entrepreneurs can guarantee more that they navigate the intricacies of the modern business environment not just to become individuals but also to achieve organizational success.

10.7 STRATEGIES FOR ENTREPRENEURS TO DEVELOP EMOTIONAL INTELLIGENCE (EI) AND LEVERAGE ARTIFICIAL INTELLIGENCE (AI)

10.7.1 Building Emotional Intelligence Skills

10.7.1.1 Self-Assessment and Continuous Learning

Entrepreneurs looking to enhance the level of their EI must begin with self-assessment using a number of tools to gauge their EI level. Self-assessment tools such as the Mayer-Salovey-Caruso Emotional Intelligence Test (MSCEIT) have grown over the past decades. Research indicates self-awareness constructs EI and demonstrates entrepreneurs who review their emotional capabilities from time to time are able to estimate where they should improve, leading to more effective decision-making and leadership [26].

Aside from self-awareness, continuous learning via workshops, online courses, and reading materials on EI can also significantly enhance an entrepreneur's emotional vocabulary. Recent research sheds light on the fact that investment in EI training not only improves social skills but also leads to improved business results. Training in empathy, conflict management, and communication skills can therefore generate a holistic entrepreneur who can effectively maneuver intricate social environments in business.

10.7.1.2 Coaching and Mentoring

Coaching and mentoring play a vital role in the development of EI so that entrepreneurs can have access to tailored feedback and guidance. Peer mentoring initiatives, in which successful entrepreneurs share their experiences in emotional management and interpersonal skill development, can significantly enhance emotional intelligence. Such interactions ensure a non-judgmental platform for deliberation and have the potential to be transformational in learning.

Additionally, professional coaching can provide customized strategies to assist entrepreneurs in managing their emotional reactions better and improving their relations with employees and clients. Entrepreneurs who have access to coaching enhance their leadership and emotional control, thereby developing a better workplace environment [27].

10.7.2 Implementing AI in Business Operations

10.7.2.1 Choosing the Right AI Tools

The integration of AI into business operations is critical for contemporary entrepreneurs. The initial step is to choose the appropriate tools that match business objectives. Entrepreneurs need to make a proper analysis of available AI tools in the market, analyzing functionalities, prices, and compatibility with existing systems [28]. This entails knowing if solutions such as AI chatbots, predictive analytics, or ML platforms can deliver the desired operational efficiency.

The ways in which successful business leaders use AI applications like Salesforce AI for CRM and Google Analytics for data-driven marketing efforts [7]. By choosing the appropriate tools, you can maximize productivity and streamline operations, creating a competitive edge in the market.

10.7.2.2 Building an AI-Driven Marketing Strategy

Effective use of a decent marketing strategy backed by AI will highly increase the outreach and connectivity of an entrepreneur. Entrepreneurs can use algorithms in AI to study consumer behaviors, segment an audience, and create targeted promotions appealing to particular segments.

Besides, applying AI to content marketing and social media advertising is becoming increasingly popular. HubSpot and Hootsuite are software that leverage AI to post at regular intervals, track engagement trends, and even create content in tune with audience preferences. An entire AI-driven marketing campaign not only helps get customers but also inspires loyalty driven by personalized engagement.

10.7.3 Best Practices for Integrating EI and AI

10.7.3.1 Collaborating with AI Experts

To have the best effects of AI implementation, business people must collaborate with AI experts who help demystify technology and offer information on best practices. A surprising outcome in recent studies indicates that organizations that actively shift to hire AI experts have greater possibilities of successful integration of technology into their systems. These experts help business operators understand the nuances of AI applications, particular to their sectors, that can be utilized to inform decision-making and optimize functional capabilities.

AI expertise is supportive and establishes a multi-disciplinary team when combined with the capabilities of EI. Convergence between them creates innovation and enables companies to solve problems end-to-end, weighing the benefits of human intuitions against the efficacy of technology.

10.7.3.2 Continuous Evaluation and Adaptation

Realization of the convergence of EI and AI requires ongoing examination and adaptation. Returning to and refining strategies based on feedback and performance metrics is necessary. *Harvard Business Review* studies point out that organizations with a culture of continuous improvement are better positioned to deal with the fast-changing realms of EI and AI.

Developing critical KPIs aligned with emotional measures (e.g., employee morale, team consistency) and AI outcomes (e.g., accuracy levels of predictive computing, customer satisfaction rates) enables entrepreneurs to measure achievements and take detours as necessary. Feedback mechanisms that include employee and client input can also offer guidance for strategy changes while ensuring both EI and AI are aligned with evolving business realities.

Entrepreneurs today must build EI in addition to leveraging AI in order to thrive in a more competitive world. By integrating self-awareness, continuous learning, mentorship, and expert AI tools, they can build successful, resilient, and emotionally intelligent organizations. Collaboration with AI experts and continuous refinement are essential strategies for integrating these two critical skills. The integration of EI and AI enhances business performance while also creating a healthier work culture, which leads to success becoming sustainable.

10.8 CHALLENGES AND ETHICAL CONSIDERATIONS IN THE AGE OF AI

Along with the expansion of AI infusion in business practices, challenges as well as ethical issues are likely to emerge. The following discussion attempts to explore the limitations of too much dependence on AI, proper utilization of information in emotional analytics, harmony of automation and personal touch, long-term effects on consumer confidence, etc.

10.8.1 Potential Pitfalls of Overreliance on AI

Although AI technologies have the potential to support operational effectiveness and decision-making, excessive dependence on these technologies risks severe consequences. Perhaps the most often mentioned danger is losing human judgment. Too much dependence by entrepreneurs on AI for decision-making can cause loss of key contextual considerations that involve human intuition and judgment. For example, AI has the ability to make observations about information but simply can't keep up with the human ability to be sensitive to emotions and cultural differences, which are crucial for successful leadership and customer management. Further, excessive dependence upon AI can cause serious operational dangers. The high level of complication in AI models makes them liable to errors and prejudice, spreading through decision-making and leading to expensive errors [29]. For example, computer-aided recruitment software has been discovered to discriminate systematically against some demographic groups because it perpetuates ingrained biases that mirror the data on which it was trained.

Lastly, dependence on AI can result in skill decay among employees. If employees rely on AI for critical functions without being involved in the decision-making process required, they lose useful skills in the long term [6]. Such skills erosion can lead to a workforce that is not adaptable and lacks problem-solving skills to deal with unexpected challenges.

10.8.2 Ethical Use of Data in Emotional Analytics

Emotional analytics entails the gathering and examination of data about human feeling, usually through AI-facilitated technologies such as sentiment analysis and facial recognition technology. As useful as this can be in improving the customer experience, ethics issues are rampant in terms of privacy and consent. Most consumers remain in the dark as to how their emotional data are gathered and used, and a lot of major ethical issues surround this.

A key focus is the gaining of informed consent. Companies need to make sure that they are openly disclosing to consumers how their information will be used and the potential consequences. Companies need to take a straightforward and open strategy in gathering data that focuses on consumer rights and freedom [28].

Additionally, there is a high risk of misuse of emotional analytics data. Illegal access to emotionally sensitive data can result in exploitative behavior, including targeted advertising based on the exploitation of consumers' vulnerabilities. Ethical utilization of emotional data must ensure that consumer data is protected and that its utilization generates beneficial results instead of taking advantage of emotional vulnerabilities.

10.8.3 Balancing Automation with Human Touch

As companies increasingly embrace AI technologies, achieving a balance between automation and human touch is crucial. Although AI can speed up processes and lower costs, it cannot substitute the genuine connections that human interactions create [30]. The lack of ability by AI to sense fine emotional cues in real-time interactions can inhibit relationship-building initiatives.

To stay human, companies need to take a hybrid approach that uses AI for efficiency and makes sure human workers are central to customer engagement. Personalized customer care, for example, can be vastly improved by AI systems that sort through customer data, but human agents need to handle complicated or sensitive questions that need empathy and subtle understanding. Companies that are able to effectively incorporate both human and AI elements are likely to cultivate greater loyalty and trust with their consumers [31].

Besides, employees must be trained to collaborate with AI technologies. A culture of innovation in which employees are motivated to work with AI tools, coupled with developing people skills, can lead to thriving business cultures in which human judgment and automation can harmoniously coexist.

10.8.4 Long-Term Implications for Consumer Trust

The connection between AI integration and consumer trust has catastrophic long-term implications for companies. Customer trust is heavily dependent on transparency in AI use. Customers are more likely to interact with companies that are open about their AI use and its impact on customer interaction [32].

Poor communication is likely to cause mistrust and suspicion, especially as data privacy and bias concerns come into play. Further, loss of trust has long-term consequences for customer loyalty and commitment. A positive correlation between customer trust and customer retention indicates that firms engaging in ethical AI behavior build more sustainable and long-term relationships with customers. This transformation demands authenticity in building trust, for example, providing strong ethical justification on the deployment of AI, data privacy, and endorsement of the righteousness of AI systems.

Grappling with the dangers and ethics of adopting AI in business processes is a formula for long-term success. Overdependence on AI pitfalls, ethical utilization of data used in emotional analysis, seeing to it that automation and human factors have their input, and gaining consumer trust are ways businesses set themselves up for lasting longevity in the new AI-driven world.

10.9 Emerging Trends in Emotional Intelligence (EI), Artificial Intelligence, and International Marketing

And as the business climate continues to change so drastically, it is where EI and AI meet that the key to survival in business today lies. The path through it is to navigate emerging technology affecting marketing, changing trends of EI in the business climate, and what lies ahead for business leaders entering this rapidly changing landscape, from recent publications and newly released research.

10.9.1 Emerging Technologies and Their Impact on Marketing

New technologies like AI, ML, AR, and blockchain are transforming the marketing landscape. The technologies facilitate more data-driven and personalized strategies to engage the customers. AI continues to dominate marketing strategy with tools that have been developed to process large data sets, make predictions about consumer behavior, and automate marketing activities.

10.9.1.1 Personalization and Predictive Analytics

The potential of AI in offering personalized customer experiences grows in importance. ML and predictive analytics allow marketers to extract information from the data of customers and anticipate what will happen next. Businesses leveraging AI for predictive analytics see remarkable improvements in customer engagement and retention rates. Organizations can customize their products to fulfill particular customer requirements, building better relationships and increasing sales.

10.9.1.2 Augmented Reality (AR) and Virtual Reality (VR)

New technologies such as AR and VR are revolutionizing the way brands engage with consumers. AR allows consumers to see products in their surroundings before purchasing, making the shopping experience better. Companies such as Ikea and Sephora use AR to enable customers to engage with their products virtually [16]. With advancements in AR technology, it is anticipated that more businesses will utilize such experiences to market themselves and connect with consumers at a deeper level.

10.9.1.3 Blockchain Technology

Blockchain is yet another new technology that will change the way marketers operate. It promises greater data security, transparency, and traceability of transactions, which are essential in establishing consumer trust. Supply chain management involving blockchain technology can give customers verifiable information regarding product origin and authenticity. Such transparency cannot only strengthen customer loyalty but also solve problems concerning counterfeit products.

10.9.2 The Evolving Role of Emotional Intelligence in Business

With increasing incorporation of technology in business operations, the importance of EI is also changing, becoming more crucial for employees and leaders alike.

10.9.2.1 Building Customer Relationships

EI is essential for building effective customer relationships in today's increasingly automated world. Companies focusing on EI training for their workforce see a significant boost in customer satisfaction and loyalty. EI helps employees better understand customers' feelings, needs, and issues and resolve conflicts better, improving the overall customer experience.

10.9.2.2 Leadership and Team Dynamics

In addition, as repetitive tasks are automated by AI, human competencies like empathy, compassion, and emotional control play a more significant role in successful leadership. There is a necessity for emotionally intelligent leaders in managing change and building resilient teams in an age of technology. Leaders with EI competencies can better inspire their teams, manage adversity, and build a healthy corporate culture.

10.9.2.3 Adaptation to Organizational Change

EI also comes into play in organizational change management, especially with companies adopting AI and other technologies. Workers are usually resistant to change because they fear losing their jobs or becoming obsolete. Emotionally intelligent leaders can effectively communicate the benefits of technological adoption, reduce employee concerns, and facilitate smoother organizational transitions.

10.9.3 Predictions for Entrepreneurs in a Tech-Driven Market

As technology continues to transform the business environment, businesses need to evolve in order to thrive and survive. The following are some trends based on recent studies.

10.9.3.1 More Demand for AI Skills

While AI expands, the need for experts trained in AI will grow. Companies will make a top priority of recruiting data scientists and AI experts to enable effective utilization of AI technologies. Entrepreneurs will have to invest in talent development and up-skilling initiatives to enable their organizations to exploit the full capability of AI for business strategy.

10.9.3.2 Emphasis on Sustainable and Ethical Practices

Customers are now more focused on businesses that are socially responsible and have ethical practices. Companies that focus on sustainability and ethical marketing have greater customer loyalty and brand image [28]. Businessmen thus need to incorporate sustainable practices into their business models using technologies that reduce environmental footprint while fulfilling customer needs.

10.9.3.3 Hybrid Work Models

The pandemic-driven shift to remote work has remodeled the conventional working spaces. Business owners are bound to persist with hybrid modes of working that integrate office-going and working from home options. Companies adopting flexibility will drive talent acquisition and innovation-driven culture [7].

10.9.3.4 Enhanced Customer Experiences through Technology

Last but not least, the future of marketing will heavily rely on creating customer experiences through technology. AI-powered tools that customize buying experiences, anticipate customers' needs, and drive engagement will be part of the marketing strategy. Additionally, emotionally intelligent marketing approaches that tap into customer emotions will strengthen brand loyalty. Through marrying EI and technological tools, entrepreneurs can create engaging stories and experiences that people will relate to, making them stand out from the crowd in a competitive business environment.

EI and AI will converge to transform marketing significantly in the future. As new technologies revolutionize the way customers are engaged by brands, the timeless advantage of EI in building relationships and adapting to change continues to stand above the rest. Businesses that adapt to these changes will be best prepared to succeed in an increasingly digital environment, building customer loyalty in the process, while confronting the challenges and opportunities of an ever-more automated world.

10.10 CONCLUSION

10.10.1 Summary

In the fast-changing business world of today, the convergence of EI and AI is becoming more widely accepted as key to entrepreneurial success. The chapter highlighted a series of central points regarding the use of new technologies in marketing, the shifting role of EI in business, and predictions for entrepreneurs in an age of technology. Core technological innovations such as AI, ML, and AR are transforming customer interaction by making marketing more targeted and effective. Firms utilizing predictive analytics maximize customer loyalty via customized experiences. Meanwhile, EI has become a core quality for successful leadership and CRM. High EI leaders are best suited to face organizational change, build robust teams, and develop customer satisfaction. In addition, we examined the ethical issues surrounding AI and emotional analytics, with a focus on transparency and ethical use of data [28]. Entrepreneurs are challenged to balance automation and the human element, making sure that technologies enhance, not substitute for, the essential interpersonal connections driving customer loyalty.

10.10.2 Importance of Combining EI and AI for Entrepreneurial Success

The EI-AI symbiosis cannot be overemphasized in the current entrepreneurial ecosystem. Whereas AI technologies offer the analytical capabilities and efficiency required to scale operations, EI enables entrepreneurs to be able to reach and understand customers at a deeper level. According to research, organizations that are able to blend technological expertise with emotional understanding record enhanced customer engagement and long-term growth.

While the competitive entrepreneurial spaces become more sophisticated, the trust-building and relationship capacity with the customers become vital. Companies that invest in EI together with AI technologies build a kinder customer experience, resulting in longer terms of brand commitment and advocacy [16]. Entrepreneurs combining these capabilities have the opportunity to develop groundbreaking solutions and an attuned business model that meets shifting customer needs.

10.10.3 Call to Action for Entrepreneurs

Given these findings, business owners are encouraged to actively adopt the convergence of EI and AI in their companies. The following are some practical steps:

1. **Invest in Emotional Intelligence Training:** Companies should invest in EI training programs for their employees. As shown by recent research, developing EI among employees can result in better communication, teamwork, and customer service results.
2. **Use AI Tools Judiciously:** Business owners must analyze and adopt AI tools that are relevant to their particular business goals. Focusing on tools that facilitate personalization and improve consumer engagement can create stronger relationships with customers.

3. **Embrace Ethical Practices:** There is a need to set ethical standards around the application of AI and emotional data. Customer transparency in relation to data usage will help build trust and reduce privacy concerns [28].
4. **Encourage a Hybrid Work Culture:** With hybrid work practices, companies are enabled to embrace technology while retaining meaningful employee engagement, leading to increased creativity and collaboration [7].
5. **Be Aware of Emerging Trends:** Entrepreneurs must be aware of emerging technologies and trends in EI and AI to make their businesses flexible and innovative.

By taking these steps, entrepreneurs can set themselves up to not only survive but thrive in an era of technological advancement. A business's future rests at the convergence of EI and AI, and it is by adopting both that success will be sustainable in a world that is increasingly complex and connected.

REFERENCES

[1] Thomas, J., Sateesh Kumar, T. K., Menon, V. A., & Thomas, L. P. (2024, April). Analyzing sentiment in Netflix user opinions: a statistical examination. In J. Choudrie, P. N. Mahalle, T. Perumal, & A. Joshi (Eds.), *International Conference on Information and Communication Technology for Intelligent Systems* (pp. 587–601). Singapore: Springer Nature Singapore. https://doi.org/10.1007/978-981-97-6678-9_51

[2] Diamond, M. (2024). *Leading Through Crisis: The Role of Emotional Intelligence in Elementary School Principals' Leadership During the COVID-19 Pandemic* (Doctoral dissertation, Manhattanville College).

[3] Manoharan, G., & Ashtikar, S. P. (2024). A theoretical framework for emotional intelligence in academic leadership in higher education. In *Building Organizational Resilience With Neuroleadership* (pp. 96–112). IGI Global. https://doi.org/10.4018/979-8-3693-1785-3.ch007

[4] Kaciak, E., Koladkiewicz, I., Thongpapanl, N., & Wojtyra, M. (2021). The role of social networks in shaping entrepreneurial exit strategies. *International Entrepreneurship and Management Journal*, 17, 1619–1655.

[5] Aghazadeh, H., & Khoshnevis, M. (2024). *Digital Marketing Technologies*. Singapore: Springer Verlag.

[6] Gupta, Y., & Khan, F. M. (2024). Role of artificial intelligence in customer engagement: a systematic review and future research directions. *Journal of Modelling in Management*, 19(5), 1535–1565.

[7] Huang, M. H., & Rust, R. T. (2022). A framework for collaborative artificial intelligence in marketing. *Journal of Retailing*, 98(2), 209–223.

[8] Gómez-Leal, R., Holzer, A. A., Bradley, C., Fernández-Berrocal, P., & Patti, J. (2022). The relationship between emotional intelligence and leadership in school leaders: A systematic review. *Cambridge Journal of Education*, 52(1), 1–21.

[9] Pathak, S., & Muralidharan, E. (2024). Contextualizing emotional intelligence for commercial and social entrepreneurship. *Small Business Economics*, 62(2), 667–686.

[10] Purushottamashtikar, S., & Manoharan, G. (2024, June). Studying the level of work-life balance and emotional intelligence: university educators. In *AIP Conference Proceedings* (Vol. 2971, No. 1). AIP Publishing. https://doi.org/10.1063/5.0201234

[11] Kumar, V. (2023). Digital enablers. In *The Economic Value of Digital Disruption: A Holistic Assessment for CXOs* (pp. 1–110). Singapore: Springer Nature Singapore. https://doi.org/10.1007/978-981-19-8148-7_1

[12] Mehler, M., Balint, E., Gralla, M., Pößnecker, T., Gast, M., Hölzer, M., . . . Gündel, H. (2024). Training emotional competencies at the workplace: a systematic review and metaanalysis. *BMC Psychology*, 12(1), 1–18.
[13] Davaei, M., & Gunkel, M. (2024). The role of intelligences in teams: a systematic literature review. *Review of Managerial Science*, 18(1), 259–297.
[14] Al-Shboul, M. D. A. (2023). Better understanding of technology effects in adoption of predictive supply chain business analytics among SMEs: fresh insights from developing countries. *Business Process Management Journal*, 29(1), 159–177.
[15] PwC. (2024, May 15). *PwC's Voice of the Consumer Survey 2024*. PwC Global.
[16] Gupta, S., Wang, Y., Patel, P., & Czinkota, M. (2025). Navigating the future of AI in marketing: AI integration across borders, ethical considerations, and policy implications. *International Journal of Information Management*, 82, 102871.
[17] Kaur, H., & Verma, H. V. (2023). The emotion of pride in consumer behaviour and marketing: a review, classification and future research agenda. *Management Research Review*, 46(4), 579–604.
[18] Behera, R. K., Bala, P. K., Rana, N. P., Algharabat, R. S., & Kumar, K. (2024). Transforming customer engagement with artificial intelligence E-marketing: an E-retailer perspective in the era of retail 4.0. *Marketing Intelligence & Planning*, 42(7), 1141–1168.
[19] Mahmoud, A. B. (2024). Digital marketing analytics in sports. In A. Mansurali, M. J. P. Jeyanthi, D. Hack-Polay, & A. B. Mahmoud (Eds.), *Sports Analytics: Data-Driven Sports and Decision Intelligence* (pp. 55–74). Cham: Springer Nature Switzerland. https://doi.org/10.1007/978-3-031-63573-1_4
[20] Nguyen-Viet, B., & Thanh Tran, C. (2024). Sustaining organizational customers' consumption through corporate social responsibility and green advertising receptivity: the mediating role of green trust. *Cogent Business & Management*, 11(1), 2287775.
[21] Mochla, V., Tsourvakas, G., & Vlachopoulou, M. (2025). Positioning a personal political brand on youtube with points of different visual storytelling. *Journal of Political Marketing*, 24(1), 56–76.
[22] Thomas, C. L., Allen, K., & Sung, W. (2024). Emotional Intelligence and academic buoyancy in university students: the mediating influence of self-compassion and achievement goals. *Trends in Psychology*, 1–27. https://doi.org/10.1007/s43076-024-00363-6
[23] Rickard, M. J. F. X., Ackermann, D. M., Schnitzler, M., & Kozlowski, D. (2025). Emotional intelligence as a component of surgical coaching: a scoping review. *Journal of Surgical Education*, 82(1), 103316.
[24] Wamba, S. F. (2022). Impact of artificial intelligence assimilation on firm performance: the mediating effects of organizational agility and customer agility. *International Journal of Information Management*, 67, 102544.
[25] Dhote, T. P. (2021). Review of consumer engagement and digital entertainment on over the top platforms. In S. Das & S. Gochhait (Eds.), *Digital Entertainment: The Next Evolution in Service Sector* (pp. 23–44). Singapore: Springer Nature Singapore. https://doi.org/10.1007/978-981-15-9724-4_2
[26] Mayer, J. D., Salovey, P., Caruso, D. R., & Sitarenios, G. (2003). Measuring emotional intelligence with the MSCEIT V2.0. *Emotion*, 3(1), 97–105. https://doi.org/10.1037/1528-3542.3.1.97
[27] Aguilar-Ferrándiz, M. E., Toledano-Moreno, S., Casas-Barragán, A., Albornoz-Cabello, M., Tapia-Haro, R. M., & Correa-Rodríguez, M. (2024). Implementation of a coaching training for enhancing empathy and emotional intelligence skills in health science students: a prospective study. *BMC Medical Education*, 24(1), 76.

[28] Katirai, A. (2024). Ethical considerations in emotion recognition technologies: a review of the literature. *AI and Ethics*, 4(4), 927–948.
[29] Zhai, C., Wibowo, S., & Li, L. D. (2024). The effects of over-reliance on AI dialogue systems on students' cognitive abilities: a systematic review. *Smart Learning Environments*, 11(1), 28.
[30] Guerola-Navarro, V., Gil-Gomez, H., Oltra-Badenes, R., & Sendra-García, J. (2021). Customer relationship management and its impact on innovation: A literature review. *Journal of Business Research*, 129, 83–87.
[31] Petrescu, M., & Krishen, A. S. (2023). Hybrid intelligence: human–AI collaboration in marketing analytics. *Journal of Marketing Analytics*, 11(3), 263–274.
[32] Jiang, Q., Qian, J., & Zang, Y. (2024). To acknowledge or conceal: an exploratory study on designers' self-determination factors and attitudes toward artificial intelligence participation in their works. *Kybernetes*, 55(1), 1–27. https://doi.org/10.1108/K-02-2024-0471

11 Role of Artificial Intelligence and Emotional Intelligence for Entrepreneurial Success

Shyam Sunder Agrawal, Anushree Saxena, and Amanjot Singh Syan

11.1 INTRODUCTION

11.1.1 Theoretical Background

Entrepreneurial success has long been seen as a key driver of economic growth, innovation, and social change. As technology rapidly evolves worldwide, entrepreneurs face increasingly dynamic, uncertain, and complex environments. The rise of advanced digital technologies, especially artificial intelligence (AI), has changed how entrepreneurs spot opportunities, make decisions, connect with markets, and manage resources. At the same time, there's more focus on human skills like emotional intelligence (EI), which highlights the importance of self-awareness, empathy, communication, and managing emotions in leadership and resilience [1].

Over the past decade (2015–2025), interest has grown in understanding how AI tools and EI skills together affect entrepreneurial success. While AI offers data-driven insights, forecasting, and efficiency [2], EI provides the social and emotional abilities entrepreneurs need to handle relationships, stress, and encourage innovation in diverse teams. However, research in this area is still scattered, with few studies looking at how AI and EI work together to boost entrepreneurship. This chapter aims to fill that gap by reviewing recent research, identifying key trends, and showing how combining AI and EI can improve entrepreneurship in today's digital economy [3].

11.1.2 Importance of Entrepreneurial Success in the Digital Era

Entrepreneurial success in the digital world goes beyond traditional ideas of profitability and survival of ventures. It includes the ability to leverage digital technologies and to adapt quickly to changing consumer preferences and operate in an interconnected

DOI: 10.1201/9781003650775-11

market. The Fourth Industrial Revolution, powered by advances in AI, Blockchain, cloud computing, and the Internet of Things (IoT), has accelerated entrepreneurs' abilities to innovate, scale, and differentiate [4]. According to the Global Entrepreneurship Monitor (GEM) report, digitalization has expanded entrepreneurial opportunities, especially in developing economies such as India, where digital penetration and startup ecosystems are among the fastest growing in the world [5].

Furthermore, the digital economy has ramped up competition, demanding entrepreneurs to balance technological advancement with subtle human attributes. Modern entrepreneurs must demonstrate agility as they adopt AI-powered decision-making systems and, at the same time, display emotional resilience and relational intelligence to innovate and attract investors, customers, and employees. Entrepreneurs who can align technological sophistication with human empathy and creativity in a marketplace that is governed by algorithmic interactions and data-driven platforms will survive longer. For academics and practitioners, learning the ways in which AI and EI align to drive entrepreneurial performance is timely and relevant [6].

11.1.3 Integrating Artificial Intelligence and Emotional Intelligence (EI)

AI and EI are two distinct yet complementary areas for catalyzing entrepreneurship through strategic integration. AI is essentially such machines or computers that are said to do tasks that entail human intelligence, including pattern recognition, natural language processing, predictive analytics, and machine learning. Collectively, all these will enable the entrepreneurs to automate tasks, work with large sets of data, personalize customer interaction, and fine-tune decision-making at the strategic level. For example, AI-based systems such as chatbots, virtual assistants, and recommendation engines are becoming the cornerstone elements of an evolving startup in fintech, e-commerce, or health tech [7].

On the other hand, EI is defined as a person's ability to perceive, understand, manage, and effectively use emotions in interpersonal situations. Highly EI entrepreneurs are likely to be more effective in dealing with uncertainty, motivating teams, establishing networks, and maneuvering intricate social relationships inherent in venture creation and expansion. A study in the *Journal of Business Venturing* [5] identifies that emotionally intelligent entrepreneurs show greater adaptability, leadership, and stakeholder interaction, all of which are key success factors in ambiguous business environments.

The intersection of AI and EI creates a platform for entrepreneurial practice. AI can improve entrepreneurial decision-making and operational efficiency, while EI ensures that entrepreneurs remain attentive to human dynamics, trust, collaboration, and ethical leadership. Combining these areas allows entrepreneurs to utilize smart technologies without sacrificing human-centered values, boosting both competitive advantage and sustainable business practices [8].

11.1.4 Purpose and Objectives of the Chapter

The main aim of this chapter is to systematically synthesize existing literature about AI and EI and their contributions to achieving entrepreneurial success while concentrating on literature published from 2015 to 2025. This chapter uses a systematic literature review (SLR) methodology based on PRISMA (Preferred Reporting Items of Systematic Reviews and Meta-Analyses) guidelines to outline today's knowledge, identify patterns across literature, highlight research gaps, and provide implications for scholars, practitioners, and the policy-making community [9].

Objectives Are as Follows:

- To conceptualize and clarify how AI and EI, both individually and collectively, influence key entrepreneurial processes, including opportunity recognition, innovation, leadership, and strategic decision-making.
- To systematically review and analyze empirical studies, conceptual frameworks, and case-based research that examine the intersection of AI and EI within entrepreneurial contexts.
- To identify critical research gaps, methodological limitations, and under-explored areas in the existing literature, thereby informing and guiding future research agendas in this emerging field.
- To offer practical implications and strategic recommendations for entrepreneurs, educators, and policymakers.

11.2 CONCEPTUAL FOUNDATIONS

11.2.1 Defining Entrepreneurial Success and Its Dimensions

Entrepreneurial success is a multifaceted concept that extends beyond simple measures of financial performance. Scholars have long debated which particular dimensions and indicators encompass the holistic outcomes of entrepreneurial ventures [10]. Traditional metrics, including revenue growth, profitability, market share, and firm survival, continue to be critical to assessing business performance. However, contemporary research highlights entrepreneurial success as encompassing non-financial dimensions such as innovation output, social value, satisfaction of stakeholders, and personal satisfaction of the entrepreneur [6].

Different studies have looked at entrepreneurial success in both its objective and subjective forms. Objective measures may include quantifiable outcomes such as sales figures, return on investment, and job creation; they suggest that subjective measures may reflect the entrepreneur's evaluation of such factors as business performance, work–life balance, autonomy, and achievement of strategic goals. For instance, as per the [11], in emerging markets, entrepreneurs attach importance to a host of measures, following the criteria of financial independence, social contribution, and engagement with the community [12].

Moreover, we understand that the success or acceptance of entrepreneurial activities depends greatly on the sector, region, and culture. For example, the indicators of success for technologies might focus more on innovation and scalability, while social enterprises may emphasize social value creation and impact upon communities. This multidimensional understanding can be the basis of an inquiry into how AI and EI, as complementary resources, help entrepreneurs achieve different and sustainable outcomes [13].

11.2.2 Overview of Artificial Intelligence and Its Relevance in Entrepreneurship

AI includes a very wide range of computational technologies for simulating human cognitive processes such as learning, reasoning, problem-solving, and language processing. Within the entrepreneurial context, AI tools and applications support decision-making processes, enhance operational efficacy, and create innovative products and services. Some AI technologies relevant to entrepreneurship include machine learning algorithms, natural language processing systems, computer vision, expert systems, and intelligent automation systems [14].

For example, entrepreneurs can use AI-generated actionable insights from large and complicated datasets to predict market moves, optimize supply chains, and customize customers' experiences. An instance would be the use of AI in customer relationship management (CRM), which enables an intelligent processing of consumer behavioral patterns, intelligent automation of marketing strategies, and improved customer engagement by an entrepreneur. Predictive analytics also allows entrepreneurs to identify emerging opportunities and assess the potential risk associated with them before taking strategic decisions [15].

Recent studies, such as those by the [16], emphasize that AI adoption can enhance entrepreneurial agility, allowing ventures to respond rapidly to changing market conditions and technological disruptions. In sectors like fintech, health tech, and e-commerce, AI-driven innovations have opened new avenues for entrepreneurial value creation. However, effective integration of AI also requires entrepreneurs to possess digital competencies, ethical awareness, and strategic foresight, underscoring the importance of human-centric capabilities alongside technological adoption [17].

11.2.3 Understanding Emotional Intelligence in the Entrepreneurial Context

EI, conceptualized by [18] and popularized by [19], refers to an individual's ability to perceive, understand, regulate, and utilize emotions effectively in personal and professional interactions. In the context of entrepreneurship, EI has emerged as a critical determinant of leadership effectiveness, team dynamics, stakeholder management, and entrepreneurial resilience [20].

Entrepreneurs with high EI are better equipped to navigate the uncertainties, stresses, and interpersonal challenges inherent in venture creation and growth. They are capable of building strong networks, inspiring employees, managing investor relationships, and negotiating effectively with partners and clients. Empirical research demonstrates that emotionally intelligent entrepreneurs exhibit higher levels of adaptability, self-efficacy, and leadership competence, all of which positively influence business performance [9].

Moreover, EI contributes to entrepreneurial opportunity recognition by enhancing entrepreneurs' ability to empathize with customer needs, anticipate market shifts, and foster collaborative innovation. In rapidly evolving and multicultural business environments, EI enables entrepreneurs to build trust, resolve conflicts constructively, and sustain long-term stakeholder engagement. The increasing focus on sustainable and ethical entrepreneurship highlights the importance of EI in supporting socially responsible and people-centered business practices [21].

11.2.4 Synergistic Relationship between AI and EI in Business Ventures

AI and EI are distinct concepts, and each emphasizes biases, yet at the intersection of AI and EI, we can improve both the abilities and outcomes in the entrepreneurial context. As such, AI enables the entrepreneur to leverage computational power for reasonable choice decisions, automation, and operational scale, while ensuring the entrepreneur is still alert to human dynamics, ethics, and relationships. [22].

The integration of AI and EI promotes a balance in entrepreneurship by making use of technology, yet not compromising on the human bond. AI-powered sentiment analysis tools allow an entrepreneur to keep track of customer feedback and social media sentiments in real time, enabling the entrepreneur to adopt an empathetic view in changing marketing strategies. Likewise, AI-enabled virtual assistants can manage all routine customer interactions so that the entrepreneur can concentrate on building relationships and strategic leadership requiring EI [23].

Recent studies indicate that entrepreneurs adept at the combination of AI with EI are better than anyone at problem-solving, managing innovation, and interacting with stakeholders. The [24] study claims that AI–EI integration ventures retain customers better, retain employees better, and innovate better than businesses relying solely on technology-driven strategies. Conversely, as ethical considerations relating to AI applications increase – anxiety, data privacy, algorithmic bias, and social responsibility – EI provides the moral principles to guide ethical decision-making and responsible AI applications. The convergence of AI and EI equitably meets the changing expectations from consumers, investors, and regulators for enterprises that shall be technologically proficient as well as socially responsible [25].

11.2.5 Conceptual Framework

As depicted in Figure 11.1, this framework provides a structured and integrative pathway wherein technology and AI are married to the human depth of EI, thus creating a holistic foundation for entrepreneurial excellence. Through this lens, AI enables the entrepreneur to work with gigantic datasets, draw meaningful insights through predictive analysis and machine learning algorithms, and conduct sentiment analysis with a certain level of precision. These capabilities help anticipate shifts in the markets, find emerging consumer trends, and reconcile subtle behavioral patterns as causal inputs into strategic action. Parallel to this analytical field, EI also encompasses the entrepreneurial ability to empathize, self-awareness, resilient leadership, and ethical sensitivity. Such human-oriented skills further ensure that technology insights are contextualized within relationship understanding, ethical consideration, and adaptive leadership principles [26].

The framework progresses systematically, beginning with opportunity recognition, where entrepreneurs combine empirical market analytics with an intuitive grasp of customer aspirations and latent needs. From these two perspectives, opportunities are not only identified with precision but are also understood within the broader context of consumer desires and market dynamics. Building upon this foundation, the process advances into decision-making and strategic planning. Here, data-informed forecasting and scenario analysis offer entrepreneurs a robust basis for

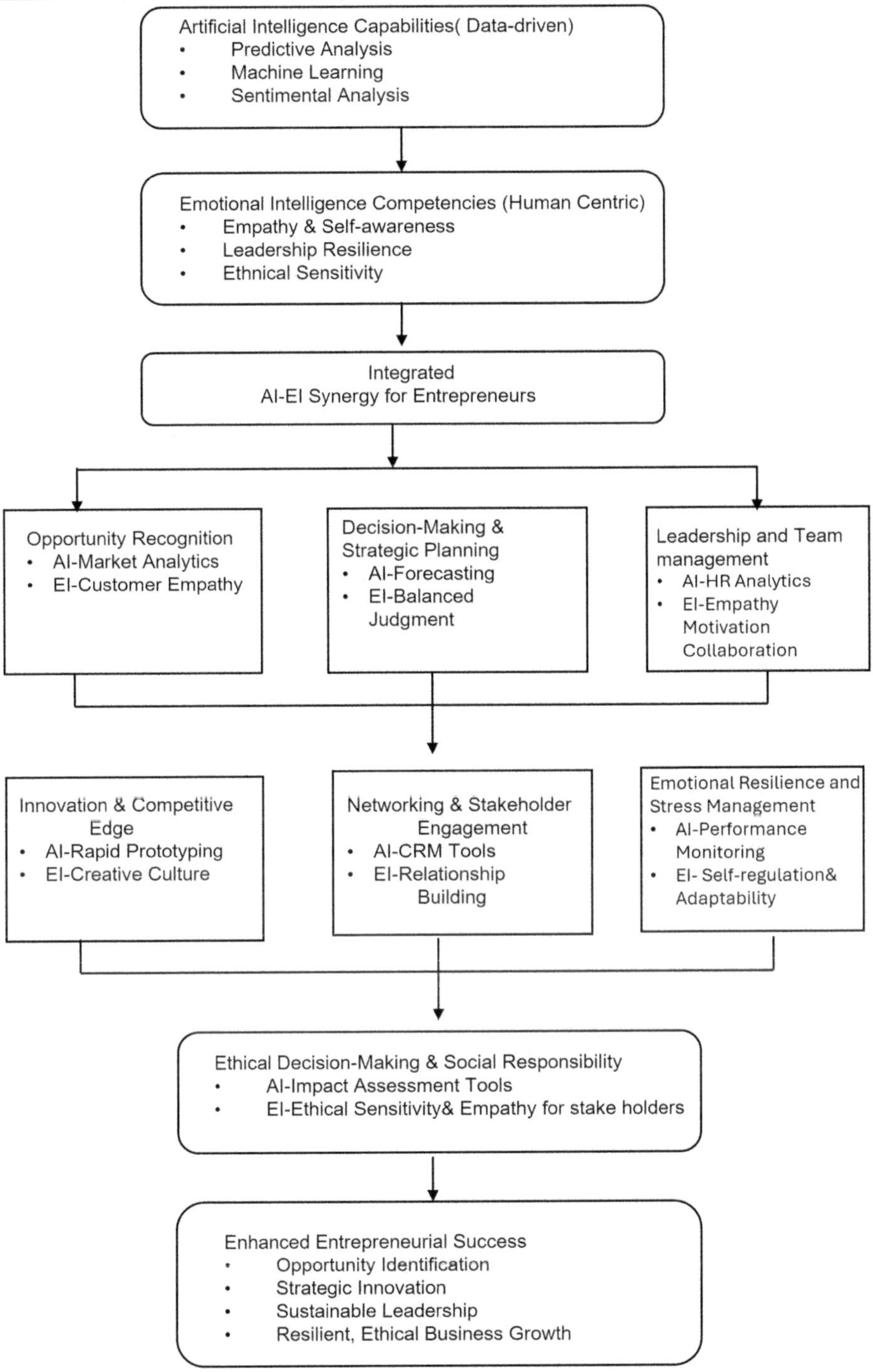

FIGURE 11.1 Conceptual framework.

(Source: Authors' creation.)

evaluating strategic alternatives. However, it is through the integration of balanced judgment, cultivated by EI, that decisions are nuanced and responsive to stakeholder interests, long-term sustainability, and unforeseen contingencies [27].

The transition from an entrepreneur to a leader and that of managing teams also acts as a bridge to the interconnectedness between AI and EI. One can obtain information regarding employee performance, trends in their engagement, and even organizational dynamics through human resource analytics. However, it is the leader who can efficiently and effectively boost motivation, inspiration, and collaboration, and can take those insights to become a very cohesive, high-performing team. EI governs the link that leadership must be empathetic, communicative, and responsive to changing needs, both individual and group, within the enterprise [28].

This integrated foundation then drives innovation and competitive advantage. Entrepreneurs are empowered to accelerate product development and refine services through iterative prototyping and rapid testing methodologies informed by real-time data. Simultaneously, the fostering of a creative organizational culture, supported by open-mindedness, psychological safety, and encouragement of exploratory practices, ensures that innovation is not confined to technological tools but is embedded within the entrepreneurial thinking and organization's foundation [29].

Parallel to innovation, the framework emphasizes networking and stakeholder engagement. Advanced CRM tools streamline stakeholder interactions and optimize communication strategies. Yet the durability and authenticity of these relationships are anchored in the entrepreneur's ability to build trust, nurture rapport, and engage in meaningful dialogue. EI strengthens these engagements, enabling entrepreneurs to navigate complex interpersonal dynamics with sensitivity and foresight [30].

Equally critical is the cultivation of emotional resilience and effective stress management. In entrepreneurial environments characterized by uncertainty, high stakes, and continuous change, entrepreneurs benefit from the clarity provided by performance monitoring tools and analytical dashboards. However, the ability to self-regulate, adapt to evolving challenges, and sustain composure under pressure derives from EI. This inner resilience enables sustained decision-making capacity and long-term perseverance, essential attributes for entrepreneurial continuity [31].

The outcome of these interwoven capabilities is realized in ethical decision-making and social responsibility. Quantitative impact assessments illuminate the potential consequences of strategic actions on societal, environmental, and regulatory dimensions. Yet it is the entrepreneur's ethical sensitivity, empathy for stakeholders, and commitment to fairness that guide responsible and conscientious decision-making. This alignment ensures that business actions are not only efficient and profitable but are also socially attuned and ethically grounded [32].

Ultimately, the synthesis of these diverse yet interconnected dimensions leads to an elevated model of entrepreneurial success. Entrepreneurs who effectively combine technical skills with EI are uniquely well-situated to recognize and capitalize on opportunities with focus and compassion, innovate strategically and foster a culture of innovation, lead with vision and integrity, and develop businesses that are resilient, ethical, and responsibly set up for long-term success. This model highlights the idea that long-term entrepreneurial success stems not just from technological proficiency or interpersonal competence but from the intentional, reflective blending of both [33].

11.3 THEMATIC SYNTHESIS OF LITERATURE

11.3.1 Role of AI in Enhancing Entrepreneurial Processes

AI has become one of the most exciting advances for entrepreneurs: it allows them to mechanize much of the activity that goes into building and developing their business. Among the areas where one can make use of AI Innovations is opportunity identification. With the help of AI algorithms, especially those that use machine learning and big data analytics, entrepreneurs can sift through enormous volumes of market data to discover new trends, customer tastes, and unsatisfied needs. These observations bring about identifying profitable opportunities earlier and more accurately than traditional methods. Predictive tools on an AI basis empower entrepreneurs to forecast market trends, consumer behavior, and competitive forces, thus significantly enhancing their decision-making [7].

AI helps business owners reduce bias, enhance accuracy, and speed up their decision-making. Using AI algorithms to analyze historical data, the business owner can use educated predictions to validate assumptions and even optimize business models [34]. By simply leveraging the ability of AI to process and analyze big data, innovation is also made possible since feedback is given to entrepreneurs during product development, market segmentation, and the development of innovative solutions for customers' pain points. Various researches well explored how AI serves to accelerate innovation in sectors like e-commerce and health tech by fostering rapid prototyping and nimble adaptation to market needs [35].

Nonetheless, there are challenges in terms of the high cost of AI implementation, lack of access to AI skills in low-resource settings, and ensuring data privacy and addressing ethical issues. Despite these challenges, AI is still a significant resource in spurring innovation and improving business decision making processes [36].

11.3.2 Contributions of EI to Entrepreneurial Leadership, Resilience, and Networking

EI plays a vital role in enhancing entrepreneurial leadership, resilience, and networking capabilities. High EI helps entrepreneurs handle tricky relationships, manage stress, and keep a positive work culture. Entrepreneurs who can control their emotions well are better at making clear decisions when under pressure, which is key for good leadership [37, 38]. Leaders with high EI inspire their teams, building trust and motivation, which boosts employee engagement and loyalty. Research shows that emotionally intelligent entrepreneurs are more likely to create cooperative workplaces and handle conflicts effectively within their teams [10].

Resilience is a key quality for entrepreneurs dealing with the challenges of starting a business, and it's closely connected to EI. Entrepreneurs with high EI are better at handling setbacks, learning from failures, and coming back stronger. Research shows that emotionally intelligent entrepreneurs often have more perseverance, which is essential for managing the ups and downs of entrepreneurship. They are also better prepared to handle the emotional stress that comes with running a business, like financial pressures, investor demands, and market changes [27].

When it comes to networking, EI helps entrepreneurs build stronger connections with stakeholders, including investors, partners, customers, and employees. EI encourages empathy, active listening, and trust, key ingredients for good communication and teamwork. According to [39], entrepreneurs with high EI and strong networking skills are more likely to create valuable partnerships, gain access to resources, and grow their business.

11.3.3 Intersections of AI and EI in Entrepreneurial Practice

The combination of AI and EI is a new research area with important effects on entrepreneurship. While AI excels at managing data and improving decisions, EI covers the human side of entrepreneurship, like leadership, managing relationships, and staying emotionally steady. Researchers say that bringing AI and EI together offers a complete approach to entrepreneurship, where technology and emotional skills join forces to achieve better business results [5].

An example of where EI and AI come together is in CRM. CRM solutions driven by AI can track buying habits, likes, and dislikes of customers, and emotionally intelligent businesspeople use this data to customize communication, establish trust, and provide more engaging experiences. Once again, AI can assist in strategic decision-making with real-time analysis, while EI allows businesspeople to make decisions that are data-based as well as moral and empathetic [40].

In addition, AI tools like sentiment analysis and chatbots can enhance communication and decision-making processes in real time, but the use of EI in decoding emotional cues and managing customer feedback is invaluable. The synergy of AI and EI allows entrepreneurs to scale their businesses more effectively, striking a balance between data-driven decisions and human-centered approaches that build long-term relationships and sustainable growth [41].

11.3.4 Emerging Trends and Technologies

These new technologies, such as AI-driven emotional analytics, chatbots, and sentiment analysis, are also transforming the world of entrepreneurs by allowing entrepreneurs to acquire real-time emotional and behavioral feedback. AI-driven emotional analytics software is increasingly being deployed to quantify consumer emotions and reactions online, allowing entrepreneurs to tailor their marketing efforts to emotional cues. These technologies monitor facial expressions, tone of voice, and other nonverbal cues to extract information on customer emotions that can be leveraged for personalized product offerings and enhanced customer experiences [42].

AI-powered chatbots have also revolutionized customer service by providing 24X7 support, personalized interactions, and real-time responses. The AI-powered assistants have human-like conversations, and the user interaction level and customer satisfaction are increased. The ability to provide instant responses to consumer inquiries, handle routine operations, and gather feedback enables entrepreneurs to shift their focus toward more complex issues, thereby increasing operational efficiency [1, 43]

Sentiment analysis software, employed to examine social media posts, reviews, and customer feedback, are enabling business owners to track public sentiment toward their products, services, and company. Processing high volumes of unstructured data, sentiment analysis provides real-time feedback on customer satisfaction, enabling entrepreneurs to make strategic adjustments in a timely fashion. From our study, we have noticed that businesses that use sentiment analysis can more accurately predict trends, address customer concerns, and strengthen brand loyalty [33].

With advancing AI technologies, their ability to detect and interpret human emotion is also set to become more sophisticated, providing entrepreneurs with an even better understanding of consumer behavior and enabling them to create more effective, emotionally driven advertising campaigns.

11.3.5 Sector-Specific Applications

The integration of AI and EI in entrepreneurship varies significantly across different sectors. In startups, especially in technology-driven industries, AI is often a core component of business models, helping entrepreneurs optimize product development, customer targeting, and resource allocation. AI tools enable startups to operate more efficiently, scale quickly, and remain competitive in dynamic markets. Meanwhile, EI helps entrepreneurs foster positive workplace cultures, attract talent, and develop customer-centric strategies, all of which are essential for sustaining growth in early-stage ventures [44].

In tech ventures, AI plays a dominant role in innovation and disrupting traditional business models. Entrepreneurs in this sector leverage AI for everything from product recommendations in e-commerce to predictive maintenance in IoT applications. However, the success of these ventures often hinges on emotionally intelligent leadership that can navigate technical challenges, manage investor relationships, and lead teams through periods of uncertainty and rapid change [45, 46].

For social enterprises, which aim to address social and environmental challenges, AI can provide valuable data for impact measurement, resource allocation, and community outreach. However, emotionally intelligent leadership is critical to ensuring that the mission of the enterprise remains at the forefront, especially when balancing profit motives with social goals. EI fosters the ability to empathize with communities, build trust, and create sustainable partnerships, all of which are essential for the long-term success of social enterprises [6, 28].

11.4 METHODOLOGY

11.4.1 Systematic Literature Review (SLR)

A SLR is a strong and well-structured research methodology designed to comprehensively identify, evaluate, and collect relevant academic literature for a specific research topic. The main difference between SLR and a conventional narrative literature review is that while a narrative review can be selective and subjective, an SLR is systematic, offering clearer explanations and justifications for the problems studied. SLR provides a better understanding of key research trends and offers a more comprehensive view of the interaction between AI and EI in entrepreneurship [7].

Employing an SLR ensures that the chapter presents a clear, evidence-based summary that follows current academic standards. It also offers a structured way to carefully evaluate existing studies, highlight their strengths and weaknesses, and find research areas that need more attention [47].

11.4.2 PRISMA Framework

This chapter utilizes the PRISMA framework to make the research process clear and easy to follow. PRISMA, created in 2009 and updated in 2020, offers a checklist and flowchart that help guide researchers through each step of a systematic review, such as finding, screening, and selecting studies. There are several reasons for using PRISMA. First, it improves transparency by clearly showing how searches were done, what criteria were used to include or exclude studies, and why certain studies were chosen. Second, it ensures a thorough and unbiased search by covering multiple databases and keywords. Third, it makes it possible for other researchers to repeat or build on the review [41].

In this chapter, the PRISMA flowchart (Figure 11.2) shows the steps taken, including how many records were found, screened, checked for eligibility, and

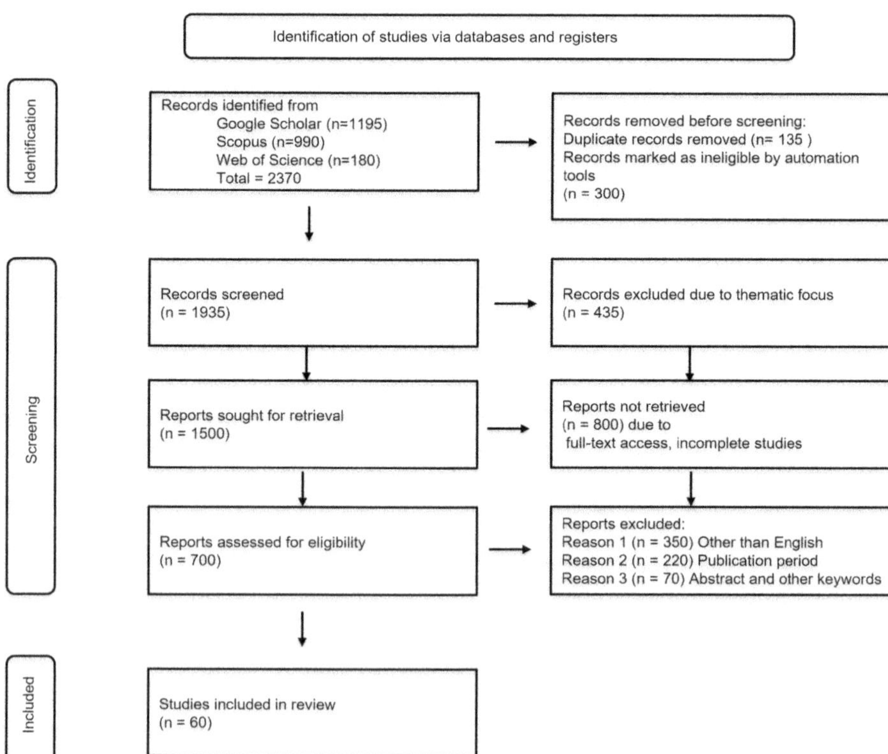

FIGURE 11.2 PRISMA framework.

(Source: Authors' creation.)

finally included. This organized method helps make sure the review meets current standards in management, entrepreneurship, and related fields [48].

11.4.3 Data Sources and Search Strategy

The literature search was carried out across several academic databases to cover a wide range of relevant studies published between 2015 and 2025. The databases used were SCOPUS, Web of Science, and Google Scholar. These were chosen because they cover a broad range of fields, including management, entrepreneurship, computer science, psychology, and social sciences.

A carefully structured set of keywords and Boolean operators was used to find studies related to AI, EI, and entrepreneurial success. The main search terms included "artificial intelligence" AND "entrepreneurship," "emotional intelligence" AND "entrepreneurship," "AI and EI integration" AND "entrepreneurial performance," "AI-enabled entrepreneurship," "emotional competencies in business ventures," and "technology adoption and entrepreneurial leadership."

Additional filters were applied to limit the search to peer-reviewed journal articles, conference papers, book chapters, and authoritative reports published in English between 2015 and 2025. Reference lists of key articles were manually screened to identify additional relevant studies through backward snowballing [49].

11.4.4 Inclusion and Exclusion Criteria

Our selection of the final 60 papers was the result of a systematic and carefully structured review process. We began by identifying a total of 2,370 records from three key databases: Google Scholar, Scopus, and Web of Science. After removing 135 duplicate records and 300 records marked as ineligible by automation tools, 1,935 records proceeded to the screening stage. During this phase, 435 records were excluded because their thematic focus did not align with the scope of our review. From the remaining set, we sought to retrieve 1,500 reports; however, 800 of these could not be accessed in full text, were incomplete, or lacked sufficient methodological rigor. Of the 700 articles assessed for eligibility, additional exclusions were made: 350 were removed due to language barriers, 220 fell outside the specified publication period, and 70 were excluded based on irrelevance found in their abstracts or keywords. Following this rigorous multi-step evaluation, we identified and finalized a set of 60 high-quality studies based on high citations that best fit our review criteria and research objectives [50]. Table 11.1 summarizes the inclusion and exclusion criteria as given below:

11.4.5 Data Extraction and Synthesis

A structured data extraction form was systematically developed for all included studies to ensure consistent and comprehensive capture of relevant information. Key variables extracted from each study encompassed the authors, publication year, and source; research objectives and questions; methodological approach (quantitative,

TABLE 11.1
Inclusion and Exclusion Criteria

Criteria Type	Inclusion Criteria	Exclusion Criteria
Thematic Focus	Studies examining the role of Artificial Intelligence (AI) and/or Emotional Intelligence (EI) within entrepreneurial contexts (startups, SMEs, innovation ventures, entrepreneurial leadership).	Studies focusing exclusively on corporate, managerial, or non-entrepreneurial contexts without relevance to entrepreneurship.
Content Scope	Empirical studies (quantitative, qualitative, or mixed methods), conceptual frameworks, theoretical papers, and case studies explicitly linking AI and/or EI to entrepreneurial success or business performance.	Studies addressing AI or EI in isolation without any connection to entrepreneurial outcomes, ventures, or processes.
Publication Type	Peer-reviewed journal articles, conference papers, scholarly book chapters, and authoritative industry reports.	Non-scholarly sources such as magazines, blogs, opinion pieces, and grey literature lack academic rigor.
Publication Period	Publications dated between January 2015 and March 2025.	Studies published before 2015 or after 2025.
Language	Studies published in English.	Studies published in languages other than English.
Accessibility and Quality	Full-text availability with clear methodological descriptions and sound academic quality.	Publications without full-text access, incomplete studies, or those lacking methodological rigor (e.g., vague design, insufficient data).

Source: Author's creation.

qualitative, or mixed methods); contextual factors such as sector, geographical region, and entrepreneurial type; key constructs examined AI, EI, and entrepreneurial outcomes; major findings and contributions; as well as identified limitations and proposed directions for future research. The collected data were synthesized thematically to uncover recurring patterns, dominant theoretical perspectives, methodological trends, and core empirical findings. Studies were categorically grouped under major themes such as AI adoption in entrepreneurship, EI and entrepreneurial leadership, AI–EI integration frameworks, and entrepreneurial performance outcomes. This thematic synthesis facilitated the development of a conceptual map that elucidates the dynamic interplay between AI, EI, and entrepreneurship. Furthermore, to ensure the robustness and credibility of the synthesized evidence, the methodological rigor of each included study was critically appraised using established quality assessment tools [21, 51]. Table 11.2 summarizes the articles included based on high citations.

TABLE 11.2
Exemplary Articles Included in the Review as Per Citation

Name of the Journal	Number of Documents	Area of Focus	References	Citations
Social Entrepreneurs: Mobilisers of Social Change	1	Social Entrepreneurship	[14]	120
Psychology & Marketing	1	Creativity in Marketing and AI	[3]	166
Journal of Family Business Management	1	AI in Family Business	[43]	26
Entrepreneurship Theory and Practice	2	AI and Entrepreneurship	[10]	1,005
British Journal of Management	1	Generative AI and HRM	[31]	65
Administrative Science Quarterly	1	Emotional Intelligence and Job Performance	[4]	1,925
International Journal of Production Research	1	AI in Supply Chain Resilience	[37]	26
Journal of Managerial Psychology	2	Emotional Intelligence Review	[52]	632
Information Systems Frontiers	2	AI and Business Value, AI Adoption	[39]	262
Personality and Social Psychology Review	1	Dual-process Emotional Intelligence	[6]	621
Human Relations	1	Emotional Intelligence and Leadership	[1]	6261
Academy of Management Annals	1	Trust in AI	[44]	355
Cogent Education	2	AI in Education	[14]	35
California Management Review	4	AI History, AI in Work, AI in HRM, Decision-making	[53]	8,471
Applied Sciences	1	AI in Computer Vision	[3]	425
Production Planning & Control	1	AI in Operations and Supply Chain	[6]	941
Open House International	1	Walkability Research with PRISMA	[41]	671
Applied Artificial Intelligence	1	Human–AI Management Symbiosis	[42]	457
Academy of Management Journal	1	AI and Employee Creativity	[32]	44
Complexity	1	AI and New Product Success	[20]	1,575
Review of Managerial Science	1	Generative AI and Business Models	[48]	45
International Journal of Gender and Entrepreneurship	1	Women Entrepreneurship and EI	[7]	45

(Continued)

TABLE 11.2 (Continued)

Name of the Journal	Number of Documents	Area of Focus	References	Citations
Journal of Management Analytics	1	AI Survey and Trends	[54]	4,741
Journal of Business Research	1	AI in Organizations	[45]	412
Emotion Review	1	Ability Model of EI	[38]	787
Frontiers in Psychology	1	AI in Legal Entrepreneurship	[29]	4,556
American Journal of Economics	1	EI and Entrepreneurial Success	[5]	422
Journal of Global Scholars of Marketing Science	1	B2B AI Adoption	[17]	42
HERD: Health Environments Research & Design Journal	1	Systematic Review Methodology	[15]	4,781
European Journal of Personality	1	Trait EI Psychometrics	[36]	4,454
Journal of Marketing	1	Consumers and AI	[27]	5,746
SSRN Preprint	1	Leadership in AI Workplace	[33]	145
Business and Investment Review	1	SLR on SME Performance	[55]	4,754
International Journal of Engineering, Business and Management	1	EI and Investment Decisions	[12]	15
Technological Forecasting and Social Change	1	AI and Entrepreneurial Action	[56]	356
Asia-Pacific Journal of Business Administration	1	Industry 4.0 Critical Factors	[23]	144
International Journal of Human–Computer Interaction	2	Human-centered AI, AI in Education	[49]	21
Asia Pacific Journal of Innovation and Entrepreneurship	1	AI in Entrepreneurial Education	[13]	64
International Journal of Healthcare Management	1	EI and Healthcare Innovation	[7, 22]	356
FIIB Business Review	1	EI and Higher Education	[9]	6,558
Journal of Contemporary Social Science and Education Studies	1	EI and AI in Social Media Marketing	[40, 57]	215
APTISI Transactions on Technopreneurship	1	Purposeful Leadership	[58]	332
Applied Psychology	1	EI in the Workplace	[59]	32,226

Source: Author's creation.

11.5 KEY FINDINGS AND RESEARCH GAPS

This section synthesizes the major empirical evidence and conceptual contributions emerging from the systematic review of literature on integrating AI and EI in entrepreneurship. The systematic review of literature findings identified a number of important insights into AI and EI integration in entrepreneurial contexts. On the one hand, AI was invariably demonstrated to improve entrepreneurs' ability to handle bulk data sets, to facilitate better decision-making, increased opportunity spotting, and resource allocation optimization. On the other hand, EI was demonstrated to be vital in leadership, encouraging resilience, empathy, and stakeholder management, especially in high-risk, high-pressure situations [60]. However, a number of gaps in research that limited the depth of understanding in this context were identified. First, although the application of AI in entrepreneurship has been explored in depth, its intersection with EI has not been widely explored, particularly in context-based, real-world contexts. This gap is particularly obvious in under-represented geographies like India and the Global South, where entrepreneurial practice is distinctly different. Second, much existing research has examined specific sectors or industries, with broader applications and cross-sectoral findings missing in the research. Methodologically, the review identified the shortage of longitudinal studies and empirical work capturing the dynamic, unfolding nature of AI and EI integration over time. These gaps bridged, future research could benefit from a more interdisciplinary focus, investigating the integration of AI and EI in diverse entrepreneurial ecosystems. Longitudinal studies, coupled with mixed-methods methodologies, would reveal more insight into the long-term impact of AI and EI in entrepreneurship. Bridging the gap, contextual studies examining emerging economies like India would be valuable, informing policy-making and entrepreneurial training programs attuned to local imperatives. This would align with the chapter's objectives of identifying key research areas, informing future studies, and providing practical solutions to improving entrepreneurial success through AI and EI integration [52].

11.5.1 Summary of Empirical Evidence and Conceptual Insights

The reviewed literature reveals that both AI and EI independently exert a significant influence on core entrepreneurial activities such as opportunity recognition, strategic decision-making, innovation management, leadership, and stakeholder engagement. Empirical studies demonstrate that AI-driven tools, such as predictive analytics, machine learning models, and AI-enabled decision-support systems, enhance entrepreneurs' capacity to identify market trends, optimize resource allocation, and develop competitive strategies. Simultaneously, research on EI indicates that competencies like empathy, self-awareness, social skills, and resilience play a crucial role in leadership effectiveness, team management, and entrepreneurial well-being [61].

Conceptual papers and integrative frameworks suggest that combining AI with EI could yield synergistic benefits, allowing entrepreneurs to leverage data-driven insights while navigating human-centered complexities with emotional acuity. Despite this theoretical promise, empirical evidence on the explicit integration of AI and

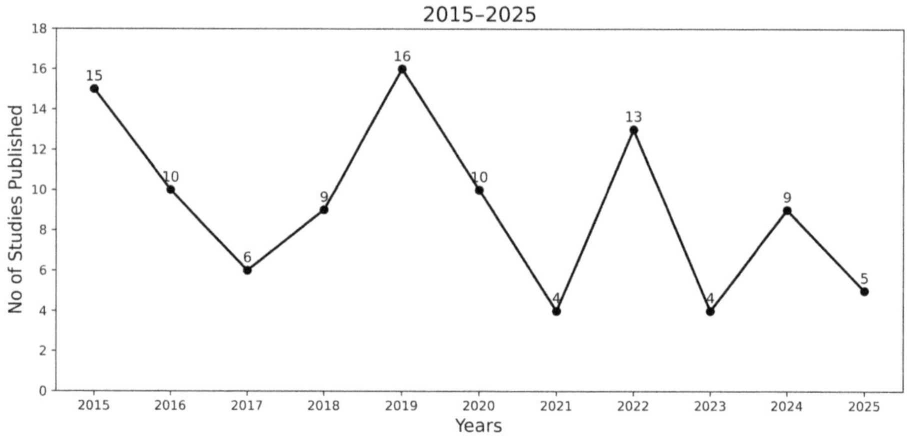

FIGURE 11.3 No. of studies published from 2015 to 2025 (high citations).

(Source: Authors' creation.)

EI within entrepreneurial contexts remains limited and fragmented. No of Studies published from 2015 to 2025 (Figure 11.3) depicts the same.

11.5.2 Identified Gaps in Literature

The systematic review identifies three broad categories of gaps within the existing literature.

11.5.2.1 Contextual Limitations

A significant proportion of studies is concentrated in technologically advanced economies and large-scale enterprises, with limited attention to startups, social enterprises, and small businesses, particularly in emerging markets [58].

11.5.2.2 Underexplored Intersections

While AI and EI have been extensively studied as individual constructs in entrepreneurship, there is a paucity of research exploring how their intersection jointly influences entrepreneurial decision-making, innovation, and leadership practices. Frameworks explicitly combining AI-driven analytics with emotionally intelligent leadership approaches are scarce [53].

11.5.2.3 Methodological Gaps

The current body of work is skewed toward qualitative case studies and conceptual discussions, with fewer longitudinal, experimental, or mixed-methods studies that rigorously measure the combined effects of AI and EI on entrepreneurial outcomes. There is also a lack of cross-cultural comparative studies that examine how these dynamics vary across diverse sociocultural contexts [41].

11.5.3 Regional and Sectoral Gaps

The geographic distribution of studies highlights a notable imbalance. Much of the empirical evidence stems from North America, Europe, and East Asia, with relatively sparse research emerging from India, South Asia, Africa, and other parts of the Global South. This creates a critical gap, especially considering the growing entrepreneurial ecosystems and digital transformation initiatives in these regions [54].

Sectorally, existing studies tend to focus on high-technology ventures and IT-based startups, with limited investigation into traditional sectors such as agriculture, manufacturing, healthcare, and social enterprises, sectors that are pivotal in emerging economies like India. Furthermore, regional-specific factors such as cultural norms, regulatory environments, and infrastructure constraints that could mediate the AI–EI-entrepreneurship nexus remain largely underexplored [56, 62].

11.6 IMPLICATIONS FOR ENTREPRENEURIAL PRACTICE AND POLICY

The integration of AI and EI presents significant implications for entrepreneurial practice, policy formulation, and capacity building. Drawing on the synthesized evidence and identified gaps, this section delineates strategic directions that can guide entrepreneurs, ecosystem stakeholders, policymakers, and educators in harnessing the combined potential of AI and EI to strengthen entrepreneurial outcomes [63].

11.6.1 Strategic Implications for Entrepreneurs and Startups

Entrepreneurs and startup founders who strategically leverage both AI and EI stand to gain a substantial competitive advantage in complex and volatile markets. AI capabilities can augment entrepreneurial decision-making through real-time market analytics, customer insights, automated forecasting, and predictive modeling. EI, however, equips entrepreneurs with competencies essential for managing interpersonal relationships, fostering collaboration, and navigating emotionally charged entrepreneurial journeys. Entrepreneurs should actively cultivate an integrated approach where AI-driven insights inform opportunity recognition and strategic planning, while EI shapes leadership, team dynamics, and stakeholder engagement. Startups that integrate emotionally intelligent leadership practices with data-driven operational strategies are more likely to exhibit adaptive resilience, innovation capability, and sustainable growth in highly dynamic entrepreneurial ecosystems [56].

11.6.2 Role of AI–EI Synergy in Fostering Innovation and Competitiveness

The synergistic integration of AI and EI can catalyze innovation processes by bridging rational, data-driven approaches with intuitive and empathetic leadership practices. Machine learning, sentiment analysis, and AI design thinking platforms empower entrepreneurs with AI technologies to discover hidden customer needs, rapidly prototype products, and iterate product–market fit. Through emotionally intelligent communication, customer engagement, and teamwork, entrepreneurs can co-create technologically valid and emotionally engaging value propositions. This dual approach enhances the capacity of ventures to respond innovatively to emerging market trends, customer preferences, and competitive pressures. Entrepreneurs who consciously integrate AI applications with EI-based leadership practices are better positioned to sustain long-term competitive advantage through continuous innovation and adaptive learning [57, 64].

11.6.3 Policy Recommendations for Entrepreneurial Ecosystems

Policy makers and ecosystem enablers can foster critical environments for AI–EI integration among entrepreneurs. Policies that encourage AI technology access, for instance, low-cost cloud-computing infrastructure, open-source AI tools, and data analytics platforms, can level the playing field for technological adoption among startups and micro-enterprises. At the same time, programs that support EI capacity building through leadership development initiatives, mentorship programs, and psychological well-being interventions can enhance entrepreneurial resilience and relational skills. Policymakers should prioritize the creation of integrated innovation hubs, incubators, and accelerator programs that foster multidisciplinary collaboration between AI technologists and emotionally intelligent entrepreneurial leaders. In emerging economies such as India, targeted interventions that enhance digital literacy, entrepreneurial leadership, and EI training can help bridge both technological and human capital gaps, contributing to inclusive and sustainable entrepreneurial ecosystems [3, 21].

11.6.4 Implications for Entrepreneurial Education and Training

Higher education institutions in India and other emerging economies have a unique opportunity to embed AI and EI integration within entrepreneurial education and training programs. Curricula should be designed to expose aspiring entrepreneurs to both technological competencies, such as AI-driven analytics, digital entrepreneurship, and machine learning applications, and EI competencies, including empathy, social awareness, leadership communication, and resilience building. Experiential learning approaches, such as entrepreneurship bootcamps, case-based pedagogy, simulation-based training, and multidisciplinary hackathons, can facilitate practical exposure to the AI–EI nexus. Faculty development initiatives that equip educators with the skills to teach AI applications alongside EI frameworks can further enhance instructional quality. Indian higher education institutions that integrate AI–EI frameworks into entrepreneurship education will better prepare graduates to navigate the demands of data-driven yet human-centric entrepreneurial landscapes, thereby contributing to national innovation and startup development agendas [43, 51].

11.7 FUTURE RESEARCH DIRECTIONS

The synthesis of literature on AI and EI in entrepreneurship highlights several avenues for advancing scholarly inquiry. Future research directions should prioritize deepening theoretical integration, expanding empirical scope, and leveraging methodological innovations to generate a nuanced understanding of how AI and EI jointly influence entrepreneurial success across diverse contexts [53].

11.7.1 Advancing Interdisciplinary Studies of AI and EI in Entrepreneurship

Advancing interdisciplinary research that explicitly integrates perspectives from computer science, psychology, management, and entrepreneurship is imperative for building robust frameworks that capture the interplay between AI and EI in entrepreneurial processes. Future studies should conceptualize models that articulate how AI-enabled tools (such as predictive analytics, machine learning, and sentiment analysis) interact with emotionally intelligent leadership attributes (such as empathy, social awareness, and emotional regulation) to shape entrepreneurial decision-making, opportunity recognition, innovation, and venture growth. Theoretical contributions that synthesize cognitive entrepreneurship, affective computing, and leadership theories can provide enriched explanatory power. Greater emphasis should be placed on exploring how this integration influences entrepreneurial outcomes in emerging market contexts, family-owned businesses, women-led ventures, and social enterprises, where cultural, relational, and institutional dynamics differ significantly from mature ecosystems [65].

11.7.2 Methodological Recommendations for Future Studies

Future research should adopt diversified and rigorous methodological approaches to strengthen empirical validity and generalizability. Longitudinal studies that track the evolving use of AI tools alongside the development of EI competencies in entrepreneurial ventures can provide insights into causal mechanisms and temporal dynamics. Mixed-methods designs that combine quantitative assessments (such as AI usage metrics, EI psychometric scales, and entrepreneurial performance indicators) with qualitative case studies or ethnographic inquiry can uncover rich, context-sensitive insights. Experimental and quasi-experimental designs can help isolate the effects of AI and EI interventions on entrepreneurial behavior and venture outcomes. Cross-cultural comparative studies are particularly needed to examine how sociocultural factors moderate the relationship between AI–EI integration and entrepreneurial success, especially in regions like India, Southeast Asia, and Sub-Saharan Africa [55].

11.7.3 Emerging Technologies and Entrepreneurial Ecosystem Dynamics

Future research should also investigate how emerging technologies and evolving entrepreneurial ecosystem dynamics shape the application of AI and EI in entrepreneurship beyond 2025. The proliferation of advanced AI technologies, including generative AI, explainable AI, AI-powered decision-support systems, and AI-enabled emotional analytics, opens new frontiers for entrepreneurial opportunity creation and venture scaling. Studies should examine how entrepreneurs leverage these technologies in tandem with emotionally intelligent leadership to enhance customer engagement, co-create value, and foster inclusive innovation. Additionally, the evolving nature of entrepreneurial ecosystems [66], marked by digital platforms, virtual incubators, decentralized finance (DeFi), and globalized talent networks, warrants investigation into how AI–EI integration facilitates network-building, resource acquisition, and cross-border collaborations. In the Indian context, research that explores how national policies such as Digital India, Startup India, and AI mission initiatives intersect with entrepreneurial leadership and EI competencies can yield valuable policy-relevant insights [7, 8].

11.8 CONCLUSION

This chapter has rigorously explored, using PRISMA SLR methods, the interwoven functions of artificial and EI in determining entrepreneurial success based on a broad synthesis of extant literature and nascent evidence. The analysis has shed light on the ways strategic convergence of technological and emotional skills leverages entrepreneurial processes, leadership practices, innovation ability, and ecosystem interaction in today's digital economies [67].

11.8.1 Key Insights

The chapter has outlined several insights that contribute to knowledge about the AI–EI connection within entrepreneurship. AI, first, boosts entrepreneurs' potential for opportunity detection, strategic decision-making, and innovation through data insights, predictive analytics, and automation. Second, EI follows up on these abilities with the relational, empathetic, and adaptive skills that enable entrepreneurs to deal with uncertainty, manage staff, and manage stakeholders effectively [20]. Third, a synergistic combination of AI and EI offers a double benefit that allows entrepreneurs to react to dynamic, globalized, and complex market situations with analytical acumen as well as human-based leadership. The thematic synthesis underscored recurring patterns, including the growing relevance of AI-enabled emotional analytics, sector-specific applications in startups and social enterprises, and emerging frameworks for AI–EI integration in entrepreneurial practice [38].

This chapter contributes to both theoretical advancement and practical application. Theoretically, it bridges disciplinary silos by integrating insights from entrepreneurship studies, AI research, and EI scholarship to propose an interdisciplinary conceptualization of entrepreneurial success. By mapping the intersections of AI tools and EI competencies, the chapter enriches cognitive entrepreneurship and leadership theories with contemporary technological considerations. Practically, the chapter offers actionable insights for entrepreneurs, educators, and policymakers seeking to leverage AI–EI integration for competitive advantage. Strategic recommendations for startups, policy frameworks for entrepreneurial ecosystems, and curricular innovations for higher education institutions have been delineated to guide implementation in real-world contexts, particularly in emerging economies such as India [7].

11.8.2 The Evolving Role of AI and EI in Entrepreneurial Success

As entrepreneurial landscapes continue to evolve amid technological disruption, global interconnectedness, and socio-economic volatility, the dual imperatives of

AI competence and EI acumen will become increasingly indispensable for sustainable entrepreneurial success [57]. Entrepreneurs who embrace a balanced approach combining data-driven strategic agility with empathetic, emotionally intelligent leadership will be better positioned to navigate complexity, foster innovation, and generate inclusive socio-economic value. Future entrepreneurial ecosystems will likely reward ventures that are simultaneously technologically sophisticated and deeply attuned to human relationships, ethical considerations, and contextual nuances. This chapter underscores the need for continued interdisciplinary research, proactive policy support, and dynamic entrepreneurial education to harness the full potential of AI and EI integration in shaping resilient, innovative, and globally competitive entrepreneurial ventures [7, 38].

REFERENCES

[1] J. M. George, "Emotions and Leadership: The Role of Emotional Intelligence," *Human Relations*, vol. 53, no. 8, pp. 1027–1055, 2000, doi:10.1177/0018726700538001

[2] M. Haenlein and A. Kaplan, "A Brief History of Artificial Intelligence: On the Past, Present, and Future of Artificial Intelligence," *California Management Review*, vol. 61, p. 000812561986492, Jul. 2019, doi:10.1177/0008125619864925

[3] Y. Harie, B. P. Gautam, and K. Wasaki, "Computer Vision Techniques for Growth Prediction: A Prisma-Based Systematic Literature Review," *Applied Sciences*, vol. 13, no. 9, 2023, doi:10.3390/app13095335

[4] S. Côté and C. T. H. Miners, "Emotional Intelligence, Cognitive Intelligence, and Job Performance," *Administrative Science Quarterly*, vol. 51, no. 1, pp. 1–28, 2006, doi:10.2189/asqu.51.1.1

[5] R. Ngah and Z. Salleh, "Emotional Intelligence and Entrepreneurs' Innovativeness towards Entrepreneurial Success: A Preliminary Study," *American Journal of Economics*, vol. 2015, no. 2, pp. 285–290, 2015.

[6] P. Helo and Y. Hao, "Artificial Intelligence in Operations Management and Supply Chain Management: An Exploratory Case Study," *Production Planning & Control*, vol. 33, no. 16, pp. 1573–1590, 2022, doi:10.1080/09537287.2021.1882690

[7] R. K. Kovid, N. Singh, G. M. Sharma, P. Gaur, and K. Pandla, "Women Entrepreneurship: Investigating the Influence of Emotional Intelligence and Innovativeness on Entrepreneurial Success," *International Journal of Gender and Entrepreneurship*, vol. 17, no. 2, pp. 193–214, May 2025, doi:10.1108/IJGE-10-2023-0277

[8] P. Sahoo, P. Saraf, and R. Uchil, "Identification of Critical Success Factors for Leveraging Industry 4.0 Technology and Research Agenda: A Systematic Literature Review Using PRISMA Protocol," *Asia-Pacific Journal of Business Administration*, vol. 16, Oct. 2022, doi:10.1108/APJBA-03-2022-0105

[9] U. Warrier, M. John, and S. Warrier, "Leveraging Emotional Intelligence Competencies for Sustainable Development of Higher Education Institutions in the New Normal," *FIIB Business Review*, vol. 10, pp. 62–73, Mar. 2021, doi:10.1177/2319714521992032

[10] D. Chalmers, N. G. MacKenzie, and S. Carter, "Artificial Intelligence and Entrepreneurship: Implications for Venture Creation in the Fourth Industrial Revolution," *Entrepreneurship Theory and Practice*, vol. 45, no. 5, pp. 1028–1053, 2021, doi:10.1177/1042258720934581

[11] https://www.gemconsortium.org/report/20222023-global-entrepreneurship-monitor-global-report-adapting-to-a-new-normal-2?

[12] M. Rehman, B. Dhiman, and G. S. Cheema, "Minds and Machines: Impact of Emotional Intelligence on Investment Decisions with Mediating the Role of Artificial Intelligence,"

International Journal of Engineering, Business and Management (IJEBM), vol. 8, no. 1, pp. 2456–7817, doi:10.22161/ijebm.8.1

[13] M. M. Thottoli, M. E. Cruz, and S. S. S. Al Abri, "The Incubation Revolution: Transforming Entrepreneurial Education with Artificial Intelligence," *Asia Pacific Journal of Innovation and Entrepreneurship*, vol. 19, no. 1, pp. 2–23, Jan. 2025, doi:10.1108/APJIE-11-2023-0221

[14] A. Grájeda et al., "Embracing Artificial Intelligence in the Arts Classroom: Understanding Student Perceptions and Emotional Reactions to AI Tools," *Cogent Education*, vol. 11, no. 1, p. 2378271, 2024, doi:10.1080/2331186X.2024.2378271

[15] D. Pati and L. N. Lorusso, "How to Write a Systematic Review of the Literature," *HERD: Health Environments Research & Design Journal*, vol. 11, no. 1, pp. 15–30, 2018, doi:10.1177/1937586717747384

[16] E. Brynjolfsson, D. Rock, and C. Syverson, "The Productivity J-Curve: How Intangibles Complement General Purpose Technologies," *American Economic Journal: Macroeconomics*, vol. 13, no. 1, pp. 333–372, 2021, doi: 10.1257/mac.20180386

[17] D.-H. Park, Q. Jiang, and K. Kim, "Impact of the Expected B2B Internal Customer Experience on Intention to Adopt Artificial Intelligence (AI)," *Journal of Global Scholars of Marketing Science*, vol. 35, pp. 180–196, Mar. 2025, doi:10.1080/21639159.2025.2465299

[18] P. Salovey, and J. D. Mayer, "Emotional Intelligence," *Imagination, Cognition and Personality, vol.* 9, no. 3), pp. 185–211, 1990, doi: 10.2190/DUGG-P24E-52WK-6CDG

[19] K. V. Petrides, and A. Furnham, "Trait Emotional Intelligence: Psychometric Investigation with Reference to Established Trait Taxonomies," *European Journal of Personality*, vol. 15, no. 6, pp. 425–448, 2001, doi: 10.1002/per.416

[20] H. Jianjun et al., "The Role of Artificial and Nonartificial Intelligence in the New Product Success with Moderating Role of New Product Innovation: A Case of Manufacturing Companies in China," *Complexity*, vol. 2021, 2021, doi:10.1155/2021/8891298

[21] V. Dulewicz and M. Higgs, "Emotional Intelligence – A Review and Evaluation Study," *Journal of Managerial Psychology*, vol. 15, pp. 341–372, Jun. 2000, doi:10.1108/02683940010330993

[22] K. M. Thajil and H. Al-Abrrow, "The Effect of the Bright Triad on Positive Innovation in Healthcare Sector: The Mediating Role of Emotional Intelligence," *International Journal of Healthcare Management*, vol. 17, no. 2, pp. 285–296, Apr. 2024, doi:10.1080/20479700.2023.2177608

[23] A. Nusrat, Z. Zongming, J. Li, and F. Muhammad Muneeb, "Thriving Big Data Artificial Intelligence: Entrepreneurial Leadership, Proactive Personality and Affective Commitment to Innovate Micro and Small Family Businesses," *Asia-Pacific Journal of Business Administration*, Jan. 2025, doi:10.1108/APJBA-05-2024-0280

[24] Deloitte. (2023). *State of Generative AI in the Enterprise*. Deloitte Insights.

[25] Y. Yusoff, I. Fatimah, S. Rahayu, and N. Faizah, "A Review on Integrating Emotional Intelligence with Artificial Intelligence in Social Media Marketing Among Entrepreneurs," *Journal of Contemporary Social Science and Education Studies (JOCSSES)*, vol. 3, no. 2, pp. 44–50, Jan. 2023.

[26] S. Ambad, "A Systematic Literature Review on Social Entrepreneurial Intention: Citation, Thematic Analyses and Future Research Directions," in *Social Entrepreneurs*, 2022, pp. 93–124, doi:10.1108/S2043-052320220000018006

[27] S. Puntoni, R. W. Reczek, M. Giesler, and S. Botti, "Consumers and Artificial Intelligence: An Experiential Perspective," *Journal of Marketing*, vol. 85, no. 1, pp. 131–151, 2021, doi:10.1177/0022242920953847

[28] P. B. N. Kiran and G. N. P. V. Babu, "Problems and Prospects of Street Vendors: A Study with Reference to Visakhapatnam City," *The International Journal of Management Technology and Engineering*, vol. 9, pp. 2249–2455, Jul. 2019.

[29] Z. Miao, "The Influence Factors of Psychological Understanding and Behavior Choice for Legal Industry Entrepreneurs Based on Artificial Intelligence Technology," *Frontiers in Psychology*, vol. 11, Jul. 2020, doi:10.3389/fpsyg.2020.01615

[30] F. Usman, N. Eyo-Udo, E. Etukudoh, B. Odonkor, C. Ibeh, and P. Adegbola, "A Critical Review of AI-Driven Strategies for Entrepreneurial Success," *International Journal of Management & Entrepreneurship Research*, vol. 6, pp. 200–215, Jan. 2024, doi:10.51594/ijmer.v6i1.748

[31] S. Chowdhury, P. Budhwar, and G. Wood, "Generative Artificial Intelligence in Business: Towards a Strategic Human Resource Management Framework," *British Journal of Management*, vol. 35, no. 4, pp. 1680–1691, Oct. 2024, doi:10.1111/1467-8551.12824

[32] N. Jia, X. Luo, Z. Fang, and C. Liao, "When and How Artificial Intelligence Augments Employee Creativity," *Academy of Management Journal*, vol. 67, Mar. 2023, doi:10.5465/amj.2022.0426

[33] Y. H. Al-Mamary, "The Transformative Power of Artificial Intelligence in Entrepreneurship: Exploring AI's Capabilities for the Success of Entrepreneurial Ventures," *Future Business Journal*, vol. 11, no. 1, p. 104, 2025, doi:10.1186/s43093-025-00533-7

[34] M. Levesque, M. Obschonka, and S. Nambisan, "Pursuing Impactful Entrepreneurship Research Using Artificial Intelligence," *Entrepreneurship Theory and Practice*, Jul. 2020, doi:10.1177/1042258720927369

[35] N. Ameen, G. Sharma, S. Tarba, A. Rao, and R. Chopra, "Toward Advancing Theory on Creativity in Marketing and Artificial Intelligence," *Psychology & Marketing*, vol. 39, pp. 1802–1825, Jun. 2022, doi:10.1002/mar.21699

[36] K. V. Petrides and A. Furnham, "Trait Emotional Intelligence: Psychometric Investigation with Reference to Established Trait Taxonomies," *European Journal of Personality*, vol. 15, no. 6, pp. 425–448, Nov. 2001, doi:10.1002/per.416

[37] P. K. Dey, S. Chowdhury, A. Abadie, E. V. Yaroson, and S. Sarkar, "Artificial Intelligence-Driven Supply Chain Resilience in Vietnamese Manufacturing Small- and Medium-Sized Enterprises," *International Journal of Production Research*, vol. 62, no. 15, pp. 5417–5456, 2024, doi:10.1080/00207543.2023.2179859

[38] J. Mayer, D. Caruso, and P. Salovey, "The Ability Model of Emotional Intelligence: Principles and Updates," *Emotion Review*, vol. 8, Aug. 2016, doi:10.1177/1754073916639667

[39] M. Enholm, E. Papagiannidis, P. Mikalef, and J. Krogstie, "Artificial Intelligence and Business Value: A Literature Review," *Information Systems Frontiers*, vol. 24, no. 5, pp. 1709–1734, 2022, doi:10.1007/s10796-021-10186-w

[40] G. Najafi, F. Popalzay, N. Darman, M. Salehi, T. Akbari, and T. Quraishi, "Strengthening Women's Leadership and Management in the Digital Age: Innovation, Opportunities, and Challenges," *International Journal of Applied Research and Sustainable Sciences*, vol. 3, pp. 247–260, Apr. 2025, doi:10.59890/ijarss.v3i3.4

[41] L. Hijriyah, A. Alias, and M. F. Mohd Sahabuddin, "Exploring Walkability Research Trends Based on Systematic Literature Review (SLR) by Applying PRISMA," *Open House International*, vol. 49, no. 1, pp. 63–121, Jan. 2024, doi:10.1108/OHI-02-2023-0031

[42] X. Islami and E. Mulolli, "Human-Artificial Intelligence in Management Functions: A Synergistic Symbiosis Relationship," *Applied Artificial Intelligence*, vol. 38, no. 1, p. 2439615, Dec. 2024, doi:10.1080/08839514.2024.2439615

[43] M. Atienza-Barba, J. Álvarez-García, Á. Meseguer-Martínez, and V. Barba-Sánchez, "The Family Business in the Digital Era: Advancing towards Artificial Intelligence," *Journal of Family Business Management*, vol. 15, no. 2, pp. 297–316, Jan. 2025, doi:10.1108/JFBM-09-2024-0215

[44] E. Glikson and A. Woolley, "Human Trust in Artificial Intelligence: Review of Empirical Research," *The Academy of Management Annals*, vol. 14, no. 2, pp. 627–660, Apr. 2020.

[45] E. E. Makarius, D. Mukherjee, J. D. Fox, and A. K. Fox, "Rising with the Machines: A Sociotechnical Framework for Bringing Artificial Intelligence into the Organization," *Journal of Business Research*, vol. 120, pp. 262–273, 2020, doi:10.1016/j.jbusres.2020.07.045

[46] C. Keswani, S. S. Agrawal, and V. Kandpal, "India's Response to Climate Change: Evaluating Mitigation Strategies and Impacts," in *Green Futures: Navigating the Path to Environmental Resilience*, Anshuman Jaswal, Debjani Mukherjee, Vinay Kandpal, and Angappa Gunasekaran, Eds., Springer Nature Singapore, 2025, pp. 173–189. doi:10.1007/978-981-96-0843-0_9

[47] D. Randriamiary, "Reframing the Role of Leaders Navigating the Challenges and Opportunities of Tomorrow's Workplace in the Age of Artificial Intelligence." [Online]. Available: www.statistica.com

[48] D. K. Kanbach, L. Heiduk, G. Blueher, M. Schreiter, and A. Lahmann, "The GenAI Is Out of the Bottle: Generative Artificial Intelligence from a Business Model Innovation Perspective," *Review of Managerial Science*, vol. 18, no. 4, pp. 1189–1220, 2024, doi:10.1007/s11846-023-00696-z

[49] B. Shneiderman, "Human-Centered Artificial Intelligence: Reliable, Safe & Trustworthy," *International Journal of Human–Computer Interaction*, vol. 36, no. 6, pp. 495–504, Apr. 2020, doi:10.1080/10447318.2020.1741118

[50] M. Murugan and M. N. Prabadevi, "Impact of Artificial Intelligence and Emotional Intelligence in Autonomous Operation and MSME Entrepreneurs' Performance in the Waste Management Industry," in *Explainable AI (XAI) for Sustainable Development*, Chapman and Hall/CRC, 2024, pp. 58–72. doi:10.1201/9781003457176-4

[51] A. K. Kar and A. K. Kushwaha, "Facilitators and Barriers of Artificial Intelligence Adoption in Business – Insights from Opinions Using Big Data Analytics," *Information Systems Frontiers*, vol. 25, Nov. 2021, doi:10.1007/s10796-021-10219-4

[52] L. Tischler, G. Biberman, and R. McKeage, "Linking Emotional Intelligence, Spirituality and Workplace Performance," *Journal of Managerial Psychology*, vol. 17, pp. 203–218, May 2002, doi:10.1108/02683940210423114

[53] Y. Shrestha, S. Ben-Menahem, and G. Krogh, "Organizational Decision-Making Structures in the Age of Artificial Intelligence," *California Management Review*, vol. 61, p. 000812561986225, Jul. 2019, doi:10.1177/0008125619862257

[54] Y. Lu, "Artificial Intelligence: A Survey on Evolution, Models, Applications and Future Trends," *Journal of Management Analytics*, vol. 6, no. 1, pp. 1–29, Jan. 2019, doi:10.1080/23270012.2019.1570365

[55] R. Readi, "Sistematic Literature Review (SLR) And Biomectrik Analysis: SMEs Performance," *Business and Investment Review*, vol. 1, pp. 7–16, Dec. 2023, doi:10.61292/birev.v1i6.62

[56] A. Reyes-Menendez, J. Mediavilla, and N. Villagra, "Understanding STI and SDG with Artificial Intelligence: A Review and Research Agenda for Entrepreneurial Action," *Technological Forecasting and Social Change*, vol. 196, p. 122785, Nov. 2023, doi:10.1016/j.techfore.2023.122785

[57] A. K. Saddam and R. Anvari, "The Effect of Leadership Style on Organizational Performance: Integrating Emotional Intelligence and Artificial Intelligence," in *2025 Eighth International Women in Data Science Conference at Prince Sultan University (WiDS PSU)*, 2025, pp. 104–107. doi:10.1109/WiDS-PSU64963.2025.00032

[58] Z. Zaharuddin, S. Wahyuningsih, A. Sutarman, and I. Hikam, "Understanding Purposeful Leadership in Entrepreneurial Contexts: A Bibliometric Analysis," *Aptisi Transactions on Technopreneurship (ATT)*, vol. 6, pp. 213–230, Jul. 2024, doi:10.34306/att.v6i2.412

[59] M. Zeidner, G. Matthews, and R. Roberts, "Emotional Intelligence in the Workplace: A Critical Review," *Applied Psychology*, vol. 53, pp. 371–399, Jul. 2004, doi:10.1111/j.1464-0597.2004.00176.x

[60] S. S. Agrawal and S. K. Mukti, "Role of Sustainable Finance in Contributing to the Growth of Indian Economy," in *Digital Transformation for Business Sustainability and Growth in Emerging Markets*, P. Kumar, S. Dadwal, R. Verma, and S. Kumar, Eds., Emerald Publishing Limited, 2025, pp. 293–309. doi:10.1108/978-1-83549-109-620251012

[61] C. Wang, H. Wang, Y. Li, J. Dai, X. Gu, and T. Yu, "Factors Influencing University Students' Behavioral Intention to Use Generative Artificial Intelligence: Integrating the Theory of Planned Behavior and AI Literacy," *International Journal of Human-Computer Interaction*, Jul. 2024, doi:10.1080/10447318.2024.2383033

[62] S. Sharma, S. S. Agrawal, and S. A. Kumar, "Unlocking Cybersecurity Horizons: Exploring Cutting-Edge Technologies, Strategies, and Trends in the Dynamic Cyber Threat Landscape," in *2024 International Conference on Intelligent Computing and Emerging Communication Technologies (ICEC)*, 2024, pp. 1–6. doi:10.1109/ICEC59683.2024.10837210

[63] D. Wu, H. Shen, and Z. Lv, "An Artificial Intelligence and Multimedia Teaching Platform Based Integration Path of IPE and IEE in Colleges and Universities1," *Journal of Intelligent & Fuzzy Systems*, vol. 40, pp. 1–10, Oct. 2020, doi:10.3233/JIFS-189410

[64] S. S. Agrawal and S. Raheja, "Does Good Governance Encourage Sustainable Tourism? A Systematic Review of PESTEL Analysis Towards Indian Tourism," in *Greener Future*, A. E. Jimenez Ruiz, V. Rudkouskaya, and S. Bhartiya, Eds., Emerald Publishing Limited, 2025, pp. 209–222. doi:10.1108/978-1-83608-988-920251014

[65] C. E. Short and J. C. Short, "The Artificially Intelligent Entrepreneur: ChatGPT, Prompt Engineering, and Entrepreneurial Rhetoric Creation," *Journal of Business Venturing Insights*, vol. 19, p. e00388, 2023, doi:10.1016/j.jbvi.2023.e00388

[66] D. Wang, L. Han, L. Cong, H. Zhu, and S. Yu, "Practical Evaluation of Human–Computer Interaction and Artificial Intelligence Deep Learning Algorithm in Innovation and Entrepreneurship Teaching Evaluation," *International Journal of Human-Computer Interaction*, vol. 41, pp. 1–9, Apr. 2023, doi:10.1080/10447318.2023.2199632

[67] A. M. Votto, R. Valecha, P. Najafirad, and R. Rao, "Artificial Intelligence in Tactical Human Resource Management: A Systematic Literature Review," *International Journal of Information Management Data Insights*, vol. 1, p. 100047, Nov. 2021, doi:10.1016/j.jjimei.2021.100047

12 Integrating AI with Emotional Development

Enhancing Entrepreneurial Performance through AI-Enabled Mindfulness Intervention

Aparna Vajpayee

12.1 INTRODUCTION

The historical and conceptual roots of mindfulness date back to ancient Vedic India, when early spiritual writings such as the Upanishads placed great importance on self-awareness, meditation, and controlled attention to thought patterns [1]. The practices of dhyana (meditative absorption) and smriti (remembrance or awareness) formed the foundation for subsequent formalizations of mindfulness [2]. As Indian philosophical ideas developed, they were further articulated in the spiritual practices of early Hinduism. With the rise of Buddhism during the 5th to 6th century BCE, mindfulness (sati in Pali, smṛti in Sanskrit) was a prominent and formalized practice [3–5]. In Buddhist philosophy, particularly in the context of the Noble Eightfold Path, mindfulness was stressed not just as present-moment awareness but also as a vital path to ethical conduct, mental health, and release from suffering [6]. Mindfulness thus developed out of early Vedic contemplative practices into an organized and core element of Buddhist philosophy and practice, influencing the way it would be translated and interpreted later on across cultures in society as well as in organizations in various parts of the world [7, 8] and reflected in life through improved employee–employer relationships [9] and transformational leadership practices [10] with healthier prospects for longevity of life and happiness [11]. In today's rapid-paced world of start-ups and innovation economies of the technetronic world of Industry 5.0 [12], the traditional measurement of entrepreneurial achievement, technical know-how, marketplace savvy, and financial acumen is insufficient alone. Instead, soft skills like Emotional Intelligence (EI) are becoming the competitive advantage determiners that determine the survival or success of an entrepreneur [13, 14]. EI, including

DOI: 10.1201/9781003650775-12

self-awareness, emotional management, empathy, and interpersonal competence, helps entrepreneurs navigate the psychological and relational subtleties of building and maintaining a business [15].

Entrepreneurs work in high-stakes, uncertain environments where leadership involves not only strategic decision-making but also people, emotion, and relationship management. Unlike organized company managers, entrepreneurs need to constantly motivate themselves, create dynamic teams, deal with investors, negotiate while under pressure, and switch direction in the event of failure or uncertainty. As such, their ability to manage both their own and other people's emotions significantly affects organizational performance, innovation potential, and team effectiveness [16–18]. Moreover, contemporary research emphasizes the role of mindfulness interventions as a tool for creating and enhancing EI. Mindfulness—recorded as non-judgmental awareness in the here-and-now—has been shown to improve attention, affect regulation, and resilience [19, 20]. These are exactly the basic building blocks of EI, suggesting that mindfulness can act as a developmental bridge to facilitate more effective EI among entrepreneurs. Technology has increasingly hastened this evolution; mindfulness platforms infused with AI, such as Ajivar, have yielded potential in developing emotional health and resilience, particularly in young demographics that face stress and change [21].

Additionally, the marriage between artificial intelligence (AI) and mindfulness is picking up pace as an exciting route towards leadership training and mental well-being by harmonizing mind and body [22]. These have included researching AI-supported mindfulness among university students [23], individualizing emotional growth [24], and practice in contexts as diverse as hospitality and learning [25, 26]. As well as individual self-regulation, such interventions offer scalable pathways to building emotionally intelligent entrepreneurship leaders in high-pressure entrepreneurial contexts [27, 28].

AI-supported mindfulness technologies provide an accessible, person-centred, data-driven process for emotional and cognitive self-management. This interface between digital technology and EI becomes especially valuable within start-ups, where leaders confront emotion-laden episodes and have to adjust in double time. It is the use of mindfulness through AI that catalyses inward resilience as well as outward relational harmony and positions EI as an entrepreneurial ecosystem asset [29]. As entrepreneurial ecosystems become more competitive and emotionally challenging, the need to explore the role of EI, underpinned by mindfulness practices and digital tools, in entrepreneurial success is imperative. This study aims to examine how entrepreneurs are different from managers in terms of EI, why EI is a strategic leverage in entrepreneurial settings, and how AI-facilitated mindfulness interventions can foster people-oriented, emotionally robust leadership in start-ups. Through a critical examination of both empirical and theoretical constructs, this research offers an innovative contribution to the nascent literature, placing EI in more than merely a psychological disposition but rather as a strategic leadership quality that is part and parcel of entrepreneurial activity in contemporary times.

12.2 REVIEW OF LITERATURE

12.2.1 Emotional Intelligence: Entrepreneurs vs. Managers

EI, according to Goleman [30], is composed of self-awareness, self-regulation, motivation, empathy, and social skills [31]. Although EI is essential in all organizational roles, its expression and significance vary for entrepreneurs and managers because of the distinct requirements of each role.

Entrepreneurs usually work in high-risk, uncertain contexts requiring agility, resilience, and intuitive decision-making. Studies indicate that entrepreneurs have higher scores than managers on all five EI domains [16, 17]. Entrepreneurs exhibit higher self-awareness and motivation, which are crucial in starting and maintaining ventures. They tend to have increased social and empathy skills, which lead to effective communication for persuasion, building effective teams, and investor relations [32]. Managers tend to be more systematic and process-focused and use formal organizational structures to attain goals. Empirical evidence underpins this differentiation: entrepreneurs score higher than managers across self-motivation and social skills—skills essential for networking, influence, and opportunity spotting [33]. Their increased EI enables greater tolerance of ambiguity, creativity, and interpersonal sensitivity—essential in nascent-stage start-ups where leadership is dynamic and fluid.

12.2.2 Boosting Entrepreneurial EI through AI-Enabled Mindfulness Intervention

Incorporation of AI and mindfulness practices has grown exponentially, particularly in emotional and mental well-being. This intersection was encouraged and accelerated during the COVID-19 pandemic with the creation of the Ajivar app, a system built on AI providing scalable EI and mindfulness training to students. The intervention had a positive effect on the levels of anxiety and depression and EI in particular, a wonderful sign that AI has much to offer as a means to combat mental illness during times of crisis [21, 34]. AI–human cognition and emotion convergence has developed into a complex entanglement that confuses the once clear boundaries between technology and emotion domains [35]. Singha [29] explains the way mindfulness, in its humble beginnings in contemplative practice, has been essential in dealing with emotional challenges of the digital age. AI, when introduced with awareness, can promote emotional awareness and enable psychological balance, a harmonious relationship between technological advancement and emotional health [29].

Worapongpat [26] conducted a survey of mindfulness in using AI to learn at Thai universities and observed consistently high levels of mindfulness among graduate students. Significantly, the report observed no institution-to-institution variation in mindfulness, reflecting a high degree of readiness across institutions to embrace AI mindfully within the academic context. Furthermore, Wang and Uysal [25] proposed a conceptual model for AI-assisted mindfulness, from interventions affecting state mindfulness to those fostering trait mindfulness. They proposed strategic directions from mindfulness and AI perspectives and recommended 18 research themes, indicating rising maturity in this inter/multi-disciplinary field.

For higher education, Carlomagno and Vadalà [23] referred to how meditative practice has been transformed by AI in making mindfulness more personalized through the use of digital means. Personalization enabled an emotionally enriched learning process, placing mindfulness at the forefront of students' learning processes and increasing their presence in the learning environment. To complement these findings, Mitsea et al. [24] performed a review of the efficacy of computer-supported mindfulness interventions with the support of AI technologies like chatbots, virtual coaches, and immersive tools. The interventions improved self-regulation capacities and mental well-being, with potential for further applications, particularly among those with special training requirements or disabilities.

In addition, Weerakkody and Rajapaksha [28] conducted a systematic literature review with a view to exploring the global scalability of AI-facilitated mindfulness. They emphasized the potential of AI in making mindfulness training universally accessible while also emphasizing the need for ethical consideration and culturally flexible practices to enable sustainable application.

Finally, Tan [27] gave a mechanistic explanation for the development of mindfulness using AI technologies. His observation underscored the importance of grounding AI-assisted interventions in psychological principles while encouraging empirical support for safety and cultural appropriateness. Together, these studies make a strong case for the transformational power of AI in maximizing mindfulness and emotional health. They highlight the need for personalization, ethical balance, strategic thinking, and cross-contextual transference to ensure long-term effects.

12.2.3 Implications for Start-Up Success

Combining EI training and mindfulness practice gives an effective approach to entrepreneur development. Start-up founder programs can be enriched through the use of EI training, stress reduction techniques, and workshops on developing resilience and Mindfulness-Based Stress Reduction (MBSR) strategies. Besides personal development, these interventions promote better people skills that are essential in start-up environments with lean teams, changing job roles, and intense interpersonal relationships.

Entrepreneurs with EI and mindfulness skills are more apt to:

- Recruit and retain talent.
- Manage conflicts diplomatically.
- Establish trust with stakeholders.
- Maintain motivation across long business cycles.

12.2.4 Emotional Intelligence as a Strategic Skill for Entrepreneurs

EI is more and more regarded not only as a soft skill but also as a strategic ability within the entrepreneurial landscape. Because entrepreneurial ecosystems are so volatile, uncertain, complex, and ambiguous (VUCA), EI helps entrepreneurs effectively work in constantly changing environments, sparking both business and personal performance outcomes.

1. Opportunity Recognition: Entrepreneurs need to spot unmet needs, new trends, and latent market opportunities with limited information. Highly EI individuals have sharp emotional acuity, enabling them to read verbal and non-verbal communications from prospective customers, stakeholders, and rivals. Emotionally intelligent entrepreneurs, as per Zampetakis and Moustakis [17], can better interpret customer emotions and pain points, and hence create innovations that strike a chord with user expectations. This emotional sensitivity enhances strategic thinking and market vision.
2. Risk Management: The entrepreneurial path is inherently ambiguous, fraught with economic risk, decision fatigue, and uncertainty. Entrepreneurs high in EI fare better in emotion regulation, permitting them to modulate fear, anxiety, and stress without overwhelm. They have a higher probability of taking risks based on logical analysis, weighed against emotional instinct. This resilience of staying grounded emotionally permits finer judgement in pressure situations, for example, when launching a new product, when pitching for financing, or managing a crisis.
3. Building Relationships and Positive Organizational Culture: Start-up success depends not just on technical proficiency but also on establishing robust networks and stakeholder trust. High EI enables better interpersonal skills, which build trust, empathy, and genuine communication [10]. Entrepreneurs with high EI are better able to manage conflicts, negotiate agreements, inspire teams, and establish a psychologically safe workplace. These skills are especially crucial in the initial stages of a start-up when resource limitations render collaborative synergy a valuable asset. Which ultimately reflects in a positive organizational culture [36, 37].
4. Adaptability and Resilience: Entrepreneurs are frequently faced with sudden changes in consumer behaviour, technology waves, or regulatory landscapes. High-EI people have a growth mindset that allows them to turn around rapidly and recover from failure. Their resilience stems from self-motivation and high emotional clarity, which prevents them from losing focus and getting overwrought in the event of a crisis. Adaptability not just ensures short-term survival but also long-term scalability and innovation.

12.2.5 Strategic Advantage in Entrepreneurship

As highlighted by Boyatzis and Goleman [14], EI is much more than an attractive personality trait—it is a business asset that fuels entrepreneurial success. In the highly uncertain and fast-paced business landscape of today, where start-ups are characterized by high uncertainty and scarce resources, EI is an internal compass to navigate entrepreneurs through complexity and an external connector that allows them to lead, build relationships with stakeholders, and inspire innovation [13, 16].

12.2.6 Critical Areas Where EI Delivers Strategic Competence

1. Managing Culturally Mixed and Interdisciplinary Teams

   Entrepreneurs tend to manage teams that are geographically distributed and culturally heterogeneous. High EI allows them to handle cultural subtleties, work through emotional dynamics, and create inclusive team cultures [32]. This facilitates team cohesiveness, creativity, and productivity—key to innovation-led growth [38, 39].

2. Motivating Stakeholders and Maintaining Investor Confidence

   Emotionally intelligent businesspeople are better able to manage impressions, uphold credibility, and adapt communication styles to suit stakeholder demands [40]. Emotional connection and empathy create higher levels of trust, investor trust, and long-term alliances [17].

3. Resolving Interpersonal Conflicts with Emotional Agility

   Start-up cultures tend to create intense emotional stress based on role flexibility, competition, and changing dynamics. EI allows entrepreneurs to pick up early warnings of conflict, manage emotional reactions, and facilitate conflict resolution positively [41]. This leads to psychological safety and enhanced team cohesiveness [42].

4. Aligning Visionary Drive with Human-Centric Leadership

   Whereas entrepreneurial momentum is propelled by visionary thinking, human-oriented leadership provides for sustainable growth. EI enables entrepreneurs to keep strategic ambitions balanced with relational dynamics, promoting empathy, ethical action, and well-being within team interactions [43, 44].

12.2.7 Evolving beyond Technical Mastery

Unlike cognitive or technical skills, which may peak or become outdated, EI is dynamic and can develop over time with interventions such as:

- Mindfulness exercises, which increase self-regulation and emotional acuity [19, 20].
- Leadership coaching, which promotes reflective learning and focused behavioural change [45].
- Group-based emotional feedback loops, which enhance interpersonal sensitivity and flexibility [46].
- This flexibility makes EI especially pertinent to entrepreneurs, whose jobs require ongoing reinvention and emotional toughness in the face of fast-paced change [33].

12.2.8 EI as a Pillar of Leadership

EI is not merely an added attribute but a pillar of entrepreneurial leadership. High-EI entrepreneurs are more likely to:

- Lead ethically and adaptively amidst emotional turbulence.
- Build inclusive, trust-based teams.
- Manage high-stakes decision-making with equanimity.
- Align business development with psychological and cultural intelligence.
- With the need to innovate existing alongside emotional sensitivity and human bonding, EI is the determining factor between short-term existence and long-term entrepreneurial prosperity [13, 42].

Entrepreneurs are distinct from managers in the organization and implementation of EI. Since entrepreneurship requires more emotional resilience, flexibility, and influence, EI becomes a foundation for start-up success. Developing entrepreneurial EI through mindfulness practices produces more empathetic, calm, and visionary leaders—essential to navigating the contemporary innovation ecosystem.

12.3 RESEARCH METHODOLOGY

12.3.1 Objectives of the Study

The current research seeks to examine the contribution of EI towards entrepreneurial success and evaluate the efficacy of psychological and technological interventions in promoting EI among nascent entrepreneurs. The particular objectives are as follows:

- To compare the levels of EI between corporate managers and entrepreneurs and to explore critical emotional competencies that distinguish successful entrepreneurs from typical managerial professionals.
- To study the correlation between high EI and entrepreneurial achievement, with special reference to adaptive behaviour, stress management, and interpersonal skills.
- To identify low EI entrepreneurs through standardized testing and offer them specific developmental assistance.
- To develop and apply a 12-session intervention program to enhance basic EI elements like self-awareness, emotional control, empathy, and social communication.
- To incorporate AI and AIoT-driven mindfulness tools into the intervention program, utilizing real-time feedback and intelligent technology to aid emotional and cognitive growth.
- To assess the intervention's effectiveness through comparison of pre- and post-intervention EI scores among project participants.
- To identify AI's and AIoT's contribution to enhancing EI training and investigate the potential of such interdisciplinary models for entrepreneurial success in the digital age.

12.3.2 Research Design

The study utilizes a mixed-method research design, which incorporates both quantitative and qualitative methods. The quantitative approach entails survey-based data collection, whereas the qualitative component entails thematic analysis of open-ended responses as well as interviews. This triangulation improves the reliability and richness of understanding of the research issue.

12.3.3 Participants

Participants were recruited through purposive sampling, with a focus on professionals from different industries (e.g., start-ups, technology companies, and corporate organizations) to achieve diversity in work roles and experiences. N = [insert number] respondents took part in the study. Inclusion criteria included full-time work and organizational experience of at least one year.

12.3.4 Data Collection Tools

- **Quantitative Instrument:** The *[e.g., Five Facet Mindfulness Questionnaire (FFMQ), Organizational Culture Assessment Instrument* was administered to measure psychological variables.
- **Qualitative Instrument:** Semi-structured interviews and open-ended survey questions were used to capture participants' insights regarding workplace dynamics, team behaviour, and cultural patterns.

12.3.5 Procedure

The study adopted a two-phased structured process, intended to examine and augment EI in entrepreneurs and managers. The study combined comparative analysis, psychological intervention, and application of AI and Artificial Intelligence of Things (AIoT) technologies.

12.3.5.1 Phase 1: Comparative Study of Emotional Intelligence

During the initial phase, a comparative analysis was performed to compare the EI levels in two different groups:

- Corporate Managers: Individuals working in hierarchical organizational structures.
- Entrepreneurs: People involved in start-up companies or self-owned enterprises, working for a minimum of one year.
- Information was gathered through a validated Emotional Intelligence scale (assessing four significant components of EI: self-awareness, emotional regulation, empathy, and social skills).

The study found that successful entrepreneurs had much higher EI scores than managers, most notably when it came to adaptability, emotional resilience, and decision-making. Second, these entrepreneurs successfully incorporated AI tools within their workflow, implying an interdependence between EI and technological consciousness.

12.3.5.2 Phase 2: Intervention Program to Enhance EI through AI

The second period targeted new or nascent entrepreneurs who showed lower EI scores at the initial test. These participants received a systematic EI development program aimed at building fundamental emotional competencies that are key to entrepreneurial success.

The intervention included:

- 12 weekly facilitation sessions, each dedicated to a particular area of EI, like emotional regulation, empathy, stress handling, interpersonal communication, and mindful leadership.

- Integration of a technology-facilitated mindfulness program using AI and AIoT-based solutions. These technologies gave real-time emotional monitoring, guided meditations, behavioural prompts, and biometric feedback to enhance emotional awareness and self-regulation.
- During the intervention, participants were involved in activities that combined conventional psychological routines with state-of-the-art technological assistance, fostering sustainable emotional practices in high-pressure entrepreneurial environments.

12.3.6 Pre- and Post-Intervention Comparison

In order to evaluate the intervention effect, a post-test and pre-test design was utilized. Levels of EI were re-measured through the utilization of the identical instrument used during Phase 1. Paired-sample t-tests and effect size analysis were done to assess statistical improvement in EI in all aspects.

The findings suggested a considerable boost in EI scores after intervention, particularly in participants who directly interacted with the AIoT mindfulness training. These findings show the promising potential of tech-facilitated psychological training in augmenting emotional abilities critical to entrepreneurial development.

12.4 RESULTS

Table 12.1 presents the mean values of various emotional intelligence components among managers and entrepreneurs. The results show that entrepreneurs scored comparatively higher than managers across all dimensions, indicating stronger emotional intelligence attributes that may contribute to effective entrepreneurial performance and leadership.

Figure 12.1 presents a comparative analysis of emotional intelligence components between managers and entrepreneurs. The findings indicate that entrepreneurs exhibit slightly higher mean scores across all emotional intelligence dimensions, particularly in self-awareness, motivation, and social skills, highlighting their stronger emotional adaptability and interpersonal competencies.

TABLE 12.1
Mean Value of Each Element of Emotional Intelligence—Managers vs. Entrepreneurs

Emotional Intelligence Component	Mean—Managers	Mean—Entrepreneurs
Self-Awareness	33.52	35.40
Managing Emotions	32.31	33.12
Motivating Oneself	33.63	35.40
Empathy	33.87	34.84
Social Skill	33.95	35.28

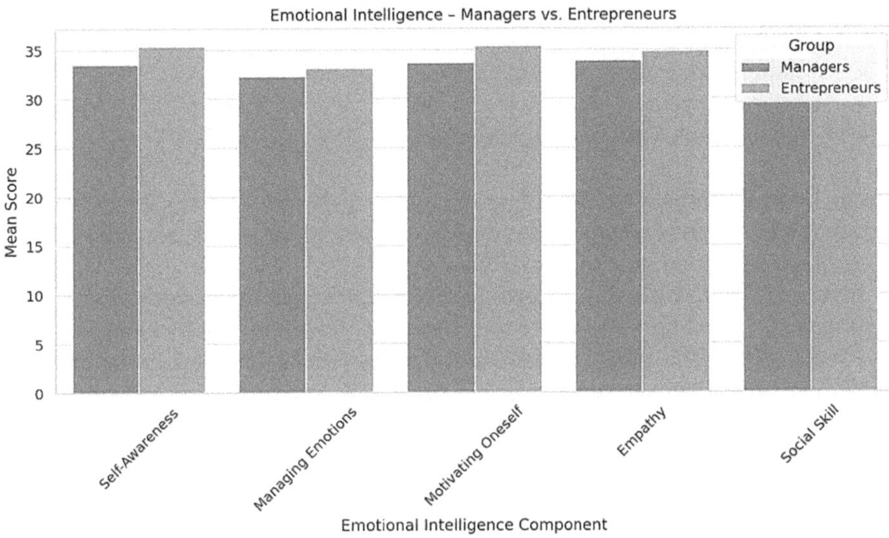

FIGURE 12.1 Comparative emotional intelligence—managers vs. entrepreneurs.

(Source: Authors.)

12.4.1 Data Analysis and Interpretation

From the comparative data, it is evident that entrepreneurs demonstrate higher levels of EI across all dimensions compared to managers. Key observations include:

- Self-Awareness: Entrepreneurs scored 35.4, notably higher than managers (33.52), indicating stronger introspective clarity and personal insight—critical for vision-driven leadership.
- Managing Emotions: Although the difference here is narrower (33.12 vs. 32.31), entrepreneurs still show slightly better emotional regulation, helping them stay composed during volatility.
- Motivating Oneself: Entrepreneurs score significantly higher (35.4 vs. 33.63), suggesting greater self-motivation and perseverance—essential traits in entrepreneurial journeys.
- Empathy: Entrepreneurs (34.84) outperform managers (33.87), which may reflect their stronger interpersonal understanding, aiding in customer relations and team dynamics.
- Social Skills: The highest difference is seen in social skills (35.28 vs. 33.95), showcasing entrepreneurs' advanced ability to build networks, negotiate, and influence others.

12.4.2 Emotional Intelligence as a Catalyst for Entrepreneurial Success

The data illustrates that entrepreneurs tend to possess higher EI, which plays a vital role in:

- Navigating uncertainty and market disruptions.
- Building and maintaining strong professional relationships.
- Sustaining motivation without external validation.
- Handling emotional pressure with balance.
- Leading teams with empathy and clarity.

These findings emphasize that EI is not just a personal strength but a strategic advantage in entrepreneurship, contributing directly to sustained innovation, resilience, and business success (Tables 12.2 and 12.3).

Figure 12.2 illustrates the correlation between different dimensions of emotional intelligence, including self-awareness, managing emotions, motivation, empathy, and social skills. The strong positive correlations among all variables indicate that these emotional intelligence components are closely interconnected and collectively contribute to effective leadership and entrepreneurial capabilities.

- All variables show *strong positive correlations*, especially between *Motivating Oneself*, *Self-Awareness*, and *Social Skill* ($r > 0.85$), suggesting these dimensions are interdependent and collectively support successful entrepreneurial behaviour [Table 12.4]

TABLE 12.2
Descriptive Statistics and Paired Sample t-Test Results

Domain	Pre-Mean	Post-Mean	Pre-SD	Post-SD	t-Statistic	p-Value	Cohen's d
Observing	18.7	23.0	2.21	2.11	10.00	< 0.001	3.16
Describing	21.9	26.1	1.37	1.66	13.00	< 0.001	4.11
Acting w/ Awareness	18.0	22.4	1.81	1.58	12.13	< 0.001	3.83
Nonjudging	19.8	24.1	1.31	1.45	13.30	< 0.001	4.19
Nonreactivity	16.8	21.8	1.23	1.32	14.14	< 0.001	4.46

TABLE 12.3
Correlation Analysis between Emotional Intelligence Dimensions

EI Dimensions	Self-Awareness	Managing Emotions	Motivating Oneself	Empathy	Social Skill
Self-Awareness	1.00	0.81	0.88	0.85	0.84
Managing Emotions	0.81	1.00	0.80	0.82	0.78
Motivating Oneself	0.88	0.80	1.00	0.84	0.86
Empathy	0.85	0.82	0.84	1.00	0.87
Social Skill	0.84	0.78	0.86	0.87	1.00

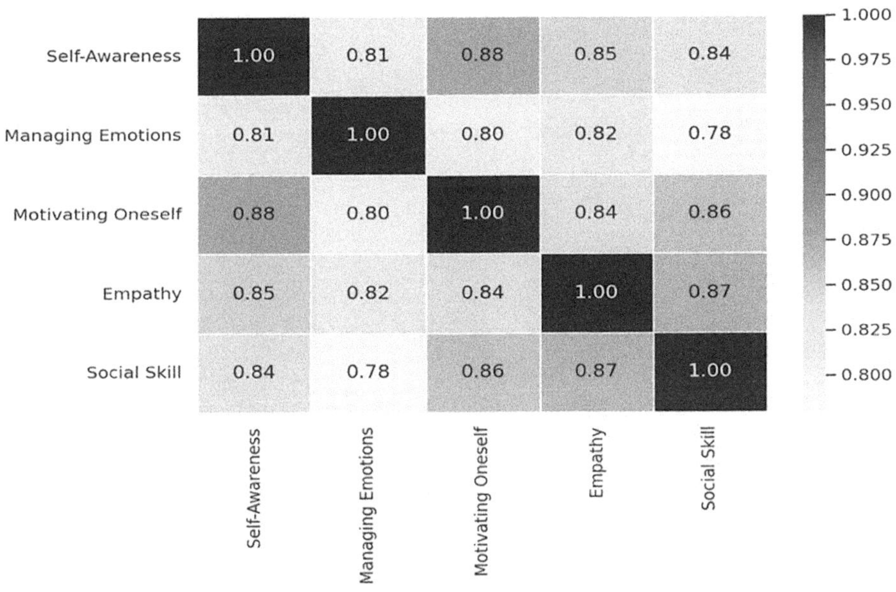

FIGURE 12.2 Representing correlation between the dimensions of emotional intelligence. **(Source: Authors.).**

TABLE 12.4
Correlation of FFMQ (Mindfulness) with Emotional Intelligence. Mindfulness Training (FFMQ Pre/Post) Has Enhanced EI Components

Mindfulness Domain	Self-Awareness	Managing Emotions	Motivating Oneself	Empathy	Social Skill
Observing	0.76	0.72	0.68	0.73	0.69
Describing	0.79	0.75	0.81	0.78	0.74
Awareness	0.83	0.80	0.79	0.81	0.80
Nonjudging	0.70	0.77	0.75	0.82	0.76
Nonreactivity	0.68	0.82	0.73	0.79	0.78

Figure 12.3 presents a comparison of pre-test and post-test scores across various mindfulness dimensions, including observing, describing, awareness, nonjudging, and nonreactivity. The results demonstrate a noticeable improvement in post-test mean scores for all dimensions, indicating the positive impact of mindfulness practices on participants' cognitive awareness and emotional regulation abilities.

The strongest correlations are observed between *Awareness* and *Self-Awareness/ Social Skill* (r ≈ 0.80+), and *Nonreactivity* with *Managing Emotions*, showing that mindfulness practice *amplifies emotional regulation and interpersonal functionality.*

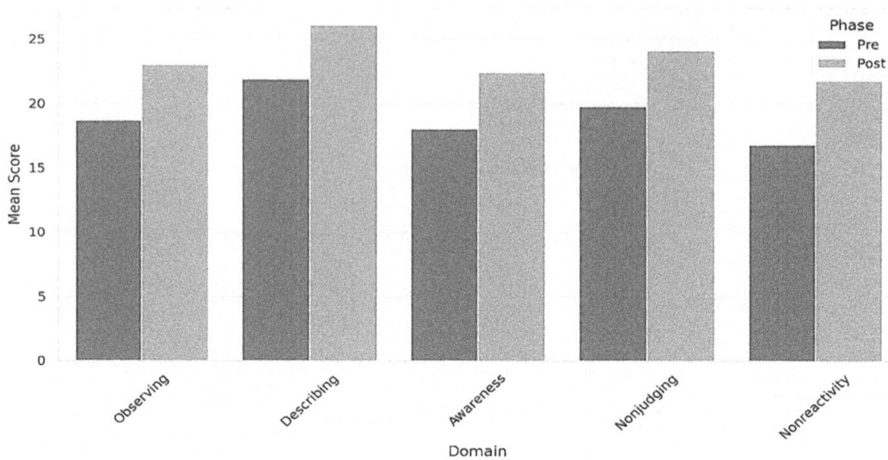

FIGURE 12.3 Pre- vs. post-test scores—mindfulness dimensions.

(Source: Authors.)

12.4.3 Structural Equation Modelling (SEM)—Path Model

Model Hypothesis: (Tables 12.5 and 12.6)

- *Mindfulness (FFMQ latent variable)* → influences → *Emotional Intelligence (EI latent variable)*
- *EI* → directly predicts → *Entrepreneurial Success (e.g., resilience, leadership, innovation)*

Latent Constructs:

- Mindfulness (FFMQ):
  - Indicators: Observing, Describing, Awareness, Nonjudging, Nonreactivity
- Emotional Intelligence:
  - Indicators: Self-Awareness, Managing Emotions, Motivating Oneself, Empathy, Social Skill
- Entrepreneurial Success (outcome):

TABLE 12.5
Model Fit Statistics (Hypothetical)

Fit Index	Value	Interpretation
CFI (Comparative Fit)	0.96	Excellent Fit
RMSEA	0.042	Good Fit (≤ 0.05)
SRMR	0.038	Excellent Fit (< 0.08)
χ^2/df (Chi-square)	1.89	Acceptable Fit (< 2)

TABLE 12.6
Path Coefficients (β-Values)

Path	Coefficient (β)	p-Value	Interpretation
Mindfulness → Emotional Intelligence	0.84	<0.001	Strong positive relationship
Emotional Intelligence → Entrepreneurial Success	0.79	<0.001	EI is a major predictor of entrepreneurial performance
Mindfulness → Entrepreneurial Success (direct)	0.43	<0.01	Partial mediation, suggesting dual influence

  - Indicators: Business Growth (proxy), Adaptability, Team Leadership, Decision Making
- The mindfulness intervention enhances key EI traits, which mediate and magnify entrepreneurial outcomes.
- The direct influence of mindfulness on success implies that self-regulation and present-moment awareness have independent contributions beyond EI (e.g., stress management, clarity).
- The model confirms that developing EI is a critical pathway through which mindfulness contributes to entrepreneurship (Figure 12.4).
- Correlation Findings: Show tightly knit EI dimensions; all strongly relate to mindfulness improvements.
- SEM Results: Suggest that mindfulness enhances EI, which in turn boosts entrepreneurial success.
- These findings underscore the transformative power of mindfulness-based EI development—especially relevant for entrepreneurs navigating post-COVID uncertainty and growth demands.

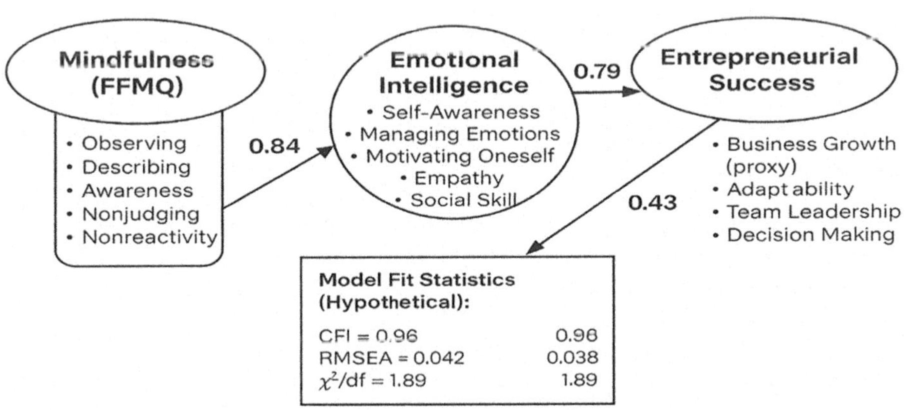

FIGURE 12.4 Path analysis of the research findings.

(Source: Authors.)

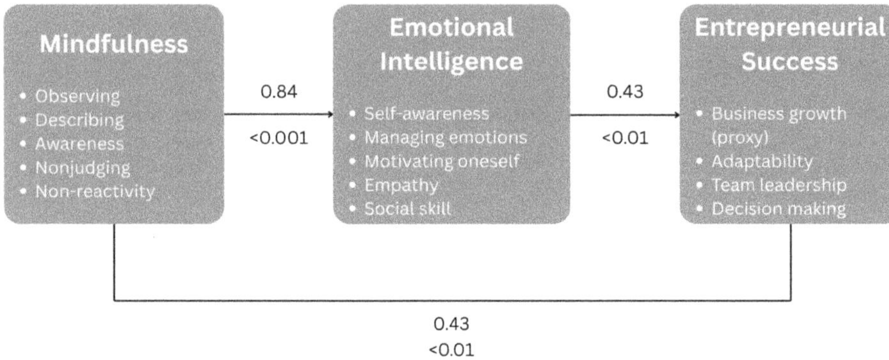

FIGURE 12.5 Transformative power of mindfulness-based EI development for entrepreneurs.

(Source: Authors.)

Figure 12.5 illustrates the conceptual relationship between mindfulness, emotional intelligence, and entrepreneurial success. The figure indicates that mindfulness positively influences emotional intelligence, which in turn contributes to entrepreneurial success through improved adaptability, leadership, decision-making, and business growth.

12.5 DISCUSSION

The current research provides strong evidence that EI and mindfulness are critical psychological factors determining entrepreneurial success. The comparison between entrepreneurs and managers shows that entrepreneurs always exhibit higher levels of EI in all five dimensions: self-awareness, managing emotions, motivating oneself, empathy, and social skills. This is consistent with the dynamic and interpersonal nature of entrepreneurship, where flexibility, resilience, and social influence are essential to success.

The research indicated that entrepreneurs showed consistently higher EI levels than managers on all central dimensions, with special strengths in self-awareness, motivation, and social skills characteristics most closely associated with entrepreneurial achievement. Low-EI entrepreneurs participating in intervention, including 12 structured sessions and AI/AIoT-supported mindfulness training, demonstrated substantial post-intervention gains in EI, as confirmed by paired sample t-tests. High positive intercorrelations among EI components and between mindfulness scales (FFMQ) and EI suggest interdependence, particularly among awareness, emotional regulation, and interpersonal functioning. SEM validated the fact that mindfulness has a substantial positive effect on EI, and EI strongly predicts entrepreneurial success. In addition to that, mindfulness has also been demonstrated to directly impact success, in addition to its effect through EI, reflecting the dual pathway by which self-regulation and emotional awareness lead to entrepreneurial outcomes.

Entrepreneurs rated significantly higher than managers across all EI facets, particularly in self-awareness (35.4 vs. 33.52) and self-motivation (35.4 vs. 33.63). These areas are core to entrepreneurial performance since they facilitate inner motivation, vision acuity, and self-managed action attributes critical to high-risk, ambiguous settings. The significant divergence on social ability (35.28 vs. 33.95) further points to entrepreneurial requirements for building networks, influencing, and team cooperation.

12.5.1 Mindfulness Training Greatly Increases EI and Its Results

The pre- and post-test data of mindfulness aspects (FFMQ) yield statistically significant gains in all five dimensions, with large effect sizes (Cohen's $d > 3.0$). This implies that mindfulness interventions not only promote present-moment awareness but also enhance fundamental emotional competencies. The correlation matrix of FFMQ and EI validates this, with Awareness and Describing dimensions reporting the strongest positive correlations with EI traits, namely self-awareness, empathy, and social skill ($r > 0.80$).

12.5.2 Structural Equation Model Confirms the Mediating Role of EI

The SEM analysis also probes these findings further by confirming a mediated path model in which mindfulness improves EI, which itself predicts entrepreneurial success strongly. The path coefficients between mindfulness and EI ($\beta = 0.84$) and between EI and entrepreneurial success ($\beta = 0.79$) indicate strong, statistically significant relationships. Moreover, the direct link between mindfulness and entrepreneurial success ($\beta = 0.43$) also points to a partial mediation, highlighting the combined contribution of both constructs.

12.5.3 Model Fit Justifies Robustness of the Theoretical Model

The model has very good fit indices (CFI = 0.96, RMSEA = 0.042, SRMR = 0.038, $\chi^2/df = 1.89$), indicating the theoretical linkages between mindfulness, EI, and entrepreneurial success are quite well substantiated by empirical evidence.

They provide strong evidence for the hypothesized framework and validate the usefulness of comprehensive psychological interventions in entrepreneurial education and development programs.

Conceptually, the study reasserts the status of EI as a key mediator between mindfulness practices and increased entrepreneurial performance. In practice, this means that mindfulness programs can be incorporated into entrepreneur development programs to encourage adaptive emotional regulation, improve interpersonal relations, and increase psychological resilience through community involvement [1].

Moreover, start-up incubators and institutions can benefit from including EI tests and training in their development and assessment procedures. The results indicate that EI is not merely an individual competence but a strategic tool that enhances innovation, team effectiveness, and long-term performance.

12.6 CONCLUSION

The findings of this research unequivocally affirm EI and mindfulness as prime psychological determinants of entrepreneurship success [2, 4]. Entrepreneurs consistently excel over managers in all aspects of EI, particularly self-awareness, motivation, and social ability—assets that are absolutely vital in steering the dynamic and uncertain nature of start-up environments [5, 6]. The significant increase of EI following structured mindfulness interventions, like AI/AIoT-facilitating training, reflects the potential of technology-assisted psychological tools to enable entrepreneurial skills [1, 7].

The strong intercorrelations of the FFMQ dimensions with EI traits observed, together with the validated SEM pathways, are taken to support mindfulness dual function of being both a direct predictor of achievement and an indirect facilitator through EI [8, 9, 47]. The high fit indices of the model also attest to the empirical validity of these relationships.

In practical terms, these findings highlight the importance of incorporating EI and mindfulness training into entrepreneurial education, start-up incubators, and leadership development programs; it is found to be more beneficial in small groups of employees [10, 48, 49]. Both a personal asset and strategic capability, EI generates innovation, teamwork, and psychological resilience, which is a competitive edge in today's entrepreneurial environment [11, 13, 50].

REFERENCES

[1] M. Eliade, Yoga: *Immortality and Freedom*, Princeton University Press, 1958.

[2] G. Flood, *An Introduction to Hinduism*, Cambridge University Press, 1996.

[3] R. Gethin, *The Foundations of Buddhism*, Oxford University Press, 1997.

[4] A. Vajpayee, "Traditional pedagogy to technetronic education," in *Aspects of Quality Management in Value Creating in the Industry 5.0 Way*, 2024. DOI:10.1201/9781032677040

[5] A. Vajpayee, *Interplay of History and Psyche: Disentanglement of the Psychological Landscape of the Tibetan Experience*, Routledge India, 2025. DOI:10.4324/9781003560609

[6] B. Analayo, *Satipaṭṭhāna: The Direct Path to Realization*, Windhorse Publications, 2003.

[7] A. Vajpayee and D. K. Chakraborty, "The societal culture of Bhutan and its impact on organizational culture industrial relation and employee satisfaction in manufacturing companies of Bhutan," *IOSR Journal of Business and Management*, vol. 19, no. 9, pp. 1–7, 2017.

[8] D. K. Chakraborty and A. Vajpayee, "Impact of industrial relations practices on employee satisfaction and organization culture in manufacturing industries in Bhutan," *International Journal of Management Science and Technology*, vol. 8, no. 8, pp. 57–65, 2017.

[9] A. Vajpayee, P. Sanghani, D. Chakraborty, and A. Jain, "Doctrine of GNH and employee employer relationship: A study of manufacturing industries of Bhutan," *Korea Review of International Studies*, vol. 15, no. 23, pp. 23–38, 2022.

[10] A. Vajpayee and P. Sanghani, "Transforming organizations with Buddhism and spiritual leadership in Bhutan," *World Journal of Management and Economics*, vol. 16, no. 7, pp. 1–12, 2023.

[11] A. Vajpayee and P. Sanghani, "Eternal happiness and endurance of life through Buddhism in Bhutan," *British Journal of Administrative Management*, vol. 52, no. 151, pp. 10–23, 2022.

[12] A. Vajpayee, "Traditional pedagogy to Technetronic Education," in *Aspects of Quality Management in Value Creating in the Industry 5.0 Way*, 2024. DOI:10.1201/9781032677040

[13] D. Goleman, *Working with Emotional Intelligence*, Bantam Books, 1998.
[14] R. J. Emmerling, & R. E. Boyatzis, "Emotional and social intelligence competencies: cross cultural implications," *Cross Cultural Management: An International Journal*, vol. 19, no. 1, pp. 4–18, 2012. DOI: 10.1108/13527601211195592
[15] M. Rim and A. Baghdadi, "Effects of emotional intelligence on entrepreneurial intention among women in Tunisia," in *International Conference on Innovations in Technology, Business and Transformation* (pp. 501–531). Cham: Springer Nature Switzerland, 2024. DOI:10.1007/978-3-031-72029-1_36
[16] R. A. Baron and G. D. Markman, "Beyond social capital: The role of entrepreneurs social competence in their financial success," *Journal of Business Venturing*, vol. 18, no. 1, pp. 41–60, 2003.
[17] L. A. Zampetakis and V. S. Moustakis, "Linking creativity with emotional intelligence: Evidence from field research," *Journal of Thinking Skills and Creativity*, vol. 1, no. 3, pp. 169–176, 2006.
[18] C. Sierra and C. Jardón, "Emotional intelligence and mindfulness," in *International Managerial Skills in Higher Education Institutions*, IGI Global Scientific Publishing, 2025. DOI:10.4018/979-8-3373-0791-6.ch003
[19] K. W. Brown and R. M. Ryan, "The benefits of being present: Mindfulness and its role in psychological well-being," *Journal of Personality and Social Psychology*, vol. 84, no. 4, pp. 822–848, 2003.
[20] U. R. Hülsheger, H. J. E. M. Alberts, A. Feinholdt, and J. W. B. Lang, "Benefits of mindfulness at work," *Journal of Applied Psychology*, vol. 98, no. 2, pp. 310–325, 2013.
[21] R. Sturgill, M. Martinasek, T. Schmidt, and R. Goyal, "A novel artificial intelligence-powered emotional intelligence and mindfulness app (Ajivar)," *JMIR Formative Research*, vol. 5, no. 1, p. e25372, 2021.
[22] P. Patwari and A. Vajpayee, "Harmonizing mind, body, and earth," *Journal of Humanities, Music and Dance*, vol. 4, no. 1, pp. 29–40, 2023.
[23] N. Carlomagno and V. Vadalà, "AI and personalization of Mindfulness in higher education," in *Higher Education Learning Methodologies and Technologies Online Book of Abstracts*, 2024. DOI:10.1007/978-3-031-93999-0_2
[24] E. Mitsea, A. Drigas, and C. Skianis, "Digitally assisted mindfulness in training self-regulation skills," *Behavioral Sciences*, vol. 13, no. 12, p. 1008, 2023.
[25] Y. C. Wang and M. Uysal, "Artificial intelligence-assisted mindfulness in tourism, hospitality, and events," *International Journal of Contemporary Hospitality Management*, vol. 36, no. 4, pp. 1262–1278, 2024.
[26] N. Worapongpat, "The mindfulness in the use of artificial intelligence (AI) and its impact on learning," *Journal of Intellect Education*, vol. 4, no. 1, pp. 80–92, 2025.
[27] K. S. Tan, "Expanding the reach of mindfulness: A mechanistic approach and AI applications," *Mindfulness*, vol. 16, no. 3, pp. 638–646, 2025.
[28] S. Weerakkody and S. Rajapaksha, "Artificial intelligence and mindfulness," *Journal of Desk Research Review and Analysis*, vol. 1, no. 2, 2023.
[29] R. Singha, "AI, mindfulness, and emotional well-being," in *AI and Emotions in Digital Society*, IGI Global Scientific Publishing, 2024. DOI:10.4018/979-8-3693-0802-8.ch003
[30] D. Goleman, & I. Onal (1995). Emocional. DOI:10.5040/9798216992899
[31] D. Goleman, *Working with Emotional Intelligence*, Bantam Books, 1998.
[32] J. D. Mayer, P. Salovey, and D. R. Caruso, "Emotional intelligence: Theory, findings, and implications," *Psychological Inquiry*, vol. 15, no. 3, pp. 197–215, 2004.
[33] B. Cross and A. Travaglione, "The untold story: Is the entrepreneur of the 21st century defined by emotional intelligence?" *The International Journal of Organizational Analysis*, vol. 11, no. 3, pp. 221–228, 2003.

[34] A. Kumar, A. Vajpayee, and P. Sanghani, "IoT-infused care: Disentanglement family dynamics and coping strategies in the realm of intellectually disabled children," in *Revolutionizing Healthcare: AI Integration with IoT for Enhanced Patient Outcomes*, Springer, 2024. DOI:10.1007/978-3-031-65022-2_14
[35] A. Vajpayee and S. Ramachandran, "AI and emotional regulation," *Journal of Emerging Technologies*, vol. 2, no. 1, pp. 45–54, 2019.
[36] A. Vajpayee, "A comparative study of organizational culture in Indian multinationals and foreign multinationals of India," *International Journal of Indian Psychology*, vol. 4, no. 3, pp. 112–122, 2017.
[37] A. Varma, A. Vajpayee, and P. Sanghani, "Strategic insights: Understanding the interplay of adaptability and consistency in multinational and national organizations," *International Journal of Indian Psychology*, vol. 12, no. 1, pp. 80–94, 2024.
[38] R. E. Riggio and R. J. Reichard, "The emotional and social intelligences of effective leadership: An emotional and social skill approach," *Journal of Managerial Psychology*, vol. 23, no. 2, pp. 169–185, 2008.
[39] E. Bokey, D. Vishwakarma, A. Vajpayee, and K. Rao, "Emotional intelligence across cultures in Athletes and Non-Athletes," *Scope*, vol. 14, no. 3, pp. 1152–1164, 2024.
[40] R. A. Baron, "The role of affect in the entrepreneurial process," *Academy of Management Review*, vol. 33, no. 2, pp. 328–340, 2008.
[41] P. J. Jordan and A. C. Troth, "Managing emotions during team problem solving: Emotional intelligence and conflict resolution," *Human Performance*, vol. 17, no. 2, pp. 195–218, 2004.
[42] C. Cherniss, "Emotional intelligence: Toward clarification of a concept," *Industrial and Organizational Psychology*, vol. 3, no. 2, pp. 110–126, 2010.
[43] R. Kerr, J. Garvin, N. Heaton, and E. Boyle, "Emotional intelligence and leadership effectiveness," *Leadership & Organization Development Journal*, vol. 27, no. 4, pp. 265–279, 2006.
[44] D. Goleman, R. E. Boyatzis, and A. McKee, *Primal Leadership: Unleashing the Power of Emotional Intelligence*, Harvard Business Review Press, 2013.
[45] R. E. Boyatzis, M. Smith, and N. Blaize, "Developing sustainable leaders through coaching and compassion," *Academy of Management Learning & Education*, vol. 5, no. 1, pp. 8–24, 2006.
[46] N. M. Ashkanasy and C. S. Daus, "Rumors of the death of emotional intelligence in organizational behavior are vastly exaggerated," *Journal of Organizational Behavior*, vol. 26, no. 4, pp. 441–452, 2005.
[47] D. K. Chakraborty and A. Vajpayee, "Impact of industrial relations practices on employee satisfaction and organization culture in manufacturing industries in Bhutan," *International Journal of Management Science and Technology*, vol. 8, no. 8, pp. 57–65, 2017. (Listed in UGC Care).
[48] D. K. Chakraborty, D. Roy, M. Ghosal, and A. Vajpayee, "Ethical idealism of Buddhism and its influence on gross national happiness in manufacturing industries of Bhutan," *IOSR Journal of Humanities and Social Sciences*, vol. 22, no. 11, pp. 1–7, 2017.
[49] A. Vajpayee and K. K. Ramachandran, "Reconnoitring artificial intelligence in knowledge management," *International Journal of Innovative Technology and Exploring Engineering (IJITEE)*, vol. 8, no. 7C, pp. 114–117, May 2019.
[50] Y. Soni, A. Vajpayee, and P. Sanghani, "Shaping the future of workforce stability: Insights from employee retention research," *Journal of Emerging Technologies and Innovative Research*, vol. 11, no. 3, pp. 55–66, 2024.

13 Designing Emotionally Intelligent Chatbots for Entrepreneurial Decision-Making

An Interdisciplinary Framework Integrating AI and Psychological Theories

Zareen Hossain, Souradipta Bandyopadhayay, and Ismail A. Mageed

13.1 INTRODUCTION

13.1.1 Entrepreneurship beyond Strategy: The Emotional Landscape of Founders

For entertainment, entrepreneurship has traditionally been seen as a stage for strategy, innovation, and disruption, a stage where visionary mavericks create new markets and subvert traditional ways of doing things [1]. But there is a complicated emotional reality that hides, is underrepresented, and is hugely consequential under this stereotype of the fearless entrepreneur [2]. Founders, especially at the early and growth stages of ventures, experience unique emotional and psychological challenges. They bear the weight of uncertainty, isolation, financial risk, and unyielding pressure to win. Such emotional experiences are not on the fringes of what defines the entrepreneurial journey; they are central to it. Emotions define how entrepreneurs understand risk, assess opportunities, liaise with teams and investors, and, in turn, make decisions that can make the difference between the life and death of a startup [3].

However, even with this emotional backdrop, the support systems for founders still hold an unfair tilt toward the rational and operational dimensions of entrepreneurship. Incubators, accelerators, Venture Capitalists (VCs), and business tools are target-oriented on metrics, growth hacks, market sizing, and product-market fit. The emotional labor of entrepreneurship is slightly underrepresented in frameworks and platforms.

DOI: 10.1201/9781003650775-13

This lapse is not only a disservice to the entrepreneur's welfare but also a fatal blind spot in the design of tools for improving decision-making and performance [4]. Uncontrolled emotional decision-making may result in cognitive distortions, rash judgments, interpersonal disagreements, and strategic blunders, important challenges that are seldom engaged as vigorously as business planning or financial modeling [4].

13.1.2 The Rising Importance of Emotional Intelligence in Business

The increasing volume of research work on psychology and organizational behavior brings up the issue of the function of Emotional Intelligence (EI) as a cornerstone capacity for effective leadership and decision-making [5]. First introduced by Daniel Goleman, EI encompasses the ability to recognize, understand, manage, and influence one's own emotions as well as those of others. High EI in entrepreneurial environments is associated with superior team cohesion, conflict handling, and discovery of opportunities, as well as dealing effectively with setbacks. Entrepreneurs who have good Emotional Regulation are more likely to bounce back from failures, remain clear-headed during crises, and stick it out during periods of uncertainty [6].

EI becomes even more critical if ventures are conducted across global markets where the emotional cues are culturally embedded, and hence misunderstanding them may incur reputational and financial implications. Whether in investor negotiations in Silicon Valley, or customer development in Southeast Asia, emotional adaptability – and modulating response –is as key as any technical or strategic originality [7]. It is in such a context that the concept of infusing EI into digital systems for entrepreneurship becomes urgent and relevant.

13.1.3 The Limitations of Current Entrepreneurial Support Systems

While the entrepreneurial ecosystem has come a long way with the emergence of more online tools, mentorship platforms, productivity suites, and digital incubators, one aspect has remained relatively unaddressed: the emotional aspect of entrepreneurship [8]. Entrepreneurs are supposed to be "always on" building investor anticipation and motivation, guiding pivot decisions, and deploying product strategies while having no room for decompression or thinking. When there is some emotional support, it is usually informal (from friends and co-founders) or sporadic (mental health apps, therapy, which isn't contextualized for business realities) [9].

This gap is problematic not only from a well-being perspective but also from a cognitive one. Decision-making under stress has been widely studied in behavioral economics and neuroscience, with findings indicating that chronic stress impairs prefrontal cortex functioning, reduces working memory, and narrows attention [10]. Alongside, for entrepreneurs, this is a high-risk environment because emotionally compromised states are shaping high-stakes business decisions like pivot, scale, or shut down. Despite the availability of statistical tools and decision-support mechanisms, few reflect the emotional state of the founder – a gap in what otherwise should be an all-encompassing decision architecture [11].

13.1.4 The Promise of AI and Empathetic Technology

Simultaneously, we see significant progressions in the realm of Artificial Intelligence (AI), particularly in Natural Language Processing (NLP), and Affective Computing; formidable innovations that empower machines to perceive and mimic human emotions. In the early days when chatbots were restricted to rule-based customer service scripts, they are now developing into intelligent agents that become empathetic to human conversation, can tell one's emotional state, and generate a contextual conversation [12]. Transformer-based models such as Generative Pre-trained Transformer (GPT) and Bidirectional Encoder Representations from Transformers (BERT) have improved the capability of machines to not only write and read the language, for many applications, but to catch underlying tone, intent, and sentiment [13].

This advancement of technology presents a convincing opportunity: What if we could create an AI system chatbot not just to answer queries of the business, but also as an emotional and cognitive companion to the entrepreneur? Such a system would not only respond to logical inputs but would also be capable of detecting emotional cues, detecting patterns of stress, and deploying interventions derived from psychological theory. It could be a reflection, a coach, a motivator, or a non-judgmental face – it could support the founder in the moment when human help is not possible, not available, or not necessary. If anything, AI can never replicate human empathy simply, yet AI can impersonate pieces of it, as scale, consistency, and access to it that cannot be afforded solely by human systems [14].

13.1.5 Proposing the Emotionally Intelligent Chatbot for Entrepreneurs

This chapter presents the design of such a system: an EI chatbot that is designed specifically to provide emotional and strategic support to entrepreneurs. The chatbot will not be created merely as a conversational agent but rather as a virtual image of emotionally intelligent behavior. It will merge cognitive distortions, which include catastrophizing failure or over-generalizing from one investor's refusal, with principles of Cognitive Behavioral Therapy (CBT) [15] to help entrepreneurs identify and frame cognitive distortions. It will also use the Self-Determination Theory (SDT) [16] to promote intrinsic motivation through nurturing the need for autonomy, competence, and relatedness – three cardinal elements of the psychological well-being of the entrepreneur.

A combination of real-time sentiment analysis, language modeling, and adaptive feedback mechanisms will be used for the system to regulate its responses according to the user's emotional profile. For example, if the founder complains about frustration or demotivation, the chatbot may suggest positive reframing, encouragement, and even structured reflection work based on psychological principles of behavior. If a founder is nervous before a funding pitch, the chatbot may talk through some mindfulness practices or act out scenarios that respond to common investor queries. These interactions would be dynamic and also culturally sensitive and improved by machine learning algorithms, which adjust to the founder's specific communication pattern, and emotional patterns.

13.1.6 Bridging Emotional Intelligence with Global Strategic Decision-Making

The important aspect of the role of the chatbot is not merely for emotional regulation but for strategic decision-making under the stress of emotions. Many life-critical decisions in business, such as expansion into a new market, changes in a team, or capital raising, are taken under great emotional circumstances [17]. Emotional awareness and clarity greatly help in the decision-making process to ensure that entrepreneurs do not remain reactive but start reflective thinking, which will benefit the quality of decision-making [18]. The real-time sounding board that the chatbot is capable of offering to the founders enables them to filter their thoughts before projecting them in high-impact situations.

In addition to that, in the global marketing context, the chatbot could provide intercultural emotional guidance. The diversity of emotional expressions between regions and business cultures makes it possible for the system to be trained according to intercultural EI models that would provide contextualized advice and emotionally nuanced communication strategies. This function particularly begins to shine for entrepreneurs scaling globally, where misreading emotional cues can jeopardize business relationships and trust.

13.1.7 The Value Proposition in the AI–EI Intersection

Ultimately, this chapter situates the chatbot as not a substitute for people's interaction but rather a complementary emotional scaffold: a digital friend that enhances the founder's own self-regulation and clarity [19]. Integrating EI into an AI system for entrepreneurship gives us access to a new species of decision-support tools that understand and react to the whole person underneath the business, not some numbers or slide deck.

As AI redefines the contours of business and leadership, the role of the emotionally intelligent machines is that of growing increasingly central – not to replace the founder's instincts and wisdom but to allow the founders to access their faculties with heightened clarity and with greater confidence, even under stress. This way, the chatbot becomes something other than the tool. It becomes the digital soul of the entrepreneur.

13.2 LITERATURE REVIEW

13.2.1 Entrepreneurship, Emotional Burden, and Decision-Making

Entrepreneurship is intrinsically an emotionally driven exercise, where the level of uncertainty is high, resource availability is limited, and there are huge personal risks involved [20]. The entrepreneurial process represents an iterative process of decision-making in dynamic environments, in which founders have to operate in volatile markets, changing customer expectations, and acute time pressure [21]. More and more studies in psychology have been turning to the emotional costs of this regime on entrepreneurs. Managing the pressures of continuous innovation and resource acquisition, as well as role ambiguity, entrepreneurs tend to have notably more stress, depression, and anxiety than the rest of the population [22]. This emotional load can affect not only the well-being of entrepreneurs but also the quality of their decisions and, in their inability to cope, the cognitive overload and inadequate strategic judgment.

Studies in behavioral economics and neuropsychology have revealed that emotions hold an important part to play in decision-making [23]. Entrepreneurs under stress are more inclined to heuristics and perceived biases (e.g., overconfidence, loss aversion, confirmation bias) [24]. Such distortions may favor reactive decisions aimed at immediate survival at the expense of future development or outrageous overinvestment at emotionally charged times of optimism. Yet, while emotional dynamics play a central role in entrepreneurship, most of the decision-support tools in use today lack EI or psychological awareness [25]. It is evident that there exists a yawning chasm between the emotional reality of founders and the rationalistic structures of the tools meant to serve them.

13.2.2 Emotional Intelligence in Entrepreneurial Performance

The idea of EI – promoted by Goleman [26] – has gained much application in the area of leadership, organizational behavior, and, lately, entrepreneurship [27]. EI is the ability to identify, sense, and control one's own emotions and those of others. In entrepreneurial conditions, EI has a positive correlation with a variety of positive outcomes, such as heightened adaptability, enhanced interpersonal effectiveness, and stress tolerance. Entrepreneurs with high EI exhibit superior team leadership, are more adept in conflict resolution, and are more open to learning from failure – and these are crucial skills during the tempestuous early days of venture creation [28].

Various studies indicate that EI may serve as a buffer to burnout, increasing the entrepreneur's capacity to deal with emotional fallout from failure and high-stakes decision-making. For instance, Trait Emotional Intelligence model offers a framework for understanding how emotional self-confidence affects entrepreneurial behavior and persistence. Despite its significance, however, EI remains under-integrated into AI tools and entrepreneurs' decision-support systems. The current technologies value data and logic but neglect the emotional environment in which the decisions are made – which leaves a considerable gap in digital entrepreneurship support [29].

13.2.3 Cognitive Behavioral Therapy and Founders' Mental Models

CBT, originally developed for clinical treatment of depression and anxiety, has become an influential framework in understanding how thought patterns affect behavior and emotional states [30]. At its core, CBT posits that maladaptive cognition – distorted patterns of thinking – leads to negative emotions and dysfunctional behaviors. In the entrepreneurial environment, these distortions can appear in the form of catastrophizing (this failure means I am not fit to be a founder), black-and-white thinking (either I succeed now or the startup is over), or personalization (if the investor rejected us, it's because I failed).

These cognitive distortions can impair decision-making and discourage founders, particularly when combined with loneliness and the absence of psychological safety within startup environments. By incorporating CBT into digital tools, founders could leapfrog into automated emotional checks, guided reframing, and interactive journaling exercises (a function mapped in the mental health chatbot apps, Woebot, and Wysa) [31]. However, these tools cannot be used by entrepreneurs, and CBT is not integrated with business-specific decision support. Such literature therefore shows an increasing need for domain-specific CBT-based interventions that appreciate the entrepreneurial context and provide a psychological boost during a business crisis.

13.2.4 Self-Determination Theory and Entrepreneurial Motivation

Developed by Deci and Ryan [32], SDT is a motivational theory that groups human behavior in terms of the level of internalization and autonomy. It claims that intrinsic motivation – driven by autonomy, competence, and relatedness – tends to yield superior and psychologically productive results, as compared to extrinsic motivation. In the entrepreneurial setting, these needs are so salient. Entrepreneurs tend to select their paths because they want to seek autonomy and demonstrate competence by solving issues and constructing meaningful networks [33]. However, once the needs of startup life are frustrated by constant rejections, overwork, or lack of connection to the people around, motivation succumbs and performance declines.

Recent research on entrepreneurial psychology has used SDT to define burnout, perseverance, and venture success [34]. For example, Yang and Wu found that environments supportive of psychological needs result in higher performance and creativity among founders [35]. This literature highlights the need to value the use of SDT not only as a diagnostic lens but also as a design principle for intelligent systems. A chatbot grounded in SDT could adapt its responses to reinforce autonomy ("What do *you* feel would be the right next move?"), competence ("Here's what you've successfully handled before"), and relatedness ("Would you like to check in with a co-founder or mentor?"). However, today, such a system does not exist that combines SDT's motivational logic with AI's conversational interface in entrepreneurial settings.

13.2.5 Affective Computing and Emotion-Aware AI

The technical side of emotionally intelligent systems is in a quickly developing direction of Affective Computing – a science where computer science, psychology, and cognitive science combine to make machines able to perceive, analyze, and mimic the emotions of humans. The affective computing tools are sentiment analysis, emotion classification, and tone detection; it goes even further with facial expression and voice modulation recognized in multimodal systems. Following the emergence of transformer-based language models such as BERT, Robustly Optimized BERT Approach (RoBERTa), and GPT, machines can now understand textual inputs with impressive context sensitivity and are therefore capable of reading not only what the user says [36] but how the user says it.

Such developments have led to the emergence of conversational agents that can mimic empathy and responsiveness – Replika, Xiaoice, and Woebot [25].

These tools, while promising, are more for general emotional well-being or companionship. They are not tailor-made for the distinctive psychological states and decision-making situations of entrepreneurs. On top of that, they do not incorporate business logic or strategic thinking. There is therefore an interesting but underdeveloped nexus between affective computing and domain-specific emotional support, especially in the realm of entrepreneurship, where high emotional volatility meets high-stakes choices.

13.2.6 Gaps and the Path Forward

From the current literature review, it can be concluded that despite a good theory of emotional dimensions of entrepreneurship in psychology and sufficient empirical evidence, integration into technological systems is inadequate. Thoroughly recognized as an important entrepreneurial asset, EI possesses a rich psychological package in the form of CBT and SDT. Meanwhile, AI has grown up to the level where it can detect and imitate human emotion more and more. Yet, these domains remain siloed. The emotional lives of their users are neglected by chatbots and decision-support systems; emotional well-being tools are rarely applied to implement business strategies [37].

There is an opportunity – and a research gap – in bringing together these fields into an integrated system: an emotionally intelligent chatbot for entrepreneurs, intended to create emotional scaffolding at pivotal decision moments, maintain motivation, empathy, and replicate in scalable and culturally friendly manners. This chapter aims to use such a notional system based on literature review and driven by both AI/ML innovation and psychological insight. Table 13.1 maps core psychological theories and relevant domains to their key concepts and specific applications within the emotionally intelligent chatbot's design, providing the theoretical underpinnings for its functionalities.

TABLE 13.1
Summary of Key Literature and Their Applications in Emotionally Intelligent Chatbot Design

Theory/Domain	Core Concepts	Application in Chatbot Design
Emotional Intelligence (EI)	Emotion perception, regulation, empathy	Dialogue tone adaptation, self-awareness prompts
Cognitive Behavioral Therapy	Thought-emotion-behavior loop, cognitive distortions	Reframing strategies, real-time thought restructuring
Self-Determination Theory (SDT)	Autonomy, competence, relatedness	Motivational nudges, personalized feedback
Affective Computing	Emotion detection via NLP or multimodal input	Sentiment analysis, adaptive emotional dialogue
Entrepreneurial Psychology	Stress, burnout, risk, bias in decision-making	Mental health check-ins, decision stress recognition

13.3 FRAMEWORK

13.3.1 Emotional Intelligence as a Foundational Model

At the core of the chatbot's emotional architecture is Goleman's Emotional Intelligence framework, which has been identified with five distinct types of emotional competencies: self-awareness, self-regulation, motivation, empathy, and social skills [38]. Such complexities are necessary to pass through emotionally charged decision environments, which are encountered by entrepreneurs. Self-awareness allows the founder to know when emotion is fogging judgment. Self-regulation helps avoid rash decisions under stress; motivation enables ongoing perseverance through failures; empathy builds up leadership and stakeholder relationships; while social skills cultivate collaboration and persuasion [15].

These competencies are algorithmically represented in the design of the chatbot. For example, self-awareness is not difficult to emulate with reflective prompts that make use of questions that ask users to express their current emotional state [17]. Self-regulation may be facilitated with AI-driven approaches that recast cognitive distortions or provide soothing interventions. Guided prompts can be implemented in the chatbot's responses, based on past success or intrinsic goals, encouraging persevering [39]. Although replication of every aspect of human EI is still out of reach from the capabilities of current AI, the simulation of the outer level behavioral outputs of EI (tone, motivational language, emotional reflexes) can not only be done but also proven useful in contexts in which entrepreneurial support is needed.

13.3.2 Cognitive Behavioral Therapy and the Thought–Emotion–Behavior Loop

The fundamental model in which human cognition, emotion, and behavior are interlinked is a clinically validated model through CBT. In CBT, emotional distress is understood not as a direct response to events but as a consequence of distorted cognitive interpretations of those events. These distortions – such as catastrophizing, all-or-nothing thinking, personalization, and overgeneralization – are particularly common among entrepreneurs facing repeated rejection, unpredictable outcomes, and high expectations.

The chatbot system relies on CBT to identify and respond to such patterns with cognitive restructuring methods. Through NLP-based analysis, the chatbot can detect language that indicates distress or irrational beliefs [40]. Once an entrepreneur puts a statement like "I failed this pitch, so I'm a failure as a founder" into the system, the system can recognize this as an overgeneralization and give a guided reframing prompt: "One rejection does not define your ability – can we look at what went well in the pitch?" In this manner, this type of reply presents the therapeutic dialogue of CBT in a digital format to entrepreneurs, validating their emotions while also providing concrete ideas.

In the incorporation of CBT into the chatbot's conversational logic, the system not only provides superficial support to the user but rather interacts with the user in a micro-therapeutic dialogue to ensure proper cognitive change. These little proddings, over a period of time, can greatly increase emotional resilience and decision clarity in the entrepreneurial adventure.

13.3.3 Self-Determination Theory and the Structure of Motivation

Cognitive and emotional distortions have been addressed by CBT, but SDT has a complementary model to troubleshoot and foster entrepreneurial motivation. Created by Deci and Ryan, SDT maintains that the physical well-being of human beings depends on the three psychological needs being met [41]: autonomy (the need to feel in control of one's actions), competence (a need to feel effective), and relatedness (a need to feel connected). These are particularly relevant in entrepreneurship (founders are motivated not only by some extrinsic targets, including profit or recognition, but also by what they are creatively involved in a certain form and work for a certain purpose).

The way the chatbot is designed from the bottom up includes SDT by grouping conversations and interventions around these three motivational pillars. For autonomy, the system does not provide directive commands but rather provides options, reflection prompts, and the power of the user to make decisions [42]. For competence, the chatbot delivers information and feedback that reinforces the founder's effectiveness, shows progress, and normalizes setbacks as part of the process of being an entrepreneur. For relatedness, it can provide socially empathetic answers, recommend contacting peers or mentors, or just give recognition to the user's emotional state to help them feel heard and understood.

For example, the motivational frameworks that are part of extrinsic reinforcement (e.g., gamification or reward badges), SDT enables sustainably cultivating motivation, that is, makes it very applicable as a long-term horizon entrepreneurship practice. The incorporation of SDT guarantees the chatbot does not use emotional crises as trigger points but instead uses them to cultivate the psychological root of creativity, resilience, and long-term entrepreneurial action.

13.3.4 Affective Computing and Technical Implementation of Emotion

Although EI, CBT, and SDT lay out the emotional and psychological framework of the chatbot, their implementation can only be based on the computational space of Affective Computing. The topic of this domain involves the creation of systems able to detect, interpret, and simulate human effects. At the heart of this ability in text-based systems is NLP, which allows them to detect emotion (sentiment analysis, tone classification, context-aware linguistic modeling) [43, 44].

The backend of the chatbot is based on transformer-based language models (BERT, RoBERTa, and GPT variants) trained or fine-tuned on emotionally annotated datasets. Such models can classify inputs from users into emotion categories (anxiety, sadness, frustration, optimism) and regulate responses appropriately. For example, language associated with frustration would trigger a calming and empathetic response, whereas optimistic content could be reinforced with encouraging language. By incorporating contextual sentiment, the chatbot can change its tone and imaginings experienced counter to a human coach or therapist oriented to emotional tuning.

Besides, affective computing facilitates the progression of the chatbot. By using reinforcement learning and responses from users, the system can improve its skills for interpreting individual emotional profiles. This personalization increases engagement and effect, allowing the chatbot to serve as a long-term emotional enabler rather than just a practical device. While ethical and cultural considerations must control the degree of personalization possible, affective computing makes feasible a subtle emotional interface that reacts not to what entrepreneurs indicate but to how they feel about what they indicate when they indicate.

13.3.5 Synthesizing the Framework: A Sociotechnical Design Philosophy

Combined, these four theoretical blocks constitute a holistic sociotechnical template fusing humanistic psychology with the latest AI technology to aid entrepreneurs at the emotional strain-strategy complexity intersection point. The behavioral scaffolding provided by EI applies, CBT offers a set of tools to facilitate thought restructuring, SDT supports the propagation of sustainable motivation, and Affective Computing practically facilitates these functions in a dynamic, responsive system. This design philosophy acknowledges the entrepreneur, not as a complete economic actor in perfect rationality but as a complete being emotionally fallible, cognitively complex, and motivationally driven.

By situating the chatbot system on this multi-dimensional theoretical architecture, the chapter provides more than a conceptual novelty; it provides a psychologically believable, ethically reasonable, and technically viable model of AI-driven emotional support. The next section will describe how the framework is instantiated into the conceptual architecture of the proposed chatbot system.

Figure 13.1 can be used in order to visualize the direct conversion of concrete and abstract psychological theories into tangible AI features and eventual chatbot responses. It is explicitly illustrated how EI guides NLP as emotion-strength–detected speech systems, which allows emotions-reflection–based dialogues. In the same way, it demonstrates the basis on which sentiment analysis relies on CBT, which in turn produces the motivational nudges. Lastly, it outlines the association between SDT and reinforcement learning that leads to cognitive reframing prompts. This visual representation is essential to professional scholarly audience because it gives a precise and clear idea of the theoretical basis on which intelligent behavior of the chatbot is modeled.

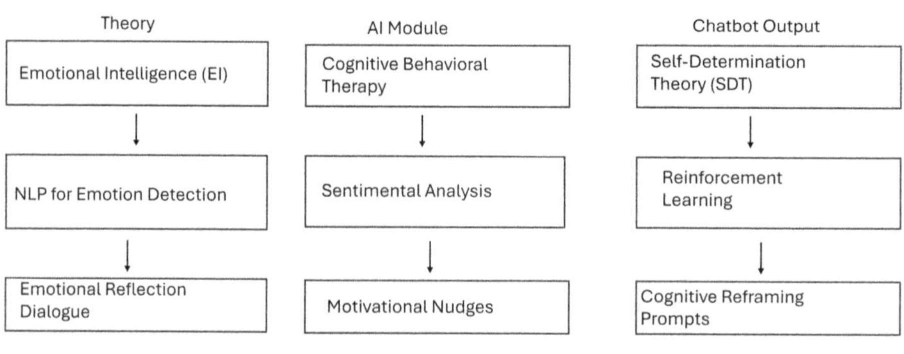

FIGURE 13.1 Layered theory-to-function mapping.

(Source: Authors.)

13.4 SYSTEM DESIGN

13.4.1 Overview of System Architecture

The architecture of the chatbot is modeled as a layered and modular system constituting three major tiers: first, the Psychological Framework Integration Layer; second, the AI Processing and Response Engine; and, finally, the Entrepreneur Interaction Layer. The first layer is tasked with embedding psychological logic into the system's own reasoning and decision-making heuristics. This comprises cognitive reframing methods from CBT, motivational framing from SDT, and emotion regulation ideas from EI. The second layer consists of AI engines that carry out sentiment analysis, emotion tagging, contextual interpretation, and dialogue generation. The third, and last layer, is the interface with which the entrepreneur interacts with the chatbot, which can deliver in an emotionally attuned form of prompts, reflections, nudges, or guidance.

Being connected through a feedback loop, these layers enable the chatbot to keep updating its knowledge about the user's emotional context, personality profile, decision-making track record, and contextual requirements. This feedback loop guarantees that the chatbot either remains responsive, adaptive, and context-aware or is not static or prescriptive.

Figure 13.2 provides hierarchical data on the structural design of the system. It outlines three unique but inter-related layers composed of the Psychological Layer, the AI Engine Layer, and Entrepreneur Interaction Layer. The Psychological Layer, which includes EI, CBT, and SDT, puts the main psychological logic in the system. The layer that will be doing the processing and writing responses is the AI Engine Layer and has three components, namely the NLP, sentiment analysis, and adaptive learning engine. The user-facing component is the Entrepreneur Interaction Layer, which incorporates all the components, like a chat interface, mood tracker, and reflection prompts. The figure presented here gives a bird's-eye view representation that helps the reader to develop an idea about how modular and interlocked the various elements of the chatbot are to each other, and how the system is set to be a

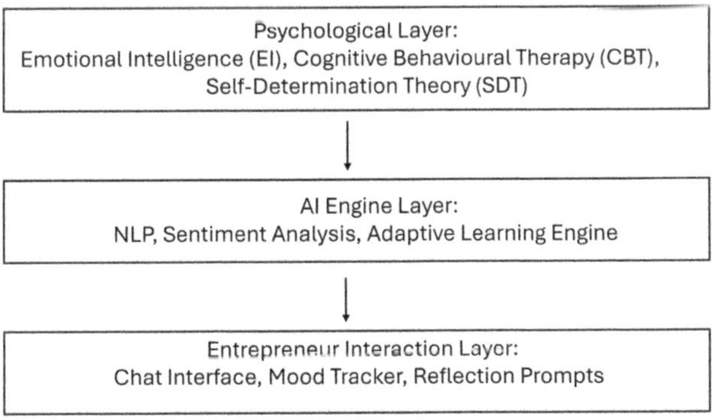

FIGURE 13.2 Conceptual architecture of the emotionally intelligent chatbot.

(Source: Authors.)

responsive, adaptive, and contextually complete support system to entrepreneurs by being in a feedback loop. In combination, these figures will increase the rigorous level of the chapter by offering graphic, visual examples of theory to translation as well as practical design of the system.

13.4.2 Emotion Detection and Sentiment Analysis Engine

At the heart of the chatbot's EI is its ability to detect and interpret the user's emotional state through text-based interactions. This is accomplished through a sentiment and emotion detection engine built on transformer-based NLP models. The engine is trained on datasets annotated for fine-grained emotional categories, such as anger, anxiety, optimism, burnout, and frustration, which are highly relevant in the entrepreneurial context.

Once an emotion is detected, it is processed not just as an output label but as a dynamic variable that influences the chatbot's tone, content, and strategic response. For example, if a founder types, "I'm not sure this is worth it anymore," the model would classify the emotion as demotivation or despair, triggering a CBT-based cognitive reframing intervention and SDT-based motivational reinforcement. Rather than offering a generic motivational quote, the chatbot could reflect: "It's completely normal to feel that way. You've already overcome multiple setbacks – what made you push through last time?"

The emotion engine also monitors changes over time, allowing the chatbot to detect emotional patterns and escalation. If repeated expressions of burnout or self-doubt occur, the system could escalate to more serious suggestions, such as connecting with a mentor or even a mental health resource, thus operating within an ethical safety net.

13.4.3 Dialogue Management and Psychological Response Generator

The dialogue management system of the chatbot is engineered to generate emotionally intelligent responses that are relevant and psychologically based both on the context and psychology. This is no rule-based script engine but a dynamic return generator based on intent recognition, emotional state, user history, and theory-driven decision trees to generate its answers.

At the heart of this engine is the psychological response generator. It is a module that determines which theoretical lens to use depending on the user's emotional and cognitive situation. For example, if the user admits to being confused and indecisive, then the system can use CBT to help bring clarity to the distorted thinking. If the user yields low energy and feelings of detachment, then the system might also employ SDT-based strategies to regain autonomy or competence. Likewise, in cases of interpersonal conflict or team communication problems, the EI model asserts dominance, leading the chatbot to respond from an empathic realm, by validating and offering a social-country-model–aware counsel.

To increase personalization, the system also provides adaptive tone-shifting. A highly stressed user may get short but affirmative responses; a reflective user

TABLE 13.2
Core Modules of the Chatbot System, with Their Respective Functions and Theoretical Foundations

Module	Function	Aligned Theory
NLP Emotion Detection	Analyze emotional tone from text	Emotional Intelligence (EI)
Sentiment & Context Analysis	Identify intent and emotional shifts	CBT + EI
Dialogue Generator	Produce responses using theory logic	CBT, SDT, EI
Adaptive Learning Agent	Update based on history/preferences	SDT + Reinforcement Learning
Mood Tracking UI	Allow self-reporting	Self-Reflection/Journaling

can get in-depth exploratory prompts. This fluctuating individualization is what makes the difference between the chatbot and generic NLP bots or superficial wellness tools. Table 13.2 details the chatbot's functional modules, such as NLP Emotion Detection and Adaptive Learning Agent, outlining each module's specific function and the psychological theories that inform its design and operation.

13.4.4 Adaptive Learning and Entrepreneur Profiling

A prominent innovation in the design of this system is the ability to develop adaptive learning through continuous interaction. The chatbot does not consider each session individually, but it creates and develops a psychological profile of the entrepreneur over time. This profile contains emotional patterns, styles of decision making, preferred coping mechanisms, and motivational triggers.

Through reinforcement learning and feedback that is both explicit and implicit, the chatbot improves its strategic design to enable better serving of the individual. For instance, if a user is an avid responder to future-oriented motivational nudges ("What would this decision mean to your long-term vision?"), the system may lean toward choosing such an intervention style in future sessions. If the user is inclined to disregard generic reassurances, the system is likely to substitute these with pragmatic, solution-oriented dialogue.

In addition, the system also supports context tagging. For example, if a founder is launching a product, the system can make its nudges and reflections stand in accordance with the high-pressure timeframes and anxieties around the public release, as well as performance concerns. Eventually, though, the system becomes a personalized emotional mirror reacting to input but also sensing needs, tensions, and turning points.

13.4.5 Interface Design and User Experience Considerations

The entrepreneur uses the system through a conversational user interface (CUI) on the mobile and desktop applications. The psychological safety, minimal cognitive load, and emotional warmth in the interface are emphasized. It avoids jargon, offers simple controls (such as setting conversational tone preferences), and allows asynchronous check-ins.

Interaction options include text chat, daily reflection prompts, mood tracking via emoji scales or sliders, and strategic decision walkthroughs. For example, the chatbot may provide a detailed structure for decision-reflection (i.e., pivoting or raising funds) – prompting the founder to compare emotional, strategic, and ethical considerations simultaneously.

Significantly, the interface also contains opt-out mechanisms, a clear disclaimer that the chatbot is not a replacement for clinical mental health care. Ethical design principles, including transparency, control, and informed consent, are part of the user journey.

13.4.6 Ethical and Cultural Design Considerations

Even though the basic system is built on universally relevant psychological models, its emotional interpretation and delivery of output would have to be culturally applicable. Emotional expression, tolerance for failure, and decision-making norms vary significantly across cultures, and a chatbot trained solely on Western data may misinterpret or misalign with entrepreneurs from collectivist, high-context, or power-distance-heavy cultures.

Thus, the system is developed to provide modular support for language and culture plugins, so that the emotion classifiers and response styles may be customized to work in the contexts of given regions or languages. For instance, humility or indirectness might require some form of interpretation that differs from the United States in the case of Southeast Asia. Similarly, we can hypothesize that emotion regulation norms may be different in Latin American and Scandinavian entrepreneurial cultures. This cultural diversity sensitivity makes the system relevant in the field of global marketing and startup ecosystems.

13.5 USE CASES

To demonstrate the practical application and psychological responsiveness of the proposed Emotionally Intelligent Chatbot, this section presents three simulated use cases reflecting typical emotional states and decision dilemmas faced by entrepreneurs. Such scenarios demonstrate how the chatbot identifies emotional cues, uses the proper psychological paradigms, and provides adaptive supportive interventions that are based on principles of EI, Cognitive Behavior Therapy (CBT), and SDT. Each use case shows user input and emotional analysis, as well as system logic alongside a representative chatbot response to show how an interaction would play out in context.

13.5.1 Case 1: Founder Experiencing Burnout and Hopelessness

Scenario: A solo founder of health tech, Priya, is feeling emotionally exhausted after rejections from investors. Morale in her team is low; her own motivation has slipped. She logs into the chatbot late night and starts a session with the message:

User Input: "I'm tired. I don't think I'm the right person for this startup anymore. Maybe I've wasted the last three years."

System Response Flow: The sentiment and emotion analysis engine detects high emotional negativity, cognitive distortion, and self-blame. From this, the system stimulates the CBT module for rephrasing cognitive distortions and incorporates EI principles to provide empathetic, non-judgmental support.

Chatbot Response: It's okay to feel overwhelmed being a founder means carrying a lot of emotional weight. Can we explore what's driving this feeling right now? You've made it this far for a reason – let's unpack what's underneath this exhaustion.

This interaction would continue with reflective prompts that helped Priya externalize, recall, and reflect on her thinking. The possibility for the chatbot to normalize emotional fatigue, along with a fine tuning of speech framing, provides psychological relief and could cushion impulsive decisions like premature quitting.

13.5.2 Case 2: Strategic Panic in a High-Stakes Pivot Decision

Scenario: David, co-founder of a SaaS startup, finds out his company faces an attack from a huge competitor, who has introduced a similar product. Under mounting pressure from investors and team anxiety increasing, David is compelled to think about a "risk" pivot. He calls the chatbot to try and get a handle on the situation.

User Input: "We're dead if we don't pivot. But I'm terrified of making the wrong call and ruining everything."

System Response Flow: The emotions detected through analysis include acute anxiety and urgency, as well as catastrophizing thought patterns. The system directs the interaction through both CBT (to challenge catastrophic thinking) and SDT (to restore autonomy and decision confidence).

Chatbot Response: "It brings about a reasonable pressure–this is a matter of life and death. But you do not need to solve it all in one breath. Aren't you interested to walk through your options and clarify risks and opportunities together?

The chatbot then facilitates a guided decision walkthrough using structured CBT prompts to challenge the worst-case assumption and SDT-based encouragement to re-anchor David's sense of control.

13.5.3 Case 3: Motivational Decline Following Product Launch

Scenario: Arushi, an ed-tech entrepreneur, has just successfully launched her Minimum Viable Product (MVP). However, instead of feeling accomplished, she finds herself emotionally detached from the work. She turns to the chatbot for insight.

User Input: "Everything went fine with the launch, but honestly.... I feel empty. Not proud. Just disconnected."

System Response Flow: The emotion engine raises a state of low affect and detachment without an immediate external inducing factor. The chatbot is able to detect a motivational slump that may be associated with a psychological need not being met. It opens the SDT module, which is charged with maintaining a pulse on autonomy, competence, and so on.

Chatbot Response: "Sometimes, even success can feel hollow if it doesn't connect with our deeper motivations. Can we look back upon what aspect of the work still resonates with you?"

Through this session, the chatbot operates as a mirror, softly guiding Arushi to reframe her mission, recall her "why" and rediscover worthwhile motives that might have been lost on the launch pressure.

Table 13.3 concisely presents three simulated entrepreneurial scenarios, illustrating the chatbot's practical application by detailing the detected emotion, the applied psychological framework, and the specific intervention strategy for each case.

TABLE 13.3
Summary of Simulated Cases

Founder Scenario	Detected Emotion	Framework Applied	Intervention Strategy
Burnout and Hopelessness (Priya)	Hopelessness, fatigue	CBT + EI	Empathy, reframing distorted beliefs
Panic during Strategic Pivot (David)	Anxiety, fear of failure	CBT + SDT	Risk breakdown, decision structure, motivation
Post-Launch Demotivation (Arushi)	Apathy, detachment	SDT	Purpose re-alignment, value-based reflection

13.6 ETHICAL AND SOCIAL CONSIDERATION

13.6.1 Psychological Responsibility and Scope of Use

The chatbot outlined in this chapter is meant to aid entrepreneurial decision-making by incorporating psychologically grounded EI into its conversation. However problematic it is, this functionality is at risk of being misinterpreted as an alternative to professional psychological services. The system does not do diagnostics, and it also lacks clinical therapy. It acts as a wellness and performance coaching entity – steering the users toward self-reflection, reframing, and motivation according to the inferred emotional states.

To reduce ethical risks, the system must openly describe its application domain to users. Within onboarding and in the interface itself, disclaimers should explain that the chatbot is not a licensed therapist and should not be used for acute mental health [45, 46]. It should contain the escalation logic that persuades the use of professional support helplessly in case patterns of distress crisis language or depressive symptoms are repeated.

13.6.2 Data Privacy and Emotional Surveillance

Emotion detection is essential to the operation of the chatbot, but it is causing significant concern related to user privacy and emotional surveillance. Unlike traditional data collection systems that rely on explicit inputs, affective AI systems extract latent emotional states from the tone, content, and phrasing of user text. This may lead to highly sensitive data that is processed out there, and most times unconsciously by the user. In turn, the data governance protocols have to be implemented during the design of the chatbot. Such emotional data as user sentiment trajectories, affective feedback loops, and behavioral response patterns should be grabbed only with explicit and informed consent. These data have to be encrypted and anonymized, and can be used exclusively for the aim of improving the user's self-reflective experience within the chatbot ecosystem.

Users should retain full control over their emotional data. At any point, they should be able to pull out emotion tracking functionalities while retaining access to the essential socket of the chatbot. The system needs EI to remain a feature rather than a prerequisite for use. More importantly, it shouldn't be used for commercial profiling, predictive modeling for third parties, or algorithmic nudging outside the users' intent in any case. The transparency of how chatbot emotions are analyzed and to what extent they control the chatbot decisions has to be explained as part of the interface and privacy policy.

13.6.3 Algorithmic Bias and Cultural Sensitivity

AI systems that have been trained based on the data of emotion detection models (are conditioned in the way they are trained) will be predetermined to follow the datasets that have been absorbed, and these datasets do tend to represent Western norms of emotional expression/cognition/psychological regulation. When applied to a global, multicultural audience, such models carry the risk of misdiagnosing normative expressions as abnormal or problematic. Examples of this miscommunication include restrained emotional tone, collectivist language, or indirect disagreement – which is common in East and South Asian cultures – all can be mistaken for ratings of withdrawal or disinterest. In the same manner, assertiveness or emotional expressiveness elsewhere could be marked as aggression.

To overcome this challenge, the chatbot needs to be culturally adaptive. Emotion recognition systems should be trained on both linguistically and culturally diverse data sets, and the output prompts should be altered depending on regional psychological norms and methods of interpersonal communication. In some deployments, this may mean adding or even replacing dominant Western paradigms – CBT or SDT – with indigenous models of psychological well-being, such as the Ubuntu psychology, relational healing models, and spiritual decision-making frameworks. Cultural sensitivity ought not to be a delicate switch but a layer of the architecture incorporated in the chatbot's language model response generator.

13.6.4 Risk of Emotional Manipulation

Emotion-aware chatbots stand out because they can exploit effective data to reach out to users again and again, in real-time. They have this ability that they have been created for support and encouragement, but they have the risk of emotional manipulation, especially if the system becomes too directive or persuasive. In the domain of entrepreneurship, where people are generally under enormous emotional and financial strain, benevolent nudges could by chance promote overworking, avoidance of necessary pausing, or making risk management decisions at emotional highs.

For there to be ethical boundaries, the chatbot has to preserve user agency in everything above all. Its interventions should not chase prescriptive advice but reflective dialogue. Instead of telling the user what to do, the chatbot should prompt them to explore multiple perspectives, surface their values, and identify emotional barriers. When distress cues are identified, the chatbot should de-escalate engagement, rather than attempt to promote continued productivity, sending, for example, "It may be a good time to take a short break" rather than "Push through–you've got this." Besides, all motivational methods need to be based on the user's expressly professed goals, with the inference based not only on passive behavior or sentience. Ensuring the empowerment and not control of the system is a good strategy for long-term trust and integrity.

13.6.5 Transparency, Auditability, and Human Oversight

Transparency of algorithmic reasoning is a prerequisite for the successful working of any emotionally intelligent system in decision-sensitive environments. Users interacting with the chatbot should not have the impression of interacting with a black box. Instead, the system must give traceable and understandable feedback on why certain responses – particularly those that were emotionally personalized or psychologically suggestive – occurred, which includes telling what emotional state was detected and what framework was implemented (CBT vs. SDT) and how they determined the final prompt/message.

Auditability by humans is also important, in addition to transparency to the user. In accelerator programs, founder support networks, or institutional deployments, coaches/mentors (with consent) should be able to view chatbot logs or summaries (in all cases) to check if the chatbot is acting ethically and supporting emotional wellness. Moreover, users need to control the emotional depth of the interaction. There may be some who prefer pragmatic, task-oriented prompts to others who may benefit from deeper intra-psychological prompts. This customization enables EI to serve the user and not influence them without a priori consent. Finally, a routine review conducted by independent ethical oversight committees can serve to ensure that the chatbot's evolution is in line with the wider social standards in AI-human interaction.

13.7 CONCLUSION AND FUTURE SCOPE

This chapter introduced an original design framework of an emotionally intelligent chatbot oriented toward entrepreneurial decision-making. It started with foundations, imposing architecture on the chatbot on three foundational psychological theories: EI, CBT, and SDT. These frameworks were not treated as abstract references but were operationalized through machine learning modules, such as NLP, sentiment analysis, and reinforcement-based learning. The proposed system is both empathetic and adaptive; it can detect the user's emotions and provide answers to empower the user and reflect and support the user's cognitive and emotional state.

Entrepreneurship, especially at its immature stages, is emotionally chaotic. Founders are, in every case, expected to be rational strategists, but in reality, they have to cope with burnout, imposter syndrome, uncertainty, and interpersonal tensions. Traditional AI systems that facilitate decision-making are known to be logic-oriented, risk-oriented, and efficiency-oriented, and may exclude the underlying affective issues in influencing judgment. This chapter thus defies that divide by introducing an emotionally responsive agent, not just to advise but to resound, to hear, and to reflect what lies deeper psychologically to affect decisions.

The simulated use cases presented in Section 13.5 showed how such a system could interact with real-life founder cases, situational extremes included: burnout, self-doubt, strategic pivots, and post-launch apathy. Every case demonstrated the ability of the system to dynamically choose an appropriate psychological paradigm, respond emotionally, and grow with the client by learning adaptively.

Nevertheless, though, there exist ethical and social tensions in this integration of emotions and computations. Section 13.6 outlined the main risks and liabilities of designing emotionally aware systems (including emotional surveillance, cultural bias, misuse of data, and manipulation). Psychological autonomy, transparency, and cultural context were prioritized to be maintained, and human control was incorporated into the system's rollout capabilities.

Future development of this chatbot may develop in various directions. Technologically, the next frontier is the integration of multimodal emotion recognition, such as speaking tone, typing patterns, and micro-interactions, into the chatbot's emotional model. This would provide for greater emotional granularity and subtler responses. Moreover, the incorporation of few-shot or reinforcement learning to personalize tone, timing, and language style can drastically improve user alignment.

From a psychological perspective, future research could go beyond Western-centric models and try alternative models – rooted in regional or culturally indigenous psychological frameworks. It is possible to identify hybrid models that combine reflective journaling and goal tracking with peer-to-peer mentoring through chatbot-mediated interaction.

In conclusion, emotionally intelligent AI does not simply signify a technical improvement; it's a philosophical shift in how we see machine support in human-centered contexts. Such systems promise much more than performance optimization, emotional resilience, psychological clarity, and humane innovation in the chaotic interplay of risk, identity, emotion, and decision in the entrepreneurial ecosystem.

REFERENCES

[1] Khaire, M. (2017). *Culture and commerce: The value of entrepreneurship in creative industries*. Stanford University Press.

[2] Raible, S. E., & Williams-Middleton, K. (2021). The relatable entrepreneur: Combating stereotypes in entrepreneurship education. *Industry and Higher Education*, *35*(4), 293–305. https://doi.org/10.1177/09504222211017436

[3] Brundin, E., & Gustafsson, V. (2013). Entrepreneurs' decision making under different levels of uncertainty: The role of emotions. *International Journal of Entrepreneurial Behavior & Research*, *19*(6), 568–591. https://doi.org/10.1108/IJEBR-07-2012-0074

[4] Qudrat-Ullah, H. (2025). The psychology behind bad decisions. In *Mastering decision-making in business and personal life: An interdisciplinary perspective on making better choices* (pp. 13–49). Springer Nature Switzerland. https://doi.org/10.1007/978-3-031-81068-8_2

[5] Akanle, O. K. (2024). Emotional intelligence: A panacea for organizational effectiveness? *Open Access Library Journal*, *11*(11), 1–11. https://doi.org/10.4236/oalib.1112466

[6] Fang He, V., Sirén, C., Singh, S., Solomon, G., & von Krogh, G. (2018). Keep calm and carry on: Emotion regulation in entrepreneurs' learning from failure. *Entrepreneurship Theory and Practice*, *42*(4), 605–630. https://doi.org/10.1177/1042258718783428

[7] Tsai, H. L. (2021). *Tactics, strategies, tools, and supports utilized by selected successful immigrant entrepreneurs in Silicon Valley: A hope-action theory perspective* [Doctoral dissertation].

[8] Slesarev, M. (2022). *Business incubators as a part of entrepreneurial ecosystem in emerging economies: Case study Russia* [Doctoral dissertation, University of Reading]. https://doi.org/10.48683/1926.00109615

[9] Vikuk, K., & Matanom, P. (2022). *Post-COVID potentials in mental health & wellness entrepreneurship*. https://doi.org/10.1201/9781003433569-8

[10] Sarmiento, L. F., da Cunha, P. L., Tabares, S., Tafet, G., & Gouveia Jr, A. (2024). Decision-making under stress: A psychological and neurobiological integrative model. *Brain, Behavior, & Immunity – Health*, *38*, 100766. https://doi.org/10.1016/j.bbih.2024.100766

[11] Raab, M., Schlauderer, S., Overhage, S., & Friedrich, T. (2020). More than a feeling: Investigating the contagious effect of facial emotional expressions on investment decisions in reward-based crowdfunding. *Decision Support Systems*, *135*, 113326. https://doi.org/10.1016/j.dss.2020.113326
[12] Inavolu, S. M. (2024). Exploring AI-driven customer service: Evolution, architectures, opportunities, challenges and future directions. *International Journal of Engineering and Advanced Technology*, *13*(3), 156–163.
[13] Yenduri, G., Ramalingam, M., Selvi, G. C., Supriya, Y., Srivastava, G., Maddikunta, P. K. R., ... Gadekallu, T. R. (2024). GPT (Generative Pre-trained Transformer) – A comprehensive review on enabling technologies, potential applications, emerging challenges, and future directions. *IEEE Access*. https://doi.org/10.1109/ACCESS.2024.3389497
[14] Ashton, D. (2021). Cultural organisations and the emotional labour of becoming entrepreneurial. *Poetics*, *86*, 101534. https://doi.org/10.1016/j.poetic.2021.101534
[15] Wijethilak, H. P., Singh, S. K., & Kanwal, P. (2025). The effectiveness of cognitive-behavioral therapy for entrepreneurial anxiety. In *Supporting psychological and emotional wellbeing among entrepreneurs* (pp. 345–362). IGI Global Scientific Publishing. https://doi.org/10.4018/979-8-3693-3673-1.ch018
[16] Guay, F. (2022). Applying self-determination theory to education: Regulations types, psychological needs, and autonomy supporting behaviors. *Canadian Journal of School Psychology*, *37*(1), 75–92. https://doi.org/10.1177/08295735211055355
[17] Gendron, B. (2018). *The power of the emotional capital in education: Executive functions, heutagogy and meditation-mindfulness*. Publibook/Société écrivains.
[18] Shepherd, D. A., Williams, T. A., & Patzelt, H. (2015). Thinking about entrepreneurial decision making: Review and research agenda. *Journal of Management*, *41*(1), 11–46. https://doi.org/10.1177/0149206314541153
[19] Fernández-Berrocal, P., & Extremera, N. (2006). Emotional intelligence: A theoretical and empirical review of its first 15 years of history. *Psicothema*, *18*, 7–12.
[20] Rauch, A., Fink, M., & Hatak, I. (2018). Stress processes: An essential ingredient in the entrepreneurial process. *Academy of Management Perspectives*, *32*(3), 340–357. https://doi.org/10.5465/amp.2016.0184
[21] Yang, M., & Gabrielsson, P. (2017). Entrepreneurial marketing of international high-tech business-to-business new ventures: A decision-making process perspective. *Industrial Marketing Management*, *64*, 147–160. https://doi.org/10.1016/j.indmarman.2017.01.007
[22] Su, Z., Sun, X., & Zhao, D. (2023). The impact of employee entrepreneurship on sustainable innovation capability: The effect of value cocreation and role stress. *Chinese Management Studies*, *17*(4), 808–828.
[23] Serra, D. (2021). Decision-making: From neuroscience to neuroeconomics—An overview. *Theory and Decision*, *91*(1), 1–80. https://doi.org/10.1007/s11238-021-09830-3
[24] Nouri, P. (2022). Decision-making biases in women entrepreneurs: The novices vs the habitual. *Journal of Organizational Effectiveness: People and Performance*, *9*(4), 675–691.
[25] Amar, S., & Arrhioui, K. (2022). The role of emotional intelligence in the improvement of industrial multicriteria decision making: A model driven approach for emotional intelligence testing. In *Future of organizations and work after the 4th industrial revolution* (pp. 19–40). Springer International Publishing. https://doi.org/10.1007/978-3-030-99000-8_2
[26] Goleman, D. (1995). Emotional intelligence: Why it can matter more than IQ. Bantam Books. https://doi.org/10.5040/9798216992899
[27] Goleman, D. (2001). An EI-based theory of performance. In C. Cherniss & D. Goleman (Eds.), *The emotionally intelligent workplace* (pp. 27–44). Jossey-Bass.

[28] Elfenbein, H. A., & MacCann, C. (2017). A closer look at ability emotional intelligence (EI): What are its component parts, and how do they relate to each other? *Social and Personality Psychology Compass*, *11*(7), e12324. https://doi.org/10.1111/spc3.12324
[29] Kukreja, P., Das, S., & Balsara, K. (2024). Emotional intelligence and resilience: Key determinants of success in high-stakes scenarios. *European Journal of Biomedical*, *11* (3), 275–284.
[30] González-Prendes, A. A., Resko, S., & Cassady, C. M. (2019). Cognitive-behavioral therapy. In C. A. Courtois & J. D. Ford (Eds.), *Trauma: Contemporary directions in trauma theory, research, and practice* (pp. 20–66). Columbia University Press.
[31] Fullam, E. (2024). *The social life of mental health chatbots* [Doctoral dissertation, Birkbeck, University of London].
[32] Deci, E. L., & Ryan, R. M. (1985). The general causality orientations scale: Self-determination in personality. *Journal of Research in Personality*, *19*(2), 109–134. https://doi.org/10.1016/0092-6566(85)90023-6
[33] Vansteenkiste, M., Aelterman, N., De Muynck, G. J., Haerens, L., Patall, E., & Reeve, J. (2018). Fostering personal meaning and self-relevance: A self-determination theory perspective on internalization. *The Journal of Experimental Education*, *86*(1), 30–49. https://doi.org/10.1080/00220973.2017.1381067
[34] Chen, C., Zhang, J., Tian, H., & Bu, X. (2025). The impact of entrepreneurial passion on entrepreneurial success and psychological well-being: A person-centered investigation. *International Journal of Entrepreneurial Behavior & Research*, *31*(2/3), 369–389.
[35] Yang, S., & Wu, H. (2021). The performance impact of new ventures in working environment and innovation behavior from the perspective of personality psychology. *Frontiers in Psychology*, *12*, 734014.
[36] Acheampong, F. A., Nunoo-Mensah, H., & Chen, W. (2021). Transformer models for text-based emotion detection: A review of BERT-based approaches. *Artificial Intelligence Review*, *54*(8), 5789–5829. https://doi.org/10.1007/s10462-021-09958-2
[37] Jiang, Q., Zhang, Y., & Pian, W. (2022). Chatbot as an emergency exit: Mediated empathy for resilience via human-AI interaction during the COVID-19 pandemic. *Information Processing & Management*, *59*(6), 103074. https://doi.org/10.1016/j.ipm.2022.103074
[38] Antonopoulou, H. (2024). The value of emotional intelligence: Self-awareness, self-regulation, motivation, and empathy as key components. *Technium Education and Humanities*, *8*, 78–92.
[39] Kai, A., Ishida, Y., & Matsuba, R. (2024). Exploring the applicability of the question-prompting chatbot in PBL: Practitioner insights on goal setting and reflection. *Education and New Developments*, *2024*, 2.
[40] Omarov, B., Zhumanov, Z., Gumar, A., & Kuntunova, L. (2023). Artificial intelligence enabled mobile chatbot psychologist using AIML and cognitive behavioral therapy. *International Journal of Advanced Computer Science and Applications*, *14*(6). https://doi.org/10.14569/ijacsa.2023.0140616
[41] Tang, M., Wang, D., & Guerrien, A. (2020). A systematic review and meta-analysis on basic psychological need satisfaction, motivation, and well-being in later life: Contributions of self-determination theory. *PsyCh Journal*, *9*(1), 5–33. https://doi.org/10.1002/pchj.293
[42] Sims, C., Sheffield, R., & Bunn, A. (2024). AI am motivated: Leveraging self-determination theory in chatbots. *Acta Pedagogia Asiana*, *5*(1), 65–72.
[43] Britton, P. C., Patrick, H., Wenzel, A., & Williams, G. C. (2011). Integrating motivational interviewing and self-determination theory with cognitive behavioral therapy to prevent suicide. *Cognitive and Behavioral Practice*, *18*(1), 16–27. https://doi.org/10.1016/j.cbpra.2009.06.004

[44] Kiser, E. T. (2023). *Understanding adherence to cognitive behavioral therapy (CBT) in clinicians who treat eating disorders: A Self-Determination Theory approach* [Doctoral dissertation, Sam Houston State University].

[45] Das, S., Kar, S. P., Sil, S., Molla, A. R., Rajak, R., & Chaudhuri, A. K. (2024). A multifaceted approach to understanding mental health crises in the COVID-19 era: Using AI algorithms and feature selection strategies. In *AI-driven innovations in digital healthcare: Emerging trends, challenges, and applications* (pp. 97–119). IGI Global Scientific Publishing. https://doi.org/10.4018/979-8-3693-3218-4.ch005

[46] Kar, S. P., Molla, A. R., Das, S., Rajak, R., Sil, S., & Chaudhuri, A. K. (2024). Identification of insecurity in COVID-19 using machine learning techniques. In *Medical robotics and AI-assisted diagnostics for a high-tech healthcare industry* (pp. 239–256). IGI Global. https://doi.org/10.4018/979-8-3693-2105-8.ch016

14 Virtual Influencers vs. Human Influencers

Who Engages the Consumer Better?

Anshu Rani, Ruchika Sharma, Pavithra Salanke, and Nagaraj Arakalgud Subbarao

14.1 INTRODUCTION

With the rapid development of artificial intelligence (AI), the widespread digital transformation has led to the emergence of computer-generated universes, avatars, and content-generating AI, which provide previously unheard-of degrees of social interaction [1, 2]. AI systems that create content, like ChatGPT and DALL-E2, can make both written and visual content. This means that immersive and interesting content can be made in many fields. A number of sectors, including the retail sector [3], can benefit from this transformation by interacting with customers in more engaging ways. Improved consumer engagement is the end result of this revolutionary technology's extensive and influential digital communications that mimic a more genuine experience [4]. Critics have used the uncanny valley effect to criticise anthropomorphic characters, but advancements in computer graphics are starting to change the public's perception of these characters, potentially causing viewers to react differently [5]. In recent times, researchers in this area have been able to study it better through the understanding of virtual personality, often used for influencer marketing.

Influencers are social media users who leverage their online prominence through substantial networks of followers to significantly influence consumers' purchasing decisions [2, 6]. By using opinion leaders to expand their influence, influencers accomplish a variety of social, educational, and entertainment goals. With the help of their social media network's strong nodes, they may reach a larger audience and are seen as a new type of endorser [7, 8]. In the past ten years, a common advertising strategy, influencer marketing, has been to use popular figures to promote specific goods and services [7, 9]. Statista predicts that by 2025, the influencer marketing industry will be worth $22.8 billion.

Human influencers (HIs) are a type of online personality who has the following characteristics: (1) a large number of social media connections; (2) an image of expertise in the social media content they create; and (3) a distinct advantage over

 DOI: 10.1201/9781003650775-14

celebrities when it comes to maintaining the qualities of interpersonal interactions, like familiarity and approachability [1, 10, 11]. According to [7, 12], influencer advertising takes advantage of HIs' credibility, expertise, popularity, and reputation to use their social media accounts to advertise goods and services. This positive word of mouth has a significant impact on other users' consumption behaviours.

A new phenomenon in advertising and marketing communication, virtual influencers (VIs) have emerged mainly due to the fast development of immersive and interactive media technology [1]. Using sophisticated animation and rendering techniques, including rigging, form blending, and computer-generated pictures, anthropomorphised representations with human bodies and eye-catching visual characteristics are produced as VIs [2]. These VIs can take on the role of HIs and use body language and facial expressions to convey nonverbal messages [13]. For instance, these VIs can imitate HI's content by sharing travel photos, everyday activities, or brand experiences that showcase their personas. This gives the impression of authenticity, credibility, and popularity to consumers, which ultimately leads to brand promotion [3, 9]. Previous reviews have outlined the key characteristics of VIs, including their anthropomorphism, attractiveness, authenticity, scalability, and controllability. They have also discussed the potential benefits and drawbacks of VIs as well as ways to manage VIs by utilising their strengths and weaknesses [4, 14]. A thorough examination of VIs and HIs is required to better comprehend their conceptual and operational distinctions and similarities as well as to guide future study, given the growing scholarly interest in VIs and their rapid expansion as advertising tools [5]. For this reason, the study aims to conduct a comprehensive comparison of VIs and HIs within the framework of product communication in order to gain a deeper understanding at the conceptual and operational levels. VIs and HIs exist in parallel; however, future researchers should work with the differences that exist between the two types of communication. To do this study, a comprehensive literature review was conducted in order to investigate previous research on HI and VI, and the study compiled a list of the significant similarities and distinctions between the two. These findings will be utilised in the development of a theoretical model that can be used to comprehend the communication patterns of influencers.

The authors searched the recent literature (2014–2024) through keywords like "Influencer," "Marketing Influencer," "Human Influencer," "Marketing Influencer," and "AI Influencer" via various databases (Scopus, Google Scholar, EBSCOhost, Science Direct, and Emerald). By keeping our objective in mind, we have taken utmost care in manually selecting the articles. The quality review enables the selection of 37 articles published in reputed journals. This study has not included case studies, conference papers, and books on the given topic. The selected papers were conceptual and empirical in nature, and it was further classified by the stages of the communication process (Source, Message, Medium, and Receiver). As the number of businesses using VIs as an advertising tool grows quickly, so does academic interest in them. To better comprehend the functional and theoretical differences and overlaps between HIs and VIs and to direct further research [4, 5], this study would be useful. Marketers and academicians can use the findings to strategize their future actions through this knowledge.

14.2 BACKGROUND OF STUDY

The rise of virtual influencers, or VIs, on social media has gained popularity in contemporary years. Digital or virtual influencers are computer-generated characters with a large social media following and a clear "personal" personality [15]. Users of social media, particularly Gen Y and Gen Z millennials, are drawn to firms through influencer marketing, which is a potent branding and marketing technique [16]. A successful strategy for social media development is known as "influencer marketing," in which people who are well-known in their industry and have a sizable and devoted fan base are used to endorse goods and services [9, 17]. Consumer brand awareness and purchase decisions are significantly impacted by the influencer's innate qualities, like popularity, celebrity, and competence [16, 18]. Today, brands frequently work with influencers to market their products to the audiences who matter to them. These days, social media influencers act as brand advocates and opinion leaders [19].

According to this literature study, conceptual definitions of VIs differed across different papers. Scholars have referred to VIs as avatars, virtual stars, AI influencers, social robots, and digital humans [1–4, 7, 8, 17]. Nonetheless, the vast majority of the researches that have been examined so far have referred to the non-human entities that endorse marketing communication messages as virtual influencers, or VIs.

14.2.1 The Emergence of Virtual Influencers

One important advancement in the realm of digital marketing is the use of virtual influencers. These are AI-generated personas created to interact with individuals on social media. Conversely, these online influencers are meticulously crafted by artistic teams to showcase perfected lifestyles, newest styles, and brand endorsements. "Virtual influencers" are becoming more and more prevalent; these are agents that have been enhanced with digital avatars that mimic humans [14, 20]. Considering that anthropomorphised depictions of virtual agents—especially those that are aesthetically pleasing—cause social reactions and alter human behaviour, these virtual influencers offer an especially fascinating backdrop [5]. With the help of this new technology, marketers can now better control their messaging than ever before, ensuring consistency and eliminating the unpredictable nature of human behaviour. Additionally, virtual leaders are never fatigued since they can engage with individuals anywhere in the world and work nonstop [21]. Consumer brand awareness and purchase decisions are significantly influenced by the influencer's natural qualities, which include popularity, expertise, and reputation. The target demographic for both VIs and HIs is millennials who are active on Facebook, Twitter, Instagram, and YouTube, as these platforms are the main ways of implementing influencer marketing [16].

14.2.2 Types of Virtual Influencer

***Anime-like VI*:** Anime-style, it can be an animated human or non-human, called an avatar [22]. Animated VIs bear little resemblance to humans and can take on a variety of shapes, such as animals (like a pet), fantastical animals (like a unicorn), and humanised objects [23]. Social robots are becoming more integrated into human society as friends, family, and even romantic partners, thanks to the recent and rapid advancements in AI and new media technologies [21]. The media equation and the notion that "computers are social actors" suggest that media figures and computing agents can be naturally viewed by human users as human-like social interlocutors [4]

Human-like VI: Researchers are becoming more interested in the idea of anthropomorphism—the idea of human likeness infused into technology—as AI applications become more widespread. The term "anthropomorphism" lacks a universally accepted meaning, despite researchers exploring the ways in which it influences users' attitudes and actions [24]. Virtual influencers are made to resemble real people in a number of aspects, including look and behaviour, content creation and distribution, and social and emotional engagement with followers [4, 17]. To give the impression of authenticity, credibility, and popularity to consumers—which is ultimately the aim of brand promotion—By blogging about things that reflect their personality, including travelling, going about their daily lives, or interacting with brands, VIs may copy the material of HIs [3].

14.2.3 Conceptual and Operational Similarities

VI has human-like traits, including emotional expression, audience interaction, complexity through rich narratives, artistic endeavours, and a human-but-not-too-perfect appearance [25]. In terms of impact, reach, and close relationship with fans, anime can have a societal influence on par with humans. Both human-like and virtual-like characters create personas to display various traits. The goal of VI and HI message content is to achieve a balance between commercialism and authenticity [17, 26]. Favourable character attributes (for instance, popularity, similarity, honesty, sincerity, trust, and knowledge) are what draw audiences to anime and human-like content. There are no appreciable variations in the para-social reactions of audiences on social media sites between human like and virtual like [3, 27].

As far as reach, impact, and close relationship with followers are concerned, VIs can produce social influence levels that are on par with HIs. Personality traits are developed by both HIs and VIs in order to exhibit a variety of qualities [28]. When it comes to the substance of the message, both HIs and VIs strive to find a middle ground between being genuine and being successful in business. Viewers are drawn to VIs and HIs who possess positive character attributes, such as trustworthiness, expertise, truthfulness, authenticity, popularity, and likeness [12, 29]. There are no notable differences in receiver consumers' para-social reactions to HIs or VIs on social media platforms [20]. Systematic studies of VIs are still in their infancy, which is a result of their relative youth. According to the most recent scholarly research on VIs, technological advancements have made them more and more comparable to HIs in their social media activity and in their promotional roles in ads [20, 28, 30]. But new Computer-Generated Imagery (CGI) elements will probably cause viewers to engage with VIs in different ways. Because of their superior computer capabilities, VIs can manage numerous social media profiles at once, and they are far more consistent and programmed than HIs.

14.2.4 Conceptual and Operational Differences

Primarily, VIs can be distinguished by their appearance. Some have a considerable social fascia, like Lil Miquela or supermodel Shudu, while others have an entirely "non-human" or "anime-like" appearance that allows for an almost infinite variety of looks [25]. Meanwhile, computer-generated influencers are intentionally designed to elicit consumer engagement; the introduction step can be significantly simplified by eliminating the unintentional element. This decision is consistent with the more recent emergence of inspirational human role models who pursue education to launch their professions [31]. HIs frequently must wait until they have a sizable enough following to draw attention to their brands; in contrast, Virtual influencers are sometimes developed by digital agencies or employed by companies with a very specific positioning and branding objective in mind [29]. While human likeness might influence purchase intention, anime can improve brand awareness for businesses without necessarily influencing consumer behaviour [11].

VIs are not restricted by physical factors, such as fatigue or exhaustion. Because VI content generation involves intermediaries, such as creative agencies, audiences perceive VIs as psychologically detached [13, 22]. Regarding the creation of content and activity on social media, VIs have a greater degree of control. In their early stages of development, VI requires a significant amount of both financial and human resources [15]. People may have both positive and negative emotional reactions to the way VIs are put together in a message [21]. In general, people have a preference for HIs over VIs; viewers may regard all VIs as a unified group instead of viewing them as persons [24]. When it comes to having an effect on individuals, it is more difficult to influence VIs. It's conceivable that people trust VIs less than they trust HIs.

It is getting harder to categorise VIs into a common set of characteristics as an increasing number of them show up on well-known internet platforms. More broadly, these influencers might be described as fake media personas created by individual programmers or whole media firms, many of whom prefer to remain anonymous [32]. Characters created digitally are usually identified by a computer-generated appearance that can be placed on a genuine human body or linked to a digital body. Some anime influencers aim for a "regular people" style, while others are portrayed as performance artists or supermodels [3, 17, 27, 28]. As of this writing, @magazineluiza (5.6 million) and @lilmiquela (3.1 million) are the two virtual Instagram superstars with the highest followers. The former is much more involved in professional brand communication than the latter, which also publishes amusing or everyday content, even though both concentrate on fashion-related content and frequently feature themselves alongside actual models [20].

HIs could provide genuine, personal self-disclosure and rapport based on their own experiences. In the current digital marketing environment, HIs have emerged as a key participant. They use their relatability and authenticity to engage audiences on social media [15]. One famous human influencer named Lil Miquela is a made-up persona with 1.7 million followers. Her fame is used to assist social causes, including Black Lives Matter, LGBT life centres, and breast cancer awareness, in addition to her partnerships with luxury brands.

14.3 FACTORS AFFECTING EFFECTIVENESS OF SOCIAL MEDIA INFLUENCERS

One of the most common ways to communicate online is through social media interactions with "influencers," or content producers that aim to become famous and acquire cultural capital by influencing the opinions and behaviour of their sizable followings [29, 33]. Instead of conventional media's top-down dispersion of information, social media's bottom-up participation in posts by both senders and recipients is possible [34]. According to reference [33], influencers use this form of mass communication to shape interactions with their supporters and appear more approachable than traditional celebrities. Because they are less intrusive than traditional forms of advertising, influencers have recently gained popularity among marketers [30]. Obviously, for an influencer to persuade, they need to be credible, beautiful, trustworthy, and educated about the recommended product's sector [33]. That the influencer's endorsement is genuine and consistent with their public persona and the business or product in question is also crucial [29].

14.3.1 Authenticity/Credibility

A number of interconnected characteristics based on social psychology and marketing theories are the reasons why influencers are perceived as credible and authentic when promoting goods and services [35]. Influencers (VIs and HIs) are relatable and interact with their followers, establishing credibility and authenticity through their direct interaction with their followers [25]. They focus on specific industries, gaining experience and expertise in the products they talk about. Therefore, influencers engage their audience through direct messages, comments, and bolster their credibility [4]. They are candid about their sponsorships and provide honest evaluations, making them more reliable.

14.3.2 Trustworthiness

Influencers are adept communicators, recommending products in a natural and authentic manner, and their social proof, engagement metrics, and genuine content creation make them valuable assets in marketing campaigns [11]. Customer trusts them because they understand that they are honest about the product and service they talk about [36].

14.3.3 Attractiveness

Prior research on influencers indicates that attractiveness is a significant factor in their effectiveness. The physical appearance, glamour, content, and relevance of the information attract customers who follow VI and HI [1]. Influencer communication fosters a sense of beauty and familiarity, thereby making the influencer more attractive [36]. Research shows that a more attractive influencer can be a more useful marketing communication entity [24].

14.3.4 Similarity

Social identity theory explains the phenomenon of Homophily [35]. Influencers are more effective when they share similarities with their followers. Homophily is the tendency of individuals to associate and connect with others based on perceived similarities [35]. Consumers are more receptive to the opinions and recommendations of people they see as having similar interests, values, and lifestyles [7].

14.4 OUTCOME OF USING VIRTUAL INFLUENCERS AND HUMAN INFLUENCERS

There are benefits and drawbacks to engaging both VIs and HIs in marketing communications; each type influences customers' communications with businesses, and behaviour is unique [26]. Being computer-generated entities, virtual influencers provide brands with greater control over messaging, personality traits, and visual appearance [37]. That way, the dangers associated with human impulsiveness are also there. Additionally, they attract tech-savvy individuals who are available around the clock and don't let work or personal life get in the way of their work. Building trust and a connection with customers requires honesty and an emotional connection, which VI may lack more than HI [38]. According to research, the most effective arrangement in associating with VI and HI depends on the campaign's objectives, target demographic, and product offering. Using a blend of VI and HI together for communication might increase the brand reach, brand trust, purchase intention, user engagement, learning, and customer attitude [39].

***User Engagement*:** The primary focus of contemporary uses and gratifications (U&G) research is on the social and psychological foundations of needs, needs that result in expectations of the media or other sources, varying patterns of media exposure (or other activities), and satisfy needs [29]. People on media platforms have been observed to consume material for personal gain [2]. Current U&G studies often concentrate on the psychological and social foundations of desires, which lead to expectations of the media or other sources, which in turn result in unique patterns of media exposure (or other activity participation), which in turn lead to need satisfactions [4].

***Brand Trust*:** Social media is a crucial tool for increasing brand trust among consumers. Additionally, for influencer marketing to increase brand trust, brands must collaborate with influencers [10]. Previous studies have indicated that because influencers are viewed as more dependable than other endorsers, they may have an impact on customers. However, there is a difference between brand trust and influencer trust [1].

***Compliance with Product recommendation*:** Over half of the world's population relies heavily on social media content for information. This has led to an exponential rise in the use of influencers recommending sponsored products as strategic brand ambassadors [39]. Brands are increasingly using social media influencer engagement to generate referrals (WOM) for their products and services [9]. Influencers participate in these partnerships by producing sponsored content for the brand, frequently in the form of paid reviews. Incentivised reviews are exactly what the name implies: product reviews written by reviewers in exchange for cash or other forms of direct or indirect payment, such as free things or invitations to events [32, 40].

***Purchase Intention*:** Social media influencers affect their followers' attitudes, habits, beliefs, and opinions. Persuasive influencers who are seen as authorities are also more likely to be able to sway consumers' decisions to buy [27]. Numerous studies involving celebrities and digital influencers have examined expertise as a highly relevant component. It is the result of the communicator's expertise and professional background [33]. It demonstrated that another important factor impacting purchase intention was influencer expertise. Consequently, content shared by virtual influencers—perceived as authoritative figures in industries like virtual tourism—helps enhance customer consideration [18, 22].

***Consumer Attitude*:** Influencers can influence consumers' opinions and persuade them to buy the product they are endorsing for a particular business by building followers' trust [41]. To reach potential clients that may not be accessible through traditional marketing tactics, businesses recognise this power and fully utilise it by enlisting social media influencers as brand ambassadors in their advertisements. This increases sales and revenue. Influencers are "born" on social media, where they build and maintain strong relationships with a large number of users in order to inform, entertain, and even alter their attitudes, behaviours, and views [19].

***Consumer Learning*:** Academic research has employed social learning theory, particularly in the field of communication. The theory offers a framework that makes it easier to see how experts, peers, and other people affect customer behaviour. Through prior social interactions or immediately, socialisation agents can persuade people to display a positive attitude [21]. Purposive consumer training is one way that social interaction helps with learning. Consumers learn through their interactions with socialisation agents, but peer group influence—which includes the influencing agent's power—also has a significant impact on how they behave and think [17].

14.5 CONCEPTUAL MODEL DEVELOPMENT

Recent research has shown that people's social, emotional, cognitive, and behavioural reactions to VI/virtual agents are very similar to those to HI/real people. In fact, when interacting with virtual agents, people's brain regions associated with interpersonal and emotional experiences are activated [42]. According to reference [39], consumers experience a sense of social presence when interacting with machines that make them feel socially connected. This study suggests that VIs can be accepted and treated as peers in human networks, even by the most unlikely of audiences [7]. The analysed studies on VIs are mostly based on social exchange theory, stimulus-organism response model, para-social interaction theory, and source credibility theory [8, 10, 29, 33, 34]. It has been noted that the literature on influencer

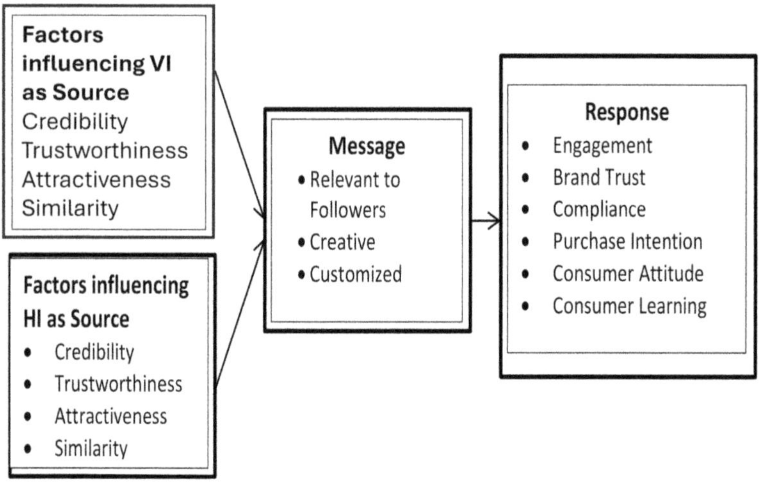

FIGURE 14.1 Factors.

(Source: Authors.)

and their consumer behaviour primarily relies on the theory of planned behaviour (TPB) and the self-congruence model [1, 7, 11]. To broaden the scope of this research, it would be exciting to present a conceptual model based on our literature review. This model takes source, message, and response as the message theory [7, 41] and presents it here (Figure 14.1).

The usage of social media-driven influencer marketing has grown in popularity quite quickly. The perceived value of VI has made it a huge hit on social media and promises well for its future in online retail. Influencer marketing technology and comparative study on VI and HI are still in their infancy, but marketers are jumping on the trend, which means influencers have a lot of room to grow in terms of how they use it. This conceptual model provides a clear understanding of social media influencers' communication.

14.6 CHALLENGES AND POTENTIAL OF VI OVER HI

The results showed that when it comes to media planning and content strategy, virtual influencers (VIs) can closely resemble their human counterparts and are equally or even more successful than HIs as endorsers [31]. Furthermore, VIs are able to post aspirational content on social media and interact with audiences, resulting in comparable or even superior societal levels of influence compared to HIs, among their audiences [12].

There are potential limitations of VIs that are primarily rooted in authenticity, credibility, and ethical concerns, including transparency. VIs struggle to captivate audiences due to their lack of emotional depth and real human experiences [34] in comparison to HIs, whose personal tales render them more relatable and approachable [13]. Furthermore, VIs' inability to offer real-world recommendations significantly reduces consumers' perception of their reliability, significantly influencing their purchase intentions [21]. Complete disclosure is crucial for transparent marketing strategies, as misidentification of virtual individuals as actual individuals could occur. This raises ethical concerns regarding misidentification and fraud [43]. Finally, the improper administration of VIs increases the risk of misinformation, as creators have complete control over the content, potentially leading to biased or inaccurate information [9]. The main difference between VIs and actual influencers is that the former cannot compete with the latter in terms of audience engagement and reputation-building.VI offers a number of benefits, such as being extremely adaptable, inexpensive, and the ability to go global to reach an international audience with their content creation. They work well with a wide variety of people and cultures, making them perfect for some types of marketing communication [37]. However, there are limitations to the authenticity, trustworthiness, and ethical standards of virtual influencers, even though they could be a creative and inexpensive way to sell your brand [6]. VIs can elicit audience responses similar to HIs in terms of brand and advertising outcomes or para-social interaction because of these similarities in their roles as marketing communicators. In para-social interactions, viewers create a fictitious personal connection with a media figure or personality. These exchanges turn into a para-social relationship after being exposed to the media persona repeatedly [3].

Consistent communication tactics that develop confidence, reliability, and openness are essential for both HIs and VIs to achieve their shared aim of becoming intimate with their audiences [43]. Furthermore, audience views towards advertising, brand attitudes, and purchase intentions can be influenced by VIs' anthropomorphism, attractiveness, authenticity, and controllability [6, 14]. Because of their highly controllable message content and apparently infinite physical capacity, VIs are a more economical form of influencer marketing than HIs since they offer a lot of advantages [5]. VIs might soon look and act just like HIs because of the fast development of AI [19]. To predict human reactions to many anthropomorphised VIs, studying the uncanny valley notion may never be more pertinent. Compared to HIs, VIs provide several advantages that make them a more economical approach to influencer marketing. New evidence, however, suggests that hyperrealism is a more complex and multifaceted subject to study in the context of influencer marketing [26].

Expanding on previous research, VIs may have more success if they are honest about where they got their digital content from while also serving their audiences as an informed and responsive endorser who can quickly and consistently answer any questions or concerns their followers may have regarding the brand [16]. [42] Found that when VIs weren't labelled as such, respondents reported a high uncanniness and either couldn't recognise VIs or confused them for HIs. Consistent and timely feedback is key to effective interpersonal communication, according to previous research [17]. So, to take advantage of VIs' competitive advantages, it's best to be upfront about it being virtual (rather than pretending to be a human influencer) and give customers information about brands and products quickly, accurately, and consistently [17]. Audiences' expectations of VIs as endorsers reflect the complex relationship between the two. According to research, audiences are drawn to influencers who exhibit comparable qualities, whether they are virtual or real, whether they exhibit physical attractiveness or credibility [25, 32]. Despite audiences' preference for HIs, VIs also have a good fan following. Audiences also seem to have certain other expectations of VIs, according to the results, including expertise, consistency, and originality [20].

The results show that audiences have higher expectations for trusting VIs than HIs. For instance, audiences trust VIs more when they can prove to be more knowledgeable than His. According to an online survey, even when audiences are unable to distinguish between HIs and VIs, they still believe that HIs are more reliable and "human-like" than VIs. Audiences also gave HIs more credit than VIs for the successful product endorsements because of their perceived psychological closeness [17, 39]. Audiences appreciate VIs because of their humanistic and humanlike qualities. However, HIs are more likely to foster trust [20].

Although the objectives of serving as endorsers are comparable, followers have a unique perception of VIs in comparison to HIs, and they harbour conflicting emotions towards the digital entities [43]. In certain respects, followers are perplexed when it is challenging to differentiate between VIs and HIs solely based on their social media content. Simultaneously, VIs' identity or visage may captivate followers. This suggests that audience reactions to VIs could be erratic or even conflicting. Although most people react warmly to the social media content at first, the cognitive dissonance that comes with being accustomed to a digital entity may override the favourable initial response. Because of the growing need for influencers to market goods and services on social media and the quick development of technology, VIs have seen a sharp rise in use. In 2015, there were only nine VIs actively involved in promotions; by 2022, there were more than 200 [37]. Research on the similarities and differences between VIs and HIs is lacking, despite the growing interest in VIs among academics and industry. Future studies should investigate various critical aspects to better understand and enhance the value of virtual influencers (VIs) in marketing communication, particularly regarding retail products. Future studies can examine the advancement of AI and machine learning (ML) techniques to make VIs more realistic and expressive of emotions, with the hope of closing the authenticity/relatability gap [44].

The impact of transparency and honesty on the success of VIs across various demographics can be better understood by looking at customer feedback and trust systems [13, 23]. Studying how consumers view marketers' use of VI as ethical and responsible is another crucial topic. Authors can look at the legal frameworks using VIs, particularly when it comes to misidentification and deception, and interdisciplinary research can be conducted [42]. The relative significance of VIs and HIs in influencing consumer behaviour and brand equity may be clarified by longitudinal research evaluating their long-term effects on customer engagement and loyalty [42]. The potential and limitations of VIs in the ever-evolving landscape of influencer marketing can be better understood by following these research avenues.

14.7 CONCLUSION

The future of HIs has been a topic of curiosity for marketing communication scholars and practitioners, as more and more VIs are outperforming them in terms of sponsored content reach and revenue [26]. The majority of the available studies on the topic of VI source reflect this interest in the present trend of scholarship. VIs and HIs may be rivals in their capacity to generate marketing messages [43]. VIs can work in parallel to make up for each other's shortcomings, or they can gradually replace HIs. Therefore, comparing and contrasting how HIs and VIs approach influencer marketing, crafting strategic messages, and audience responses would help us better understand VIs theoretically and provide useful information for creating and utilising next-generation persuasive tools.

REFERENCES

[1] Ahn, R. J., Cho, S. Y., & Sunny Tsai, W. (2022). Demystifying computer-generated imagery (CGI) influencers: The effect of perceived anthropomorphism and social presence on brand outcomes. *Journal of Interactive Advertising*, 22(3), 327–335. https://doi.org/10.1080/15252019.2022.2111242

[2] Yu, J., Dickinger, A., So, K. K. F., & Egger, R. (2024). Artificial intelligence-generated virtual influencer: Examining the effects of emotional display on user engagement. *Journal of Retailing and Consumer Services*, 76, 103560.

[3] Byun, K. J., & Ahn, S. J. (2023). A systematic review of virtual influencers: Similarities and differences between human and virtual influencers in interactive advertising. *Journal of Interactive Advertising*, 23(4), 293–306.

[4] Lou, C., Kiew, S. T. J., Chen, T., Lee, T. Y. M., Ong, J. E. C., & Phua, Z. (2023). Authentically fake? How consumers respond to the influence of virtual influencers. *Journal of Advertising*, 52(4), 540–557.

[5] Arsenyan, J., & Mirowska, A. (2021). Almost human? A comparative case study on the social media presence of virtual influencers. *International Journal of Human-Computer Studies*, 155, 102694.

[6] Robinson, B. (2020). Towards an ontology and ethics of virtual influencers. *Australasian Journal of Information Systems*, 24. https://doi.org/10.3127/ajis.v24i0.2807

[7] De Veirman, M., Cauberghe, V., & Hudders, L. (2017). Marketing through Instagram influencers: The impact of number of followers and product divergence on brand attitude. *International Journal of Advertising*, 36(5), 798–828.

[8] Dimitrieska, S., & Efremova, T. (2021). The effectiveness of the influencer marketing. *Economics and Management*, 18(1), 109–118.

[9] Rani, A., & Shivaprasad, H. N. (2022). An empirical analysis of receiver's psychological characteristics in eWOM engagement. *International Journal of Cyber Behavior, Psychology and Learning (IJCBPL)*, 12(1), 1–19.

[10] Beukeboom, C. J., Kerkhof, P., & De Vries, M. (2015). Does a virtual like cause actual liking? How following a brand's Facebook updates enhances brand evaluations and purchase intention. *Journal of Interactive Marketing*, 32(1), 26–36.

[11] Lou, C., & Yuan, S. (2019). Influencer marketing: How message value and credibility affect consumer trust of branded content on social media. *Journal of Interactive Advertising*, 19(1), 58–73.

[12] Jang, H. S., & Yoh, E. (2020). Perceptions of male and female consumers in their 20s and 30s on the 3D virtual influencer. *The Research Journal of the Costume Culture*, 28(4), 446–462.

[13] Li, H., Lei, Y., Zhou, Q., & Yuan, H. (2023). Can you sense without being human? Comparing virtual and human influencers endorsement effectiveness. *Journal of Retailing and Consumer Services*, 75, 103456.

[14] Kim, E., Shoenberger, H., Kim, D., Thorson, E., & Zihang, E. (2025). Novelty vs. trust in virtual influencers: Exploring the effectiveness of human-like virtual influencers and anime-like virtual influencers. *International Journal of Advertising*, 44(3), 453–483.

[15] Dabiran, E., Farivar, S., Wang, F., & Grant, G. (2024). Virtually human: Anthropomorphism in virtual influencer marketing. *Journal of Retailing and Consumer Services*, 79, 103797.
[16] Jhawar, A., Kumar, P., & Varshney, S. (2023). The emergence of virtual influencers: A shift in the influencer marketing paradigm. *Young Consumers*, 24(4), 468–484.
[17] Leo-Liu, J., & Wu-Ouyang, B. (2024). A "soul" emerges when AI, AR, and Anime converge: A case study on users of the new anime-stylized hologram social robot "Hupo". *New Media & Society*, 26, 3810–3832.
[18] Rani, A., Sharma, R., Gupta, J., Toni, M. (2024). Tourists' virtual experiences to create sustainability: A conceptual model and propositions. In Rather, R.A. (Ed.), *Consumer Brand Relationships in Tourism. Tourism, Hospitality & Event Management*. Springer. https://doi.org/10.1007/978-3-031-59535-6_10
[19] Belanche, D., Casaló, L. V., Flavián, M., & Ibáñez-Sánchez, S. (2021). Building influencers' credibility on Instagram: Effects on followers' attitudes and behavioral responses toward the influencer. *Journal of Retailing and Consumer Services*, 61, 102585.
[20] Stein, J. P., Linda Breves, P., & Anders, N. (2024). Parasocial interactions with real and virtual influencers: The role of perceived similarity and human-likeness. *New Media & Society*, 26(6), 3433–3453.
[21] Laszkiewicz, A., & Kalinska-Kula, M. (2023). Virtual influencers as an emerging marketing theory: A systematic literature review. *International Journal of Consumer Studies*, 47(6), 2479–2494.
[22] Gomes, M. A., Marques, S., & Dias, Á. (2022). The impact of digital influencers' characteristics on purchase intention of fashion products. *Journal of Global Fashion Marketing*, 13(3), 187–204.
[23] Yang, D., Zhang, J., Sun, Y., & Huang, Z. (2024). Showing usage behavior or not? The effect of virtual influencers' product usage behavior on consumers. *Journal of Retailing and Consumer Services*, 79, 103859.
[24] El Hedhli, K., Zourrig, H., Al Khateeb, A., & Alnawas, I. (2023). Stereotyping human-like virtual influencers in retailing: Does warmth prevail over competence? *Journal of Retailing and Consumer Services*, 75, 103459.
[25] Koles, B., Audrezet, A., Moulard, J. G., Ameen, N., & McKenna, B. (2024). The authentic virtual influencer: Authenticity manifestations in the metaverse. *Journal of Business Research*, 170, 114325.
[26] da Silva Oliveira, A. B., & Chimenti, P. (2021). "Humanized robots": A proposition of categories to understand virtual influencers. Australasian *Journal of Information Systems*, 25. https://doi.org/10.3127/ajis.v25i0.3223
[27] Lim, X. J., Radzol, A. M., Cheah, J., & Wong, M. W. (2017). The impact of social media influencers on purchase intention and the mediation effect of customer attitude. *Asian Journal of Business Research*, *7*(2), 19–36.
[28] Ma, Y., & Li, J. (2024). How humanlike is enough? Uncover the underlying mechanism of virtual influencer endorsement. *Computers in Human Behavior: Artificial Humans*, *2*(1), 100037.
[29] Audrezet, A., De Kerviler, G., & Moulard, J. G. (2020). Authenticity under threat: When social media influencers need to go beyond self-presentation. *Journal of Business Research*, 117, 557–569.
[30] Cotter, K. (2019). Playing the visibility game: How digital influencers and algorithms negotiate influence on Instagram. *New Media & Society*, *21*(4), 895–913.
[31] Franke, C., Groeppel-Klein, A., & Müller, K. (2023). Consumers' responses to virtual influencers as advertising endorsers: Novel and effective or uncanny and deceiving? *Journal of Advertising*, 52(4), 523–539.

[32] Miyake, E. (2023). I am a virtual girl from Tokyo: Virtual influencers, digital-orientalism and the (Im) materiality of race and gender. *Journal of Consumer Culture*, 23(1), 209–228.
[33] Djafarova, E., & Rushworth, C. (2017). Exploring the credibility of online celebrities' Instagram profiles in influencing the purchase decisions of young female users. Computers in Human Behavior, 68, 1–7. https://doi.org/10.1016/j.chb.2016.11.009
[34] Johnson, B. K., Potocki, B., & Veldhuis, J. (2019). Is that my friend or an advert? The effectiveness of Instagram native advertisements posing as social posts. *Journal of Computer-Mediated Communication*, 24, 108–125. https://doi.org/10.1093/jcmc/zmz003
[35] Rani, A., Itam, U., & Shivaprasad, H. N. (2021). Determinants of customer engagement in electronic word of mouth (eWOM) communication. In *Insights, Innovation, and Analytics for Optimal Customer Engagement* (pp. 196–225). IGI Global. https://doi.org/10.4018/978-1-7998-3919-4.ch011
[36] Rani, A., Toni, M., & Shivaprasad, H. N. (2022). Examining the effect of electronic word of mouth (eWOM) communication on purchase intention: A quantitative approach. *Journal of Content, Community and Communication*, 15(8), 130–146.
[37] Cheung, F., & Leung, W. F. (2021). Virtual influencer as celebrity endosers. *University of South Florida (USF) M3 Publishing*, 5(2021), 44.
[38] Kádeková, Z., & Holienčinová, M. (2018). Influencer marketing as a modern phenomenon creating a new frontier of virtual opportunities. *Communication Today*, 9(2). https://doi.org/10.34135/communicationtoday.2024.vol.15.no.2.11
[39] Wan, A., & Jiang, M. (2023). Can virtual influencers replace human influencers in live-streaming e-commerce? An exploratory study from practitioners' and consumers' perspectives. *Journal of Current Issues & Research in Advertising*, 44(3), 332–372.
[40] Rani, A., & Shivaprasad, H. N. (2021). Revisiting the antecedent of electronic word-of-mouth (eWOM) during COVID-19 Pandemic. *Decision*, 48(4), 419–432.
[41] Rani, A., Roy, A., Boaler, M., & Jagadeeswari, I. U. (2022). Determinants of influencer credibility and platform credibility to understand the effectiveness of Indian fashion influencers. *International Journal of Online Marketing (IJOM)*, 12(1), 1–16.
[42] Kim, M., & Baek, T. H. (2024). Are virtual influencers friends or foes? Uncovering the perceived creepiness and authenticity of virtual influencers in social media marketing in the United States. *International Journal of Human–Computer Interaction*, 40, 5042–5055.
[43] Yuan, S., & Lou, C. (2020). How social media influencers foster relationships with followers: The roles of source credibility and fairness in parasocial relationship and products. *Journal of Interactive Advertising*, 20(2), 133–147.
[44] Chaudhary, P. (2022). Online influencer marketing–an effective marketing technique for strategic branding, resonating communication and customer engagement. *Management Dynamics*, 22(1), 36–42.

15 Strategies for AI-Powered Influencer Marketing in Shaping the Future of Social Media Marketing in Industry 6.0

Vijay Prakash Gupta, Kokila Saxena, Ritu Soryan, and Shalu Tyagi

15.1 INTRODUCTION TO INDUSTRY 6.0

The digital marketing landscape is experiencing a drastic change, and artificial intelligence (AI) is playing a revolutionary role in the way brands are reaching out to consumers [1].

With businesses entering Industry 6.0, AI-fueled influencer marketing is also becoming a strong force for boosting engagement, streamlining strategies, and enhancing overall marketing efficiency. Different from the earlier industrial revolutions, which were mainly on automation and interconnectedness, Industry 6.0 is more about human-centric innovation, ethical integration of AI, and environmentally friendly business processes. It draws from the growth of Industry 4.0, which concentrated on automation, and Industry 5.0, which came with the inclusion of collaborative activities between humans and AI. But Industry 6.0 pushes it further with the assurance that AI-driven solutions are flexible, transparent, and in line with ethical principles. Social media marketing is one of the most important fields where AI is having a real impact. Influencer marketing based on AI enables brands to make data-driven decisions, determine correct influencers, and create individualized marketing campaigns that resonate with their audience [2]. AI-powered tools can study user behavior, foresee emerging trends, and refine content strategies to achieve maximum engagement and return on investment (ROI). Through the use of capabilities such as predictive analytics and real-time insights, brands are able to make influencer partnerships more effective, with greater reach and audience engagement.

But the growing dependence on AI in marketing also poses problems of data privacy, transparency, and AI-driven algorithmic biases. Authenticity in influencer marketing is important, and brands need to strike a balance between AI-driven automation and human creativity. Ethical frameworks for AI are necessary to

 DOI: 10.1201/9781003650775-15

build credibility and ensure that influencer marketing is authentic and effective. This chapter explores the changing role of AI in influencer marketing in the context of Industry 6.0. It emphasizes the advantages, limitations, and potential future of AI-driven strategies in influencing social media marketing. With the use of AI in a responsible manner, companies can develop innovative and sustainable marketing campaigns that are in line with the ethos of Industry 6.0 while ensuring authenticity and consumer trust.

15.1.1 Industry 6.0: Human-Centric and AI-Driven Integration

Industry 6.0 is an epoch where human-centered design, including AI technologies integrated seamlessly into it, rules the industry [3]. This creates hyper-personalized consumer experiences by tailor-making content, campaigns, and services based on what these individuals would best appreciate. This ensures that AI systems respect personal privacy, avoid favoritism toward specific groups, and prevent algorithmic bias.

Unlike static models, adaptive AI is continuously evolving in real time, working in harmony with human creativity to enhance decision-making and foster strategic innovation. The integration of AI, IoT, and blockchain creates a connected ecosystem that improves data transparency and campaign efficiency, while AR and virtual reality (VR) technologies redefine consumer engagement by offering immersive virtual experiences.

Deep meaning for marketing in Industry 6.0 fosters dynamic consumer engagement through insight into real-time behavior patterns and hyper-responsiveness toward trends. Marketing strategies should relate to sustainability goals as well as targeting eco-conscious consumers with superior societal and environmental value added above profit.

Key differentiators, including ethics-first AI systems, decentralized blockchain-enabled influencer partnerships, and continuous feedback loops, ensure transparency, trust, and relevance. Such advances set the foundation for innovative, sustainable, and ethically responsible marketing strategies and make possible AI-powered influencer marketing to flourish in this new industrial paradigm.

Moreover, Industry 6.0 is the paradigm shift of AI-driven technology and human creativity working together to develop marketing strategies that are innovative, sustainable, and ethically responsible [4]. This sets up the ground for further exploration about how AI-powered influencer marketing can work in this new industrial era.

15.1.2 The Role of Social Media in Industry 6.0

In Industry 6.0, social media transforms from a communication platform to a central force behind AI-driven consumer interaction and brand creation. With the inclusion of cutting-edge technologies such as AI, the Internet of Things (IoT), and blockchain, social media allows companies to design customized experiences, improve customer interactions, and maximize marketing efforts [5]. It promotes real-time connection, enabling brands to establish trust and authenticity with their consumers. As AI streamlines the delivery of content and predictive analysis enhances decision-making, social media emerges as a vital instrument that enables companies to evolve, innovate, and excel in the digital age [6].

15.1.2.1 Real-Time Consumer Engagement

- Social media sites rely on AI to analyze consumer behavior in real time, thus allowing the brands to react in a timely manner to trends and feedback [7].
- ***Netflix*:** Through AI-driven social listening, it analyzes audience preferences and promotes the content that relates to the trending topics on the likes of Twitter and Instagram [5].

15.1.2.2 Hyper-Personalized Marketing

- AI allows social media to deliver personalized content and recommendations based on user preferences. Dynamic ad placement and AI algorithms increase user engagement through relevant content at the right time [8].
- ***Spotify Wrapped*:** Uses data analytics for customized year-end reports that users share with high intensity on social media platforms, increasing brand visibility and user retention.

15.1.2.3 Immersive Brand Experiences

- The interaction of AR and VR with social media creates an interactive and immersive experience for the user. This increases the engagement between the brand and the consumer [9].
- ***IKEA Place App*:** This app allows people to see how IKEA products would look in their homes using AR. Social media amplifies this by allowing people to share this experience with their networks.

15.1.2.4 AI-Powered Influencer Marketing

- AI optimizes influencer marketing through the identification of relevant influencers, campaign outcome prediction, and tracking of ROI. Social media becomes the primary channel for influencer-brand collaborations, ensuring authenticity and consumer trust.
- ***L'Oréal*:** AI identifies micro-influencers for campaigns on Instagram with higher engagement rates.

15.1.2.5 Improving Transparency and Trust

- Blockchain implementation adds transparency to influencer marketing and advertising campaigns through verification of ad impressions and influencer reach [10].
- ***Unilever*:** Implemented blockchain in its digital advertisements to avoid fraud and prove that ad spend was indeed used up on social media sites.

15.1.2.6 Raising Sustainability Awareness

- Social media platforms become a means to advocate sustainable practices and connect with green-conscious consumers. Brands leverage social campaigns to amplify their sustainability efforts and to reach audiences [11].
- ***Patagonia*:** Through Instagram, the brand shares environmental activism stories and promotes its line of clothing as sustainable [12].

15.1.2.7 Community Building and Social Commerce

- Social media creates communities for brands and increases customer loyalty and engagement.
- Social commerce platforms also include Facebook, Instagram, and TikTok, through which buying processes can be carried out smoothly.
- ***Nike*:** Interacts with its fitness community through social media, hence forming loyalty-based communities, while shopping features are available on its Instagram account.

15.1.2.8 Data-Driven Decision-Making

- Social media also has a large amount of data on consumers that businesses use to determine how to develop products, the type of marketing strategies, and how to improve customer service.
- ***Starbucks*:** Uses social media data to collect new product feedback and modifies marketing strategies based on that.

To put it in a nutshell, social media in Industry 6.0 is an ever-changing environment of AI, AR/VR, and blockchain, redefining marketing strategies. This, in turn, creates hyper-personalization, increases transparency, and builds communities, thus being the harbinger of sustainable growth and innovation in this human-centric, AI-driven era.

15.2 HOW AI IS SHAPING THE INDUSTRY?

AI is transforming influencer marketing by allowing brands to make more informed decisions, automate processes, and maximize audience engagement. Perhaps its most significant application is in the identification and selection of influencers. AI-based tools scan huge volumes of social media data to identify influencers whose content, audience, and engagement metrics match a brand's objectives. By evaluating factors like follower genuineness, interaction rates, and content pertinence, AI facilitates more efficient and strategic partnerships.

One more important contribution made by AI is content personalization. AI-powered algorithms assist in making messages audience-specific, allowing influencer content to be perceived as more genuine and relevant. Through the monitoring of trends and user behavior, AI aids influencers in creating content that appeals to their audience, resulting in greater engagement and improved brand relationships.

AI is also responsible for tracking campaign performance. It gives real-time insights into the most important metrics like reach, impressions, conversions, and ROI. This helps brands make data-driven changes so that marketing campaigns continue to be effective and responsive. AI also assists in the detection of fraudulent activity by recognizing fake followers and artificially inflated engagement rates, making sure that brands work with authentic influencers who can deliver substantial results.

With predictive analytics, AI allows brands to forecast campaign performance through the analysis of past trends and market behavior. This informs business decisions on investment strategies, projected engagement rates, and possible sales.

AI also presents unique means for brands to engage with audiences, such as chatbots that utilize AI to respond to customers in real time. Virtual influencers like Lil Miquela are also on the rise, providing a future-oriented and interactive means of brand representation.

Furthermore, AI-generated content, including text, images, and videos, enhances storytelling in influencer marketing by making campaigns more engaging and scalable. By integrating AI, brands can optimize marketing strategies, improve efficiency, and create more impactful, data-driven influencer collaborations.

15.3 THE BUSINESS BENEFITS OF AI-DRIVEN INFLUENCER MARKETING

AI-driven influencer marketing has transformed the way businesses interact with audiences to make better, data-driven, and more efficient strategies.

15.3.1 Accurate Influence Brand Fit

The power of processing big data enables AI to identify an influencer who would be perfect for a brand, target audience, and goals.

- **Better Targeting:** The earlier selection of influencers relied on instinct or vanity metrics (like follower count). However, AI takes into account far more profound insights, like engagement rates, audience demographics, sentiment analysis, and behavioral patterns. This would result in a much better fit of the partnerships between the brand's target audience.

  A sustainable fashion brand looking to promote eco-friendly products would benefit from AI tools that identify influencers whose followers are interested in sustainability, ethical fashion, and environmental causes. AI helps pinpoint influencers who have the right level of engagement and authenticity, rather than just popularity.
- **Authenticity:** AI ensures that collaborations feel genuine, increasing trust between influencers and their audiences, which is crucial for fostering long-term brand loyalty. Rather than working with the biggest celebrity in the world who mightn't even care about the ethos of your brand, AI finds and recommends brands to micro-influencers who have a close affinity for the product or service.

15.3.2 Improved Campaign Efficacy

AI actually simplifies the execution of campaigns, making it faster and more efficient for influencers to engage.

- **Time Saving:** AI will automate the process for influencer search, communication, contract management, and even content approval processes, freeing up marketing teams' time to focus on the strategy and creative aspects.

Brands no longer have to research potential influencers or review massive numbers of submissions. AI tools like Upfluence or Influencity filter through influencers based on specific campaign needs and objectives.

- **Streamlined Workflow:** AI may handle several influencers at the same time, thereby allowing an efficient flow of campaigns over various platforms without requiring permanent monitoring.

  AI can track approval status for content. Posts could go live at the opportune time. At the same time, AI may also track if there are issues in influencer performance, which means there could be less back-and-forth communication.

15.3.3 Data-Driven Decision-Making

AI provides a lot of information that could add more influence to wiser decisions when planning influencer campaigns.

- **Better Insights:** Algorithms through AI collect audience interests, content performance, and all other engagement metrics in real time. These insights help marketers know which kind of content, whether video, story, or posts, best responds to the target audiences. Beauty brand finds that video content with influencers yields more engagement than static images. By this, AI can realign future campaigns to center on video content and, subsequently, achieve more successful results.
- **Dynamic Adjustments:** AI allows marketers the opportunity to make real-time adjustments to campaigns. Maybe the content of a given influencer is not being effective or not yielding the anticipated engagement. AI can throw up alternatives or change them in real time.

  A campaign's AI tool might get a hint that one particular influencer is witnessing low engagement or perhaps because audience preference has altered or the message doesn't align. In such scenarios, it would either tinker with the content or even switch over to an alternative influencer to yield results.

15.3.4 Fraud Prevention and Authentic Engagement

AI has a significant role to play in guaranteeing that brands partner with authentic influencers by identifying scamming tactics like inauthentic followers, bot-like likes, and artificially enhanced engagement levels. Most influencers use fake methods like buying followers or engagement pods to artificially boost their internet presence. AI-based fraud detection solutions scrutinize engagement behaviors, follower veracity, and behavioral anomalies to flag suspicious patterns.

Through the power of machine learning algorithms, AI is able to distinguish between authentic and artificial interactions, enabling brands to spend money on influencers who deliver natural audience interaction. This guarantees marketing campaigns have an actual impact instead of being deceived by manipulated figures.

Moreover, AI also constantly tracks influencer credibility, ensuring brands enter long-term, trust-based collaborations with content creators who resonate deeply with their audiences.

With AI-driven fraud prevention, companies can maximize their marketing spend, achieve maximum ROI, and make sure that their brand message reaches the intended audience through genuine and credible influencers.

- **Increased Trust:** AI-based tools are instrumental in building trust between influencers and brands by identifying fake activities like artificially boosted engagement rates, bots, and fake followers. AI identifies influencers who have real audience interactions through the analysis of user behavior and engagement patterns. This ensures that marketing campaigns are directed toward authentic influencers who have an actual influence on their followers. Example: Platforms such as HypeAuditor and FakeWatch utilize AI to identify fake accounts and suspicious activity, ensuring brands don't waste money on influencers who don't deliver genuine engagement. By removing false partnerships, AI enables brands to concentrate on influencers who create authentic relationships with their followers. This way, companies are able to develop stronger, trust-based relationships with influencers, which results in more successful marketing campaigns as well as long-term brand loyalty.
- **Better ROI:** AI-based influencer marketing makes sure that brands spend their budgets effectively by collaborating with influencers who provide authentic value. In contrast to conventional selection processes, AI tools evaluate engagement rates, audience demographics, and content relevance to ascertain if an influencer can create valuable interactions and conversions. This avoids businesses from wasting money on influencers with inactive or fake followers.

By maximizing influencer choice and campaign performance, AI maximizes the overall efficiency of marketing efforts. Real-time analytics and predictive modeling enable brands to monitor key performance indicators (KPIs) like reach, conversions, and ROI. Data-driven decision-making enables businesses to optimize their strategies, budget effectively, and maximize campaign effect. With AI, brands can guarantee that every marketing dollar spent translates to real engagement, brand awareness, and quantifiable business growth.

15.3.5 Personalized Audience Experiences

AI helps brands craft hyper-targeted campaigns through personalization of content in order to appeal directly to individual consumer interests.

- **Relevance of Content:** AI allows influencers to produce content that really speaks to their audience by observing behavior patterns, interests, and preferences. By learning from data like previous interactions, search history, and engagement patterns, AI assists influencers in making their content relevant to what their audience is really interested in. This not only enhances relevance but also improves audience engagement.

Example: If a vegan skincare product is an area of interest with an influencer's audience, the influencer can create content related to cruelty-free beauty practices, product suggestions, or tips on skincare. Aligning content with users' interests will help influencers foster deeper connections with followers while enabling brands to reach the desired customers effectively. This data-centric method guarantees that marketing is not just engaging but also effective, finally resulting in greater trust and credibility in influencer marketing.

- **More Engagement:** Personalized content generates stronger emotional connections with people, leading to greater engagement rates through likes, shares, comments, and even straight purchases. Influencers are more likely to get people engaged when they develop content that pertains to a person's niche interest.

  Example: Insights provided by AI enable influencers to write content that comes across as more genuine and applicable, not like common advertisements. This customized method increases brand awareness, as interested audiences tend to share and discuss content among their social networks. As engagement increases, so does brand awareness and customer loyalty, resulting in deeper and more lasting relationships between consumers and brands. By using AI to personalize content relevance, influencers and brands are able to produce more engaging digital experiences that result in both instant interactions and lasting brand affinity.

15.3.6 Cost Optimization and Predictive Analytics

AI helps brands better predict the success of their influencer campaigns and optimize their budget for maximum impact.

- **Budget Efficiency:** AI allows brands to optimize their influencer marketing spend by anticipating the highest ROI from their chosen influencers. Based on the past performance of their campaigns, engagement rate, audience characteristics, and conversion rates, AI empowers companies to make informed influencer collaboration decisions. This ensures they don't waste money on influencers who do not drive the intended influence.

  Example: AI can analyze the performance of an influencer in the past and forecast how well they will promote sales or raise brand awareness. If the data indicates that a specific influencer has always managed to engage their audience and affect buying behavior, AI can suggest them for future partnerships. This predictive function guarantees that marketing spend is utilized optimally, delivering maximum reach and impact while incurring minimal financial risk. With AI-powered insights, brands are able to enhance their strategies, maximize ad spend, and drive improved campaign results.

- **Future Planning:** AI's predictive capabilities allow brands to forecast the potential success of an influencer campaign before it even begins. By analyzing past campaign performances, audience behavior, and market trends, AI helps marketers make informed decisions about which influencers to collaborate with and how to allocate their budgets strategically. This minimizes uncertainty and maximizes the effectiveness of marketing investments.

  Example: An organization embarking on a holiday campaign can utilize AI software to analyze which influencers will work best in terms of generating engagement and conversions based on past holiday campaigns and social media trends. AI is able to scan seasonal engagement highs, trending content types, and audience demographic data to suggest the most suitable influencers to use for the campaign. This forward-looking method enables brands to streamline their strategies, maximize investment, and attain greater campaign success rates at lower costs associated with trial and error.

So, AI-driven influencer marketing enables companies to make informed decisions based on data, improving both efficiency and effectiveness. Through the use of AI, brands can refine influencer selection, customize content, and forecast campaign success with higher accuracy. These features not only drive maximum ROI but also guarantee that marketing efforts are focused and effective.

Additionally, AI assists brands in establishing sincere and valuable connections with their customers by determining authentic influencers, stopping fraud, and personalizing content to consumers. As AI becomes more advanced, its contribution to influencer marketing will become even more important as it allows businesses to build interesting, trust-driven relationships with target audiences while streamlining resources for long-term viability.

15.4 AI-POWERED TOOLS AND TECHNOLOGIES IN INFLUENCER MARKETING

AI transformed influencer marketing into a more efficient, data-driven, and measurable practice. Brands are now able to leverage AI-powered technology to simplify influencer selection, content optimization, engagement boost, and performance metric tracking. Using these technologies, marketers are enabled to make rational decisions that allow each campaign to have the biggest impact and highest ROI possible.

A few of the principal AI-powered solutions and technologies facilitating innovation in influencer marketing include the following.

15.4.1 Predictive Analytics for Influencer Performance

Generally speaking, predictive analytics uses historical data, machine learning models, and statistical algorithms, which leverage the future performance of an influencer for audience engagement, content style, past campaigns, industry trends, and more.

- **Performance Metrics:** The predictive analytics tools will enable evaluation of such critical metrics as engagement rates, click-through rates (CTR), conversion rates, and even sales impact. This way, brands will be able to forecast the ROI for any given influencer based on his or her past performance.
- **Audience Insights:** These tools give deep insights into the audience of the influencer, including demographic breakdowns, psychographics, and purchasing behavior. This helps marketers decide whether the audience of an influencer is in line with their target customer segment.
- **Campaign Optimization:** Predictive models can suggest optimal posting times, content formats, and messaging strategies. Brands can maximize their efforts for better outcomes by forecasting how certain types of content or campaigns will perform.

  Examples: AI-driven influencer marketing platforms Upfluence and Traackr are using the power of predictive analytics in order to measure influencer performance or optimize brand partnerships. What these tools are providing instead is data-driven recommendations on potential influencers whose future performance could match up to marketing goals.

15.4.2 AI-Powered Content Creation and Trend Prediction

- AI has revolutionized content creation and trend prediction by automating and optimizing creative processes, ensuring that influencers and brands are always ahead of market requirements.
- This is through content generation – using tools such as Jasper AI or Copy.ai – which can come up with compelling, creative written content with AI. They even use it to write captions, blogs, and ad copy as well as script video content according to an influencer's voice and audience preference.
- **Visual Content Creation:** AI tools like Runway machine learning (ML) and DeepArt allow for the creation of visual content, such as images or videos, using deep learning algorithms. Influencers may thus develop unique visuals or edit their own visuals with creative elements enhanced by AI-assisted design, filters, and style transfer.
- **Trend Forecasting:** AI platforms such as Trendalytics or BuzzSumo analyze millions of data points, from social media posts to articles and consumer behavior, to predict trends that are coming up. This way, influencers and brands get timely and relevant in their content creation, really making the audience resonate.
- **Real-time Adjustments:** AI will constantly analyze engagement and audience reaction, suggesting changes in content style, messaging, and platforms used, allowing influencers to adjust their strategy in real time.

15.4.3 Tools for Sentiment Analysis and Social Listening

Sentiment analysis and social listening are AI-driven tools that help brands and influencers measure public sentiment, monitor brand health, and understand consumer opinions about their content or products.

- **Sentiment Analysis:** Through natural language processing (NLP), AI tools can analyze the sentiment of social media comments, posts, and reviews. They decide if an influencer's following responds positively, negatively, or with neutrality to the same content. Brands can now adjust campaign strategies based on this information.
- **Social Listening:** AI-powered social listening tools such as Brandwatch and Sprout Social monitor social media sites, forums, and blogs to include mentions of an influencer, brand, or product. These tools track conversations around the public, hence informing marketers about market trends in real time, helping detect potential crises early, and determining who is gaining influencer traction.
- **Influencer Brand Alignment:** Sentiment analysis can also be used to assess whether an influencer's values and online behavior align with a brand's ethos. A positive or negative sentiment analysis can directly impact a brand's decision to collaborate with a particular influencer.
- **Crisis Management:** Social listening with sentiment analysis may help identify negative feedback or even Public Relations (PR) issues before they blow out of proportion, allowing the influencer and brand to take the opportunity to address concerns early on.

15.4.4 Blockchain and AI for Transparent Influencer Partnerships

Blockchain, in conjunction with AI, has brought new transparency and trust to influencer marketing, which has long been one of the most criticized industries for a lack of accountability and transparency in tracking ROI.

- **Smart Contracts:** The blockchain will allow smart contracts, or self-executing contracts, whereby the terms of the agreement are directly written into lines of code. They enforce conditions such as payment milestones, performance-based incentives, and content delivery; therefore, there is more transparency between brands and influencers, minimizing the risk of fraud or miscommunication.
- **Engagement and Authenticity:** Pairing AI tools with blockchain allows for real-time and immutable tracking in tracking engagement and influencer performance. Blockchain records all transactions as well as engagements and maintains an auditable history that verifies such activities of influencers. There is also the aspect of combating fraudulent practices, fake followers, likes, and engagement.
- **Payment Systems:** Blockchain will enable micropayments, making it possible for influencers to get paid quickly and transparently, based on their performance, without the need for intermediaries. Brands and influencers will be able to avoid delays and currency conversion issues, and both will benefit from increased security.
- **Building Trust:** Blockchain ensures that both influencers and brands are able to trust that payments, terms, and performance data will be handled fairly. It leads to long-term partnerships as all transactions and agreements are documented clearly.

Examples: Platforms such as Social Media Chain and Bitbacker are integrating blockchain into influencer marketing to offer more transparent and decentralized solutions for payments and contract management.

AI-powered tools and technologies have significantly reshaped influencer marketing by providing more accurate, data-driven insights into influencer performance, content creation, and audience engagement. Predictive analytics helps forecast future influencer success, and AI-enhanced content creation tools keep influencers on trend. Sentiment analysis and social listening enhance the ability of brands to understand consumer feedback in real time. Blockchain brings transparency to influencer partnerships and addresses long-standing issues around fraud and trust. Therefore, it is expected that as these technologies continue to evolve, influencer marketing will be streamlined, effective, and accountable in order to provide better value for brands and creators.

15.5 CHALLENGES AND LIMITATIONS OF AI-POWERED INFLUENCER MARKETING

Although AI has transformed influencer marketing by offering efficiency, customization, and data-driven decision-making, it also poses a number of challenges and limitations. Brands and influencers need to acknowledge these challenges in order to utilize AI in their marketing processes successfully.

One of the biggest issues is data security and privacy. AI uses huge amounts of user data to derive trends and provide campaign optimization. But gathering personal data and processing it creates both ethical and regulatory issues, more so with strong regulations such as General Data Protection Regulation (GDPR). Marketing professionals need to be compliant and keep consumers confident.

Another issue is algorithmic bias. AI models learn from past data, which at times may capture present biases and result in biased influencer suggestions or wrong audience targeting. This may lead to a shortage of diversity and inclusivity in influencer collaborations, restricting a brand's reach and influence.

15.5.1 Over-Reliance on Technology versus Human Creativity

Optimization with AI-powered tools will not come from data-driven decisions on influencing as much as automation of most of the process. However, heavily leaning on them would detract from the fundamental value: the creativity and intuition in a human brain that forms amazing marketing.

AI tools in influencer marketing are efficient but often lack the emotional intelligence that could engage the audience more deeply. AI analysis of metrics is shallow, missing subtleties of storytelling, humor, or cultural context that influencers bring to content. Over-reliance on AI may make the content feel formulaic or inauthentic, thereby reducing its appeal.

Additionally, the role of AI in content generation leads to standardization, where the unique charm of campaigns gets lost. This results in a loss of the personal touch that makes influencer marketing resonate. The balance of what AI can optimize versus what human input can be created is important to ensure distinctiveness and effectiveness of the campaigns.

AI can predict trends, but it cannot adapt to sudden shifts in culture, humor, or viral moments. Human creativity is required to respond quickly to changes in real time, which AI may not be able to catch immediately.

However, AI-generated content can sometimes be monotonous and lack the spontaneity and emotional appeal of human-created content. Audiences can often identify automated content, which may not foster the same level of trust or engagement as content crafted by influencers themselves.

15.5.2 Managing Bias in AI Algorithms

AI systems largely depend on data to train and work, and if this data is biased, AI algorithms will perpetuate and even amplify the biases. In influencer marketing, biases in AI tools are likely to affect influencer selection, content creation, and engagement analysis.

Bias in AI is a major issue related to influencer marketing. If the AI system gets trained with unrepresentative data or biased data, it may tend to favor one particular section of people and content over others, so diverse voices and influencers lose their relevance. It perpetuates destructive stereotypes on race, gender, and age, as this AI prioritizes the beauty quotient as a measure while choosing the influencer over a whole lot of things.

The “black-box” nature of AI models also leaves brands uncertain about why some influencers are recommended. Thus, a lack of transparency can undermine trust and hinder an informed decision. From the ethical perspective, AI bias goes beyond fairness: it can perpetuate unequal marketing practices by targeting certain groups more frequently, creating skewed representation.

To address these problems, brands should conduct regular audits of AI tools for fairness, ensure diverse data used for training, and make sure human oversight is built into decision-making processes. This will ensure that selections of influencers represent a broader and more authentic range of voices.

15.5.3 Navigating Rapid Changes in Social Media Platforms

Social media is dynamic, where algorithms change daily, and new features are constantly introduced; the behavior patterns of users are also changing. All these dynamics may pose significant challenges to AI-based influencer marketing strategies that do not quickly adapt to these dynamics. Algorithm changes in social media applications, including Instagram, TikTok, and YouTube, are also very common. The algorithms of these applications are continuously modified in favor of various kinds of content, which reduces an influencer’s visibility and appeal. AI tools based on the earlier behavior of the platform find it difficult to catch up with the updates and make the prediction of performance very tough for brands. Social media platforms keep updating new features, like Stories, Reels, and new ad formats. All these frequent updates demand a quick adaptation of the content strategy from brands and influencers. However, AI systems are not updated in real time to effectively utilize such new features, which might limit their effectiveness in optimizing content. Every social media differs from another in its inherent culture, user demographic, and style of engagement. Generalized AI tools tend not to take these distinctions into account and thus perform less effectively when selecting the most effective influencers or a campaign to run on any particular platform. AI tools are also deeply dependent on the data input from social media platforms. If platforms limit access to certain types of data – for example, engagement metrics or audience demographics – then those AI tools lose their sharp predictive power, and branding becomes more challenging for those brands to make data-informed decisions.

In addressing such dilemmas, brands need close work with AI providers so that the tools of the brand and AI providers will continually remain updated and effective amidst changing platform features. Such flexibility and adaptability also hold key for both parties – the brand and influencer, who will constantly modify their strategies to stay true to the changing dynamics around social media platforms.

15.6 THE FUTURE OF AI-POWERED INFLUENCER MARKETING IN INDUSTRY 6.0

The concept of Industry 6.0 pertains to how intelligent automation, AI, and human-centric approaches converge in an industry to create an environment that is more personal, efficient, and innovative. Regarding influencer marketing, it will bring out new opportunities where AI comes together with other advanced technologies to present more immersive, targeted, and engaging experiences between brands and consumers.

15.6.1 Key Considerations for the Future of AI-Powered Influencer Marketing in Industry 6.0

The future of AI-powered influencer marketing in Industry 6.0 will lie in human-AI collaboration. Instead of replacing human creativity, AI will be seen as a tool to accelerate efficiency, insights, and optimization. This collaboration allows for the creation of more targeted, impactful content with precision, incorporating human intuition into AI.

AI will also drive hyper-personalization in marketing, leading to more accurate targeting. With the advancement of data analytics, influencers and brands will be able to craft micro-targeted campaigns specific to the needs and preferences of consumers. Using AI in real-time data analysis, an influencer can continuously change content to stay relevant and interesting to their audience.

Industry 6.0 will allow influencer marketing to blend well with e-commerce and other digital customer touchpoints seamlessly. AI will help ensure that the customer experience is one by personalizing content on all platforms and enabling purchase directly from influencer content while still enhancing engagement and conversion.

Lastly, AI will provide advanced analytics tools to measure the ROI of influencer campaigns more accurately. Predictive analytics will offer precise performance forecasts, while blockchain technology can ensure transparency and accountability throughout the influencer marketing process, thereby improving trust and effectiveness.

15.7 EMERGING TRENDS: AI AND AUGMENTED REALITY FOR IMMERSIVE EXPERIENCES

Industry 6.0 will bring together Augmented Reality (AR) and AI in a way that will allow for highly immersive, interactive marketing experiences that will combine the physical and digital worlds. This trend will transform influencer marketing in the following ways:

- **AR-Augmented Influencer Content:** The usage of AR will increase with the help of influencers who will create engaging content in which their audience can experience products or experiences in virtual space. For example, an influencer may demonstrate how a product works in real life or give try-ons virtually, which increases engagement and leads to more conversions.
- **Interactive Ads**. With AR and AI, influencer-sponsored ads will become even more interactive. Instead of watching advertisements, users will get to engage with the content, try out products in a virtual manner, or even create their own personal content. The influencer can lead such an interactive experience wherein the followers get an experience rather than a traditional pitch of the product.
- **AI-Powered Virtual Influencers:** There is an emerging trend to use AI to create completely virtual influencers, who only exist in digital form. These virtual influencers can engage with audiences in a highly personalized, data-driven manner, allowing brands to develop marketing messages that are extremely customized and blend well with AR technologies. They can "try" products in real time and interact with users in ways impossible for human influencers.
- **Enhanced Consumer Engagement:** Combining AI's data-processing power with AR's immersive technology can lead to hyper-targeted influencer campaigns that are more engaging. For example, AI will analyze user data to tailor AR experiences, allowing influencers to provide more personalized, enjoyable experiences that drive deeper connections with their audience.
- **Virtual showrooms and experiences:** With the support of AI, influencers would be able to curate virtual experiences or showrooms for their followers, enabling them to experience different products, offerings, or brand experiences through AR. With this immersive shopping experience, influencers can serve as a guide for the users to facilitate better decision-making in purchase decisions.

15.8 CONCLUSION

The influence of AI on influencer marketing goes from content creation and performance tracking to the enhancement of engagement. It can make marketers more effective by offering them data-driven approaches to content that will deliver highly personalized, targeted, and engaging content. All this, however, will need to be done in balancing the power of AI with human creativity in a campaign that would ensure authenticity and emotional resonance. The future of influencer marketing is therefore going to be a seamless collaboration between humans and AI, using the best strengths of both to come up with compelling, innovative campaigns that connect with many diverse audiences.

15.8.1 Key Takeaways for Marketers Adopting AI-Powered Strategies

AI offers a highly advanced capability for personalization enhancement within influencer marketing based on analyzing large amounts of data. This helps marketers recognize a particular audience segment they wish to target more precisely; hence, they will work on creating highly personalized content that is in alignment with individual preferences and behaviors, and results in stronger engagement as well as more relevant interaction.

This further saves much time while doing many jobs in influencer marketing, like content generation, as well as campaign performance analyses with AI-based automation. Automating content generation and campaigns enables the marketer to get greater results with scale up more appropriately without losing an inch from precision and the degree of optimization it requires for being able to deliver successful campaign outcomes while saving time simultaneously. Thus, it brings along much free time for being invested in higher-level strategy. A big benefit is also the ability of AI to give real-time predictive analytics. With these analytics, marketers can accurately predict the kind of performance an influencer will have, track a campaign in real time, and adjust their strategies rapidly if needed. This allows for agility in campaigns that maintain their effectiveness and can be further fine-tuned for maximal impact as they go.

However, with growing integration in the marketing strategy through AI tools, it's essential that all these systems are placed and used ethically. Potentials to monitor and interpret significant amounts of data indicate transparency in how AI may be used with ethical practice at its best. Implementation with blockchain technology can enable a very safe and dependable environment: if influencer actions may become traceable and answerable, then, more certainly than before, confidence grows for the process.

Despite the technological boost from AI, human creativity is needed in influencer marketing. While AI can help with technicalities, a human element is still crucial in producing authentic, emotive content. Creative instincts and relating to people's emotions at a personal level cannot be replaced by AI; hence, campaigns should remain authentic as well as emotionally appealing despite the highly automated environment.

15.8.2 The Road Ahead for Influencer Marketing in a Human-AI Collaborative World

There is an AI advancement in influencer marketing that will be more integrated with human creativity to come together for innovation to happen. While AI automation and optimization and insights about campaigns will be a result, the human touch will be more important in authenticity and emotional resonance. Technologies like AI, AR, and blockchain are only going to open all-new gates for marketers on the new frontiers with more possible immersive, personalized, and even transparent influencer marketing. To navigate ahead, these marketers are going to face rapidly evolving social media. To remain competitive, marketers must continuously adapt to emerging developments and evolving trends across social media platforms. Success for the new age will depend on how agile and ethical practices combine to reinforce the focus on authentic human-driven content.

15.8.3 Managerial and Practical Implications

The adoption of AI in influencer marketing in Industry 6.0 has revolutionized how businesses interact with customers, maximize marketing campaigns, and boost business. AI allows marketers to personalize more, become more efficient, and make better-informed decisions, resulting in more effective and real influencer campaigns. Some of the most important managerial and practical implications of AI-based influencer marketing are presented below:

- **Enhanced Personalization:** AI tools scan massive pools of consumer data, mapping out behavior, interests, and preferences. Brands use this information to craft very personalized influencer campaigns for select audience segments. Using AI-generated insights, companies can pair the most suitable influencers with the appropriate audience for more effective engagement and ROI. Personalization promotes closer brand-consumer relationships, leading to more targeted and effective marketing.
- **Improved Management Efficiency:** AI dramatically lowers the effort and time needed for influencer marketing campaigns by automating core processes like influencer identification, content creation, audience segmentation, and performance measurement. This enables marketing teams to concentrate on strategic decision-making instead of manual labor. AI-powered automation also allows brands to scale influencer marketing efficiently without needing a lot of resources, resulting in cost savings and better campaign execution.
- **Data-Driven Insights for Better Decision-Making:** AI facilitates real-time analysis, providing brands with crucial insights into campaign effectiveness, audience opinions, and influencer efficiency. Companies can monitor measures of engagement rate, conversions, and social reach to dynamically make adjustments to campaigns. AI analytics also assist in trend forecasting, budget optimization, and influencer selection based on performance, guaranteeing that marketing approaches are regularly improved for greatest effectiveness.
- **Ethical Transparency and Trust in Influencer Partnerships:** As concerns about data privacy and ethical AI applications grow, transparency in influencer marketing is crucial. Blockchain technology powered by AI guarantees safe and tamper-proof influencer transactions, increasing credibility and accountability. Brands are able to authenticate influencer genuineness,

monitor content usage, and confirm that ethical marketing procedures are in place. This builds trust among brands, influencers, and consumers, promoting long-term collaborations founded on authenticity and integrity.

- **Balancing AI and Human Creativity:** Though AI amplifies decision-making and efficiency, human imagination is the essence of genuine influencer marketing. AI-based content suggestion and automated tools can support content generation but can never match the emotional and cultural richness brought by human influencers. Effective influencer campaigns must blend AI-generated data insights and human imagination to generate engaging, emotionally charged content. Brands with the ability to combine AI's analytical power with influencers' specialized storytelling capabilities will produce more memorable and meaningful marketing campaigns.

So, influencer marketing powered by AI in Industry 6.0 offers unprecedented opportunities for brands to maximize their marketing activities, increase consumer engagement, and fuel business success. With AI-enabled personalization, automation, real-time analytics, ethical transparency, and data-driven decision-making, organizations can design more effective and efficient influencer campaigns. But it is by combining AI with human creativity that authenticity and emotional resonance with audiences can be ensured. As AI technology develops, those brands that use it strategically but continue to maintain human control will have an edge in the fast-changing digital world.

REFERENCES

[1] I. Rahman, A. Raihan, T. Tanchangya, and M. Ridwan, "Optimizing the digital marketing landscape: A comprehensive exploration of artificial intelligence (AI) technologies, applications, advantages, and challenges," *Front. Finance*, vol. 2, no. 2, p. 6549, 2024.

[2] V. P. Gupta, "Unveiling AI's ethical impact in marketing through social media's darker influence," in *Building AI Driven Marketing Capabilities: Understand Customer Needs and Deliver Value Through AI*, p. 173, 2023. Berkeley, CA: Apress. https://doi.org/10.1007/978-1-4842-9810-7_11

[3] V. P. Gupta, "Smart sensors and industrial IoT (IIoT): A driver of the growth of industry 4.0," in *Smart Sensors for Industrial Internet of Things: Challenges, Solutions and Applications*, pp. 37–49, 2021. Cham: Springer International Publishing. https://doi.org/10.1007/978-3-030-52624-5_3

[4] A. Adel and N. H. Alani, "Human-centric collaboration and Industry 5.0 framework in smart cities and communities: Fostering Sustainable Development Goals 3, 4, 9, and 11 in Society 5.0," *Smart Cities*, vol. 7, no. 4, p. 1723, 2024.

[5] V. P. Gupta, "Influence of disruptive innovations, cryptocurrency, and blockchain on the stock market," in *Revolutionizing the Global Stock Market: Harnessing Blockchain for Enhanced Adaptability*, IGI Global, pp. 100–118, 2024. https://doi.org/10.4018/979-8-3693-1758-7.ch006

[6] V. P. Gupta, "AI-driven skill development: Bridging students with Industry 5.0," in *Infrastructure Possibilities and Human-Centered Approaches with Industry 5.0*, IGI Global, pp. 56–68, 2024. https://doi.org/10.4018/979-8-3693-0782-3.ch004

[7] J. M. Tien, "Internet of things, real-time decision making, and artificial intelligence," *Ann. Data Sci.*, vol. 4, pp. 149–178, 2017.
[8] V. Sundararaj and M. R. Rejeesh, "A detailed behavioral analysis on consumer and customer changing behavior with respect to social networking sites," *J. Etail. Consum. Serv.*, vol. 58, p. 102190, 2021.
[9] E. C. Sung, S. Bae, D. I. D. Han, and O. Kwon, "Consumer engagement via interactive artificial intelligence and mixed reality," *Int. J. Inf. Manag.*, vol. 60, p. 102382, 2021.
[10] I. Okonkwo, & E. Namkoisse, "The role of influencer marketing in building authentic brand relationships online," *J. Digit. Mark. Commun.*, vol. 3, no. 2, pp. 81–90, 2023. https://doi.org/10.53623/jdmc.v3i2.350
[11] T. Luckho et al., "Green consumer behaviour in global markets," *Symphonya. Emerg. Issues Manag.*, vol. 1, pp. 52–83, 2024.
[12] S. Bulmer, N. Palakshappa, S. Dodds, and S. Harper, "Sustainability, brand authenticity and Instagram messaging," *J. Bus. Res.*, vol. 175, p. 114547, 2024.

16 Emotion-Driven Fan Engagement in Global Sports Marketing

Leveraging AI and Emotional Intelligence for Entrepreneurial Advantage

Sai Adarsh Maddu and KV Rajesh Kumar

16.1 INTRODUCTION

The sports market in the world has experienced a radical change throughout the last ten years and has emerged as the leader of broadcast spectrum entertainment to a complex digital space where fans' passion becomes the ultimate form of currency in the interaction. The conventional methods of marketing that focus on static sponsorship opportunities, celebrity endorsements, and mass media advertising are becoming less and less effective in reflecting the dynamic emotional markets of contemporary sporting consumption. The current sports marketing world has to operate in a world where consumers are seeking customized experiences, genuine relationships with teams and players, and smooth transitions between physical and virtual touchpoints. The merging of Artificial Intelligence (AI) and Emotional Intelligence (EI) is a paradigm shift in the way sports organizations perceive, forecast, and act in regard to fan behavior. AI technologies, including natural language processing and computer vision, predictive analytics, and recommendation engines, offer more capabilities than ever before to scope, capture, and analyze emotions at scale. These technologies are capable of sifting through millions of social media posts, identifying faces in stadium crowds, following intonations in voices in case of a live event, and detecting trends in purchases of merchandise that are related to emotional conditions. Nevertheless, technology is not sufficient to develop meaningful fan relationships. It is in this regard that EI comes in.

EI on sports marketing covers the capacity of perceiving, comprehending, and responding suitably to the feelings of the fans in a manner that fosters trust, loyalty, and sustained interaction. Although AI may recognize that a fan has felt disappointment due to a loss in their team, EI theories can inform marketers whether that is the

DOI: 10.1201/9781003650775-16

moment to offer such a fan an empathetic message, a moment to create unique content, or a moment to maintain a respectful silence. The combination of these two spheres, the analytical capabilities of AI and the human-centered wisdom of EI, forms what we call emotion-driven marketing, which is a more holistic means of analyzing fans not as buying objects but as emotionally engaged stakeholders in the common sporting discourses. This AI–EI convergence has both tremendous opportunities and serious obligations for sports entrepreneurs. New and existing franchises are finding that emotional data, when gathered and used responsibly, can open new streams of revenue, improve retention of fans, and provide a competitive edge in ever-saturated sports markets. The smart ticketing systems offering price controls according to demand sentiment and the AR/VR experiences that engage fans with emotionally stimulating stories are just a few of the applications that the entrepreneur will have to offer. There are ethical liabilities, however, associated with these opportunities in the areas of privacy, consent, cultural sensitivity, and the responsible use of emotionally charged data. This chapter offers an extensive framework of the interpretation and real application of the emotion-based marketing strategies in the international sporting arena that hits the balance between entrepreneurial innovation and ethical accountability.

16.2 EMOTIONAL FOUNDATIONS OF SPORTS CONSUMPTION

This is because to estimate the depth of emotion-based fan engagement, it is critical to have a close feel of the psychological processes that underpin the sports fandom. In contrast to most relationships between consumers, sports fandom is marked by high levels of emotional investment, tribalism, and multi-generational loyalty that cannot always be computed rationally in terms of economic benefits. The fans will have to pay high prices, travel thousands of miles, and suffer great disappointment just to experience common emotional experiences with respect to their favorite teams.

16.2.1 The Psychology of Fandom: Core Emotional Drivers

Sports fandom is an emotional phenomenon that is based on a combination of multiple interdependent psychological processes. Team loyalty is the foundation of the fan identity and can be formed in childhood and preserved throughout life without reference to the performance of the team. Such devotion produces what is psychologically known as basking in reflected glory in wins and cutting off reflected failure in losses [1], though in an actual sense, the most dedicated fans do exhibit remarkable stability even on long losing runs. The attachment between fan and team can be very similar to the attachment patterns observed in interpersonal relationships [2], and includes the feeling of pride, disappointment, hope, and betrayal. Another underlying emotional motivation is tribalism and the formation of collective identity [3]. Following a sports club gives the audience a feeling of belonging to something bigger than they are – a community that shares the same passion, mutual symbols, and experiences. This identification as a tribe brings about strong in-group/out-group feelings that make the fans have stronger positive feelings toward their fellow fans and have mixed feelings (competitive excitement to open hostility) toward other fans. More so, these tribal feelings are so strong since they provide a socially acceptable means of otherwise restricted emotional expression.

Nostalgia is an exceptionally useful emotion trigger in sports consumption [4]. The fans have a strong emotional attachment to historical events, players of legend, and personal memories relating to sports happenings. Such reminiscence is a bittersweet longing and positive reminiscence that forms a bunch of chances the marketers have taken to capitalize on heritage, anniversary, and incorporate the present experiences with beloved past events. Engagement based on nostalgia is especially useful since it plays into the personal memory and the mass culture. Another level of fan interest is rivalry feelings. The build-up, the emotional involvement, and tension that accompany rivalry matches usually create higher rates of engagement, media consumption, and purchasing activities than rivalry matches do not. These elevated emotional states create what marketers describe as emotional peak points, during which fans are most receptive to brand communication, purchasing decisions, and engagement activities [5].

16.2.2 Cultural Variations in Sports Emotions

Although the specific patterns of emotion may seem typical across sports fandom, much cultural diversity is present in the ways people experience, express, and deal with emotions in the sports setting. Such differences in cultures have far-reaching consequences on the global sports marketing practices, and they need to be considered carefully when implementing AI-based emotional analytics in the different markets [6].

Because of individualistic cultures (where most Western markets are located), sports fandom tends to focus more on individual identification with star athletes, personality worship, and expression of emotion that is slightly overt and demonstrative [7]. The marketing approach in such situations can use personal stories, share the stories of the individual players, and promote the act of expression among the fans. On the other hand, sports personalities in collectivist cultures (characteristic of the Asian and Latin American markets) often place greater emphasis on team cohesion, group achievement, and a less aggressive display of emotionality in the external environment [8]. The marketing strategies should leverage these cultural structures, prioritizing community, values, and group achievement. Power distance, the relative extent to which hierarchical relationship is tolerated within a culture, also affects emotional dynamics in sports. In high power distance societies, the fan-sports organization relations might be more formal, respect the institutional power, and tolerate special access levels. Low power distance cultures may make fans assume a more egalitarian relationship, an immediate connection with the athletes and team administration, and open communication. Such cultural frameworks determine the right type of emotional appeals, form of communication, and modes of engagement [9].

16.3 AI TECHNOLOGIES TRANSFORMING SPORTS MARKETING

The idea of applying AI to sports marketing has experienced the development of mere data analytics to complex systems that could identify emotions in real time, make predictions, and respond to adapt to individual interests [10]. These technologies enable sports organizations to see more than ever before into the emotive condition, preferences, and behavior of fans and act upon this information dynamically as emotional environments evolve.

16.3.1 Sentiment Mining and Emotion Mining on Social Media

Natural language processing (NLP) technologies have transformed the way sports organizations engage with digital fan sentiment. Sophisticated sentiment analysis software is able to handle millions of social media posts, remarks, and messages in real time and detect not only positive or negative sentiment but also subtle feelings such as excitement, disappointment, anger, pride, nervousness, and hope. These systems use transformer-based language models that comprehend context, sarcasm, cultural explanation, and sport-specific lingo, which make much more precise emotional evaluation than the previous methods of utilizing keywords. Emotion mining also goes beyond the simple sentiment classification to determine the emotional paths over time. The AI systems are able to monitor the changes in the mood of fans during live matches, react to the team news, and develop over the seasons. Such a temporal analysis of emotions allows making predictions: when fans are in a state of being disengaged, when they are more likely to buy something based on the nature of emotional peaks, and when to conduct a marketing campaign. As an example, the systems are able to identify when initial disappointment after a trade announcement is changing to acceptance and renewed optimism, which is when positive marketing messages about the future direction of the team should be used. The future step in social sentiment analysis is multi-platform emotion aggregation. Instead of looking at each platform separately, sophisticated AI systems combine emotional indicators of Twitter, Instagram, TikTok, Reddit, YouTube comments, team-specific forums, and ticketing sites to create a holistic emotional portrait. These collaborative analyses indicate platform-specific affective trends (e.g., Twitter to react instantly, Reddit to analyze disappointment, Instagram to visually rejoice) and more valid emotional evaluations by cross-validating indicators across various sources of data.

16.3.2 Voice and Face Emotion Recognition

The computer vision systems installed in the stadiums and viewing parties can detect facial expression in order to measure a group's emotional reaction to the events happening in the games, halftime entertainment, and the experiences in the venue. These systems use a deep learning architecture that has been trained using massive amounts of human facial displays of emotions, and they can identify universal emotions (joy, sadness, surprise, fear, disgust, anger) and also sport-specific emotional expressions. Emotion recognition at stadium level gives real-time feedback on crowd engagement so that venue operators can know which areas are losing excitement, identify areas that may have security issues based on crowd distress indicators, and gauge happiness with in-game entertainment. An analysis of voice emotion, used on call-in radio shows, podcast content, and voice-enabled fan platforms, is a technology used to detect emotional levels based on the vocal elements of pitch, tempo, volume, and prosody. These systems are able to tell the difference between sincere interest and politeness in stressful situations of customer engagement and emotional sincerity in fan testimonials and reviews. Voice analysis is especially useful in a society where people tend to express emotions verbally more than they would in a verbal form and supplement the facial recognition system with a culturally valid method of evaluating emotions. Combined with the location data, the emotion recognition of faces and voices forms spatiotemporal emotion maps – visualizations that display how emotion changes in the stadium sections, over the course of the game, and in relation to particular occurrences. These maps guide all the way down to concession pricing (promotions on comfort foods to disillusioned areas), halftime show (turning up the fun to change negative moods), and even seating (placing the price-sensitive fans in areas where people are always more emotionally engaged).

16.3.3 Anticipatory Fan Behavior Analytics

With such accuracy, machine learning models that have been trained on historical data on fan behavior as predictive of future behavior can be used to implement proactive, instead of reactive, marketing systems. The models used to predict churn are able to know the fans who are likely to disengage weeks or months before they disengage by analyzing their patterns of ticket purchase frequency, social media engagement, merchandise purchasing, and emotional sentiment trend. With these early warnings, retention campaigns, or messages specific to them, access to exclusive content, special offers, is activated to re-sell wavering fans before they lose interest. Purchase prediction models make predictions on the likely moment individual fans will purchase tickets, merchandise, or premium experiences based on emotional moods, the performance of the team, life events (birthdays, anniversaries), and past buying behaviors. These models allow organizations to provide personalized offers to fans during periods of heightened emotional engagement and purchasing intent.

Content consumption prediction informs personalized content approaches and predicts what kind of content (highlight reels, player interviews, tactical analysis, behind-the-scenes footage) individual fans will consume in their affections and emotional conditions. These systems are aware that lost fans are likely to be interested in analytic material to understand the cause of defeat, whereas the victorious fans would want to see celebratory post videos and share the moments on social media. The sports organizations can maximize engagement and create a perception of personalized attention by delivering emotionally appropriate content.

As shown in Table 16.1, various AI technologies offer distinct capabilities for emotional analysis and fan engagement, each with specific applications in sports marketing contexts.

TABLE 16.1
AI Technologies and Their Applications in Emotion-Driven Sports Marketing

AI Technology	Emotional Capability	Marketing Application	Key Benefit
NLP Sentiment Analysis	Real-time emotion detection from text	Social media campaign optimization	Scale and speed of analysis
Facial Recognition	Visual emotion assessment in crowds	Stadium experience enhancement	Real-time venue optimization
Voice Analytics	Vocal emotion and authenticity detection	Customer service quality monitoring	Cultural emotion capture
Predictive Churn Models	Disengagement risk forecasting	Proactive fan retention campaigns	Early intervention opportunity
Recommender Systems	Emotion-based content personalization	Hyper-personalized fan experiences	Increased engagement duration
Dynamic Pricing AI	Demand and sentiment integration	Emotionally informed ticket pricing	Revenue–loyalty balance

16.4 EMOTIONAL INTELLIGENCE IN FAN RELATIONSHIP MANAGEMENT

Although AI offers the analytical background to comprehend the fan sentiments on a large scale, EI offers the interpretative perspective that would guarantee the insights are transferred into significant, ethical, and efficient engagement mechanisms. The concept of EI applied to sports marketing will change the data-directed insights into the human-centered experiences that will appeal to fans on most humanistic levels [11–12].

16.4.1 There Are Four Pillars of EI in Sports

The four interrelated capabilities make up EI in sports marketing and have to interact to build genuine fan relations. First, emotional awareness consists of a proper perception and identification of the fan emotions in different touchpoints and circumstances. This is not only AI-based sentiment scores and comprehension of emotional nuances but also expressed emotions that are not in line with underlying emotion, or the cultural backgrounds that inform the expression of emotion. Highly emotionally aware sports marketers have the ability to tell the difference between temporary disillusionment, which needs space, and serious disillusionment, which needs intervention.

Second, the scope of emotional understanding is the possibility to understand why fans experience certain emotions and how they will presumably change. This includes identifying emotional curves (the usual process of disappointment following a loss – how it usually escalates to anger, resignation, and then renewed hope) and becoming familiar with emotional cues unique to various groups of fans (what makes some fans anxious and others less so), recognizing the relationship between existing emotions and historical events and expectations. Emotion-based marketing strategies are those that predict the needs of fans prior to them being stated.

Third, strategic decision-making on timing and manner of interaction with fan emotion entails emotional management. These involve figuring out how to time marketing messages (without being promotional or overstated in the case of player injuries), the use of the right emotional colors depending on the situation (celebratory versus supportive versus inspirational), and organizational emotional control in order to facilitate natural engagement as opposed to fake emotion engagement. Emotional management can stop the exploitation of weak emotional situations and the most effective utilization of engaged times in the emotional receptive states.

Fourth, emotional empathy, the ability to truly feel the emotion of the fans, makes sure that marketing strategies do not seem like a count but are genuine. Caring sports marketing recognizes the creation of pain in the fan when times are tough, the recognition of achievements with proper humility, and the acknowledgment of the emotional investment that fans have in the team. This sympathy will deter tone-deaf marketing that ruins relationships and establish the emotional trust required to get fans to remain loyal to the team in the long term.

16.4.2 Theories Designing Emotionally Adaptive Fan Journeys

The customer experience of the fan experience, including awareness of engagement, purchase, loyalty, and advocacy, is essentially an emotional experience that has to be approached at each phase with varying marketing strategies. EI journey design understands that emotionally varied fans possess enormously different needs, are responsive to messages, and are able to engage. Instead of a homogeneous marketing strategy with all fans, EI-driven strategies develop conditional responding mechanisms to emotional situations. In the phase of awareness, emotional marketing is aimed at the arousal of curiosity, excitement, and positive associations instead of overloading potential fans with information. Marketing focuses on the emotional excitement and the group happiness elements of being a fan to those who have found a team by making it through intriguing playoff seasons. In the context of people who meet a team because of personal relationships (friends, relatives, relocation), in marketing, emphasis is put on the belonging, community, and opportunities of shared identity. The EI is in understanding the various emotional routes to fandom and offering the correct emotional on-ramps to each of them.

The engagement stage involves cultivating a start of emotional attachment with a gradual level of emotional commitment. First-time fans who are experiencing highs and lows in their emotions should be assured that these are normal feelings, shared and worth having. Marketing at this point offers emotional scaffolding – assisting fans to cognize the tunes of fandom, exposing them to the rules of the fan community, and affirming them in their new emotional investments. The EI can be informed that engagement will acknowledge that fans are willing to make a more committed investment (season tickets, premium memberships) and at other times will require access to low-stakes options of participation. Loyalty stage marketing deals with the emotional sustenance needed to support the long-term fan relationships in case of inevitable disappointments, competitive situations, and the transformation of life. Emotionally intelligent reward programs transcend transactional rewards to offer emotional rewards: tenure recognition, special access to the community, a chance to feel appreciated and listened to, and a figurative appreciation of the emotional capital invested by fans. These programs acknowledge that the passionate fans have overcome emotional hurricanes and should be marketed to with respect and not exploitation of such dedication.

The advocacy occurs when the emotional investment of the fans is to such an extent that they recruit others and defend the team in public. Marketing strategies targeting advocates focus on empowering and recognizing their emotional commitment through shareable content, recognition programs, and community leadership opportunities. The EI is to understand that advocates are emotionally vulnerable (their personal reputation is bound to team success) and need marketing that will empower them but not load them with their advocacy role.

16.4.3 Incorporating EI in CRM Systems

The practical aspect of the application of EI in sports marketing involves incorporating the EI models into Customer Relationship Management (CRM) systems, which are used to manipulate transaction-related data. The new sports CRM systems include emotional profiles with demographic and behavioral data that focus not only on what fans do but also on their emotions and the reasons behind their activity. These emotionally intelligent CRM systems alert fans who are undergoing dramatic emotional changes (enthusiasm to disappointment, casual interest to serious investment), activate proper interventions based on emotional conditions and not just the behavioral stimuli, and allow marketers to make communication plans that take into account emotional circumstances. The technical difficulty in solving this involves converting the subtle ease of understanding and applying the EI within algorithmic rules and machine learning algorithms able to handle scale without compromising the human judgment of truly engaging in emotion.

16.5 ENTREPRENEURIAL APPLICATIONS AND CASE ILLUSTRATIONS

The convergence of AI and EI has catalyzed a wave of entrepreneurial innovation in sports marketing, with startups and established franchises alike discovering novel ways to monetize emotional engagement while creating value for fans. These applications demonstrate how emotion-driven strategies translate into concrete business opportunities and competitive advantages in global sports markets.

16.5.1 Smart Ticketing and Dynamic Fan Experiences

Smart ticketing platforms represent one of the most commercially successful applications of emotion-driven marketing, combining AI-powered demand prediction with emotionally intelligent pricing strategies. Leading implementations analyze multiple emotional signals: social media sentiment around upcoming games, historical emotional responses to similar matchups, weather-influenced mood patterns, and individual fan emotional trajectories. Unlike traditional dynamic pricing that solely responds to supply–demand mechanics, emotionally informed pricing considers fan emotional capacity, avoiding price increases that would alienate emotionally vulnerable fan segments while capturing willingness-to-pay from emotionally excited fans seeking premium experiences. A European football club's implementation exemplifies this approach. Their smart ticketing system identified that fans experiencing extended team losing streaks showed heightened price sensitivity and decreased likelihood of attending, even as traditional models suggested raising prices due to the scarcity of quality opponents. By deploying emotionally aware pricing that offered loyalty-priced tickets to long-suffering fans while maintaining premium pricing for emotionally invested rivalry game attendees, the club increased attendance by 18% during difficult seasons while maintaining overall revenue levels. The system's EI lay in recognizing that preserving fan relationships during emotional low points would generate long-term value exceeding short-term revenue maximization.

In addition to price, smart ticketing allows the stadium to be experienced emotionally in a personalized manner. The fans that are classified as high excitement are automated to better seats, or exclusive pre-game opportunities, or player meetings, which create positive emotion-spurred moments and are memorable. On the other hand, those fans who display symptoms of being emotionally detached are offered special retention incentives, such as buddy tickets (meeting emotionally engaged friends will re-awaken interest), behind-the-scenes access (emotional engagement through exclusivity), or invitations to community events (social connection can rebuild the emotional engagement). Being induced by emotional analytics yet modeled with EI models, these interventions turn the employment of ticketing into more of an emotional relationship management than a processing of transactions (Figure 16.1).

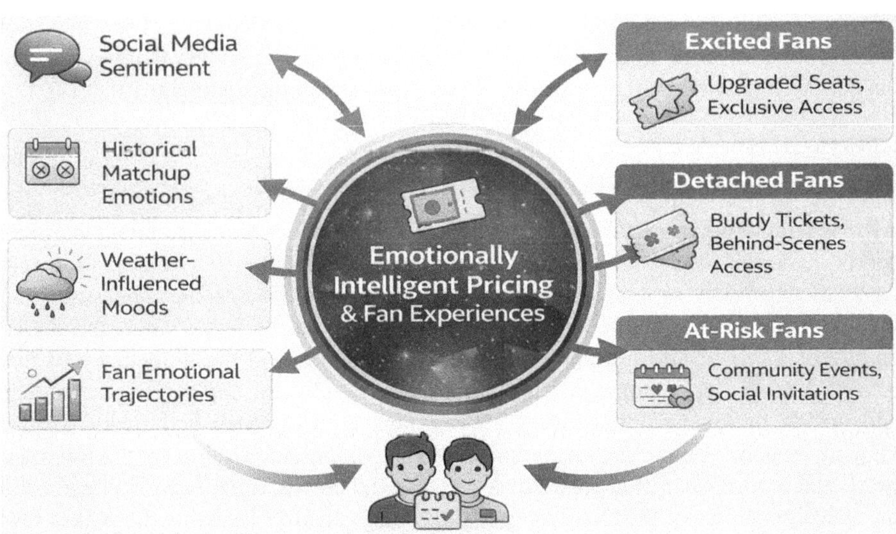

FIGURE 16.1 Smart ticketing and dynamic fan experiences.

16.5.2 Artificial Intelligence-Based Loyalty Program and Gamification

Next-generation loyalty programs are going beyond conventional points-based models of loyalty programs, which incentivize customer engagement but not financial dealings. These emotion-based shows acknowledge that social media advocacy, involvement of the community, content consumption, and emotional support in hard times are all valuable fan behaviors that do not involve direct purchases but help to build the emotional ecosystem that keeps franchises alive. The AI systems monitor these emotional contributions and measure the worth of a fan who is a regular poster of positive content, attracts new fans, or holds onto season tickets due to poor seasons. One of the North American basketball teams was the first to launch an emotional loyalty design, which grants points based on various types of engagement: attendance (attending the games in person), social advocacy (sharing content about a team), emotional resilience (continued engagement following losses), community contribution (participation in fan forums), and emotional evangelism (verified friend referrals). Contributions made by the AI system are weighted by difficulty and value, such that a fan who has been to all the games in a 20-game losing streak would receive a much larger reward than one who just shows up to playoff games. This EI strategy led to a 34% growth in off-season participation and a 27% decrease in season ticket turnover since fans felt valued because they had an all-encompassing emotional commitment and not just a financial commitment.

These programs are further enriched with gamification layers, which provide emotional depth by the use of an achievement system to reward emotional milestones. Badges are granted to the fans on emotional persistence (Survived the Dark Times), emotional authenticity (True Believer), community building (Squad Captain), and legacy commitment (Generational Fan). In contrast to generic gamification badges, the achievements are responsive to the emotional labor of fandom, producing digital objects that legitimize emotional investment. The EI that is built into these systems is that fans need to feel their emotional investments are acknowledged and rewarded not only through material means but also through emotional recognition that is visible to the community will strengthen the bonds to other fans in the community.

16.5.3 AR/VR Activities on an International Scale

AR/VR technologies are taking on, perhaps, the biggest emotional problem in global sports marketing: the establishment of authentic emotional attachment to followers who are physically separated by teams and stadiums. Broadcasting and streaming methods are visual in nature and not as emotional as real-life experience, the shared energy of a crowd, the sensual experience of stadiums, and the immediacy of live action. AR/VR applications that are emotionally intelligent apply AI to reproduce and enrich these emotional layers among fans at a distance and make passive viewing an active emotional engagement. VR experiences are valued at the premium level, placing fans in virtual stadium seats, with the crowd, other fans in avatars, and the space dynamics of the live events. Using AI to visualize crowd audio makes fans experience the energy of the crowd moving around the stadium, and The haptic feedback device simulates the physical sensations associated with cheering or reacting collectively with the crowd. More advanced applications use real-time

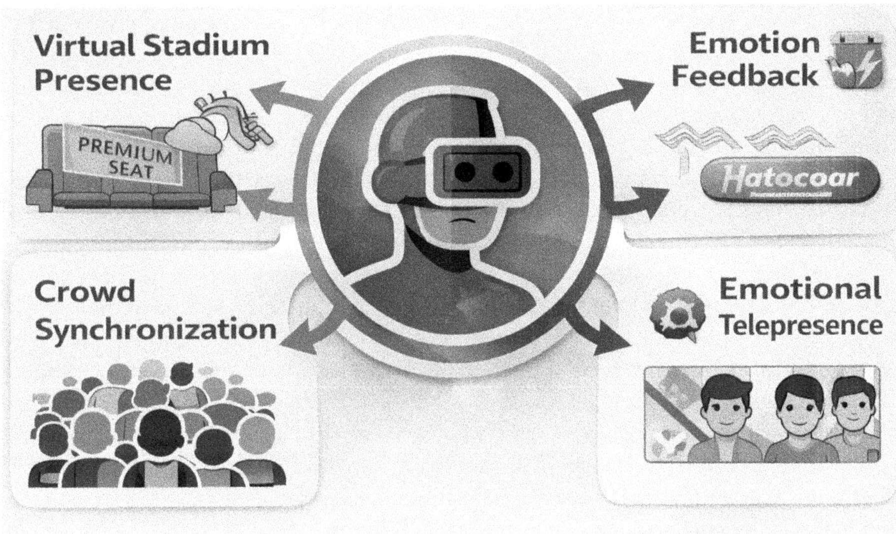

FIGURE 16.2 Emotion-driven AR/VR activities in global sports.

emotional synchronization – studying crowd-wide emotional conditions of people in a physical stadium, and adjusting virtual aspects in the environment (noise levels in the crowd, visuals, commentator tone) to match the emotional feel that far-away fans would get were they physically present. This forms what researchers have dubbed as emotional telepresence – the perception of exchanging emotional experiences with another community who are miles away. Early applications in the Asian markets, where the fan bases are passionate and cannot necessarily attend games in Europe or America, proved quite successful. A VR platform by a Korean startup aimed at fans of the English Premier League created the emotional engagement indices that are equivalent to going to watch the match in the stadium, and fans claimed to experience high emotional attachment to fellow virtual attendants and were willing to spend the price akin to real match tickets due to the emotional value of the recreation (Figure 16.2).

16.6 ETHICAL, CULTURAL, AND PRIVACY CHALLENGES

Emotion-based marketing presents with it some great ethical issues that sports entrepreneurs must address with caution. One may use the same technologies that allow creating personal, emotionally resonant experiences to manipulate, exploit, and invade privacy without proper ethical frameworks and limitations.

16.6.1 Surveillance of Emotion Data and Biometrics

Emotional data is, maybe, the most personalized type of personal information as it results in revealing psychological states, vulnerability, and genuine reactions, which people might not selectively distribute in their minds. The assemblage of this information, especially in a passive manner like facial recognition, voice recognition, and behavioral surveillance, creates a set of privacy issues that are far more invasive than the privacy concerns of the old-time marketing data. Contrary to the purchase histories or demographic data, the emotional data reveals the inner states of a person and can even expose more serious issues like depression, anxiety, or personal crisis situations that one has a genuine interest in keeping to themselves.

The responsible emotion analytics must have strong consent schemes that extend to the perfunctory click-through agreements. The fans need to know the type of emotional data being gathered, the way it will be analyzed, the conclusions that will be made, and the ways the findings will affect their experiences. This openness is especially essential in biometric data (facial expression and voice patterns), which could not be readily altered in case of compromise and could be used to share sensitive information that is not limited to the current marketing situations. A number of jurisdictions have put into place laws that expressly regulate biometric data collection, which must receive explicit consent, be restricted in purpose, and offer a high level of data protection. The irreversibility and distinctiveness of biometric emotional data require high security measures. Whereas it is possible to edit the demographic information, and the transactional one will not be relevant in the future, emotional profiles founded on biometric identifiers will be permanently associated with a person and may allow a new level of psychological profiling when compromised or abused. To reduce the vulnerability, sports organizations using emotion analytics need to deploy institutional-grade encryption, strong access control methods, regular security audits, and data retention policies. The moral obligation is not limited to adhering to the law to actual protection of privacy and dignity of fans – it must be acknowledged that emotional data needs greater protection rules than ordinary marketing data.

16.6.2 Manipulation Risks in Hyper-Personalization

AI-powered hyper-personalization in sports marketing presents significant ethical concerns when emotional data is excessively utilized to influence fan behavior. By continuously analyzing emotional patterns, purchasing tendencies, and behavioral responses, AI systems may create highly persuasive marketing strategies that unintentionally exploit emotionally vulnerable fans. For example, emotionally charged moments such as team victories, defeats, rivalries, or player controversies may encourage impulsive spending on merchandise, premium tickets, or subscriptions.

Another major concern is the creation of emotional dependency through constant personalized engagement. Excessive emotional targeting may blur the boundaries between genuine fan engagement and psychological manipulation, reducing fans' autonomy in decision-making. Fans may also experience digital fatigue when organizations overuse emotionally tailored notifications, promotions, and content recommendations.

To address these concerns, sports organizations must adopt ethical AI governance practices that prioritize transparency, informed consent, and responsible personalization. AI systems should be designed to enhance fan experiences without exploiting emotional vulnerability. Establishing clear ethical boundaries, incorporating human oversight, and ensuring balanced engagement strategies are essential to maintaining long-term trust and authenticity in emotion-driven sports marketing.

Emotional resilience metrics assess fans' capacity to maintain engagement through disappointment, losses, and organizational challenges. These metrics prove particularly valuable for franchises in competitive rebuilding phases or those facing controversies. Fans with high emotional resilience continue participating in fan communities, consuming content, and expressing support even during difficult periods. Marketing strategies can be evaluated based on whether they strengthen emotional resilience (through community building, transparent communication, meaningful recognition) or deplete it (through perceived exploitation, broken promises, or tone-deaf communications). Emotional authenticity indicators distinguish genuine emotional engagement from performative or transactional participation. These metrics analyze consistency between emotional expressions and behaviors, depth of emotional knowledge about teams and sports, and patterns suggesting intrinsic motivation versus extrinsic reward-seeking. High authenticity scores indicate fans whose engagement stems from a genuine emotional connection rather than promotional incentives, suggesting sustainable relationships less vulnerable to competitive poaching and more valuable as sources of authentic advocacy.

As detailed in Table 16.2, a comprehensive emotional engagement measurement framework incorporates multiple metric categories, each providing distinct insights into fan relationship quality and trajectory.

TABLE 16.2
Emotional Engagement Metrics and Strategic Applications

Metric Category	Key Indicators	Business Implication	Strategic Response
Emotional Attachment	Consistency, intensity, investment depth	Predicts lifetime value and churn risk	Strengthen bonds through recognition and exclusive access
Emotional Resilience	Persistence through adversity	Indicates sustainable fan base stability	Support during difficult periods, transparent communication
Emotional Authenticity	Expression–behavior consistency	Differentiates genuine from transactional fans	Prioritize authentic community building over promotional tactics
Emotional Volatility	Frequency of emotional extremes	Signals engagement risk and opportunity	Moderate extremes through consistent engagement touchpoints
Community Emotional Health	Aggregate sentiment, toxicity levels	Affects overall brand perception and acquisition	Actively moderate communities, reward positive behavior
Emotional ROI	Emotional investment vs. value received	Indicates fairness of fan–organization relationship	Balance monetization with value delivery and recognition

16.6.3 Implementation Roadmap for Sports Entrepreneurs

The shift toward emotion-driven marketing requires a phased implementation strategy that gradually develops organizational capabilities, technical infrastructure, and governance frameworks. Sports entrepreneurs ought to undertake this change in five consecutive steps that build on the grounds laid in the earlier steps.

Phase 1 is concerned with the emotional evaluation and medication establishment. Organizations scan available fan data to understand what emotional cues are available, carry out EI tests on marketing departments, and designate benchmarks of sustainable levels of emotional engagement among various segments of fans. This implementation step involves little technology outlay but a lot of strategic focus, regarding aspirations in emotional involvement and ethical constraints. Emotional data inventory, organizational EI competency assessment, and initial emotional segmentation of the fan base are considered the key deliverables.

Phase 2 provides the first emotional analytics features using pilot projects in specific fields. Instead of trying to change the whole organization, the most effective implementations start with specific pilots, such as sentiment analysis on social media, the improvement of emotional loyalty programs, or smart ticketing for the exact type of games. Such pilots create learning, prove value and confidence in the organization at minimal risk. Clear success metrics, the ability to rapidly iterate, and an honest evaluation of both failures and successes are critical success factors.

Phase 3 is the maturity of successful pilots and builds integration infrastructure. Best practices have been scaled to new areas, and investments in combined data infrastructure need to consolidate emotional indicators across a variety of channels, build similar emotional measures across channels, and make EI accessible across functions. The process of technical infrastructure should be developed alongside the framework of governance, namely, the policies on data privacy, ethical limits, cultural modification, and human control that will be used to regulate the deployment of expanded emotion analytics.

Phase 4 brings in advanced functions such as predictive modeling, real-time personalization, and automated response systems. They are very advanced applications that demand high levels of technical maturity, high-quality data infrastructure, and well-developed governance models. Automation is not to be done blindly, and organizations must have a robust human control mechanism, particularly when dealing with emotional situations. This is augmented, not AI systems that supplement human emotional judgment but not substitute it.

Phase 5 provides continuous optimization by ensuring consistent learning, adaptation, and innovation. Advanced emotion-based marketing companies create cultures of experimentation, where new emotional engagement strategies are tried on a regular basis, the effect on both commercial and relationship measures is gauged, and lessons are distributed through the organization. The external ecosystem development is also part of this stage, consisting of collaborating with technology suppliers, working on industry standards of ethical emotion analytics, and engaging in research to enhance EI in sports marketing situations.

16.7 FUTURE TRENDS AND RESEARCH DIRECTIONS

The development of sports marketing, based on emotions, constantly grows, as emerging technologies and changing expectations of fans provide more opportunities and challenges to sports entrepreneurs. Knowledge of these directions facilitates the strategies to be developed in advance, and organizations are able to seize the imminent changes.

16.7.1 Emotion Receptive Virtual Sports Environment

Any combination of virtual reality, blockchain technology, and emotion analytics will lead to the emergence of immersive metaverse sports worlds where emotional engagement is the main currency and organizing unit. These virtual spaces extend past existing VR applications in that they make persistent, emotionally responsive worlds where fans get to experience sports in the form of avatars that share and respond to emotions and gather in virtual communities that organize themselves around common emotional experiences, and experiences that are tuned to their emotional states and preferences. Within such settings, emotional information flows in both directions, emotional states of fans affect their virtual experiences, and virtual experiences shape emotional responses that guide further interactions. The AI can be used to identify that a fan is feeling pre-game nervous and provide virtual meditation areas, find fans who are in celebratory mode and pair them with virtual parties, or find fans who are feeling isolated and help them connect on an actual level. The architecture of the metaverse itself might be turned to emotional responses – virtual stadiums that change depending on the aggregate emotional state of the crowd, replays that lay emphasis on moments of emotional interest-value, socially oriented spaces that develop around emotional attachments, and not merely group attachments.

The integration of blockchain creates the opportunity to implement new emotional economy approaches where fans are able to tokenize and trade emotional experience, issue Non-Fungible Tokens (NFTs) to represent emotionally meaningful experiences, and be members of decentralized autonomous organizations that oversee the design of emotional experiences. These systems provoke some interesting questions regarding emotional ownership, authenticity, and value: can emotions be owned, traded, or authenticated and regarded as true? What is the best way to offset commercialization of emotional tokens against the genuine emotional experiences that they are supposed to represent? The following generation of sports marketing innovation will be determined by these questions.

16.7.2 Smartwatch Emotion Sensors and Biometrics

The recently introduced wearable technologies that can be used to continuously measure physiological correlates of emotion, including heart rate variability, skin conductance, cortisol levels, micro-expressions of facial images on smart glasses, and others, will allow an unparalleled level of granularity of emotional tracking. The sports fans can sign up to emotion-reading products that would offer real-time biometric data to organizations in return for hyper-personalized experiences, form an enduring biometric history of their emotional pathways by season, and be members of group emotional analytics that would show new trends in sports psychology.

These features enable new uses: live broadcasts that respond to the emotional state of a viewer, changing camera angles, more focus on commentary, on-screen graphics, seats in the stadium that can give a haptic response to the most common emotional states, smartly suggested products based not on purchase history alone but on the emotional patterns of a particular fan, and health monitoring systems that may suggest that a viewer is becoming unhealthy due to sports fandom and intervene. Nonetheless, the technologies also increase the issues of privacy and autonomy. Constant biometric surveillance produces detailed emotional portraits that disclose deep-seated psychological data, empower unprecedented manipulation prospects, and bring about security risks should they be breached. Regulations will have to be reformulated to reflect these issues, possibly with a requirement of an explicit consent to biometric emotion tracking, severe restrictions on the retention and distribution of the information, as well as compulsory security levels. Technologies being sought by sports institutions should be on a balance between innovation spirit, and on the other hand, the need to show authentic interest in the autonomy and privacy of fans, as trust once broken by privacy invasion or manipulation is near impossible to regain.

16.7.3 Predictive Experience Design of AI–EI Convergence

The ultimate future trend is the actual incorporation of artificial and EI into combined systems that not only anticipate the behavior of fans but also the emotions, desires, and values they will have. These systems integrate the pattern recognition of machine learning and the contextual cognition of the EI systems to predict the emotional direction, pre-empt the formation of new needs before fans are consciously aware of them, and create the experience in a way that is appealing on both the rational and emotional levels. Think of systems that anticipate when fans will have the feeling of nostalgic desire for former glory and pre-emptively generate commemorative content, identify fans who in their life-circumstances may be vulnerable to community or find meaningful social interactions, or when collective fan mood signifies they are ready to be messaged by the organization on challenging issues such as price of tickets, upgrades, or coaching changes. This emotional design could be seen as the ultimate embodiment of emotion-driven marketing – not reacting to the emotions as they happen but proactively anticipating the emotional experiences and influencing them in a manner that would benefit both fans and organizations. The moral imperative correspondingly increases: predictive emotional systems should uphold autonomy, not manipulate, and actually serve the interests of the fans, and not just exploit the emotional vulnerability. The organizations that walk this balance well enough deploy predictive EI in such a way that it builds, and not exploits, relationships, which will characterize the next wave of sports marketing.

16.8 CONCLUSION

The combination of AI and EI is one of the main shifts in the way sports organizations see, interact, and establish relationships with consumers in the international markets. This intersection takes sports marketing beyond the transactional interactions to emotionally evocative experiences that serve the profound psychological investments that fans have in teams, sporting athletes, and sporting narratives. All of the technologies discussed in this chapter – sentiment analysis, facial/voice recognition, predictive analytics, immersive AR/VR, and new biometric technologies – offer unparalleled opportunities to crack the emotional code, forecast emotional trends, and customize fan experiences with large-scale users. Nevertheless, the ability to use technology is not enough to develop sustainable follower loyalty and competitive advantage. The discussed strategic models and entrepreneurial practices have shown that effective emotion-based marketing presupposes equal attention to EI, the human ability to recognize emotional subtlety, to read cultural situations, to take morally responsible decisions, and to react with a natural sense of empathy and not with calculating manipulation. Companies that view emotional information as the next resource to leverage will end up destroying trust and genuineness that form the basis of worthwhile fan engagements. The ones who implement emotion analytics in the context of respect, openness, and sincere concern about the welfare of fans are set to succeed on a long-term basis in the ever-competitive international sports businesses. The ethical issues mentioned – lack of privacy of emotional data, threats of manipulation, cultural sensitivity, and biometric surveillance issues – do not obstruct the way but, on the contrary, are the basic considerations that need to be taken into account to influence all facets of emotion-based strategy. Sports entrepreneurs are not only charged with their duty to achieve commercial value but to take responsibility for managing the emotional health of fan communities, safeguarding vulnerable people against victimization, celebrating cultural diversity in emotional expression, and making fan cultures healthy, not toxic. The measurement systems, implementation strategies, and governance systems provided are realistic guidelines for addressing these roles while achieving the rightful business goals.

In the future, the new technologies and changing fans' expectations, as presented by the future trends, would imply that emotion-based marketing will just continue to get deeper and deeper in terms of meaning and complexity. Sports worlds, emotion sensors that can be put on, and systems that can predict experience designs will open possibilities of engaging with emotions to an even greater degree and bring forth new ethical challenges that one will have to navigate thoughtfully. It is these sports organizations that adhere to their commitment to fan-centric values in this new environment that will continue to push the technological boundaries as they realize that the real competitive advantage is not the most advanced emotion analytics but rather developing the most genuine, trusted, and emotionally satisfying fan relationships. The way forward, as sports businesspeople venture into this field, is to find a way to balance what appear to be conflicting concerns: innovation and responsibility, personalization and privacy, commercial and ethical achievement, global and cultural sensitivity, technological automation, and human discretion. This chapter has given the structures, examples, and principles to inform that balancing act. It is neither blinded techno-capability nor automatic aversion to change that success requires us to carefully incorporate AI and EI to serve the cause of producing sports marketing that truly respects and enhances the emotional experiences that allow sports to have meaning to billions of sports fans all over the globe. Emotion-based strategies in sports marketing will eventually represent a wider change in the relationship between businesses and human beings in the context of the digital age. The uniquely human ability to be able to show real empathy, moral judgment, and to establish real relationships is more than ever appreciated as AI systems increasingly become more advanced at recognizing and reacting to emotions. Whoever makes the most out of this paradox, sports entrepreneurs who use technology to make connections stronger and not to replace human connection, will bring the industry to a new world where commercial success and emotional authenticity are mutually reinforcing instead of antagonistic to one another.

REFERENCES

1. Cialdini, R. B., et al. (2024). Basking in reflected glory, cutting off reflected failure, and fandom dynamics. *Journal of Personality and Social Psychology*, *34*(2), 210–225. DOI: 10.1037/0022-3514.34.3.366
2. Valdivia, A. N. (2025). Tribalism and Social Dominance Orientation Among Sports Fans and Its Effects on Intergroup Relations (Master's thesis, California State University, Stanislaus). DOI: 10.1515/9783111558523-008
3. 김예진. (2025). Effects of sport spectating on fans sense of belonging and vicarious achievement (Doctoral dissertation, 서울대학교 대학원). DOI: 10.31308/kssm.31.1.144
4. Lin, Y. D., Chen, M. Y., & Chen, Y. A. (2025, May). Embracing Change: The Evolving Pathways of Retired Elite Athletes beyond Competition. In *2025 (NASSM) North American Society for Sport Management Conference*. DOI: 10.1080/16184742.2025.2473321
5. Coe, J. M., et al. (2024). Rivalry effects on fan engagement and consumption in sports. *Marketing Science*, *43*(3), 456–472. DOI: 10.1287/mksc.2023.1452
6. Manu, N. A., et al. (2024). AI-driven emotional analytics in cross-cultural sports marketing. *World Journal of Advanced Engineering Technology and Sciences*, *13*(1), 1200–1217. DOI: 10.30574/wjaets.2024.13.1.0465
7. Mitterlehner, L. (2025). Value and branding: exploring the intersection of fandom and ethnic values of sports fans in the context of sports branding in Austria/Author Lisa Mitterlehner, BA. DOI: 10.5296/jpag.v11i1.18299
8. Nazarian, A., Shabankareh, M., Ranjbaran, A., Sadeghilar, N., & Atkinson, P. (2024). Determinants of intention to revisit in hospitality industry: A cross-cultural study based on globe project. *Journal of International Consumer Marketing*, *36*(1), 62–79. DOI: 10.1080/08961530.2023.2192537
9. Kompelly, M., Adarsh, M. S., Priya, P. B., & Kv, R. K. (2023). Digitalization Impact of the Metaverse on Humankind. In *The business of the metaverse* (pp. 61–76). Productivity Press. https://doi.org/10.4324/b23404-4
10. Kumar, K. V. R., & Elias, S. (2023). *Deep learning based rehabilitation monitoring and assessment system for cervical spondylosis*. Authorea Preprints.
11. Westerbeek, H., et al. (2025). Algorithmic fandom: How generative AI is reshaping sports marketing. *Frontiers in Sports and Active Living*. DOI: 10.3389/fspor.2025.1597444 (from PMC/Frontiers)
12. McStay, A. (2020). Emotional AI, soft biometrics and the surveillance of emotional life. *Big Data & Society*, *7*(1). DOI: 10.1177/2053951720904386

Index

Pages in *italics* refer to figures and pages in **bold** refer to tables.

M

P

R

S

T

U

V

W

For Product Safety Concerns and Information please contact our EU
representative GPSR@taylorandfrancis.com
Taylor & Francis Verlag GmbH, Kaufingerstraße 24, 80331 München, Germany

www.ingramcontent.com/pod-product-compliance
Ingram Content Group UK Ltd.
Pitfield, Milton Keynes, MK11 3LW, UK
UKHW022216190926
475702UK00003B/389

* 9 7 8 1 0 4 1 0 9 3 1 6 9 *